LESS IS MORE
Developing Youth Soccer Teams

By
GEORGE WERNER

The opinions expressed in this manuscript are solely the opinions of the author and do not represent the opinions or thoughts of the publisher. The author has represented and warranted full ownership and/or legal right to publish all the materials in this book.

Less is More
Developing Youth Soccer Teams
All Rights Reserved.
Copyright © 2014 George Werner
v2.0

Cover Photo © istockphoto.com. All rights reserved - used with permission.

This book may not be reproduced, transmitted, or stored in whole or in part by any means, including graphic, electronic, or mechanical without the express written consent of the publisher except in the case of brief quotations embodied in critical articles and reviews.

Outskirts Press, Inc.
http://www.outskirtspress.com

ISBN: 978-1-4787-2729-3

Outskirts Press and the "OP" logo are trademarks belonging to Outskirts Press, Inc.

PRINTED IN THE UNITED STATES OF AMERICA

Deepest Gratitude

To Deborah Benkovich for her great graphic work.
This book would not be possible without her efforts.

TABLE OF CONTENTS

PARENTS:

Parent Evaluations	1
No Parent Zone	5
Life Lessons	7
Sideline Behavior	8
Playing Time	10
Commitment	13
Praise	17
Liking the Coach	18
Player Try Outs	19
Vigilante Parents	21
A Parent's Advice	22

THE COACH: 25

Life Lessons	25
Fun	27
Bored	29
Rec., Travel, Premier	31
Winning	32
Mistakes	33
Scrimmage	35
Teaching Every Position	36
Playing Time	37
Sideline Behavior	39
Parent Meeting	40
Master of your Profession	42

PRACTICE: 43

Do all your Teaching in Practice	43
Organize Practices	43
30 Minute Rule	46
Focus on One Segment	47
Cones	49
Coaching Moments	50
Speak with One Voice	51

PROGRAM: 52
Director of Coaching 53
Program's Four Principals 55
Soccer Skills Classes 57
Conditioning Program 63
The Technical Game 64

YEAR ONE: 66
I. Weave Play 66
II. Defensive Stance 69
III. Defense 1v1 Situation 70
IV. Defense 2v1 Situation 74
V. First-to-the-Ball Play 76
VI. 1v2 Defensive Situation 80
VII. Recovery Defenders Play 84
VIII. Add two Recovery Defenders Midfielders 90
IX. 9v9, 11v11 Play—Add Sweeper Centerback Defender 94
X. Divide Playing Fields into Thirds 102
XI. Team Formation 104
   7v7 Team Play 104
   9v9 Team Play 108
   11v11 Team Play 112
XII. Criteria for Positions 114
   Player Qualities 114
   Position Criteria 115
   Positions and Alignments 120
XIII. Shooting Play 121
XIV. Direct and Indirect Kicks 125
   Indirect—Defensive 125
   Indirect—Offensive 130
   Indirect Set Up Play 131
   Direct Kicks 137
XV. Corner Kicks 138
   Set-Up Plays 139
XVI Kickoff 144

YEAR TWO 149

I. Review Year One	149
II. The Weave	149
III. Pressure and Support Defender	153
7v7	159
9v9	164
TRANSITION PLAY	170
IV. 7v7 Transition Defensive to Middle Third	170
V. 9v9 Transition Defensive to Middle Third	191
VI. 7v7 Transition Middle to Attacking Third	209
VII. 9v9, 11v11 Transition Middle to Attacking Third	228
VIII. Finishing in the Goal Box	247
IX. Defensive Clearing	251

YEAR THREE 254

I. Review Years One and Two	254
II. Weave Play	254
III. Long Ball – Short Ball – Take-Over	255
IV. One Forward v Four Defenders	257
V. Attacking Plays	260

OBSERVATIONS and COMMENTS: 280

Passion for the Game	280
Elite Teams	283
Small Sided Games (7v7, 9v9, 11v11)	287
The Game is Always 11v11	290
Playground Mentality	290
The Elfredo Factor	292

EPILOGUE: 293

PREFACE

My wish is for every child to play soccer and understand why it is called the "beautiful game." The life lessons learned from participating are extensive. In my years of coaching high school, I began to notice that each year the players who came to me had fewer soccer skills. In 1994 I decided to open the SKILLS International Soccer Academy to teach our youth individual soccer skills. This was the first soccer academy in Rochester, New York. I analyzed the way skills were being shown to players and decided to develop a skills program using a curriculum approach, like teaching an academic subject. That would be the best way for young players to learn.

Having spent more than thirty-five years on the sidelines coaching youth players of all ages and having run many soccer camps over the years, I felt that we were not teaching the team game of soccer properly just as we had not been teaching the skills properly. Team practices consisted mostly of numerous and varied isolated drills. Never really seeing the progress that I thought a team should be making in their development, I felt that a different approach was needed in teaching teams the game of soccer. We have been teaching our players in reverse by attempting to teach them through a system of countless drills. Instead, what we need to do is to first teach them the very game of soccer itself and how it is meant to be played. Once they understand the game only then can we use various drills. If we teach the drills first and they do not yet understand soccer itself, they will be unable to associate how the drill fits into an aspect of the actual game. To achieve this end I have created a team-game concept for developing youth soccer teams. This program, like the individual skills program, also uses a curriculum approach to teaching. It limits the focus of each practice to learning only one aspect of the sport. Repetition of each element as well as simplicity is the key to developing players to play on instinct. Over stimulating the players with a multitude of activities will not achieve this goal.

I have written this book to demonstrate this alternate method for developing our youth to play soccer with an understanding of the game. The less pressure we put on our players the better they will learn to play. The simpler we keep our practices the more the player will learn, with repetition being the key. Therefore, **"Less is more"**!

George Werner

FOREWORD
By Dr. Hildegard Messenbaugh, MD

It has been the fashion in recent years to talk a great deal how self-esteem is instilled in our children. In rethinking this issue, we have invented a system that essentially says: "Let's never hurt their feelings." In order to accomplish this, in our infinite wisdom we have decided to, as much as humanly possible, only let a child win and get positive feedback and reward. We thought that surely with this would come the feeling on the child's part that he or she is therefore great, excellent, worthy and wonderful. Thus the child would then want to go forth to all endeavors with great positive self-regard. In keeping with this philosophy, we have sometimes abolished giving grades to children and in sports denying there is a winner or a loser in each game, sometimes by a very good margin even. It's taking the philosophy of: it's not whether you win or lose that counts, but how you played the game, to what appears to be its logical conclusion.

There are only two "minor" problems with this. One is that it involves lying to the child and two; the child has absolutely nothing to compare himself and his actions to.

Dissembling is involved because no one acknowledges a child's poor effort and there are no consequences to that poor effort. It also gives the impression that it does not matter really whether you did try or not, whether you did well in college or grad school, you'll still get ahead in life and people will praise you, which every adult knows assuredly will not happen. At best it is a very poor preparation for adult life. It also makes the idea of team sports ludicrous, because if it does not matter whether you win and by how much and no one keeps score, why should you help your teammate out and why should team effort matter? But if you can't play on a team, any team, even manual work becomes impossible. It is a lie to say there are no winners or losers in life. What a shock it would be to have to find out in adulthood. Would it thus not be surprising that as an adult the child would try to avoid losing at all costs?

Secondly, if a child gets rewarded and positively reinforced for even minor success, it in fact does not want to make him try. He or she then tends to think in a very narcissistic manner. If I'm already so great, how much greater do I need to become? And yet, children do compare themselves to each other and it is a burden to them to have to pretend to be so perfect already. And it is in losing and trying again that the true nature of a person is to be found. It is by real mastery of obstacles, of losses, of confronting our shortcomings that we gain real self confidence. It starts early in life when the toddler says to his mother: "Do it myself" and falls and gets up and tries again. He cries, skins his knee and tries again, and only after he masters his task does a big grin cross his face and he is ever so pleased with himself. Why are we depriving our children of this experience?

Dr. Messenbaugh is a Psychiatrist who is the Founder and Director of Third Way in Denver, Colorado whose focus is troubled adolescents. Third Way features several youth homes, a home for unwed mothers, and a high school.

PARENTS

A coaching friend of mine once stated that all youth games should be played at a time when parents cannot attend the game. Although meant as humor, I find it to be a very telling remark. Over the years I have found many coaches who feel that the problem with youth sports is the parents. Parental involvement today seems to have risen to the point where parents have a metamorphosis by changing from rational people into beings who are easily provoked, becoming belligerent, argumentative, and have a know it all attitude whose only focus is their own child.

How often have we seen parents fighting at youth games and be abusive towards the officials on the field, the coaches and even opposing players. No matter what side you are on, the other team is the one playing dirty and fouls all the time but your own team always plays by the rules. It is always the parents of the other team who are the ones yelling and acting obnoxious but never the parents from your team. The referee is always on the side of the other team thereby making favorable calls for their side but never good calls for your team. The coach knows nothing and is playing your child out of position or is not giving your child enough playing time and thereby is ruing your child's love for the sport. Your child should be on the A team but the selection system is flawed and the coach doesn't know anything. All these elements make what should be an enjoyable learning experience into something that is tension filled and confrontational.

PARENT EVALUATIONS:

The trend today is the involvement of the parents at all levels. It is a trend that is being talked about in the school systems and not just in youth sports.

Having been part of a club in which the parents evaluate a coach's performance at the end of the season, I have seen first hand some of the vile and hateful comments that parents make about a coach whose intention is to teach your child and interacts with your child. At times the coach provides rides or takes your child for ice cream after games. This same coach, who is criticized, spends time attending clinics, taking licensing courses and studying video tapes or reading books in an effort to become more qualified. This is the same coach who has VOLUNTEERED to do this job. Yet for all the coach's efforts, the reward more often than not is one of anger from the parents because of perceived treatment of their child.

I once acquired a player from a younger team who because of age had to move up to my team. During the indoor season this player showed fear and played very hesitant. This player had attended my skills academy so I knew what his skills where and thereby I had also become well acquainted with his parents. I had a discussion with this player and told him that he should not worry and do the best he can in practice. I assured him that I will not put him into situations during a game that would put him into a negative light. During the indoor games I played him only a few minutes at a time and usually with the best players. His parents would still greet me but the greetings had become formal and no longer friendly as had been the case in previous times. I could sense that they were not too happy with me but I did not care. My job was to do what I thought to be best for the child in regards to his soccer development and not worry what the parents thought of me. The parents of course wanted to see him play as much as the other players and I am sure thought me to be unfair. After all they paid the same amount of money as the other parents. As his confidence steadily grew I would increase his playing time. By the summer season he had grown to be a starter on our team. Had I given this player more playing time when he was not ready I would have ruined his desire and love for the game. Instead, I let the player grow into becoming part of the team. Once he was playing regularly the parents' greetings towards me became warm and friendly once again. The parents' opinion of me was directly related to the playing time their child had received from me. I feel certain that my parent evaluation would have been negative at the time their child was receiving little playing time but would have been positive when their child started and played regularly in games. Either way, I was still the same coach.

An incident that further illustrates the uselessness of these parent evaluations occurred one year on a 14U team when the team was without a coach the entire winter indoor season. In March I found a very experienced coach for this team. By that time this team consisted of only 10 players and was just two months away from starting their regular outdoor season. To add to the problem, most of these players were at best fourth division players or worse but had been registered to play in the third division. In order that they could field a team and play, these players recruited additional players who were recreation players and not travel players.

This new coach faced a difficult task. Not only were most of the ten veteran players not very good travel players and the recruited players only recreation players but within hardly two months time this coach had to mold this team to be able to play in the third division, a division much to strong for their abilities. These players had never been through a structured program in which they learned how to play as a team. At the age of 14, these players did not know how to kick off, how to form a defensive wall or that they even could form a wall on indirect kicks, how to execute a defensive position nor how to play as a team defensively. They had never gone through any conditioning. A very bleak picture after having so many of their developing years wasted.

The coach was in his middle thirties who had been a player since the age of seven, was an all league player, and his schools MVP. For 14 years he had taught soccer skills to players of all ages at the Skills International Soccer Academy and had coached numerous teams. His knowledge of teaching and coaching soccer is extensive. He began by developing order and discipline with these 14U players. He taught them how to organize themselves individually and as a team with the first focus being on how to defend. Although the team did not win any games they were able to achieve some ties and play all opponents to narrow scores while keeping each game manageable. With a little luck they could have won some games. By the end of the season opposing coaches would comment on how much this 14U team had improved over the course of the season.

At the end of the season a parent wrote a four page (that is correct - four pages) evaluation of this coach that criticized everything this coach had done. The parent evaluation stated that the coach should not have been teaching team tactics but instead should have taught individual soccer skills. The purpose of a team practice is to develop the tactical style of play with which the team will play the game as a unit. To develop individual soccer skills a player must attend a soccer academy which teaches those individual skills. A player must then take what is taught and practice on a daily basis. Developing individual skills requires personal hard work and dedication on a very regular basis. A player must arrive at team practice already possessing individual ball handling skills and not begin to learn those skills at team practice. This type of parent observation only shows the parent's ignorance.

This parent proceeded to attack the coach personally by stating, that the coach would walk past the players without acknowledging the players, the coach would use profanity, and that the coach would yell at the players all the time. These were all false observations made by this parent who did not attend practices on a regular basis. Most significantly, this parent never met or spoke with the coach but spoke to others behind the coach's back.

What purpose does such a negative and scathing evaluation of this coach accomplish? Keep in mind that most coaches VOLUNTEER to coach. What are a parent's soccer qualifications that would lead a parent to believe that he or she possess the ability to critique a coach? Not many parents have the qualifications to pass judgment on a coach. The knowledge parents normally have acquired regarding soccer is obtained from watching their children's youth games. Their knowledge they have gained comes having seen mostly kickball games that their child plays either in recreation leagues or travel soccer games that more often than not masquerade as real soccer games. Most parents are involved in youth soccer during the period their child is playing the sport. Once the child no longer is playing then the parents disappear from the games. Their interest is solely tied to their child's participation.

The overwhelming majority of parents have never coached in any capacity. They therefore do not know the dynamics of coaching and the wide range of coaching philosophies that are all credible methods of coaching and motivating a team. If the parent qualifications are missing then why have such a parent evaluation of coaches? These evaluations can do much harm and cause great pain to an individual who is trying to do their best. A potentially good coach can be lost as a coach. I have personally witnessed the anguish that some coaches have experienced when being confronted with such bad parent evaluations. It takes a very experienced coach who is able to realize the source of the evaluation and is thereby able to put them into a proper perspective. Personally, I have never even looked at any parent evaluation pertaining to me because they have no bearing on what I know my job to be in developing a team. I know what subject material I have to teach and how I must teach it. Most parents do not have my background in soccer. For this reason their opinions of me do not matter to me. Coaches have said to me that it is easy for me to say this since I am a professional coach. However, I say to a coach that they can have the same attitude if the coach has taken the extra time to study, attend clinics, has volunteered when others would not, and tries to do their best. The coach then has a larger investment than a parent and therefore a right to this attitude. Even if the coach's knowledge is limited it is still more extensive than the knowledge of the parents.

In 2007 I was hired to coach an 11U team. The team consisted of players from the previous year's C and B team along with a few holdover A team players. When I first saw them play I said to my assistant coach that if we are able to tie one game that season I will be happy and consider this a successful season. Their ability to play amounted to cluster soccer. I started practices and spent 50 minutes out of a one hour practice doing the same play. Six weeks later, the players were still doing the same passing play for the 50 minutes. As I found out later, the few parents that always remained at practice wondered what I was doing. They were paying me and I do the same play over and over. Had there been a parent evaluation at that time it certainly would have been negative. While doing this same drill over and over I began to demand from each player that they learn to focus and execute properly. A parent observing this and not knowing the process of developing my team will draw a wrong conclusion. They would have written a bad evaluation because I may have reprehended their child. Gradually I began to teach them how to defend as a team.

Without proper knowledge of what it takes to be a coach and how a team is developed, a parent cannot make a knowledgeable evaluation of a coach. This parent evaluation can only be biased and personal. It is graded by a parent from the point of how the coach has interacted with their particular child. Coaches should only be evaluated by a club Director of Coaching whose soccer background must be extensive to hold this position. From a Director of Coaching evaluation a coach will develop and grow as a coach. A Director of Coaching is able to spot an abusive coach or a coach with a lack of coaching ability and make adjustments to rectify a problem long before a season starts. The parent must bring any concerns to the Director of Coaching who has the ability to objectively asses the situation. By bringing a parental concern to the Director of Coaching instead of to the coach directly, the parent does not get into a confrontation with the team coach. The Director of Coaching is able to discuss the problem with the coach openly and from a position of experience while at the same time is discrete. Because of this experience by the Director the coach is therefore more receptive to any solutions. Unlike the parent, the Director of Coaching has no personal interest in any situation.

NO PARENT ZONE:

Some say that the parent pays the money to the club and therefore has every right to interfere with a coach. I question as to why they should have a say over which they have little experience and just because they pay the money? They pay for their child's school education but have no say over school coaches and school teachers. It is not any different when it comes to the child's participation in a club sport. The parent's obligation to their child is to pay the money for their child's participation and then stay out of the way. Let the child grow through their own experiences. This is all about the child's development. The achievements and experiences belong to the child alone whether the experiences are good or bad.

During the games it is most important to separate the team from the parents while both parents and team are on the same side of the field. The parents should be located on one side of the midfield line while the team should be located on the other side of the midfield line. There should be a good space between the team and parents. Team members must remain on the team side and are not allowed to go to see their parents during the game. Parents must remain on the parent side of the midfield line and short of an injury or an emergency they are not allowed to go over to the team side during a game. For example, if the player has forgotten their drink the parent cannot bring the player a drink once the game starts. The player will not forget the drink the next time.

Several years ago I was sitting in my chair on the sideline of a game. As always the parents sat on their side of the midfield line and the team sat on the opposite side of the midfield line. Between the two sides was the usual big space that I prefer. As I sat and watched my team play I was suddenly interrupted by a sound right next to me. I turned to my left to look and to my absolute surprise one parent was in the process of unfolding his chair, placed it right next to me and then sat down. I stared at him for a few moments in disbelieve then turned back to watch the game. I was stunned and my mind was no longer on the game as this was beginning to seriously disturb me. Finally I could not stand it any longer. I turned to the parent and slowly, with clenched teeth, I ask "Richard (not the real name) did you forget the rule? The rule is no parents on the team side." He turned to me and said "Shhhh, the parents told me that they would give me ten dollars if I came over here and sat next to you during the game." I asked him if I would get five of those ten dollars? He said that I would and I immediately told him to stay where he was. I not only made five dollars that day but I asked him why he hadn't thought of this at the beginning of the season so we could have been making some real money all along. After the game all the parents came up to me and laughingly told me that it would have been worth a hundred dollars just to see the expression on my face when this parent started to sit down next me. I was concerned how easily I could be bribed to compromise my rules when money was involved. The other concern to me was how quickly this conscience was dampened once I actually received the five dollars.

Several years later I was coaching a different team which of course had the same rules. At a game on an opponent's home field I started to walk back to the team side of the field just before the start of the game when I spotted an A frame type sign positioned directly at midfield. As I was walking I quickly read it. Several steps past the sign it hit me and I thought "did I really read what I think I read?" I turned around and walked back to the sign. Yes it did say what I thought it said: "George's No Parent Zone." This was amazing to me that this opposing team had the same "no parent zone rule" as I had and the coach's name was also George. I looked towards the parents section and wanted to draw their attention to this unbelievable coincidence. They were all sitting there laughing. They had made the sign and put it up. The rest of the season I brought this sign to every game and to this day I still have it.

In both situations the parents had accepted my rule. It made for a calm sideline and in the end they had fun with it as well as with me.

LIFE LESSONS:

The real purpose of youth sports is learning life lessons for both the parents and the players. The life lesson for the parent is to learn to let go from their control over their child. This is perhaps the hardest lesson for the parent to encounter but so very necessary in the growth of the child. The child's life lesson is to begin to function without the parent and to realize that the achievements and failures belong to the child. Of the two, the child's life lesson is easier to achieve since children naturally want to break from their parent while parents naturally want to hang onto their children.

The facts are that most of the youth players will never even play high school varsity. Even less will play in college and most will certainly not play at a higher level such as a professional or national team. Yet, most parents put their emphasis towards how good a player their child is. They begin to think about their child acquiring an athletic scholarship to a university. Imagine the thousands of youth players in your area alone. Then multiply this by the whole nation and you begin to realize how many children play soccer. Out of all these youth players only approximately one percent receive a soccer scholarship. A coach at the university level is hired to win games. If a coach has scholarships available that coach will first attempt to acquire an exchange student that can really play the game of soccer. How many of this one percent of scholarships will go to the players from the United States? Whenever a parent asks me about working with their child because they think the child has a chance for a soccer scholarship I tell them of the odds against it and even more importantly, their emphasis is in the wrong direction.

The parent should always emphasis first and foremost those life lessons that a child can only learn from youth team sports. The parent must learn to have faith in the child's teacher of the sport. The hardest thing for anyone is to give up control and place it into the hands of the coach. A parent must remember that the activity belongs exclusively to the child. It is the child who risks emotional uncertainties. It is the child who risks potential physical harm on the field of play. While sitting on the sideline the parent risks nothing but anguish or helplessness at a child's failure. The parent still remains unharmed. Not all the playing experiences may be good ones for the child. But as in life not all experiences will be good ones for them as adults. How the child learns to handle the positive or negative experiences as well as the pressures is what makes youth sports important.

Through this vehicle of youth sports the child learns about themselves. They can only learn this best when they are separated from the parents during this activity. Situations will arise such as dealing with something the coach said or did that require guidance for the child. The parent should then advise the child of what the parent perceives to be the best course of action for the child to take. The parent should advise the child what to say and how to say it but in the end it is the child who must handle the situation personally. The earlier that the child learns this, the better off this child will be in life.

I demonstrate this separation between parents and children at one of the first team meetings. I ask the players to form a semi circle in front of me. I then ask the parents to closely stand behind their child. I state that this is the way family works, a very tight closeness between the child and parent with the parent giving their total support to the child. Once this imagery is established I then ask the players to take five steps towards me. This demonstrates that the player is now under the coach's direction. I ask the parents to take five steps back and then proceed to walk in the space created while stressing that this space is the biggest life lesson learned in youth sports. This space that has been created gives a visual representation of what is meant by letting go and being supportive of the child from a distance. If the child should stumble the parent is not immediately there to pick the child up but instead the child has to function on his or her own while being responsible for their own actions.

SIDELINE BEHAVIOR:

At the Skills International Soccer Academy we had attached signs around the facility the stated "No Sideline Coaching." We found that parents watching their child in a class would shout instructions to their child in an attempt to be helpful. Imagine the chaos as each parent would be focused on "helping" their child. Soon you could not hear the instructor. The child would begin to listen to what the parent was saying and was no longer paying attention to the instructor. In the end the child would not be able to have learned anything and the parents wasted their money.

The same situation exists when parents start screaming out instructions to their child during a game. The child hears the parent's voice and then listens to what that voice is saying. I have seen situations where the child actually stopped playing. I recall a game where the ball had been kicked towards the goal. The mother screamed out the goalie's name, her child, and instructed the obvious by shouting "make that save!" The goalie stopped playing the ball and turned towards the sideline to hear what the mother had said. The ball went into the back of the net for a goal which would otherwise have been an easy save. The parent's instruction of "make that save" was a correct one but it was delivered strongly and at a bad moment.

From the beginning I inform my players and the parents that the players are to listen to only my voice for any soccer and game related instructions. The instructions from me will never be emotional and will always be only in reference to what we have been learning. What a parent shouts as an instruction to help their child may be technically correct but it may be something that I as the coach did not want the player to hear yet because I have not taught that yet. Instructions must never be out of context. Parents mean well but when taking it upon themselves to yell instructions they are only hurting and confusing the situation. More often than not parents associate a long kick by a player with it being a good kick. When a player boots the ball far, someone usually shouts out "Great Kick!" Most coaches have heard this. Unfortunately such a kick is usually kicked past everyone and a majority of the time is kicked to the opposing team. Such a kick is only good if the team is receiving great pressure in their defensive third of the field and needs some time to compose themselves. A big kick provides this time. As coaches we want the player to learn to control the ball and make a good pass to a teammate. When shouting out "Great Kick!" to a boom ball the parent sends a wrong message.

Shouting instructions is usually a fruitless exercise. Players do not appreciate having someone shouting from the sideline. It is distracting to the player. In most cases the player does not even hear what the parent is yelling from the sideline. Some years ago we had one of our academies located in an indoor facility right next to a large playing field. As with many indoor fields this one had walls around it with glass on top of the wooden wall. It looked like a hockey rink. One evening while we were holding classes' one father stood between our teaching area and the wall of the big rink which was only a three foot space. He was watching his son play. I studied him for fifteen minutes and the entire time he was pounding his fist onto the glass and shout instructions to his son. It was so distracting that we had to stop the class. I went over to him and informed him that he could not stand there, that his yelling is disrupting our class and that he had to remove himself to the bleacher spectator area. He gave me a look of disdain but decided to leave. As he was walking away I told him that all his antics were only disturbing us and did not help his son one bit since you cannot hear in the rink through the glass. The man had wasted his time and energy.

One of my teams had been entered into a weekend tournament. In the same age group with us was a team from Canada. These teams are generally very good and we were scheduled to play them. I decided to watch them play another opponent in our division. I positioned myself at the corner area on the Canadian team's side and away from their parents. At one point in the second half as the Canadian team attacked they played a ball to the outside on top of the opposing team's box area. A Canadian player sprinted towards the ball. The play was happening directly in front of me and coming towards me. The Canadian parents were jumping up and down screaming encouragement at the player sprinting towards the ball. The player could clearly hear this yelling and then did one of the most extraordinary things I have ever seen a young player do. As she was running towards the ball she looked right at the parents, smiled slightly and then put her index finger to her lips and taped her lips several times. She was telling her parents to be quiet. She was being distracted by their yelling. This young person was being an example of behavior to the adults on the sideline. I will always remember this incident for I consider it a privilege to have witnessed this.

Sideline behavior should be calm. Only "good job" or "nice play" should be shouted if in fact it was a "good job" or "nice play." These should not be said just for the sake of saying them. Playing instructions must never come from a parent on the sideline.

PLAYING TIME:

Playing time for each player on a team has been a serious issue for parents. Their thinking is simple; they have paid the same amount as the others therefore their child should receive the same amount of playing time as everyone else on the team. Whoa to the coach whom they feel has not given their child equaled playing time. In the eyes of the parent that coach instantly becomes a "know nothing" coach who doesn't like their child and who is out to hurt this child's self esteem. That coach is favoring other players over their child. They feel that their child is just as good or is even better than the other players on the team.

Every coach has heard of parents sitting on the sideline looking at their watch to time the amount their child played in comparison to the other players. Some parents have even gone as far as bringing a stop watch to the game. I know of coaches that have experienced this. This is a sad indictment of an adult. The image of a parent sitting on the sideline with a stop watch makes this parent out to be a somewhat pathetic person. This parent has lost sight of what youth sports is all about. To spend your time at your child's game counting seconds as opposed to enjoying what these young players are accomplishing is almost beyond comprehension. This speaks volumes about a parent's character who has failed to understand the life lesson being taught to parents by youth sports—separation from the child. However, in the eyes of the parent it is the coach's fault for this behavior by the parent. It is the coach who has forced this and is the one responsible for the action of the parent.

Athletic ability is the biggest decider of playing time. Parents do not take into consideration that perhaps their child is not as good as another player. The fact is that some will always be better players than others. Like it or not, not everyone is born with equal athletic ability. Parents must learn to face that fact. Not everyone is born with the same musical ability or math ability. For some unknown reason parents feel that everyone has the same athletic ability and believe that if it were not for the coach holding their child back then that child would be a star player. If you are not born with the ability to sing you will never be able to sing no matter how many voice lessons you take. The same holds true when it comes to athletic ability. Lack of this athletic ability does not make a child less of a person it only makes the child a lesser player on a team.

The position that a player plays on a team is another major factor as to how and when a player is given playing time. Certain positions do not lend themselves to making substitutions freely. Generally these positions are up the middle such as the sweeper, stopper, center midfielder, and especially goalie. Baring an injury, I never substitute those central positions. By their very nature the positions are anchor positions. They stabilize a team and a change at those positions will be disruptive to a team. A player may have some training at the central positions but will unlikely be playing there if the starting player does not get hurt. It takes a very focused and skilled player to play these central positions and your child may just not be best suited to play there. Just because a central player may need to come out of a game or has played the whole game does not mean that your child will go in at that position and receive more playing time. The central position players must be very consistent.

It is not as disruptive to change the outside or forward positions. The further away the position is from the own goal the easier it is to substitute at those positions. The players who play those positions usually will share playing time with other players and it is there that your child may find their playing time. The outside positions and forwards are not as multi dimensional as the central positions. Unfortunately to parents, who generally have limited soccer knowledge and are focused only on their own child, all positions are the same.

Team commitment becomes another element that dictates a player's playing time in a game. If a player misses practices more often than other players then the result is less playing time. I have always had a rule that every player on the team should receive halve the playing time if they are "in good standing". The key here is "in good standing." Parents have a tendency to overlook this part when reading about receiving halve the playing time. Missing practices does not put a player in good standing with the team.

A player's behavior while with the team will indicate the playing time. Insubordination towards a coach, general disruptive behavior, attitude towards fellow players, acting up, showing disinterest towards what the team is practicing, doing another activity while the rest of the team is doing something different. The list is endless and will not put a player "in good standing" with the team. Playing time is then limited for this player.

With all my teams I have always had a rule that if a player does not have their own uniform they cannot borrow a uniform from a teammate such as the goalie. It is the player's responsibility to come to the game prepared. Not having the uniform tells me that the player did not come prepared to the game and thereby will not receive any playing time in the game. Players must learn that they have to come prepared for the game and remain focused during the game even when on the sideline. A big life lesson!

Any player who wanders over to the parent section for whatever reason, short of an injury, might as well stay with the parents because that player will not receive any playing time the rest of the game.

There have been numerous times I have sent players to the midfield ready to be substituted into the game. Up to five or ten minutes go by and they are still standing on the sideline waiting to be called into the game. Why the delay? Players can only be substituted under certain circumstances such as their own throw in. If a circumstance does not present itself then the player cannot be called onto the field. The parent timing their child's playing time does not factor that in and draws the conclusion that their child is being shorted playing time

There are many elements that factor into the playing time of a player. The parent will still argue that since they pay the same amount as everyone else on the team their child should receive the same amount of playing time. To this I say to the parent that the fees they pay to a club are not for playing time on a team. Those fees pay for the cost an organization encounters to provide your child the opportunity to receive the life lessons they will learn through an organized team activity such as soccer. If a parent learns to separate from the child then that parent has learned a life lesson. If the player realizes they are held accountable for their behavior then that child has learned a life lesson. If a player learns that what each person does on a team effects each and every other player on the team then that player has learned a life lesson. If a player and parent learn that they are not as gifted at a sport as others then they have learned a life lesson. These life lessons are invaluable. The more life lessons that are learned by players and parents the greater the value a parent receives for their fee. Sometimes not giving a player playing time is of much greater value for a parent's fee than if a player is rewarded for an infraction with playing time.

The fee a parent pays is for their child's education that will help that child the rest of their lives.

COMMITMENT:

In all the years of coaching youth soccer I have had a rule of never coaching beyond the age of sixteen unless I was also the varsity coach at the local high school. By the age of seventeen youth players have so many other things going on in their lives that they have no time for their team activity. Most will be working at their first job for the summer. They will be driving and over the summer there will be constant social activities. This does not allow much time for soccer. By that age many will quit the sport and all that is left are those who are serious player who intend to play in college. At the age of twelve a club may have three teams, by the age of seventeen clubs usually feature only one team.

Against my better judgment, I once coached a seventeen age group team. I did it because I had taken over the team when they were at the age of sixteen. It was a team that for several years had a different coach each year. I decided to remain with the team at the age of seventeen because I did not wish to be just another one year coach. It was a huge mistake but deep down I knew that it would be. I wanted to give the team some stability and continuity it had not received in the past. Unfortunately for most practices I had only about four to five players. Numerous games were played with only eight or nine players. I was unable to teach anything. It was a very frustrating summer.

The commitment from that team had vanished. The older the age group the fewer the amount of players and consequently the fewer the teams participating. I can almost understand the lack of commitment by players at the age of seventeen. I have difficulty understanding the lack of commitment by the younger players.

Unless players play on a premier club that demands that players be fully and exclusively committed to their team, youth players do not feel a necessity to be committed to their team at the travel club or the recreation club level. The premier clubs teach their players a very large life lesson by demanding this commitment. By not making any commitment demands whatsoever, the travel clubs and recreation clubs fail to teach a child commitment which is one of the most important lessons to be learned by our youth.

Having held the position of Director of Coaching with several regular travel soccer clubs I had attempted to implement a stricter commitment policy. These attempts met with a strong resistance from the parents. Their reasoning is always the same. Their children should have the opportunity to be exposed to other sports or activities. Parents feel that this is the only way that their child will know what they would eventually like to do. During these most important development years youth players participate in a variety of activities without ever learning to understand what commitment is. Yes, they are exposed to several things and perhaps they will find something they will like to participate in over other sports. At what cost? Without first learning how to commit to something these players will only achieve the status of an average player. It is not possible to achieve superior ability without spending the time at constant practice. Without deep focus to one thing the opportunity to be considered the best at a sport is lost. Natural ability will only get you so far.

A youth player must first learn what is meant by commitment BEFORE they participate in a variety of activities. The parent should allow their child to participate in only one sport each year. What ever the child selects then this sport receives the child's complete focus and attention. The youth players must make all practices, games, practice skills on their own time, and take part in any additional developmental activity that will enhance the player's understanding and execution of the sport. This means that the youth player may have to sacrifice things such as a party, school social activity, family function, and what ever other social events that presents themselves. The player can play other sports on their own time and only when it does not interfere with the chosen main sport. The following year the parents and child can reassess their position and then perhaps commit to and try something else.

Commitment involves sacrifice and by allowing a child to participate in several sports at the same time the parent does the child a great disservice. Our youth today is insulated by parents from learning this sacrifice of commitment. Parents want to protect their child from any difficulty. Yet the difficulty of commitment is a most important life lesson that a child can learn. This life lesson will aid them greatly as they go through life and work at a job.

What is the proper age to learn commitment? I constantly hear how the players are too young at age nine or eleven or even at thirteen or fourteen. What is the magic age for a person to learn about commitment? I have always believed that the younger a person can learn something the better they will utilize the knowledge. Teach them when they know nothing else.

The old saying "Jack of all trades but master of none" holds true when a child is allowed to participate in several sports or on several teams at the same time. Let us assume that the child after a few years selects one sport to which they will devote there full attention. If they have not learned the sacrifice of commitment beforehand, then that child will not give this sport the full attention necessary to become an outstanding player. Commitment is a bigger and more important lesson to learn than permitting a child to be exposed to numerous sports just to see which sport they will prefer. The understanding of commitment will get a child through life itself.

By allowing a child to play numerous sports at the same time, a parent is telling this child that the normal physical restrictions do not apply to this child. There are only twenty four hours in a day and only seven days in a week and that fact is the same for every person living regardless of age. The child must learn this fact.

The parents who allow a child to participate in several sports do allow it because they possibly wish to brag about their child being an outstanding athlete. If the parent is living through the child then that inhibits the child's development as an individual. The truth is that those who are athletically inclined only excel in one sport. Take a look at the many great professional athletes who have tried to cross over and do a second sport at the same intensity as their main sport. They are never as good at the second sport. Most of them are average at best. If it does not work for professional athletes then why does a parent believe that it will work for their child?

A commitment of convenience has been established when a child is allowed to diversify their activities. "I will attend soccer practice if we have nothing else to do that conflict with another activity." Most coaches hear this regularly. When allowing this, the parent teaches the child to commit to soccer, for example, unless it is inconvenient to attend because another sport has their practice or game at the same time. Some allow their child to split the commitment by attending soccer one week and the other sport the next week. The child learns that it is all right to split their commitment according to how convenient it is. It is a very selfish characteristic for a child to learn. With this commitment of convenience a child learns a "me first" attitude by putting self interest ahead of a team interest. This attitude will create problems for a child when later in life they have to work with other employees who rely on each other to be an effective work force.

It is difficult for parents to look at commitment beyond their child's freedom to participate in more than one sport at a time. The bigger picture of what commitment means is simply ignored for a self centered attitude. Children will figure out in what they wish to participate on their own. Somehow they will be drawn to another sport through friends or some equipment or something they may have seen or even something they have experienced within the present sport they are participating.

I once received an invitation to attend a graduation party from high school. I recognized the name of a player who had played for me on an 11-Under team years earlier. I had not seen this player since then because I only coached this team for one season. I felt privileged that this child still remembered me after all these years and invited me on this special occasion. I rang the door bell and a tall young man with longer hair answered. He greeted me enthusiastically and was very happy that I came to his party. I did recognize him somewhat but he had grown so much. His parents I remembered immediately. Parents do not change as drastically as the players do. After some pleasant conversation, Ryan asked me to follow him into the living room for he wished to show me all the awards he had achieved during his years in high school. There were so many medals, plaques, citations, and trophies that you could hardly count them all. They were from high school events, sectional events, and state events. As I admired them Ryan said to me "Coach this all happen because of you." It was a moment I will never forget. It almost brought a tear to my eyes. Ryan and his parents then proceeded to tell me how he had learned about commitment that one year he played sweeper for me. I had not allowed the players to participate in another activity. All the players had to attend all practices and games. During my pre-season conditioning camp he learned that he had to attend every session in order to be in optimum condition to play properly.

The most amazing thing about all this was that all the medals, plaques, citations, and trophies were not for soccer at all. No, all the awards were for running. During the conditioning camp in preparation for soccer, Ryan had found out that he loved to run. He gave up soccer the next season and dedicated himself to becoming a runner. He felt that he could not have become a successful runner if he had not learned about commitment first. Ryan had learned the biggest life lesson—commitment! This is and absolute true story.

Players will find their way on their own. However, whatever they select will receive only limited attention if the player has not learned the deep meaning of commitment first.

When players are allowed to practice limited commitment of convenience they are telling a coach that the coaches' time and efforts are not important as another activity scheduled at the same time. They are telling their teammates that they are not as important as the self interest activity. Those players are showing disrespect for the coach and their teammates. It is impossible to serve two masters at the same time. By serving one you negate the other. If this is true for adults then why do parents allow their child to learn that this principal does not hold true for that child?

Parents and coaches must teach real commitment to youth players ahead of teaching anything else.

PRAISE:

As previously discussed, a youth player approaches the ball during a game and kicks it far. The ball goes out of bounds, over the players to no one, or to an opposing player. "Great kick!" is what you will hear from the parents. Yet the kick accomplished nothing beneficial to the kicker's own team.

A youth player has the ball in front of the opposing team's goal but when the player shoots on goal the kick is high over the top, very wide of the goal post, or is kicked directly at the keeper. "Nice try!" is what you will hear from the parents. But in reality the shot was terrible and an opportunity for scoring was lost.

A youth player has the ball but dribbles it out of bounds, loses it to an opponent, or makes a pass either too far ahead of a teammate or too far behind. "Good effort!" is what you will hear.

How are these good tries if the player has lost the ball?

The examples can go on. We have become a society that praises everything regardless of whether the action of a youth player was productive or not. Everything is good, great, or nice. With these comments we give our youth players a false sense of accomplishment. As a consequence they have difficulty with any criticism. As long as the player feels good about themselves that is all that matters. Only the attempt seems to be important but not the result. The youth player can feel good because the player simply tried something.

Accomplishment is not rewarded. At the youth games up to age eleven or twelve no score is kept regarding the outcome of the game. The reason given is that in this way no one will feel as a winner or a loser. This approach does not help the youth player. Part of growing up is not only learning how to handle success but also learning how to handle losing. By not keeping score in a game we have deprived the young player this valuable life lesson that the end result also matters and not only the effort. The irony of this policy is that the players do keep score themselves. They know whether or not they won or lost.

Regrettably this policy of not rewarding an accomplishment is not restricted to the keeping score at a youth game. More and more school districts are eliminating the valedictorian at graduation. They do not wish for the student body to feel bad about themselves by reminding them that someone really worked hard to achieve a high academic success. The real lesson should be to learn how to appreciate someone's achievement and success. The achievement from ones' personal work did not come at the expense of someone else. Why can an achievement therefore not be acknowledged? We have become a society where everyone gets a trophy regardless of the results. If you participated you are a winner and therefore the saying which is heard constantly today "You are all winners!" is such a popular saying.

One learns from making mistakes. If a player has done something that is not beneficial to the team play but receives praise anyhow then that player will not learn from the mistake. When coaching a team I do not correct a player during a game. I allow that player to make the mistake even though I see the problem. After the game or at practice I will explain to the player what the player had done wrong. The player now learns from that mistake. The mistake therefore was beneficial because the mistake taught a life lesson. Yes, it would be easier to yell onto the field and give the player direction. However, the lesson will be much more effective if it is taught because of the mistake instead of having saved a player from the mistake.

This false praise is in reality a lie. The message that we are sending is that it is all right to lie if it makes one feel good. The child acquires a false self esteem through these lies. Self esteem is part of a person's character. What kind of character is built upon lies? Real self esteem can only be acquired through honesty and truth. Only then will it be built onto a solid foundation. False self esteem will create a narcissistic person.

Always tell them the truth because deep inside your little darlings know that you are really lying to them when giving them false praise. We must teach them how to handle an adverse situation instead of protecting them from it by giving them praise that is not true. As with all lessons, the younger a player learns the lesson of false praise the better that lesson will be part of the character growth of this young player. They are never too young to learn a valuable lesson.

LIKING THE COACH:

"He likes his coach."

"She doesn't like her coach."

Too often a child's participation in a sport activity depends upon whether the child likes his or her coach. The coach is a good coach if the coach is liked by the child and definitely a bad coach if the child does not like the coach. To so many people the coaches' ability to coach is based on whether or not the coach is liked by the child. How have we arrived at the point where a person's ability is based on whether the person is liked or disliked?

Having been part of soccer clubs in all capacities for many years, I have often heard parents say that their child will not play on a team if a certain person is the coach. Liking the coach seems to be the requirement for a child to participate. Loving the game and wanting to participate because the child loves to compete in this game does not seem to be a factor. Should the child's love for the game not be the main reason for wanting to participate? Instead of giving in to the child the parent should instead explain this most important reason for participating.

As the child grows they will encounter many people whom they do not personally like and yet they will be required to work and deal with this person. They may not like a teacher, a fellow student, a boss or a co-worker. Will they be allowed not to attend school or not go to their place of employment? Certainly not! Why would a child then be allowed to base their decision of joining a sport and team on whether the child likes the coach?

From my personal experience I have found that usually the child does not like a coach or teacher because that person is strict and enforces the rules. Personally, I would prefer my child to be associated with a coach or teacher who has rules and requirements and enforces those rules and requirements. When the child refers to a coach or teacher as mean it usually indicates that the child has been reprimanded for behavior other than what is required and expected. In the school environment the child is not able to select their teacher or their school coach. Why is it allowed to be an issue when deciding about participating on a club team?

This is another important life lesson that is being taught within the framework of participating in a team activity. The child needs to learn that when growing up they will encounter many individuals some of whom they will like and some of whom they will not. In either case they will need to deal with a variety of people in order to live in this life. Liking a person has nothing to do with a person's ability. The main concern must be what they are able to learn from a coach and not whether they like the coach.

PLAYER TRY OUTS:

There is anxiety attached to try outs for players, parents, and coaches. For players the anxiety is making the team or if there are several teams at an age group it would be making the first team. Anxiety for the parents is the same as for the players. The coaches all anguish over having to either cut a player or move a player to the second team.

From the coach's view I can say that the placement of players was always my least favorite part of the job. You never want to hurt a young player's love for the game of soccer. It was painful for me to see the disappointment in a player's face or hear it in their voice. I would agonize sometimes for days over what to do regarding a player. The anxiety for a coach becomes even greater if that player is on the borderline. I am certain that mostly all coaches feel this way about player placement after try outs.

The players seem to adjust quickly to their placement. Their anxiety mostly exists before and during the try outs. Once they are placed they go on and integrate themselves into the team. After some initial disappointment their position falls into two categories. It either does not make much difference to the player or the player decides to work harder and make the higher team at the next tryouts. For the most part players have a better perspective regarding the outcome of try outs perhaps because they know the reasons that they are playing in the first place.

For the parents the anxiety seems to be the most severe. They take the outcome the hardest if the outcome is not what they expected. Disappointment and anger is their reaction. The coach is an idiot! The coach is blind and doesn't know what he or she is doing! The selection process was political and thereby their child had no chance! I have heard it all on many occasions. I have been on the phone with parents for as much as an hour listening to them vent. Sometimes it is heart wrenching.

To the parent it is hardly ever the lack of ability of the child. I have always found it difficult to listen when an adult compares the ability of their own child to the ability of another child. Why is there a need to belittle another child? One has nothing to do with the other child.

Regardless of the efforts in making the tryout process impartial there are other factors that go into selecting a team. The coach must be allowed to pick players for specific purpose. Some coaches look for only size, some look for only speed while others look for individual ball handling skills. I have selected players who give directions very naturally while they play. Communication that a player gives during play is for me an important quality that I look for in a player since it does not always come natural to youth players to talk to their teammates during a game. This is a quality that a parent, whose knowledge of soccer is limited, does not take into consideration when comparing their child to another.

I once had two players on the bubble after try outs. One player was very aggressive and attacked everything and one player played calm and within themselves. Both were good players but I could only select one. There is a necessity for both type of players but after much debate I decided on the player who was calmer when playing.

When I called the aggressive player to give her encouragement and let her know that she is a good player it was my misfortune to have her mother answer the phone so I never was able to speak to the child. The mother launched into major outburst that included all of the previously mentioned descriptions of me as a coach, the try out process in general and with the end result she hung up on me. In my experience this has been the most common reaction by a parent. Her child that season played on a team from another club. After not receiving satisfactory team placement the next season, they once again played for a different club.

However, I have had two outstanding experiences with parents whose children had been cut from the A team. My friend Bob Wells simply said that as long as his child was enjoying playing it did not matter on what team the child was on. He also was of the opinion that it might be in the best interest for the child to play on the B team. Regarding the second parent, I had anxiety in giving him the news that his child did not make the A team. Rich Prem had been a big supporter of the A team and the program I had initiated. Now I had to call him regarding his child's team placement. I could sense his disappointment in his silence after he received my news. But after a short pause he said very simply and in a calm voice: "Now I will see what my child is made of. Will she quit and give up trying or will she work harder and try to get back to the A team?" This response was very unusual and most refreshing.

Those two parents understood that this was about the development of their child and had nothing to do with them. They allowed their child to stand on their own feet and grow. The life lesson had been achieved and understood. What and outstanding contribution these two parents had made by their reaction. The problem arises when parents make youth sports about themselves rather than about the child. They tie themselves to the child so what happens to the child is also happening to them. Since each child is at a different level mentally, a player can sometimes develop better emotionally and physically when they move to a weaker team. The child can learn to become a leader on a B team instead of having to face a constant pressure situation on an A team. LESS pressure, the MORE room to grow. The outcome by the reaction of both parents produced a very positive result since both players made it back to the A team the following year.

VIGILANTE PARENTS:

We have all heard of the "helicopter parents" who hover over their children and protect them from all adversity. The "vigilante parent" takes this concept further and thereby becomes extremely destructive. In my many years of involvement in youth soccer I have had first hand experience of parental conspiracies against a coach. To witness a group of adults sitting on the sideline of these youth games making derogatory remarks about the coach of their child's team is a despicable characteristic that an adult can display. Possessing limited knowledge about the sport, they proceed to second guess the decisions of the coach in all aspects. It is like parents thinking that just because they attended third grade they are now able to teach third grade. Without any or very limited qualifications they believe that they know better. For whatever their reasons it usually begins with one or two parents who stir up this trouble and then it starts to affect the rest of the parent group.

Nothing or no one in life is perfect and yet these parents want perfection from the coach. One of the life lessons for the child is to learn how to deal with someone who is not like them or who does not think or act like them. But parents who make it their mission to "get the coach" deprive their child from learning how to deal with someone who is different from them and whom they might not like.

These parent vigilantes make life difficult for their own child, their team parents, their volunteer coach, and their volunteer club leaders. They do this because of their arrogant and selfish reasons. The parent who partakes in this behavior has lost all sight of what the purpose of youth sport is. These individuals must be unhappy people or they would have no need to put others down. Vigilante behavior is a most shameful and negative behavior. No matter how these parents rationalize their vigilante behavior it will always remain offensive to all human dignity.

The next segment will highlight a positive parent behavior.

A PARENT'S ADVICE:

When I began my career coaching youth soccer, I must confess that I was not the model of sideline behavior. I had a great dislike for referees. I felt that they were there to ruin the game for me. It seemed to me that every call was against my team. As a result I would harass them non stop throughout the game. Every call was bad and needed to be challenged by me. I thought all of them to be terrorists. My antics were endless.

The arguments would not end just because the game had ended. I once confronted the referee at midfield at the end of the game and proceeded to let him know what I thought of his refereeing. He started to reach into his shirt pocket to show me the red card. Being out of ear shot of everyone I told him that if he pulled the card I would kill him right then and there. He put the card back into his pocket. Success!

I had backed a referee down, or so I thought. Two days later I received the red card in the mail with a two hundred dollar fine. I had to appreciate that referee's ingenuity even though it still cost me money.

On another occasion I followed the referee to his car in the parking lot ranting my opinions all the way. It was an angry drive home. With beer in hand I plopped myself into my recliner seething over the idiotic calls this referee had made. Suddenly I realized that in my rage I had left my son behind at the soccer field. I jumped back into my car and sped back to the field where I found him casually waiting for my return. He had become used to my idiotic behavior and knew I would be back.

For many years I have been the only coach in my youth soccer district that had the distinction of having been thrown out of the game before the game even had started. That record may still stand since I have never heard of another coach who has been red carded before the game had started. Over a short period I had accumulated enough red and yellow cards to wallpaper my living room not to mention the amount of fines I had to pay. That was my legacy and reputation as a coach the first few years of my career.

I take no pride in these stories.

One summer day I was walking off the field after a game. I had been my usual argumentative self with the referee receiving my input. The mother of one of my players was walking next to me.

No words had been spoken up to this point since no one usually spoke to me after a game. But on this day I suddenly heard her call my name. I turned towards her and she calmly said, "You know George, all of the parents agree with what you say in your arguments with the referees. However, you speak so vehemently that people stop listening and just back up becoming defensive."

It was a momentous turning point in my coaching life! I thought about her words. I realized that through my eyes looking from inside out I seemed to be speaking normally. I did not see myself from the outside as others saw and heard me.

I also realized that in all my years of arguing I had never changed a referee's mind. At no time did a referee say to me that I was right and that I would receive a penalty kick in my favor to make up for a bad call.

From that moment on I began to work at ignoring the referees. There is nothing I could do about their calls or behavior. I only had control over myself. I trained myself to never confront a referee. I do not say hello, goodbye or anything else.

At the end of the game I usually thank the referee for his/her time and that is all.

Because of this parent's constructive advice my career as a youth coach has produced a calm coach during games who focuses only on the play of the game. This parent could have easily become a vigilante parent who talked with the parents on the sideline behind my back thereby creating all kinds of animosity and strife. Instead this parent was thoughtful and considerate and spoke to me personally, giving me a very important life lesson. By these few words this parent had accomplished so very much and I am forever grateful to Barbara Williams.

THE COACH

Coaches in youth sports must first and foremost be teachers.

The influence that a coach has over the youth players is vast. The child will remember the words spoken and the actions taken by the coach the rest of their lives. The question then is how do you as the coach wish to be remembered in years to come by each and every player who has been under your tutelage? Will they view you as a kind person who taught them and thereby helped them in their growth as a person or will they remember you as a tyrant who belittled them and was abusive to them.

LIFE LESSONS:

The teaching of life lessons is at the heart of being a youth coach. If a coach's focus is to teach only the sport with the intent of winning a game then that coach is a failure no matter how many games that team wins. The sport is merely the vehicle we must use to teach the many life lessons that a child learns from an organized activity such as team sports.

I once took one of my teams to a preseason scrimmage game. All the players from the team were present including our only goalie. The goalie had missed many practices over the indoor season and I couldn't remember the last time I saw our goalie at a practice. As the starting players walk onto the field, our goalie proceeded to follow them. I asked "Where are you going?" "In goal!" was the answer. I replied: "I didn't know whether you could play goal since you never attend practice" and then requested the goalie to step off the field. The rest of the players stopped and ask me who was going to play in goal? I told them that no one was playing in goal and that is why I put 11 field players onto the field. As the game began the coach from the opposing team came over to inform me that I didn't have a goalie in goal. I thanked him and stated that I knew. As the score kept mounting against us several parents came to whisper excuses into my ear regarding the goalie not having a means to come to practice. I told them that I knew all about it but that I didn't care. We had attempted to make arrangements to get the goalie to practice but the goalie didn't make the effort to take us up on it. So here we were playing with eleven field players and a fully dressed goalie standing next to me on the sideline. We lost 12 to 0. At the end of the game the players were not only tired but confused. I called them all together and informed them that on a team what one member does or does not do will affect every other team member. On a team we work together towards a common goal. It is more important to learn THAT life lesson than to win a meaningless scrimmage game. From that time on this team unified and produced their first winning season. At the end of the season the team presented me with a team picture signed by all the players. The goalie wrote on the picture thanking me for teaching this lesson. To my surprise, the word of this action had spread in the local soccer community. Many had asked me if I really played without a goalie. Winning was never a thought. Since the opportunity had presented itself I felt it more important to teach this life lesson.

Every action and every word by the coach must be geared towards the growth of the player as a person. It is this responsibility that gives great meaning to being a youth coach. Without THIS being a youth coach's focus, the job is useless. Short of the very few who will turn into professional players, no one really needs to learn to play soccer or any other youth sport. They need to learn how to read or write or do math but certainly not how to play a game. Teaching of life lessons must therefore be the constant purpose for a youth coach to make playing a youth game relevant.

The job is to make the players independent thinkers who are sure of their decisions and who understand what it is they are doing. Early on in my association with a team I begin to train my players in this lesson. It is not a separate training from the tactical or skill teaching of the sport. The two go hand in hand. It is useless to develop only a skilled player if that player is at the same time not a decisive player who cannot function without the constant guidance of the coach from the sideline.

Usually during a small sided game I begin to teach this lesson early in my relationship with the team. When I see a player make a very thoughtful play that is very well executed I stop the play and approach the player. In a very stern voice and a serious look on my face I ask the player as to what on earth they were thinking when they made that play. The player tenses up and replies with the universal catch all answer of "I don't know." I reply that this is an answer that I never wish to hear again and then I let the play continue. I will repeat this scenario as often as possible for not only the present small sided game but for any play that they are involved in over the next several practices. Each encounter is placed into my memory to be recalled at a time when I will teach this life lesson.

Once I sense that the players have become unsure of and have given me the "I don't know" answer often enough I will call them in for a discussion. I then will go through each time I had stopped play to ask a player why a particular decision was made. Because of my stern voice and demeanor each player had always backed away thinking that they had executed something wrong and that I had reprimanded them. After a slight silent pause and making eye contact with each player, I smile. I proceed to inform them that each one of the plays was an excellent decision and very well executed. The question for them is why did I stop play and appear as if I was angry at the player for having done something wrong? The answer, I approached each player in a harsh voice to see how the player will answer. What I wish to achieve is for each player to recognize and understand when they are making a good decision and executing a play very well. I want each player to learn to stand up for their action no matter who questions them even if it is the coach. They need to understand that in a game I need players who are sure of themselves and know how to play the game. In the future, they are to tell me why something was the right decision on their part and they are not to back off and say "I don't know."

From that point on I will stop a good play and approach a player for an explanation. If the player defends the decision, then this life lesson has been learned and stronger players are being developed.

FUN:

"They have to have fun!"

"Just as long as they are having fun!"

"Having fun is what it's all about!"

For many years I have heard the word "fun" used when there is a reference to a youth player participating in a sport. But what is fun? The term is used constantly but is never defined. One of the earliest responsibilities the coach faces is to teach the concept of fun in relation to the team sport. This lesson should begin at the earliest age when the players begin playing in a competitive league, usually around the age of eight.

Begin by bringing the team together and asking them what it is that they consider fun. Some of the general answers the coach can expect are:

"Fun is being with your friends."

"Fun is running around."

"Fun is doing something you like to do."

"Fun is messing around and doing what you feel like doing."

Most of the answers will center with these themes. Attempt to solicit an answer from each player. Once the answers are exhausted the job begins for the coach to guide the players to a new understanding of fun.

Remind the players that all their answers are true answers as to the meaning of fun. Unfortunately these definitions do not have the same meaning when it comes to playing a team sport. When it comes to team sports fun must include discipline. Discipline requires each player to exercise some self control. Each player's actions will affect every other player on a team. Since all players on a team depend on each other we have to look out for each other and not do something that hurts our other players. Individual actions must therefore be geared towards the common goal.

Another important element in fun regarding team sports is focus. Focus requires each player to keep their attention on the particular task that is being taught for the purpose of playing the game well. As with discipline, when one player is not focusing all the other players on a team will be affected.

When it comes to team sports the playground mentality regarding fun must now include the element of discipline and focus. When players are allowed to run around screaming or chasing each other wildly or not paying attention it will be impossible for the players to learn how to play. Discipline and focus create the atmosphere necessary for learning. Learning is in itself fun. A new fun will be found by the players when they are able to play well against another team because they learned something the other team's players do not know.

Youth players generally do not associate that learning how to play a game includes the same process as learning how to read or write. During this discussion of redefining fun I will ask the players how many play an instrument. Most of them will raise their hands. I then proceed to ask what instrument they play. After allowing them a few moments to tell me about their musical experiences I pick on one player and ask that player whether they played a song the very first time they sat down to play their instrument. The response is a smile followed by a "no." I then ask that player what was the first thing they learned when they took up the instrument. The answer is how to play the individual notes as being the first thing they learned. I now stress the point that before they could even play a simple song they had to learn the individual notes. Once they knew how to play the individual notes they learned to put a few notes together in a particular sequence and they were now playing a song. As they practiced and it became easier to string notes together they were able to play much better with the songs becoming more involved or more difficult. Finally, I ask the player as to how it felt when they had reached the point where they were playing actual songs and was that feeling fun for them?

By linking the playing of a sport to the participation of another activity, such as playing an instrument, they have an example that learning the sport is the same thing as learning to play an instrument. Without the discipline of sitting down to practice and without the focus on the notes they would have been unable to learn how to play the songs with the instrument. In the end there is great satisfaction in being able to play and with satisfaction comes fun.

Unfortunately there is the false perception that sport is running around and since all children know how to run around they automatically know how to play a sport. A sport requires the same learning process as anything else. In all probability, the coach will need to teach this lesson numerous times before it is understood by the players. The younger the team is the more often the coach must redefine fun for the players.

To participate in a sport, FUN needs to include discipline, focus and learning.

BORED:

As with fun, a youth coach must address boredom with the youth players. This subject should also be addressed at a time when they start to play soccer competitively. The younger these principals are learned, the better.

Our children grow up in a world of instant gratification. They like to play what they feel that they are good at because they will then feel good about themselves. They like to do what comes easy. As a result their attention span is very limited. To accommodate their short attention span we have developed a system of numerous short activities. Each activity will last approximately ten minutes and then we move on to the next activity for ten minutes. This continues with a variety of activities until the practice time is over.

Having observed these activity driven practices by many youth teams, I have realized that we are actually entertaining the players. As a result, if the activity is not entertaining enough to the player then that player will be bored at practice.

Several years ago I was hired by a local club to become their Director of Coaching. This gave me the opportunity to introduce my method of teaching soccer to not only the one team that I was coaching directly but to all the teams in the club. My method requires much time in teaching a tactic and demonstrating the tactic before the players actually attempt the tactic. After several weeks of practices with the numerous teams, the coaches were receiving emails from parents stating that their child is bored. All parents being soccer experts, they complained that their child is sitting down while only a few players are up and playing. Sometimes those players playing are even from another team. Of course the coaches became concerned because they do not wish to upset the parents. I had been expecting those complaints and purposely did not address the situation earlier. They will understand the explanation much better after they perceived a problem. My favorite statement was how much their child loved soccer and now the child is losing interest because the child is bored. A meeting with the parents was in order.

The first thing the parents needed to learn was that there is a big difference between kickball soccer and the actual game of soccer. The sport of soccer seems simple on the surface. Players on a team kick the ball forward, chase it, and finally kick the ball into the goal. The actual game of soccer is like an iceberg. The part of the iceberg that is showing above the water is only a small portion. Most of the massive part of the iceberg is below the surface and not visible. If we focus only on the kicking and running part of the game then we are only seeing the portion of the iceberg that is above the water.

The game of soccer is one of the most complicated of team sports. It is a very involved game that requires constant motion, deception, great individual ability on the part of each player, and a tactical plan by a team. During the course of a game all the tactical plays on offense and defense must be understood and executed by the players without taking stoppage time for discussions. All the players on the team must be in tune with one another to be able to carry out the set plays. Players must therefore learn to think on their own, recognize the set play, then reposition in reference to where the ball, the teammates, and where the spaces are. For players to learn all of this a teaching process must first take place and thereby they must be willing to sit and listen. The difficulty arises with one of the key principals to learning soccer—repetition. The last thing they want to hear is the word repetition. They always want something new.

Much of their play time has been set up to emphasis their limited attention spans. Any practices that are activity driven only encourage this limited attention span. The job of a good youth coach is to constantly work to increase their attention span by not allowing them to look towards being entertained. Do not give in to their limited attention span but drive them to expand it. The players must be taught that you as their coach are not here to baby sit them nor to entertain them. You as their coach are here to teach them and prepare them for the competitions they will be involved in.

If a player complains of being bored then that player is not learning anything. You cannot be bored when learning!

REC, TRAVEL, PREMIER:

Players and parents need to be taught that there are different levels of competition.

The recreation leagues are there for players who do not have a big interest in learning the game of soccer. This type of league exists for the players who bring only a playground mentality to the game. They are there to be mainly with their friends for fun and recreation. The atmosphere is not very restrictive and winning the game is an afterthought. It generally is a kick ball approach to soccer with the practices being activity driven. It is a perfect vehicle for those players who just wish to play with and against their friends from a particular area. They acquire simply a basic soccer knowledge from mostly parent volunteer coaches whose own experience of the sport is limited. Most participants have a limited athletic ability. The rec. leagues provide them a place to enjoy playing a sport. Laughs and ice cream are the objectives at the end of the day.

Travel soccer requires a more serious focus on part of the players. A greater athletic ability is now necessary. Teams in travel leagues play a competitive game against teams from clubs in other areas of a community. The commitment from each player must be greater than on the rec. teams. Players on travel teams are taught the game of soccer and how it is played by coaches who have greater experience and knowledge when it comes to the sport. Although it must be remembered that it is a developmental league, winning the game will be one of the objectives of the travel team. The players must dedicate themselves to learning individual skills as well as the tactical elements of the game. Player will spend time listening and learning.

Those participating on premier teams in premier clubs are considered to be the best athletes in a given city. Generally they will travel to other cities to play premier teams from those cities. The cost to the parents of premier team players can be in the thousands of dollars as opposed to the cost for travel soccer which are in the hundreds of dollars and rec. soccer which are usually sponsored by local recreation departments with a minimal fee. Premier teams require numerous practices per week which the players must attend. The commitment from each player has to be serious and complete since the games played are usually intense with winning the game as the main objective. This type of program is only for the serious soccer player.

Parents, along with the players, must understand the differences between the rec. teams, travel teams and premier teams. With each level the commitment from the parents and players becomes greater. The definition of fun changes along with how the players are instructed and what they are instructed. Too often I have seen how parents go from one level team to a higher level team and think that the fun and activity driven practices are the same as they were at the lower level team. The intensity increases with each higher level in which the player participates.

WINNING:

The trophies I have accumulated over the years, displayed in my office, do an excellent job of collecting dust. They are designed for this purpose. However, there are two which I keep in front of all the others in order that I can constantly see them. They define for me the meaning of winning.

The first is a small marble paperweight trophy. This award was given to me near the beginning of my coaching career. I was coaching one of the areas public schools. We played in a City-Parochial League. It was my second season as their coach and that particular season the team consisted of a group of very gifted athletes who were excellent soccer players. One of the players played professional soccer. As a result we produced an undefeated season and won the league championship. Being very young I was full of myself. I was the coach of a championship team. Wow! I thought that surely we had won because I was the coach. The players must have become very good because I was coaching them. Certainly they were good athletes to begin with but I was their coach and they could not have won without me. I thought to myself that I must now be a big time coach. After all this was the City-Parochial School league.

Finally, the after season awards banquet arrived and I was seated at the head table. One by one each fall sport team was acknowledged. The coaches spoke about their players and gave out the team awards. Then it was our turn. I also introduced my players and handed out the various player awards. After I was finished the athletic director called me back to the microphone and she informed everyone that the soccer team had gone undefeated and that we were the league champions. I was then presented with this paperweight award. As the AD read the inscription on the award she hesitated for a moment. With everyone applauding she handed the award to me and whispered that I needed to give her the award back after the banquet so that she could fix something. I sat down and read the inscription which stated our record and we were the champions. The name of the coach was inscribed as "GARY WERNER." They had engraved the WRONG first name!

Two months had passed when I returned to the athletic director to pick up my award. It was still engraved with the wrong name, GARY WERNER. The athletic director had forgotten what was wrong with the award in the first place and why she still had it in her possession. I took it and said nothing more about it. It occurred to me that winning was not as important as I first thought. Here the team had won a championship and they did not even know my name. This award was a terrific lesson regarding winning. I realized that other elements are much more important. Focusing on winning at the expense of teaching life lesson reduces winning to a meaningless objective. I also realized that I had very good players who produced this championship. It was a life lesson in humility that had been taught to me.

The second trophy that defines winning for me was given to me by my fellow coaches. It was a County Soccer Coaches Merit Award. The inscription read "In Appreciation for Your Contribution to Boys Soccer, and Dedication to the Development of Our Youth."

One of the interesting things about this award was that it was voted to me by my fellow coaches unbeknownst to them that I had been fired from my high school coaching position for supposed insubordination. This insubordination charge is a terrific story of school politics but irrelevant for now regarding the topic of winning.

For me this award is an honor and I have valued it above all other trophies I have ever received. The fact that my peers voted me this is by itself humbling. But this award has an even greater significance in my life because in the four years that I had coached at this school I have NEVER had a winning season. Not one winning season! Yet my peers had seen the growth in the teams that I had coached and voted me this award.

These two awards daily teach me a wonderful lesson regarding the meaning of winning. It keeps winning in its proper perspective. One award was given to me for coaching an undefeated team who became champions but in the end they never had my correct name. The second award was given to me after never having had a winning season and after I had been fired. For winning to be meaningful it has to have value. When a coach decides not to play certain players because the coach feels that those players are not that good and they are incapable of winning then that win has lost its value. Those players who were not allowed to play and who were therefore sacrificed for a win will remember the coach their entire life for this slight. The coach will have taught them a terrible life lesson in that they were viewed as less important than a win in a youth game. What coaches would want to be remembered by their youth players in such a negative light? How would a coach feel if the child slighted was their own child?

Winning must never take precedence over the positive life lessons taught to players in youth sports. If one player is scarred by a coach for the sake of winning a game then that victory will be an empty one.

MISTAKES:

There is a theory in coaching which states that if I, as the coach, put enough fear into a player regarding making a mistake then that player will not make a mistake.

Over the years I have seen coaches use this theory of coaching. After all, they reason, it is a "game of mistakes" and the team that wins is the one that makes the least mistakes. There is some truth to that. Personally I do not believe that there is any room for this type of approach in youth sports. As discussed, the emphasis is not on winning but on learning and growth.

Mistakes can be a great teaching tool and should be encouraged by a coach. Many players have come through my Skills Academy where the players learn various soccer moves. They know how to do those moves well when practicing on their own or in class. Yet you will not see them using those skills in a game. They are afraid to make a mistake. If they mess up the skill they will not be successful. That fear of being unsuccessful looms large in their thought process. They reason "What will the coach think if I am seen failing?" As a consequence they will do nothing and instead make a bad pass or kick the ball into the opponent's legs. In their mind all of this is better than being seen failing at attempting a skill.

It normally takes a great length of time until the player gains enough confidence to attempt a skill during a game. It is the coach who must encourage them to keep trying the skill even if they do not at first succeed. The youth player must understand that it may take twenty or more failed attempts. But then on the twenty first try they might suddenly be successful with their skill. This successful moment will not come unless the player is willing to pay the price of all the previous failed attempts. Complement the player for the effort if the player attempts a move but fails. It is better to fail at attempting a skill move than simply to kick the ball away with a bad pass or by kicking it into the legs of an opposing player. The player must be willing to fail if the player hopes to eventually succeed.

During a game a coaches' first instinct is to yell onto the field and send instructions if a player is seen to be out of position and thereby not defending an opponent or helping their teammate. This action by the coach does not help the player to become an independent thinker. The player will only become used to someone always directing him or her from the sideline. Let the player make the mistake even if it turns out to be a costly mistake. The correction in practice or even on the sideline when the player is removed from the game will be much more effective after a mistake. The correction is therefore not just hypothetical but has a point of reference. After a mistake the correction will have a deeper impact on a player. The chance of a player making the same mistake in the future should now be greatly reduced. During a game there is too much action around the player to give full attention to the coach's instruction. Correcting the mistake during practice or on the sideline creates the proper atmosphere for the player to absorb what needs to be learned.

Mistakes are a necessary price to pay for a player in order to not only develop and grow as a player but more importantly as a person. Give the player the freedom to make mistakes. Mistakes will breed success.

SCRIMMAGE:

The only thing youth players want to do in practice is to scrimmage. They constantly ask coaches "can we scrimmage now." This is another issue that a coach must address early and redefine for the players. Scrimmaging, as they see it, is splitting into two teams and then playing a game against each other. The coach's task is to make the players understand that everything they are learning is already part of a scrimmage. If they are learning how to pass, the pass is a part in a game. If they are learning to do a skill, the skill is part of a game. If they are learning how to defend, how to recognize when to have a hard touch or soft touch on the ball, how to shoot on goal, how to trap a ball, or all the other elements of the game, then all those things are part of the game. If all those different elements are part of the game then one must conclude that a player is already scrimmaging or playing the game when each element is learned and practiced by itself. Players must learn that any game is made up of many different elements and each one is needed to play the game properly.

Do not allow your players to think of a scrimmage as something separate from each element being taught. Using the music analogy, the players can understand how you have to learn each note separately and then the scale. Once those parts are learned, then the song can be performed. The notes are part of the song and not a separate entity. When a musician learns to play the notes, then songs are learned at the same time. Each time the notes are rearranged a new song is played. The song is the game and the individual notes are the many individual learned elements of the game.

Players are already playing the game when learning a segment of the sport.

A team scrimmage should always have a purpose other than just playing one another. The coach should require the scrimmage to include limited touch play starting with three touches where each player is allowed to touch the ball only three times before being required to pass the ball or shoot the ball. As the players become better schooled then the touches should be reduced to two touches and eventually just to one touch. Scrimmages could be played with a player being required to do a skill soccer move before passing the ball or shooting. Practice a scrimmage with the offensive players versus the defensive players. Play forced marking where each player has a specific player to mark and can only win the ball from that particular player. Require an overlapping run before one side can score. If the players are allowed to just play without a purpose then an opportunity to teach is lost.

I do not believe in playing scrimmages with other teams until I have taught the players and they have learned the elements required to play the game of soccer properly. What purpose does a scrimmage serve if the players have not learned how to play? This holds especially true if the team is very inexperienced. I once took over as coach of such a team. During the entire six month period prior to our first game I had no scrimmages scheduled against an opponent. Most parents and even coaches generally believe that the players can only get better if they play against an opponent. They reason that scrimmages are therefore necessary and important. Playing just for the sake of playing without first having learned does no good.

One week before our first game of the season I held my first scrimmage game against another team. I instructed my players that I required them to give the ball back to the other team whenever we took possession of the ball. We had been learning how to organize our defense and I wanted the team to gain experience defending in front of our goal while facing pressure. I never lost focus of the fact that this was a meaningless scrimmage that counted towards nothing. I heard my parents yelling from the other side of the field wondering what our players were doing. The parents wanted to win this scrimmage which in their eyes was a real game. Although in the end we won 1–0, my focus was not to worry about winning this game but WINNING THE SEASON. We used the scrimmage to practice what we had learning as a team. At the end of the 2007 season this 11U team ended in a tie for first place in the second division, won a tournament along the way, and was rewarded by being elevated to the first division the following year.

A scrimmage is meaningful when it is used to teach.

TEACHING EVERY POSITION TO EVERY PLAYER:

It is much easier to teach soccer through a drill format than it is to teach soccer through a system that requires all the players on the field and in position when teaching tactics.

The coach must emphasize and teach that most of the game is played by each player without the ball. It is for that reason that all the players are required to be on the field in position when they learn how to make position adjustments without having the ball at their feet. It is here, in this type of team practice, that all the players learn each position. Do not force them to play different positions during a game when a player faces numerous additional pressures such as parents on the sideline yelling, a referee who is like a policeman, an opponent whom they do not know and who is there as an enemy, and they are wearing uniforms which makes everything official. Each player must learn every position during practice where they face a calm atmosphere. By learning how to make the position adjustments they are learning how to play without the ball. The coach thereby is teaching them to let the ball do the work.

While teaching the positions to the players, the coach should identify those players who are interested in playing the goalie position. This position is one to which a player has to be born to play. Every player does not possess the special natural ability to play this position. The earlier that a coach can identify a goalie the better it is. It is in practice that other players can be allowed to gain an understanding of the goalie position. The position is too specialized to have every player taking a turn in goal during a game. I have seen players be forced into playing goalie during a game who then stand there crying. How does that teach a child to love soccer?

Each position is connected to every other position. All players in position must therefore be required to be on the field of play to understand each position.

PLAYING TIME:

The numerous reasons for playing time in a game have already been discussed in the PARENT section. From the coach's perspective, playing time should always be fifty percent for each player on the team.

By having this fifty percent rule in place, the biggest problem that parents can cause for a coach is eliminated. It is imperative that a coach goes over the playing time requirements at the parent meeting prior to the start of the season. Be aware that even though you discussed this point with them and they are agreeable, the parents seem to conveniently forget this once they perceive that their own child is being shorted playing time. At least you will be able to remind them that you had discussed this point at the beginning of the season and that you had outlined the circumstances regarding playing time for each player.

Regarding the fifty percent playing time for each player on the team, remember that you had selected each player. Once they are on your team they must be made to feel as equals. A coach must never make a player feel inferior. What message do you send to a player when you do not play that player. Once the players have been selected they must all start out as being in good standing. Their status of playing time is determined by their own actions. As long as they are in good standing then they must receive fifty percent of playing time. The coach must decide what constitutes good standing. Good standing must be outlined at the beginning of the season.

How will a player become better if that player receives no playing time? At some point of a season you will need all the players. As the season progresses players will become injured or they will miss games because they have been scheduled to attend a summer camp for example. Parents also take their vacations during the summer season and your star player will be gone. If some players have received limited playing experience your team will flounder. It is the coach's job to develop all the players on the team to be able to play to their best ability.

During a season a team will take part in several tournaments. Most tournament rules allow a team several guest players since teams often lose players for particular weekends. To fill out a roster, the coach will recruit players from another team. A coach's mind-set is to recruit the top players from that team since it will increase the chance of winning the particular tournament. Over the years I have witnessed a coach being overcome by the desire to win the tournament. Perhaps the coach is under the belief that since this is a tournament and not part of the league schedule, winning can take precedent over normal team procedure. As a result the coach will start and give major playing time to the guest players because they are better players than some of the regular members of the team. The regular team players find themselves sitting on the bench. I find this to be outrageous behavior on the part of the coach. It is inexcusable to sit regular members of a team in favor of playing the guest players. The message that the coach sends to his own players is very hurtful to each slighted player. It is a put down to the player's ability to play. It speaks poorly of a coach not only for showing such disregard for his own players but also because it says that the coach was unable to develop the players properly. Guest players should only be used as substitute players and never as primary players over the regular team players.

It is the coach's job to play a player in a way that enables the player to grow and develop. The coach must protect the players at all times. Remember that each player is different. At the younger age groups there may be some players who are inhibited in the beginning or even somewhat afraid. The result may be that this player may be unable to play fifty percent of the game. The coach must learn this about his/her players. With this type of player the coach may have to let this player play only for a short period then substitute this player out. After some period out of the game the player must be substituted back in. As the player's comfort level expands, the player's playing time can be increased. In this way the coach lets the player grow into the team and the game at the player's own pace. Your observation of the player should be discussed with the parents of the player. This type of situation has been discussed in the PARENT section.

SIDELINE BEHAVIOR:

The coach creates the atmosphere on the sideline during a game. An excitable and argumentative coach will reap a sideline that will be chaotic.

Having watched countless professional games I seldom see the head coach constantly shouting instructions out to the players on the field. For the players it is difficult to hear these instructions. In addition, players do not want someone shouting at them from the sideline while they are trying to focus on the action going on around them. It is a distraction to the players. If a coach has a running commentary with the players on the field then in short order parents will also begin shouting at their child. The end result will be a great deal of noise from the sideline with very little being accomplished.

The first order for a productive sideline is to separate the team from the parents as has been discussed in the PARENT section. By having the team on one side of the midfield line and the parents located on the other side the coach has created order. Parents are not allowed on the team side and players are not allowed on the parent side.

Parents must never be allowed to shout out any soccer instructions. Soccer related information must only come from the head coach and no one else. If the coach wishes to communicate some instruction during the game then the player should be substituted out of the game. In an orderly one-on-one setting, the head coach can now give the player the information. The player can focus on the information and digest it without also being under game pressure.

It is counter productive to pace up and down the sideline while micro managing the game. The players will soon turn a deaf ear. The coach will be tuned out. As has been stated previously, it is the coach's responsibility to create independent thinking and self functioning players. When a coach constantly shouts instructions to the players then the players will never become self reliant but will always wait for the coach to tell them what to do. The coach has thereby failed the players. I can understand this behavior by a coach who is just starting out since the coach at that phase of the coaching career is nervous and has anxiety. The constant pacing and non stop commentary is beneficial to only the coach and no one else. That phase must soon fade and a calm coach must emerge in order to become an effective coach. Panic on the part of a coach during a game will result in confusion for the players. Panic produces a situation where players are suddenly forced to play positions they are not comfortable playing.

Part of an orderly sideline is that the coach must learn to remain calm in the dealings with the referee. If a coach argues referee calls consistently then that coach can expect that the parents will begin to make comments to the referee. At the same time the players will take their cue from the coach and argue with the referee. The end result is an out of control team and therefore an out of control sideline. Coaches, players and parents must remember that there is nothing anyone can do about the referee and the calls that the referee makes. The best thing all concerned can do is to continue to play the game and not give any focus on the referee calls other than to obey them. Nothing is ever gained by arguments other than it gives the youth players a bad example to follow and a team gains a bad reputation. In my experience I have never seen a referee change the call whether the call was right or wrong.

Whenever I work with coaches I tell them that at the end of the clinic I will show them the most important game sideline tool. When that time arrives I set up my folding chair and sit down. I inform them that the folding chair is the most important sideline tool. Sit in the chair and study the game taking place in front of you. Make mental notes of what it is you need to work on at the next team practice. While being seated, the coach will now be unable to be a distraction to the players and to the spectators. The chair produces an orderly sideline as well as a less stressed out coach.

PARENT MEETING:

It is imperative for the coach to hold a meeting with all the parents of the team. At this meeting the coach must reveal what his/her expectations are from the players and the parents. This meeting will set the tone for the season. The coach must therefore be detailed in the information provided.

Parent Meeting Outline:
1. Coach should state previous playing and coaching experience.
2. This youth program is about teaching life lessons.
    • Parents separate from their children.
    • Players learn to grow as individuals.
3. Explain the type of league and division the team will play in.
4. Every player plays at least fifty percent of the game if in good standing.

5. Define good standing. Coach decides what is in good standing.
   Suggestions:
   • Player behavior towards coaches and fellow players.
   • Player behavior towards opponents and spectators.
   • Player practice habits and personal behavior.
   • Player practice attendance and team commitment.
   • Give consequences for player infractions.
     (Limited playing time or sit out a game.)
6. Expected sideline behavior by the parents.
   • Remain seated in chair.
   • Separated from the team on one side of midfield line.
   • No visiting between players and parents during the game.
   • No communicating specific soccer instructions.
   • No verbal communication with the referee.
   • No negative communication with opposing players.
   • No negative communication with opposing spectators.
7. Explain substitution policy.
8. Explain the program.
   • What will be taught to the players?
   • How the material will be taught.
   • Teach; Demonstrate; Repetition; Implementation.
   • Redefine "Fun" for players.
   • Being "Bored" is unacceptable.
   • Encourage players to try and be willing to make mistakes.
   • Meaning of "Winning" and how it is not an emphasis.
   • Importance of practice with all things taught in practice.
   • No parent input accepted regarding program and coaching.
9. Behavior of the coach during the game.
10. Open to discussing issues only at practice time.
    (Never prior, during, or after a game.)
11. Selections of tournaments to participate in.
12. Handling of player injury regarding club policy.
13. Add other points of discussion by the coach.
14. Questions?

MASTER OF YOUR PROFESSION:

You will have mastered coaching when you are able to know what material is necessary and what material has no relevance and thereby is merely busy work. Most separate drills fall into the later category. If a play does not teach the whole team how to play together in a game, then your drill is simply entertainment in value.

A coach must be willing to live through the "uglies." Most plays will look terrible when the players first learn it. However, the coach must stay with the play until the players execute the play properly. The problem with some coaches is that as soon as the play is executed poorly the coach switches to a simple drill format. Through repetition the players will learn to execute all plays properly.

The coach must coach for the future. Tactics and skills that are taught today will come to fruition tomorrow. In the beginning everything looks sloppy but gradually the players improve as they become increasingly comfortable. Never look for instant results for you will always be disappointed.

When the coach is willing to live through the "uglies", coach for the future, and is able to identify useless material, then that coach has become a "Master of the Profession." **Less** will produce **more!**

PRACTICE

DO ALL YOUR TEACHING IN PRACTICE:

Soccer is not the type of sport that lends itself to game coaching. In American sports such as football, baseball, hockey, and basketball, there are times when a player can be instructed during the game since time outs can be called or players are not in the action of the game for a period of time. Soccer is a continuous play by the same players without any time outs for a discussion as to what the next series of actions should be or how to execute them. The players must know what to do before the game begins. Therefore the coach's time to prepare the players is only in the practice. As stated before, the job of the coach is to teach the players to become independent thinkers and this objective will not be achieved if the players receive repeated instructions from the sideline during the game. This constant sideline commentary during a game serves only to distract the players from their task.

If you haven't taught it in practice you are not going to teach it during the game. The atmosphere of a game with its elevated tensions does not lend itself to learning a tactic, skill, or new position. Only the practice provides the player with a calm environment that enables the coach to teach and the player to learn. The players are relaxed and not under a microscope.

ORGANIZE PRACTICES:
PRACTICE ONLY THE WAY THE TEAM WILL PLAY!

There are numerous drills for any conceivable tactical play. The internet, soccer books and DVDs are available to provide a coach with an unlimited source of drills to be used in practice. Armed with these drills coaches lay out practice schedules of one drill after another. In the end they have become excellent drill masters. Practice has become activity driven. Yet when the players go to play the game they will generally play it with their usual kick and run style that is natural to them. On many occasions I have seen a coach be upset at this since they have practiced drills that should have eliminated this kick and run play and yet it didn't eliminate it.

Unfortunately, coaches using this drill approach when teaching average groups of players are teaching the sport in reverse. For the drills to be successful a player must already know and understand how the game of soccer is actually played.

To be an effective coach of a team with average youth players, you must have your practices organized. Each concept taught must follow in a progression from what was previously taught. Each new practice depends on the practices that came before. The coach must teach the sport as any other subject such as Math, Reading, or Music would be taught in a classroom. Those subjects are taught with each daily lesson building onto the previous lessons. If this is true with the subjects a player learns in school then why do we not teach soccer like those subjects are taught? All school subjects follow an organized progression. A sport can only be learned if it also follows an organized progression.

The practices must follow a planed out long range program with each practice building towards the goal of the program. With the variety of drills concept it is easy to plan out practices. All a coach needs to do is select a group of drills that are intended to cover a certain skill or tactic. This drills approach attempts to practice each tactic individually. The youth player then views each tactic in and of itself. Progression practices geared towards the goals of a program do not allow this thought process on the part of a youth player since the player learns that all tactics are related and connected. Therefore, the plays that are done within the context of an overall program must be set up and executed in the formation that the players will play in an actual game of soccer as has been stated earlier in the COACH section.

The coach must not plan the practices just prior to each practice. The content of each practice must be planed for the entire season with the progression adjusted depending on the ability of the players to comprehend and to execute the material. It is pointless to move on with the material if the players are unable to understand the previous segment taught. Stay with the segment until the players are able to implement it and only then do you move to the next segment of the program.

With the numerous individual drills concept, coaches tend to plan a practice filled with drills. In most cases the practice is so over stimulating to the players that they usually do not remember what was being taught. The practice becomes too busy. This over stimulated practice keeps the players entertained since it is activity driven but it doesn't teach them much.

Keep the practices simple! The material taught in a practice should only be focused towards one new element of the game. Within the practice all previously taught material must be reviewed and only then will the new segment be introduced which will advance the program's goal. This book will provide the coach with a complete soccer program. If the program is followed in its proper progression, the team will learn all phases of how the game of soccer is played.

With two hour outdoor practices when the team practices several times per week, begin each practice with conditioning for approximately twenty minutes. Players start by taking one lap around the playing field before they do their stretches. Next have the players run a distance for ten minutes which is followed by ten minutes of a series of sprints. Soccer is a running sport and the team that is better conditioned will generally win a tightly contested game. During indoor practices conditioning is a waste of time since teams will only practice once per week. Conditioning is only useful if the practices are held several times per week. A good soccer club will have a two week conditioning camp prior to the start of the outdoor season where the players spend time running everyday while alternating days between long distant running and sprint running. This camp must be held for all players of the club at the same time and at the same location.

The second twenty minutes of a practice are dedicated to ball handling during which time the player sharpens the individual ball control skills such as passing, ball moves, trapping, heading, shielding, finishing, clearing the ball, taking the ball out of the air, and so forth. All skills can be incorporated into the "Weave Play."

During the third twenty minute period split the team into defenders and forwards. Each group works on sharpening their skills required to properly play their portion of the game. The goalie's time is split between practicing with the forwards and the defenders.

The next thirty minutes are spent working on team tactic. The entire team practices together. The segment practiced will depend on what third of the field is being emphasized. Players practice exactly how each position is played during the game. It is in this segment that all players learn how to play each position. As stated earlier, the game is not the proper time to teach players new positions. The player should be left to play within their comfort zone during a game. But during practice, it is imperative that they learn each position. It is only at the practice period that a youth player's comfort zone can be expanded.

Small sided games should be played during the final thirty minute period of the practice. These small sided games must have a purpose. Restrict the touch on the ball each player is allowed to make before passing the ball by working from three to two touches and eventually to one touch. With each less touch on the ball the player has to become more aware of his teammates and must think ahead of the play. It will force player interaction and speed up the play. With unlimited touches on the ball each player can be required to execute a ball move before the ball can be passed. The small sided games are ideal for practices.

THE "30 MINUTE" RULE:

Coaches should plan and work each practice as if the team had only thirty minutes of practice time.

If as the coach I only had this limited amount of time to practice with my team would I use a system of unrelated drills or would I devote my time to working only the way the players are going to line up and play in the game? The answer of course is that I would practice only under game situations. I would have to go right to the heart of the game and run practice as close to simulating a game as is possible. The players must learn what their primary and secondary responsibilities are during a game in relation to what their game positions are. How to play your position in the defensive third, the middle third, and the attacking third of the field is what the coach needs to teach the players. This can only be understood by youth players when it is explained within the reality of the game. Players are placed into the playing field exactly where they would be in a game. Each part of a game is now learned in this context. The portion of the game they are learning is actually taught within the playing field. The drill is the playing of the game and not a separate entity.

No matter what element of the game is taught it will always include every position of the game. The youth players must learn each element of the game within this context in order for them to understand how something is executed during a game. To practice individual drills with groups made up of several players scattered around the field will not teach them how each player position is related to each other. For them they are simply executing a drill in which they are grouped with players who may not play the position that is immediate to their own position.

Practice only the way the game is played with players in specific positions and on the actual playing field. This will teach them that no matter which player has the ball every other player has a specific function related to the player with the ball and where they must be positioned for the success of the team.

Practice as if there is only a very limited time during which you can prepare the team for the game. You will soon find that within your practices there is very little irrelevant material that is being covered. Not much of valuable time will be wasted. This is even more important during indoor practices since turf time at indoor facilities is very expensive. If your practices consist of unrelated drills you will accomplish very little in preparing your team.

FOCUS ON ONE SEGMENT:

Parents and coaches attempt to cover defending, midfield play, and attacking all in a few months. After all, isn't soccer a simple game consisting of kicking the ball and then running after it? To the untrained eye this appears to be true. Unfortunately, the game of soccer is very deceiving. On the surface it does appear very simple but in fact it is a very difficult game to play that requires athleticism, constant alertness, much thought, and understanding between players in that everything that happens in a game must have purpose.

When coaching a youth team, teach only playing in one third of the field for an entire season.

Begin the first season by teaching how to play in the defensive third of the field. The following season teach playing in the middle third of the field. In the third year teach playing in the attacking third if the field. It will take a minimum of three years to learn how to organize and play in each third of the field. **Under no circumstances should the coach skip ahead** and start teaching playing in another third of the field from the one the players started learning at the beginning of the season. Once something different is introduced it will only create confusion in the minds of the players. If the organization and play in each third of the field is taught properly, the coach may find that it will take longer than one season to teach everything the players need to know to play effectively in that third of the field.

Never move on to the next segment until the players understand and can execute the material that has been taught to the present time. It is very tempting to try to cover all the elements of the sport within a short period of time because the coach knows all of the knowledge the players will need to possess in order to play the game. A coach needs to learn patience when working with youth players. Can a student learn all there is about math in a brief amount of time? Of course not and everyone understands that. One year the student will learn algebra. The next year the student will learn geometry. Teaching and learning the sport of soccer must be accomplished in the same progression as learning math. If the coach does not display patience and focus, how can it be expected from the players?

In the end the players who learned the sport of soccer in a progression over a long period of time will be able to organize and execute with greater confidence and knowledge than those players who are taught the sport through a quick time frame that tries to cover all segments of the game.

In the first season focus all your effort towards teaching how to play in the defensive third of the field. It is the first segment demonstrated in the program. The defensive third of the field must be taught first because it is the most important third. If a team knows how to organize and then defend as a team, the game will always be manageable. If the score is tied or the opponent has a one goal or even a two goal lead, then your team will always have a chance to still win. The first objective must be to defend your own side.

Good defense is never an individual effort but instead must be a group effort. Players must learn to move from being a pressure defender to a support defender and back again. Good defense is to always defend goal side of the ball. If a defender is chasing from behind the ball then the defense is in trouble and must hope that another defender has contained the attack long enough for the rest of the team to recover goal side of the ball. A mistake on defense can be costly since it can result in a goal.

Defense must be the first segment where players learn how to organize. They must learn who becomes a support defender, who becomes the pressure defender and when do the roles reverse. A straight 4–4–2 alignment at the start of the game changes to a 7–2–1 or an 8–1–1 alignment in the defensive third of the field. Players must understand this when the game has moved into this part of the field.

During the second season players can now learn how to transition into the middle third of the field. The outside game should be stressed at this stage. The players must now understand how the alignment in the defensive third now changes to a 4–4–2 when using this alignment as the basic alignment. In the first part of the season, go only from the defensive third into the middle third. Once the players understand how to recover into the defensive third, how to defend in the defensive third, and then how to transition into the middle third of the field, the players can then be taught how to transition into the attacking third of the field. The basic 4–4–2 alignment in the middle third of the field changes once again into perhaps a 3–4–3 or a 2–4–4 or a 2–3–5 depending how many players we push into the attack from the back.

The team play learned at the beginning with the recovery runs, learning how to defend, learning how to transition into the middle third and attacking third now comes full circle. We started with the recovery runs because once the attacking third is overloaded with players the team must then know how to recover back into the defensive third of the field when the opposing team takes possession of the ball.

Players must understand that a formation does not remain the same but changes depending in which third of the field the play is taking place.

If in the previous two seasons the players understand how to organize and transition from one third of the field to another, in their third season the players can now be taught set options in the attacking third of the field. In this part of the game players learn to make decisions based on what they see and what the opponent has given them. Even though they will learn to develop set plays these plays are only a variety of options. They must now decide on their own what option to create. It is for this reason that it is most important for the coach to develop the players into strong and independent thinkers.

This will never be accomplished if practices consist of individual drills that are unrelated. Practices leading to good play in a game can only be achieved when only one part of the game is taught for a season and at the same time is taught directly on the field of play with players in their proper positions.

CONES:

Having observed countless team practices, I have always found interesting the use of marking cones by coaches. Cones seemed to be place everywhere on the practice field by coaches as if they possessed stock in the cone company. Player's positions are marked by cones. The lane a player should run is marked by cones. The spot a player should run to are marked by cones. Anything conceivable a player is to accomplish on a field of play is marked by cones. Yet, I have never seen one marking cone on a field of play during a game. Why then do coaches use these marking cones during a practice? The use of cones is a big part of individual drills that coaches use in the activity driven practices. If the coach has set up the practices the way the game is actually played then the cones are no longer necessary since the players learn to recognize the significance of spaces, lanes, and positioning without any aids such as the cones.

In America the general public seems to be impressed with equipment. The more equipment a coach brings to a practice the more impressive the coach appears. I believe it is just the opposite. The less equipment a coach needs the better the coach. The objective is to teach the players to think and to function independently. It is much more difficult to teach soccer with this objective in mind. To be able to accomplish this requires great ability by the coach since the teaching must be done without the visual aids such as cones.

The usefulness of cones is restricted to laying out a boundary for a small sided game, for goal markers, or to practice a player's individual dribbling skill. The game itself is played without these markers therefore the players must learn without the use of these markers.

COACHING MOMENTS:

A coaching moment can be a good play from a player or a bad play. They are a very useful teaching tool since a coach is presented with the opportunity to teach using a player's action.

Coaching moments present themselves continuously throughout a practice. The coach must look for them and then use them as a demonstration. Whenever a coaching moment occurs in practice the coach must stop the play at that instance. Do not wait and try to point it out at a later time. The coaching moment is most affective when it is addressed at the moment it has occurred. Do not be hesitant to stop the play each and every time that such a moment presents itself even if it means stopping very frequently.

Once the coach calls for a stop to the play, the coach must then address the entire team and not just the player who is being used as the coaching moment example. Face the entire team by calling the players to you and then demonstrate. The players need to learn from each others' mistaken plays or good plays.

A coaching moment can be any action a player takes which results in a negative or positive outcome. Those moments can be a pass, a shot, a ball skill move, a trap, a player's positioning, a game tactic that the coach has been teaching and now presents itself, or any of countless circumstances. A coaching moment is not restricted to a player's bad decision but must also be used to point out a player's positive play.

Any action by a player or group of players can become a coaching moment to be used as a teaching tool for the team. The more such moments the coach can find the better the aspects of soccer will be taught to the players.

SPEAK WITH ONE VOICE:

It is easy to fall into the trap of having too many assistant coaches. Parent-volunteer-coaches want to stay in good graces with the parents and thereby accept every volunteer to be an assistant coach. It may appear that the more eyes there are the more individual coaching each player will receive. The problem that is being created with having numerous assistant coaches is confusion. If all coaches are allowed to express their opinions the practice will take on the appearance of chaos. The players will constantly hear information that is contradictory. This can only harm your practices.

Good practices demand order. To achieve this order the head coach must be the only coach who gives any instructions to the players. Assistant coaches should be limited to two coaches. The assistants must understand that they will be required to clear any instructions through the head coach before they can be given to players. If the instructions are in keeping with what is being taught, then the head coach may relay the assistant coach's observations to the players or the head coach may give permission to the assistant to proceed relaying the observation.

Speaking with one voice by the head coach avoids giving players contradictory information. Confusion on the part of players is avoided and order is maintained during a practice.

ONE QUESTION:

Teach players to always ask themselves this one question:

"Am I in a position to pass or receive the ball?"

If they are not in a position then they need to move to a new space where the opposing player is not an obstruction.

THE PROGRAM

WE MUST FIRST TEACH PLAYERS TO UNDERSTAND HOW THE GAME OF SOCCER IS PLAYED BY TEACHING THEM THE GAME ITSELF. INDIVIDUAL DRILLS CAN ONLY BE INTRODUCED ONCE THE PLAYERS UNDERSTAND THE GAME BECAUSE ONLY THEN ARE THEY ABLE TO RELATE THE DRILL TO THE ACTUAL GAME.

This is the reverse of how we teach soccer to our youth presently.

A youth soccer club must have a concise long range program in place in order to develop their youth players properly. All lessons must be related to one another. Once the decision is made to use a particular program then do not deviate from it by suddenly teaching an aspect of a different program. You must remain with the chosen program and give it time to work. Continuity is an important ingredient for success and therefore changing programs repeatedly will not benefit your players. If you deviate and introduce another approach, the players will only become confused. When teaching an Algebra course you do not suddenly introduce a lesson from a Geometry course. Your pupils will become disoriented. Students learn best when there is structure.

Why do we feel that when teaching soccer we are able to teach it through a series of isolated drills that move from one aspect to a different aspect and still to another aspect? I have witnessed countless of practices in which coaches teach soccer through the use of numerous fragmentary drills. They have learned this approach through the coaching licenses and clinics and now they in turn teach it this way. Most coaches overload their practices with drills that in the end tax the youth player's retention ability with the result being that the player learns very little or nothing at all. The player has become over stimulated and overwhelmed. **Less is much more** constructive and beneficial to the player.

In the United States we seem to focus on the new hot approach. The Brazilian System, the Dutch Method, the German approach and on it goes. My friend Dr. Laura Bourcy once described this to me as always picking up what is sexy at the time. When attaching ourselves to one of these hot programs we never take into consideration the type of player that we are teaching through our regular soccer clubs. Most of our youth players are exposed to a variety of activities. They participate in a soccer program generally because their friends are participating. The social aspect therefore plays a big part in a person's desire to join. Our youth for the most part is not exposed to the sport of soccer at a very young age as children are in the rest of the world. The interest in soccer by children around the world is addictive and thereby "it is in their blood." Their understanding of the sport is much deeper than the understanding our children have. To expect our children to be able to learn one of the "sexy" systems in the same way as a child from Brazil is foolish. Most of our children who participate in regular soccer clubs will never even play high school varsity soccer.

If we teach our children to understand the game of soccer as being more than just kicking the ball back and forth, then we can say that we have been a success as a coach. Success as a teacher for me is not about how many games my teams have won. When a child understands and recognizes that there is strategy and a thought process combined with tremendous athleticism and endurance in every soccer game, then this recognition is all we can ask from our average youth players. I can then be satisfied and feel that my job has been well done.

I. DIRECTOR OF COACHING:

For a regular soccer club to develop players properly, it is necessary to hire a Director of Coaching. It is the job of this Director to implement a concise soccer program and see this program to its fruition. Every player on every team in a club must learn from the same program.

By having a unified program in which all the players learn the same thing, continuity is established. Since all the players are taught the same material it will be easier to move players from one team to another. One group of players will not be shortchanged because of a weaker coach not teaching certain soccer concepts. The only hindrance to the player will be their own athletic limitations. The coaches within a club will become equal in knowledge and ability regarding teaching the game of soccer. A unified program prevents unevenness in ability among the coaches.

Before the start of the season, the Director must hold a series of clinics for the coaches where the program is outlined for them. Once practice for the teams begins, the Director must attend the practices and be the one to actually teach the program to the players. This must be carried out by the Director as often as every other week. The coaches will learn how to really teach the material by observing the Director interact with the players. The team coaches then work with their teams the following practice by repeating the material taught by the Director in the previous week practice.

The Director's job will be to not only teach the program and train the coaches but also to observe the practices to make certain that the emphasis in the practice remains on the club unified program. When coaches become unsure of their teaching ability they will revert to teaching the fragmentary drills they have known from the past. It is much more difficult to teach a program that instructs players how to play the game of soccer than it is to teach drills. The Director must be aware of the coaches' level of confidence in teaching a program that is geared towards teaching play of the game and be prepared to guide the coach back to the focus of the program.

The most important quality that a club must look for when searching for a Director of Coaching is the amount of experience that a person has in dealing with youth players. A former professional player or coach may not always be the wisest choice. That type of person will attempt to teach the game to youth players from the professional level. A drill system will be implemented using the drills that had been learned while a player. This drill system will work well with players who know and understand the game of soccer and thereby are able to translate the drill to the actual game play. The majority of youth players lack this understanding and are unable to see how the drills fit into the actual game. For the average youth player the drill is therefore a separate entity from the game. Players and coaches from the professional ranks in many cases have not learned how to translate their playing experiences into a teaching concept.

The Director of Coaching candidate must have a clearly written plan of how the youth players of the club will be developed in their understanding of how the game of soccer is played. The development of the players individual soccer skills are an intricate part of a solid program. The team tactical practices must teach players how they are to defend as a team, how they are to transition as a team, and how they will eventually attack the opponent as a team.

All drills must be game play oriented and therefore will be referred to in this text as a "play" in place of the label "drill."

II. THE PROGRAM'S FOUR PRINCIPALS

Each segment of the game is taught through four principals:

Teach—Demonstrate—Repetition—Implement.

The game oriented practices which are taught in the following pages are driven by these four principals. This is the opposite of the fragmentary drill oriented practices which are activity driven. Most of the world works under these four principals when developing their players.

TEACH:

The coach must teach an element of the game of soccer to the players. The purpose of an element being taught must be made clear to the players. As with a school course, the player must sit quietly and give attention to what the coach is saying. Players are learning to expand their attention span.

DEMONSTRATE:

Players who have learned this segment must demonstrate how the element is executed under game situation. Once again the student players are required to sit and observe. Their focus and attention span is expanded further which are important qualities in their development. One learns best when actually seeing how an element is played.

These first two principals of the program can produce anxiety in the parents who are observing the practice since the child appears to be inactive by sitting and listening while others who are demonstrating are playing. They reason that the child is not doing anything active therefore the child cannot be becoming better as a player. Activity oriented practices are the only thing they understand. They do not realize that activity in and of itself will do nothing towards building a better player. The coach must be aware of this potential problem and be willing to educate the parents through meetings with them.

REPETITION:

The third principal is the most disliked. Players who have grown up in a world where they have been taught that everything must be fun expect to be entertained. The variety of drills format entertains the players. They have fun and thereby are never bored since there is always something new they are doing.

Only a strong and focused coach will be able to implement this most important third principal of REPETITION. Players are resistant to repetition because it seems boring to them to do the same thing over and over. Yet, the only way a player will be able to perform an element of the sport is if the player practices the same thing repeatedly. The student's execution must become without conscious thought. In a game the player needs to be able to play on instinct. When learning a sport the student must understand that there are no shortcuts. Players will have fun when they are able to play the game because of knowledge they have worked hard to acquire. Repetition in practice by its very nature is fun because it produces the ability to play in a game with purpose. The coach must make players realize the significance of the principal of repetition.

IMPLEMENT:

When the players have reached the point where they play on instinct, they will then begin to implement into the game what they have learned. It will come naturally. Only through repetition of what has been taught and demonstrated will the player reach the comfort level to execute in a game.

My friend Deborah Benkovich summed up the meaning of the program best in an e-mail to one of her new parents from her team who did not appreciated the practices he was seeing. She started by recalling when she was a parent, before she became a coach, just sitting and watching her child practice.

> *I remember sitting as a parent watching my oldest daughter practice at U11. Every practice they did the weave and the very same recovery drill that we do almost exclusively, week after week, until the girls knew where they needed to be, they didn't have to think about it. Some practices were hard, but when they started to play games, that's when all that practice paid off. They really played well as a team and were very successful. The program is hard for a lot of parents because it is based more on a soccer regimen of repetition and discipline and doesn't play down to attention spans, instead expects the girls to grow their focus. It teaches knowledge over just activity.*

Debbie started as a coach with very limited coaching knowledge. Through learning to teach this program I have had the pleasure and privilege to see her develop into a very good youth soccer coach who now is a great asset to her youth soccer club.

The program is based on the theory that "LESS is MORE." The focus is usually on only one or two "plays" as opposed to numerous activity drills. Instead, the one or two "plays" are repeated through out the team practice and then repeated again the next practice until the players understand it and are able to execute the play during a game.

Instead of learning offense, midfield play, and defensive play all in a few months, the program focuses on only one element for the entire team season. Moving on from one segment to another will depend on how well the players grasp each segment and are able to execute it. By teaching fewer elements, but teaching each repeatedly, the players will know more and thereby understand the game of soccer better.

Debbie stated it so eloquently when she said that "It teaches knowledge over just activity."

III. INDIVIDUAL SOCCER SKILL CLASSES:

An effective club program must start with a method of training the players in individual soccer skills. Without individual soccer skills the technical portion of the overall program will be rendered almost useless.

A. MANDATORY SKILLS CLASSES:

This skills portion of an overall program needs to be **required for each individual player.** If skills are on a voluntary basis, only those players whose interest is soccer will attend skills classes. Those players that play in a club whose reasons for playing are social will chose not to attend skills classes because they will have no **desire** to learn. The result will be club teams that will be uneven regarding abilities of the players. You cannot feature successful teams with such a mixture of abilities. A team is only as strong as its weakest players because at one point of the season those weaker players need to contribute to the team with their individual abilities. If soccer skills classes are mandatory for all players, then those players who do not have a desire to attend the classes will still learn despite themselves and thereby will be able to contribute to the team play.

B. DURATION OF SKILLS CLASSES:

Soccer skills classes should be held for a minimum of ten weeks. Any period less will produce only a patchwork of results. A ten week period is long enough for players to develop the habit to do soccer skills.

The club skills sessions should be held during the indoor season. Of course the longer the period of skills classes, the more the players will benefit by learning to be comfortable with the ball. If a club has a large number of players and limited space availability, then the skills classes can be split into two ten week periods with one group learning skills one ten week period and a second group learning skills the second ten weeks.

C. CONTENT OF SOCCER SKILLS CLASSES:

The material to be taught in a skills class should be a soccer curriculum in which the material in each class follows a progression. Teaching individual soccer skills should also be the same approach as teaching a subject in an academic school.

Each class needs to be one hour in length.

The teaching portion of the class must be divided into a minimum of two segments. If the proper space exists the class should be divided into three segments.

1. The first segment must always consist of skill moves that enable the player to carry the ball and beat an opponent.

Whatever ball handling skill is taught in a lesson, it must always be repeated in the following lessons. No new ball handling skill should be added until the previous skill is mastered by the player.

This repetition may cause boredom in the players, especially those players who do not **desire** this knowledge. Like it or not, **REPETITION** is the key to becoming a successful ball handling player.

The teaching of numerous ball handling skills is not advised. It is better to know one or two ball handling skills that a player can execute in a game than it is to know ten ball handling skill moves none of which a player has developed to the point where a player is able to execute them in a game. It is not possible for the average player to master a great number of ball skill moves. The fewer the skill moves, the better a player is able to execute the moves. **Less is more!**

2. The second segment of the skills class must focus on developing a player's personal comfort with all the skills required for the player to play the game of soccer. These skills include dribbling the ball, various trapping of the ball, proper method to strike the ball, proper touch on the ball, ball preparation, heading, shielding, turning with the ball, just to name some of the numerous game skills each player must possess.

3. If the space available permits then the class is to be divided into teams of threes. Small sided 3v3 games should be played in a tight space field of play. The smaller the area of play, the more the players have to use those individual skills learned. In a confining area of play, players cannot resort to kick and run tactics. The coach must make specific demands of players to use the skills that are taught in the class.

D. GRADING THE PLAYERS:

For best results, classes should have a small teacher to student ratio. This will depend on what the total number of players will be who are participating in skill classes. The lesser amount of players per class, the more the individual will learn.

1. The coach of each team must grade the players of that team and place them into four categories:

a. Experienced Players:
Those players who have shown a desire for knowledge and who therefore possess individual soccer skills and are able to execute these skills in games. These are players who have previously attended individual soccer skill classes.

b. Average Players:
Those players who are not as athletic as the experienced players but who do demonstrate some desire for learning individual soccer skills. The execution of skills in a game is limited. These players may have attended skills classes on a limited basis.

c. Limited Players:
For those players who have social reasons as their main objective for participating in the soccer program. Their reason to join a team is because a friend is playing or the parent wants this child to play. This limited player has no desire to learn individual soccer skills. This type of player is usually disruptive in skills classes and must be kept with other players who have the same social reasons for playing.

d. New Players:
Those players who are new to playing the game of soccer and do not possess individual soccer skills. Their learning must start with level one and lesson one.

2. Grading Criteria:

How well can each player dribble the ball with the inside and outside of the right and the left foot?

- Set up a row of six cones spaced two feet apart.
- Each player dribbles through the cones with the inside of the right foot, then inside of the left foot, then outside of the right foot, then outside of the left foot.
- How many touches on the ball does the player make in getting from one side of the cone to the other side of the cone?
- Do they just kick the ball from one side of the cone to the other or are they able to make numerous touches thereby keeping complete control of the ball?

Individual Soccer Skill Moves:
- How many skill moves can a player execute efficiently?
- How well can a player execute moves with right foot then the left foot?
- Set up 1v1 play to see how well a player can execute the move against an opponent.

Ability to Pass and Touch-on-the-Ball:
- Set up the weave drill.
- How well can a player make an accurate pass?
- Make the weave circle small and then large to see how the player touches on the ball are with each distance. Do they strike the ball with the same power no matter the distance or are the players able to make soft or hard touches depending on the distance?

3v3 Games:
- How well does each player handle themselves when in a competitive play?
- Do the players possess the ability to make traps, shield the ball, head the ball, pass the ball, etc. under playing conditions?

Observing players under these simple situations should enable a coach to classify the players on the team by placing them into one of the four categories. The option must remain open for the professional skill instructor to reclassify a player after the start of the skill classes.

Age Grouping:

For the individual soccer skills classes to be successful, the players must not only be grouped according to experience and ability but must also be grouped according to age. Older players do not wish to attend classes alongside younger players and younger players are intimidated if grouped with older players. A comfort level conducive for learning will not exist if there is a wide range of ages in the same class. The problem for the scheduler of the skill classes will be not only to separate the players according to ability but also to separate the players according to age.

E. SKILLS CLASSES SPACE:

1. Individual soccer skills classes must take place during the club's indoor practices from the late fall to early spring practices. A portion of the practice area must be set aside specifically for the skills classes.

2. The area set aside for the individual soccer skills classes is divided into four equal sections:

- If dividers such as netting are available then those will isolate each section. Where dividers do not exist then temporary boundaries must be created by using cones or discs.
- Each section will be used by one of the skill groups described in section D, #1 a–d.
  Section 1—Experienced players.
  Section 2—Average players.
  Section 3—Limited players.
  Section 4—New players.
- Each group must not contain more than ten players.
- The same age players must hold their skills classes at the same time to avoid the problems of age variation as described in section D #3.
- A single professional instructor must be assigned to each specific group of players who will teach the classes. Ideally there should be a fifth instructor who will adjust to each group depending on the need of the classes and players. This will mean an expense for five professional soccer skills instructors.

3. Depending on the number of players who need to receive individual soccer skills classes, the players can be divided into two groups with one group attending one ten week period and the other group attending the second ten week period. Ideally it would be best if all players can attend the full twenty weeks.

4. Additional classes can be set up for those players who have a **desire** for more training.
- Each group of players from a team who wish more training can acquire the space and time from an indoor facility on their own and pay for this time directly to the facility from their own funds.
- One of the club professional skills instructors will then be assigned to train these players who desire this additional soccer work. This group will pay the instructor from their own funds.

5. Goalie Training:

It is most important to set aside time and space for training the club's goalies. The goalie classes should be broken apart in the same manner as the foot skill classes. First, each class must have goalies that are of the same ability. Secondly, classes must be split according to age. Both groupings are of equal importance.

As with the individual soccer skills classes, the goalie program should be one that uses a curriculum approach of teaching in which each class is built on the previous classes. It is imperative that an experienced goalie teacher will teach these goalie classes.

F. INCORPORATING SKILLS INTO TEAM PRACTICE:

1. During the indoor season the team will have limited indoor time for team practice. For that reason, the team practice must focus only on the technical aspect of playing the game of soccer. The team will have already spent time working on individual soccer skills during the skills classes.

2. During the "weave warm up" play any individual skill that has been taught in skills class can be worked into the practice without taking time away from the team practice.

3. During the "first-to-the-ball" play, the coach can incorporate the learned individual skill into this basic competitive play by demanding that specific skills must be performed before a team can score.

4. During the outdoor season more time is available for team practice. The coach can now set aside a period of time during the practice that will be dedicated to working only on individual soccer skills that have been taught in the skills classes.

G. PLAYER RESPONSIBILITY:

In the end, the success of any program will depend on the players themselves. If the player does not possess a desire to learn, no program will make the player a better soccer player. Learning individual soccer skills requires dedication and a work ethic. In these foot skill classes the players have to work. There is no where to hide since there are only a few players in the class and therefore the instructor has visual contact with all the players in the class.

Each player must take time every day to practice what has been learned in class. Without that daily practice the player will learn nothing. Attending a skills class only once per week is not enough of an effort for an individual to acquire skill. It is the responsibility of the team coach to make certain that each player on the team practices every day. It is better to practice a little amount of time every day than it is to practice for a long time only one day a week.

A man on the street asked a stranger how to get to Carnegie Hall. The stranger replied, "Practice!"

IV. CONDITIONING PROGRAM:

Player conditioning is a most important element of any club development program. Soccer is a demanding sport to play since running is a necessity for the entire game. Players must be both endurance runners as well as sprinters. These are two styles of running that are the opposite from each other. Yet a soccer player is required to do both styles of running and do them equally as well. Putting a conditioning program in place is not that difficult as long as it includes distance running and sprint running.

A. CONDITIONING CAMP:

Once the teams begin practice outside for the outdoor season, a club should sponsor a two week conditioning camp. It should be open to all the players in the club.

1. Run a distance course and a sprint course on alternating days.
a. Divide the players according to age with the cut off being twelve years. Any players younger than twelve years will run courses that are shorter and that will fit their age. Any players twelve and older will run a longer course.
b. The sprint distances will also be longer for all players twelve and older.
c. The conditioning program should run every evening Monday through Friday for one hour.
2. A festive atmosphere will be created with all the players from a club congregated in one area. It will be the only time that players of all ages will be together from the same club.
3. Make the conditioning program open to the parents.
4. Coaches should make this conditioning camp mandatory for their players. The importance for this conditioning is not only to get the players into physical condition but to also make them mentally tough.

B. CONTINUE CONDITIONING:

Once the players practice outside, every practice must contain time for conditioning the players in order to keep developing their physical endurance as well as their mental toughness. Those players who are in better shape will most likely win a close game in the end.

V. THE TECHNICAL GAME:

Teaching the technical game of soccer will take a minimum of three years. In each year the focus of training will be on only one third of the field of play.

1. Year One will focus on the play in the defensive third of the field of play.

2. Year Two will focus on transitioning from the defensive third of the field, through the middle third of the field, and into the attacking third of the field of play.

3. Year Three will focus on attacking the opponent's goal with set plays.

It must be remembered by the coach that what is taught in each year is only one method of reaching the goals of the program. There are any number of plays that will work and achieve the same ends. However, to eventually teach other set up plays, the players must first learn to execute flawlessly only one set up play. Once they know how to execute one set up play on instinct, the coach can guide them to other creative set up plays.

NOTE: The diagramed players who demonstrate each element in the following pages will be referred as a RECOVERY PLAYER.

STAY ON TASK!

KEY

Defending team

- (G) Goalie
- (D) Defender
- (PD) Pressure Defender
- (SD) Support Defender
- (CD) Center Contain Defender or Center Defender
- (RD) Recovery Defender
- (SW) Sweeper Defender or Sweeper
- (ST) Stopper Defender or Stopper
- (OD) Outside Defender
- (F) Forward
- (M) Midfielder
- (RM) Recovery Midfielder
- (OM) Outside Midfielder
- (CM) Center Midfielder
- (DCM) Defensive Center Midfielder
- (CAM) Center Attacking Midfielder
- (OCM) Offensive Center Midfield
- (RF) Recovery Forward

Attacking team

- (G) Goalie
- (A) Attacker
- (F) Forward
- (DA) Defensive Attacker
- (SW) Sweeper Attacker
- (ST) Stopper Attacker
- (MA) Midfield Attacker
- (CM) Center Midfield Attacker
- (DCM) Defensive Center Midfield

Other

- (C) Coach
- (S) Shooting Player
- (B) Ball Recovery Player
- (P) Players
- ⚽ Ball
- △ Marking Cones
- ⟶ Direction of runs
- ⇢ Direction of the ball

YEAR ONE

Year one in the development of a youth soccer team is spent on learning how to organize as a team in the defensive third of the field of play.

This defensive third is the most important part of the field. As long as the opponent can be prevented from scoring in the game, the game will remain a zero draw at worst. Therefore, the first objective of a team is to not allow the other team to score. Good defense will always keep the game manageable and provide a team with the opportunity to win the game.

The team that knows how to organize has the best chance of being successful in the game. Once the players know how to organize in the defensive part of the field, it will become easier to teach the players how to organize in the middle third of the field and eventually in the attacking third of the field. The importance of teaching players how to organize cannot be stressed enough.

The same material must be taught to players regardless of their age. For a team to become successful the elements of the foundation of the game must always be stressed and repeated. It is at the beginning that players must learn and understand the importance of repetition. NEVER move on to the next part of the program until the players can execute the present element cleanly no matter how long it takes for them to learn. The coach must gage the athleticism and ability of the players when advancing through each stage.

I. SETTING UP THE WEAVE PLAY:

I have always boasted that I could hold a team practice in any space even as small as my kitchen. It is this weave play that has enabled me to make this boast. The play was taught to me many years ago by Carlos Pachame who at that time was one of Argentina's national team coaches and a FIFA coaching license instructor. It has never become antiquated and enables a coach to teach every element of soccer in any available space. You will never need another play and it should be used to start every practice and every pre-game warm up.

1. This Weave Play is best learned with five players in a group. Four players are positioned making up a square and one player is positioned in the middle of the square.

Fig. 1   Fig. 2   Fig. 3

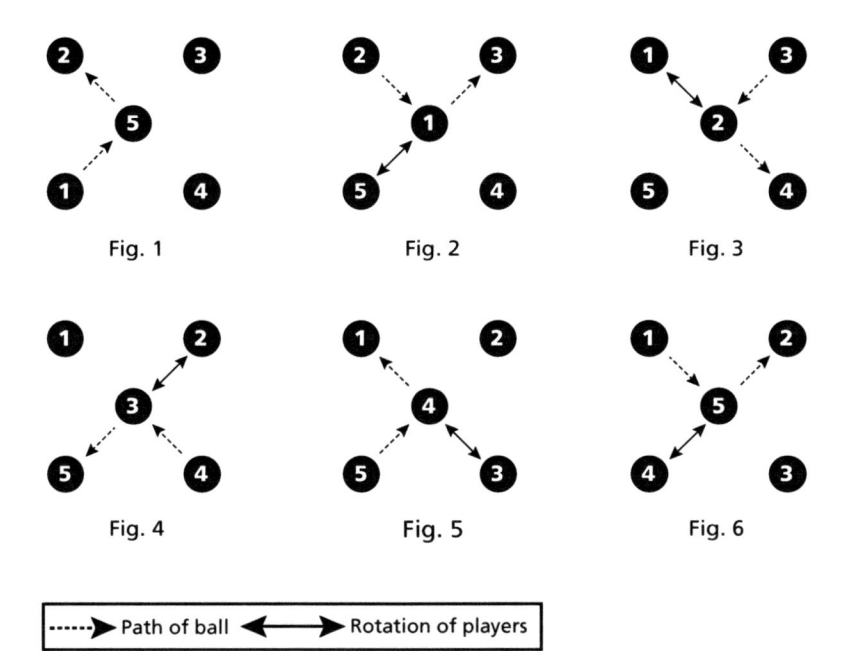

Fig. 4   Fig. 5   Fig. 6

┌───┐
│ ······▶ Path of ball   ◀────▶ Rotation of players │
└───┘

- The ball is always first played from the outside player to the middle player. Any re-start always is played from the outside into the middle
- Player 1 plays the ball from the outside to the middle player 5 (*Fig. 1*)
- Player 5 plays the ball from the middle to the outside player 2 (*Fig. 1*)
- Player 5 moves to the outside to where player 1 is positioned and while player 1 moves into the middle (*Fig. 2*)
- Player 2 plays the ball from the outside to the middle player 1 (*Fig. 2*)
- Player 1 plays the ball from the middle to the outside player 3 (*Fig. 2*)
- Player 1 moves to the outside to where player 2 is positioned while player 2 moves into the middle (*Fig. 3*)
- Player 3 plays the ball from the outside to the middle player 2 (*Fig. 3*)
- Player 2 plays the ball from the middle to the outside player 4 (*Fig. 3*)
- Player 2 moves to the outside to where player 3 is positioned while player 3 moves into the middle (*Fig. 4*)
- Player 4 plays the ball from the outside to the middle player 3 (*Fig. 4*)
- Player 3 plays the ball from the middle to the outside player 5 (*Fig. 4*)
- Player 3 moves to the outside to where player 4 is positioned while player 4 moves into the middle (*Fig. 5*)
- Player 5 plays the ball from the outside to the middle player 4 (*Fig. 5*)
- Player 4 plays the ball from the middle to the outside player 1 (*Fig. 5*)
- Player 4 moves to the outside to where player 5 is positioned while player 5 moves into the middle (*Fig. 6*)
- The whole sequence then continuous to repeat itself (*Fig. 6*)

Note:
- When first learning the Weave Play the players should be positioned approximately ten feet from each other
- When using the RIGHT foot the weave moves to the left
- When using the LEFT foot the weaves moves to the right
- The team is broken up into groups of five players
- If the passing sequences break down then always restart the play rather than allowing the play to become sloppy
- As each new element is learned the speed of the weave must be increased and lead to actual game speed.

2. Once this basic rotation is learned and understood by the players all other skills can be incorporated into this Weave Play. It must be stressed that a coach remains focused on one skill until such time that the players can execute the skill properly. Only then should a new skill be introduced. The old skills already learned must always be reviewed.

Emphasize:

a. The most important lessons learned by the players from this play is:
- *How to make good passes*
- *The player never stands still but always moves to a new space after making a pass*
- *Players must never be allowed to walk casually from position to position but must learn to move at game speed*

b. From the outset, this weave play gives the coach the opportunity to instill into the players that they must think and stay focused at all times.
- *The players are in front of the coach in small groups and therefore it is easy to capture their attention.*
- *Due to the small groups the coach has the opportunity to demand from the players proper execution.*
- *The coach is able to drive the team through this play*

3. BUILDING ONTO THE WEAVE PLAY IN YEAR ONE:

a. Using the RIGHT foot, the player traps the ball with the inside of the right foot then makes a pass to the next player in the rotation. To make an accurate pass the player's body position must be facing the player being passed to.

b. Execute the weave as stated in item #3a while using the LEFT foot for the inside foot trap and then pass.

c. Using the RIGHT foot, the players must make one touch passes without first trapping the ball.

d. Using the LEFT foot, the player must make one touch passes without first trapping the ball.

e. Using the RIGHT foot, each outside player must execute a soccer skill move with the right foot before making the pass into the middle.

f. Using the LEFT foot each outside player must execute a soccer skill move with the left foot before making the pass into the middle.

Emphasize:

Each of the above mentioned skills must be learned during Year One of a team development.

• *How fast the team progresses will depend on the athletic ability of the players.*

• *Never move to the next skill until the players have mastered each present skill.*

II. DEFENSIVE STANCE:

1. TEACH AND DEMONSTRATE PROPER DEFENSIVE STANCE:

• Legs must be apart for balance

• One leg must be placed in front of the other for maneuverability and to prevent the pall from being played between the leg

• Get into a low stance with knees bent and the upper body in a crouch

2. SET UP DEFENSIVE STANCE PLAY FOR TEAM PRACTICE:

a. Split the teams into halves.

b. Each player in one group must have a ball.

c. The group with the ball forms a line with each player standing next to each other and facing the opposite side of the field. The ball is place in front of the player. The players with the ball will be the attacking players.

d. The group without the ball will position themselves approximately three feet from the ball with each player facing one player with the ball. The players without the ball will be the defensive players.

e. The defensive players must be in the proper defensive body position.

f. The attacking players advance.

g. The defensive players keep backing up while maintaining the defensive stance but never attack the ball.

h. When the opposite side of the field is reached, the attacking players give the ball to the defensive players. The attacking players now become the defensive players while returning to the original side of the field.

i. The attacking and defensive roles become reversed.

j. Repeat this sequence numerous times.

Emphasize:
- *This is a play to instruct the players in the proper defensive stance.*
- *It is not a play for the attackers. The attackers must not attempt to beat the defenders.*
- *Start the play by first walking.*
- *Increase the speed of the play as the players comfort is increased.*
- *Never increase the speed at the expense of the proper defensive stance technique.*
- *Defensive stance must be drilled until it becomes instinctual.*

III. DEFENSIVE TECHNIQUE 1V1 SITUATION:

1. TEACH AND DEMONSTRATE:

a. Two players face each other with one player being the attacker and the other being the defender.

b. The play must take place with a goal behind the defender but the play will take place in a small contained area.

c. The attacking player must attempt to get past the defender and attack to the goal.

d. The emphasis of this play will be on the defender who must:
- Be in proper field position which is goal-side of the attacker.
- Approach the attacker in an arching run keeping possession of the center ground while giving up the less dangerous outside ground.
- Learn to be patient and contain the attacker.
- Keep the attacker to the outside by giving the attacker that open space.
- Gradually cut down the space in which the attacker can maneuver thereby cutting the attacker's time to maneuver.
- Be in a forward enough defensive position so as to prevent the attacker from playing to the center ground where the attacker becomes more dangerous.
- Remain focused on the ball so as to not react to the attacker's body fakes.

- While containing the attacker and cutting down time and space, channel the attacker as far into the corner as possible since the smaller the space the attacker has to maneuver in, the less danger the attacker is to the goal.
- Minimize the attacker's options by defending the more dangerous ground and leaving open the less dangerous ground for the attacker to play into. If the defender has given the attacker an area to play into then the defender has taken control since the defender has given the attacker only one choice. Now, the defender does not have to rely on reacting to the attacker's play.
- Be in a good defensive stance to prevent the ball from being played between the defender's legs.
- If the attacker is penetrating up the middle ground, then the defender must approach the attacker to the attacker's strong side thereby giving the attacker the space to the attackers weak side. Once the defensive position is attained, the defender must patiently channel the attacker to the outside.

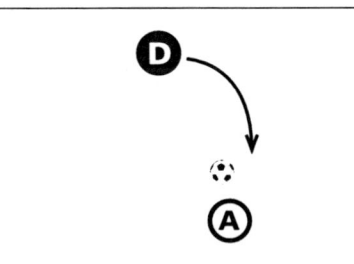

Defender approaches the attacker in an arching run thereby keeping control of the inside ground. The defender must always keep possession of the ground.

Defensive positioning is to the inside of the attacker giving the attacker the open outside territory. Defender must be positioned forward enough to prevent the attacker from playing across the defender into the middle.

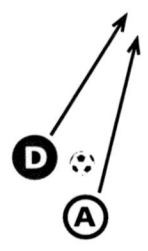

Contain and channel the attacker to the outside and as far into the corner as possible making the attacker less dangerous. Patiently cut down the attacker's time and space to maneuver.

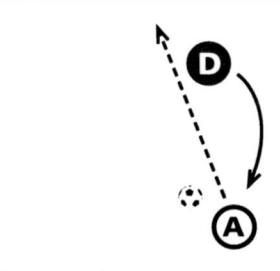

If the attacker penetrates up the middle, then the defender must play the attacker to one side giving the attacker space to the attacker's weak side and then channeling the attacker to the outside.

D Defender **A** Attacker ⚽ Ball

2. PLAY RELATIONSHIP TO THE ACTUAL GAME:

a. 1v1 is the basic confrontation in a game.

b. The attacker learns to confront a defender and become confident to:

- Hold onto the ball to buy time for the other attackers to penetrate into the attacking third of the field.
- Hold onto the ball and execute a soccer skill move to make a pass.
- To beat the defender with a soccer skill move and penetrate further into the attacking third of the field.

c. The defender learns to confront an attacker and become confident to:

- Take possession of the area of the field closest to the goal.
- Remove the attacker's choices by limiting the attacker to one area of the field.
- Contain and channel the attacker to the outside thereby limiting the attacker's time and space to maneuver.

Emphasize:

To the attacker:

- *Quickness of the soccer skill move for it to be successful.*
- *Timing of the soccer skill move for it to be successful.*
- *Be unpredictable in order to prevent the defender from dictating the area of penetration.*
- *Change of pace. Approach the defender quickly, slow down near the defender, work close to the defender, when the defender seems to be unsure then the attacker must again quicken the pace of the soccer skill move and penetrate past the defender.*
- *The attacker must be decisive in the action to be taken and where the attacker is going with the soccer skill move.*
- *Always give a body fake prior to actually executing the soccer skill move.*
- *Always work with the head up to be able to see the other players and the open spaces.*

To the defender:

- *Always get control of the territory closest to the goal.*
- *Approach the defender in an arching line.*
- *Meet the attacker as far from the goal as possible.*
- *Once near the attacker, the defender must be in a proper defensive stance and then patiently close the space between the defender and attacker.*
- *Always give the defender the outside to play into.*

- *Always be in position forward enough to prevent the attacker from playing across the middle and penetrating into the middle.*
- *Always focus on the ball.*
- *Always contain and channel the attacker to an outside position.*
- *The attacker knows what the plans are with the ball. If the defender does not limit the attacker's options by taking away some of those options, then the defender is at a great disadvantage and left to only react to what the attacker does which leaves the attacker in control of the situation.*

4. SET UP 1V1 PLAY FOR TEAM PRACTICE

- Split team into two groups.
- One group will be the defenders and form a line across the goal area with the goal behind them.
- The second group will form a line across the goal area but approximately twenty or more feet outside the penalty area. These players will be the attackers and will have the ball at their feet.
- Each attacker must be opposite one defender.
- Players must be spread out for each set of defenders and attackers to have room to play.
- Play now begins with each set of attackers penetrating toward the goal and being met by the corresponding defenders.

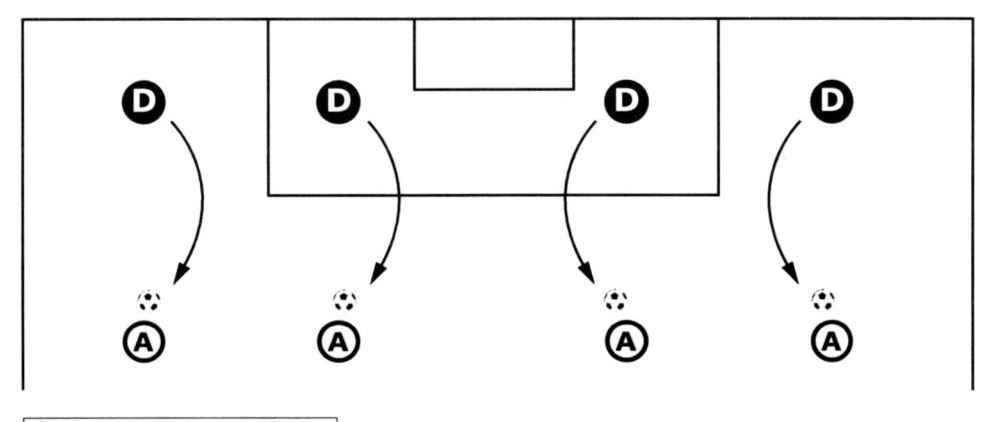

D Defender **A** Attacker ⚽ Ball

Emphasize:

Increase the defender's pressure gradually:
- *In the beginning the defender should only shadow the attacker thereby getting the attacker used to having an obstacle in front.*
- *As the players become more confident in this play, the defensive pressure is steadily increased until full game speed is achieved.*

Each player must play as the attacker and as the defender.
- *To become a good attacker one must know how the defender thinks and acts.*
- *To become a good defender one must know how the attacker thinks and acts.*
- *Attackers are the first line of defense.*
- *Defenders are the first line of the attack.*

IV. DEFENSIVE TECHNIQUE 2V1 SITUATION:

1. TEACH AND DEMONSTRATE:

a. Players required:
- Two defensive players with the first defender being the pressure defender an the second defender being the support defender.
- One attacking player with the ball.

b. See previous section III. 1. a–d.
- The play is set up as described in this section and is played in the same space.
- A support defender will be added in this segment.

c. The support defender is introduced who will be positioned behind the pressure defender and whose purpose is to assist the pressure defender in the containment of the attacker.
- Both defenders are synchronized in their movement while channeling the attacker to the outside.
- In this segment the defenders learn only pressure and support.

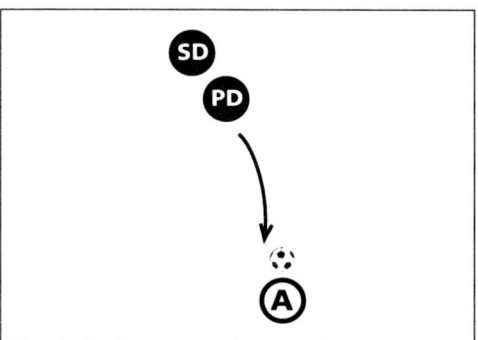

The defender approaches attacker as described in section III. The support defender takes the position behind the defender and to the inside toward the goal.

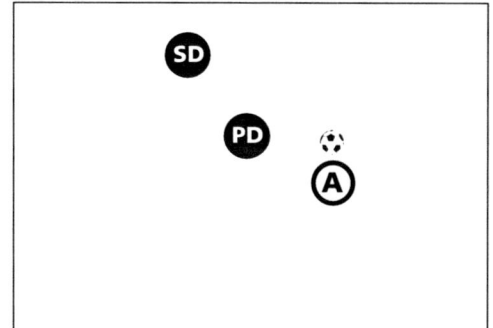

As the pressure defender moves to meet the attacker, the support defender move forward with the pressure defender. Both defenders move in unison when channeling the attacker keeping the same distance between them.

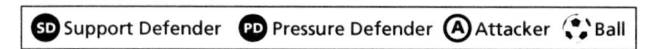

SD Support Defender **PD** Pressure Defender **A** Attacker Ball

2. PLAY IN RELATIONSHIP TO THE ACTUAL GAME:

a. The attacker learns to work against the odds by attempting to beat two defenders.

b. The defenders learn how to organize to turn the odds into their favor by always attempting to create a situation with superior numbers and positioning.

c. For the players the same qualities are present as described in section III.

Emphasize:

a. To the pressure defender:

- *It is always most important to regain possession of territory rather than to chase the attacker from behind.*
- *Always go to space first and regroup.*
- *Trust in you support players.*

b. To the support defender:

- *To take position from the pressure defender and attacker at a distance far enough so as not to be beaten at the same time as the first pressure defender.*
- *Always send verbal directions to the pressure defender which not only assists the pressure defender but will also help throw off the attacker's concentration.*
- *Stress the meaning of pressure defender and support defender.*

c. In the defensive third of the field the mid-fielder becomes the support defender.

3. SET UP THIS 2V1 PLAY AS DESCRIBED IN III. 4. FOR TEAM PRACTICE:

a. Behind every pressure defender, position a support defender.

b. The support defender must always be positioned goal-side and inside of the pressure defender.

c. Each player must be rotated in each group of three for the purpose of learning to play attacker, pressure defender, and support defender.

V. FIRST-TO-THE-BALL PLAY:

The purpose of this play is to teach the players the importance of getting to the ball ahead of the opponent while creating a 1v1 situation.

1. SET UP FIRST-TO-THE-BALL PLAY FOR TEAM PRACTICE:

❺❹❸❷❶ Ⓒ ❶❷❸❹❺

Ⓒ Coach   ❶❷❸❹❺ Players (numbered)   ⚽ Ball

a. Lay out a small playing field using discs as line markers.

b. At each end of the playing area make small goals with cones.

c. The size of this playing area will depend on the age group of the players but should never be larger than the normal goal area.

d. The players are split into two groups with one group assigned to wear pinnies.

e. The players are assembled at one side and outside of the playing field.

f. Each player from one team is given a number while each player from the opposing team is given a corresponding number.
Example: Each team will have one player with #1, #2, #3, etc.

g. One team is assembled to the left of the coach and one team is assembled to the right of the coach.

h. The coach is positioned between the two teams with numerous available soccer balls.

i. The coach calls out one of the numbers and plays a ball onto the field of play.

j. The player from each team with that number must make a run through their goal onto the playing field and attempt to get to the ball first.

k. The players with the ball become the attacker while the player without the ball must now take a defensive stance and defend against the attacker thereby preventing a goal.

l. This first-to-the-ball 1v1 game between two players concludes when one player scores a goal or the ball is played out of bounds.

m. The coach then calls out the next number and the same process begins as described in point i–k.

n. The coach should call the numbers out of sequence to teach players to stay focused.

o. Once the players know and understand this first-to-the-ball play, the coach should split the team and set up a second field. The smaller the groups on each field the more each player will have their number called.

Emphasize:

- *This 1v1 game is the most basic stage of playing the game.*
- *Players must master this 1v1 game if they are to become able players.*
- *This 1v1 play teaches the importance of gaining possession of the ball while at the same time teaches a player how to defend against the attacker.*
- *This play has acquired many names such as "Steal-the-Bacon." Whenever the coach calls a play by some cute name that focuses on entertainment, the purpose of the play is removed from the minds of the players. A play must always be titled for the purpose of teaching the players the reason for the play. This play is called "First-to-the-Ball."*
- *Players must be alert at all times because their number can be called at any given moment. This will instill into the players that during a game they must always stay focused.*
- *The coach should at times call again the number of the players who have just finished playing a 1v1 game. This will keep players even more focused.*

2. BUILDING ON THE FIRST-TO-THE-BALL IN YEAR ONE:

a. As the players become comfortable with the one set of 1v1 game, the coach can begin to throw out a second ball and call a second set of numbers thereby creating a second 1v1 game being played at the same time.

- This can be increased to a third ball being thrown out by the coach and a third 1v1 game is being played at the same time.
- *In this way more players are playing and fewer are standing while waiting for their number to be called.*

b. Once the players have become proficient with the 1v1 play, the 2v2 First-To-The-Ball Play can now be introduced.

- With the 2v2 game a support player is now introduced. This 2v2 segment must only be introduced once the players have learned about organization.
- In the 2v2 game the coach will call out two numbers and those two players must now go after one ball in the same manner as described in section V1a–n.
- The first player called is required to go for the ball while the second player called becomes the support for the attack or the support for the defender.

Emphasize:

- *The support attacker must always be in a position to receive ball.*
- *The support defender must always be behind the pressure defender, be goal side of the ball, and be in possession of the inside area of the ball and the goal.*

c. Introduce the 3v3 First-To-The-Ball Play.

- There are now two support attackers and two support defenders.
- In the 3v3 game the coach will call out three numbers and those three players must now go after one ball in the same manner as described in section V1a–n.
- The first player called is required to go after the ball while the second and third players called become the supporters for the attack and defense.

Emphasize:

- *Greater organization must now takes place for both teams.*
- *Players must now be spread out more and keep their shape.*
- *Players must now keep their attention on one opposing player when on defense and make certain that this player is defended.*
- *Defensive players must not only be responsible for their attacker but must also be in support of the other two defenders.*
- *Attacking players must always be in a position to receive a pass from the attacker with the ball.*
- *Stop play if any of these elements are not being carried out by the players.*
- *Make all corrections for all the players to hear.*
- *Make all corrections at the moment they occur.*
- *In 3v3 games all the elements of a full game take place with learning how to organize and interact with one another being the most important element to learn by the players.*
- *The 3v3 games provide a coach the opportunity to teach organization because the play takes place in a small area with the players being easily reachable by the coach.*
- *Keeping shape of the formation.*

VI. 1V2 DEFENSIVE SITUATION:

A. TEACH AND DEMONSTRATE:
Players needed: One Defender, Two Attackers, One Ball, One Goalkeeper

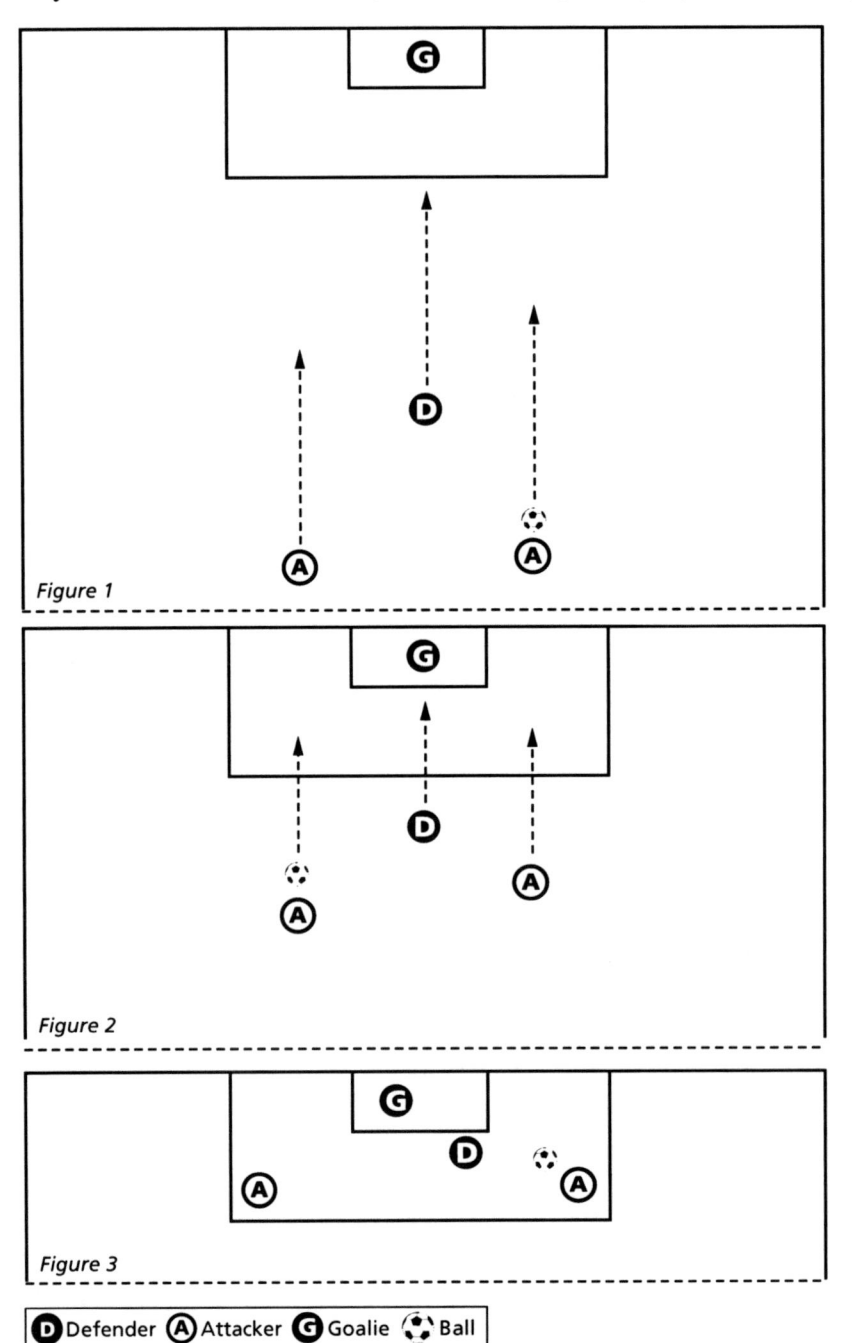

Figure 1

Figure 2

Figure 3

D Defender **A** Attacker **G** Goalie ⚽ Ball

1. The goalie is part of this defensive play who must give the defender clear instructions by repeatedly shouting for the defender to "CONTAIN." This instruction of "contain" keeps the defender focused and implants the same thought into the mind of the attackers.

2. The two attackers will start near midfield and press the attack towards goal.

3. One defender must play the two attackers by bringing them into the goal area.

a. The defender must not panic at this 1v2 situation.

b. The defender must concentrate on keeping both attackers in front and high.

c. The defender must concentrate and keep both attackers insight at all times.
   - The defender must keep backing up at the pace that enables the defender to keep both attackers in sight.
   - Once the defender permits even one attacker to play out of vision, the defender will be in trouble since the ball can now be played behind the defender with the out of sight attacker freely sprinting onto the ball.

d. The defender must always adjust slightly to ball side while at the same time keep backing up.

e. As the ball is passed back to the open attacker, the defender readjusts to ball side always backing up and keeping sight of each attacker.

f. The defender must attempt to only:
   - Contain the attackers and never commit to the ball thereby buying time.
   - Work the ball towards the goal area thereby turning a dangerous 1v2 situation into a 2v2 situation by having the goalie become a support defender.

g. Once the play has reached the goal area the defender will receive instructions from the goalie to go and pressure the ball.
   - The defender must react instantly to the goalies instructions and pressure the ball.
   - The goalie now takes a dual role by first supporting the defender in the event of a shot from that attacker while at the same time the goalie must be ready for the pass going to the open attacker who takes the shot on goal.

B. SET UP THE 1V2 PLAY FOR TEAM PRACTICE:

1. Near midfield form two attacking player lines with one positioned on the right side and one positioned on the left side.
2. Between the two attacking players lines form one defending player line.
3. It is imperative that the players rotate clockwise into the next line after each run-through of this 1v2 Defensive Play.
4. To play all the players through at a much faster pace and eliminating players standing, the team should be divided into two groups with each group playing towards the opposite goal.

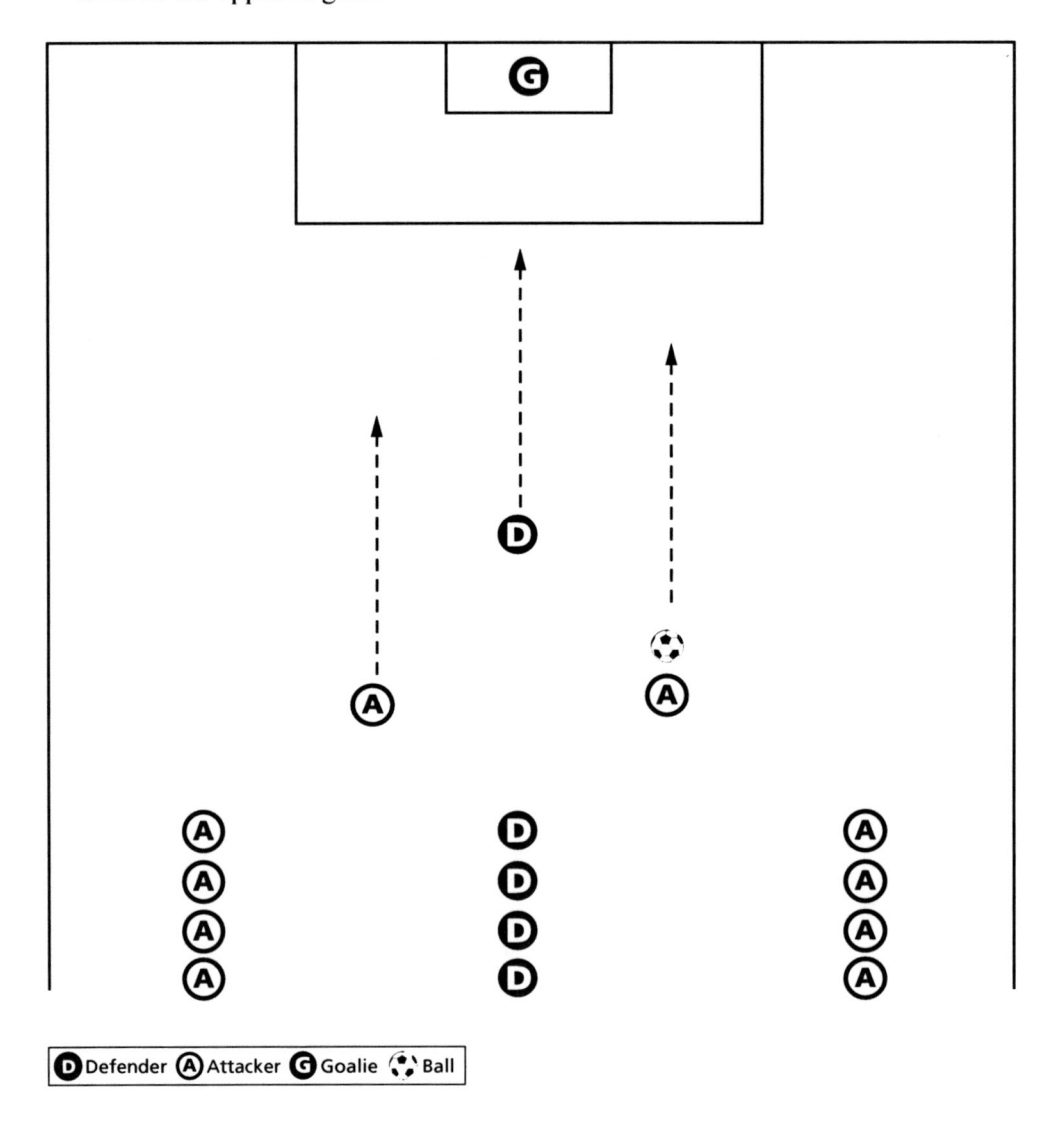

D Defender **A** Attacker **G** Goalie ⚽ Ball

Emphasize:

- *The goalie must send instruction to the defender by shouting "contain."*
- *The defender must always keep sight of both attackers by keeping them in front and high.*
- *Proper defensive stance with one leg in front of the other for good balance when backing up.*
- *Defender must not commit but just contain.*
- *Defender must buy time by backing up.*
- *Defender must shift body slightly and face towards the ball while still having sight of the open attacker.*
- *Defender must use the goalie as a support defender.*
- *Goalie must instruct the defender when to go to pressure.*
- *When defender goes to pressure the goalie must be in support of the pressure defender while being prepared to face a shot from the open attacker in the event of a pass to the open attacker.*
- *By containing the play of the attackers and bringing it into the goal area, the defender has turned a dangerous situation of facing superior numbers into a less dangerous situation of equal numbers.*
- *This is a play set up to learn defense.*
- *Organization on defense is an absolute must.*
- *Keeping shape of the formation.*

VII. RECOVERY DEFENDERS PLAY:

A. TEACH AND DEMONSTRATE:

Simulate a situation where the defense is caught on the attack and must recover goal-side to prevent a dangerous situation that could result in a goal.

Players needed: One center contain defender, two recovery outside defenders, two attackers with one ball, one goalie

1. Set up the 1v2 situation as described in the previous section VI.

2. Add the two outside recovery defenders.

a. One recovery defender on the right side and one recovery defender on the left side.

b. The line of the recovery sprint is predetermined.

- Once the defender has turned back towards the own goal, the defender picks the near post of the own goal and makes a sprint in line towards that near post.
- The defender only sprints back on that line until the defender is goal-side of the ball.
- Once the defender is goal-side of the ball, the defender turns around to face the advancing attackers.

c. If the recovery defenders can break up the attack while in the process of making the recovery run, then this can be considered a bonus.

- The first objective of the recovery defender is to regain the territory goal-side of the ball with superior numbers.
- Focus on sprinting to space first before pressuring the ball.

d. The coach will call two goes:

- On the first go the contain defender and the two attackers with the ball start to play.
- Permit these three players to advance towards goal for a short space and time.
- The coach calls a second go signaling the two outside defensive recovery runners to make their recovery runs goal-side of the ball.

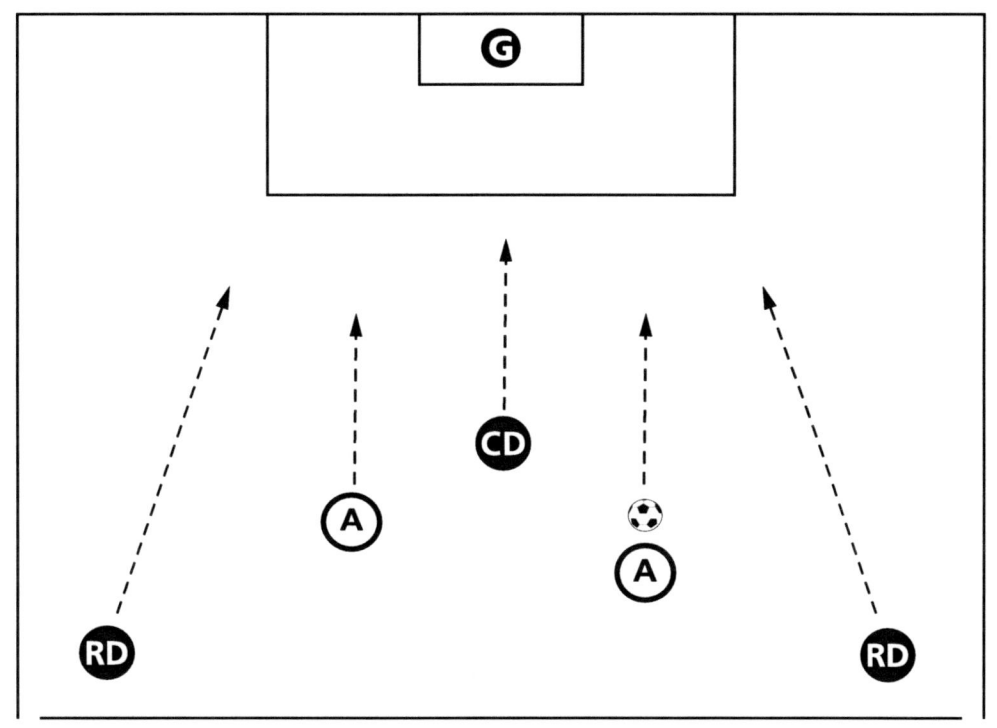

Start of play

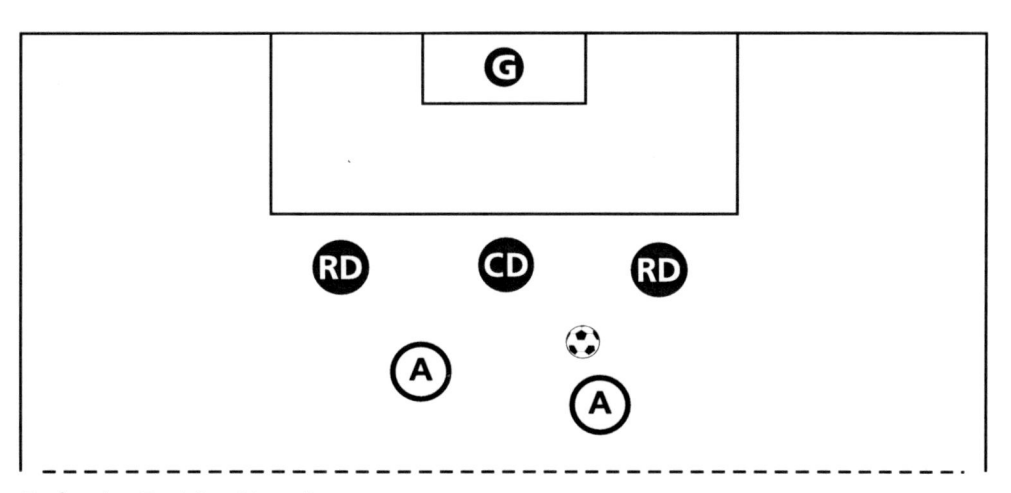

Defensive Position Near Box

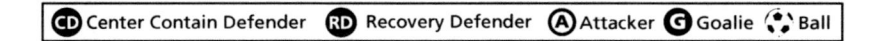

CD Center Contain Defender **RD** Recovery Defender **A** Attacker **G** Goalie ⚽ Ball

B. SET UP THE RECOVER DEFENDERS PLAY FOR TEAM PRACTICE:

1. Set up this practice recovery play as described in section VI. B.
2. On the right and left outside add the recovery defenders lines.
3. It is imperative that the players rotate clockwise into the next line after each run-through of this Recovery Defensive Play. Players must learn how to play each position.
4. To play all the players through at a much faster pace and eliminate players' standing, the team should be divided into two groups with each group playing towards the opposite goal.
5. Use two goes to signal the start of the play.
   - First go the original three players start play
   - Delay a few moments before calling the second go to give the contain defender and the two attackers time to advance.
   - On the second go the recovery defenders begin their runs.

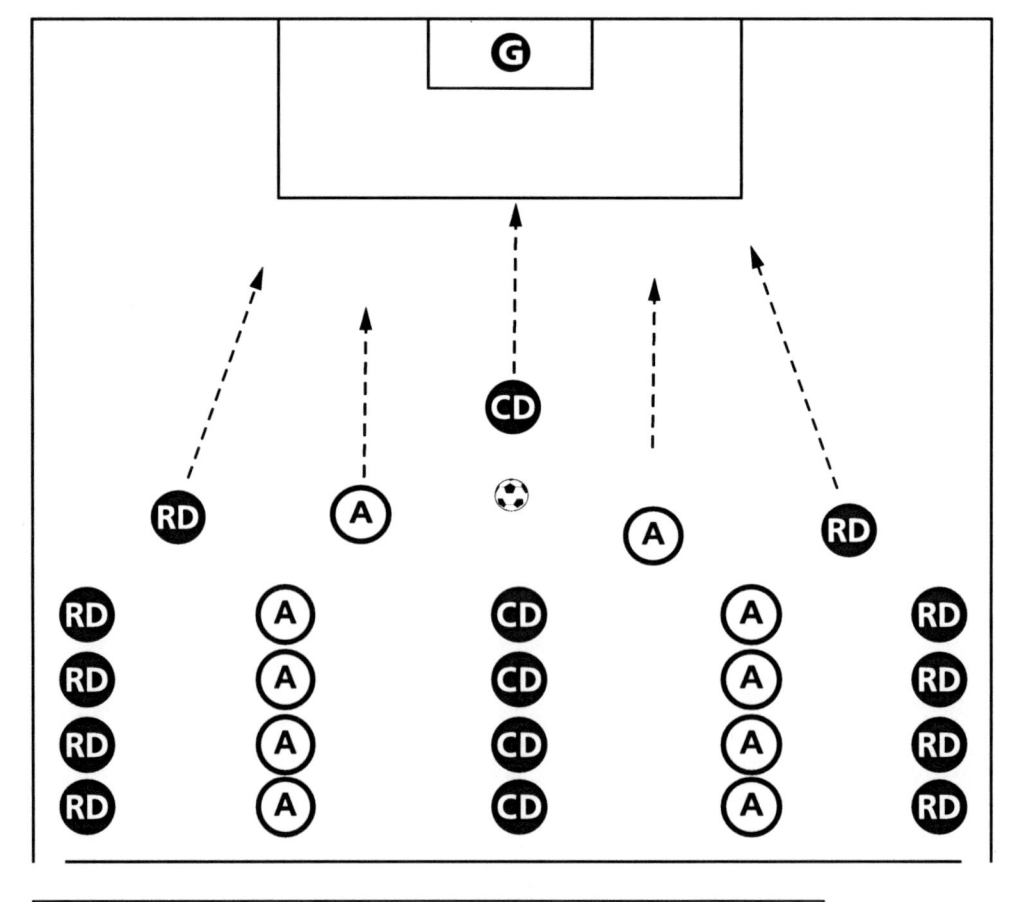

CD Center Contain Defender   **RD** Recovery Defender   **A** Attacker   **G** Goalie   ⚽ Ball

Emphasize:

- *Recovery defenders run on a predetermined line towards their near goal post.*
- *Explain that goal-side of the ball means being in position between the ball and the goal.*
- *Recovery defenders makes recovery sprint only as far as being goal-side of the ball.*
- *Once the recovery defender is goal side of the ball the defender must turn and defend against the attack.*
- *The recovery defender should make the run through the space that the attackers are playing in order to possibly break up their play.*
- *The first objective of the recovery defender is to first and foremost always regain the territory goal-side of the ball with superior numbers.*
- *Focus on sprinting to space first before pressuring the ball.*
- *The recovery runs must be an all out sprint.*
- *The reason for learning recovery runs is because eventually the players will learn how to attack from their defensive positions and thereby must know how to get back to their primary responsibility of defending.*
- *Recovery runs take place on every section of the field.*
- *We begin with practicing recovery runs in the middle section because it is the most dangerous ground.*
- *The goalie must send instruction to the contain defender by shouting "contain."*
- *The contain defender must always keep sight of both attackers by keeping them in front and high.*
- *Proper defensive stance with one leg in front of the other for good balance when backing up.*
- *Contain defender must not commit but just contain until the recovery defenders are in position to support the contain defender.*
- *Contain defender must buy time by backing up.*
- *Contain defender must shift body slightly and face towards the ball while still having sight of the open attacker.*
- *This is a play set up to learn defense.*
- *Organization on defense is an absolute must.*

NOTE:
The defense for 7v7 Team Play has now been set in a 3–2–1 alignment. The three defenders now know and understand how to organize themselves. This will make it much easier for the coach to teach a four defender alignment once the team goes to a 9v9 or 11v11 Team Play.

C. ADD ANOTHER ATTACKING MIDFIELDER:

1. Set up the team practice described in section VII. B.
   - In 7v7 the attackers consist of the forward and one mid-fielder.

2. Add the second midfielder to the attackers.
   - This second attacking midfielder will be positioned behind the two attackers and provides the two attackers the option to play the ball back when facing defensive pressure.

3. This third midfield attacker will begin play on the second go along with the recovery defenders.

4. A scrimmage game is now played in the defensive third near the goal.
   - Defenders now must defend under pressure in the most dangerous area of the field.
   - This scrimmage will build the defenders confidence to defend in the most dangerous area of the field.

5. Near the midfield area of the field, set up one small goal on the right outside and one small goal on the left outside.
   - If the defense takes possession of the ball they are now able to go on a counter attack and score on either of those small goals.
   - This will teach the defense to go on a counter attack to the outside which will be worked on in year number two when actual transition from defense to attack will be taught.

Emphasize:
- *All items from EMPHASIZE in previous section VII. B.*
- *Midfield Attacker must remain behind first two attackers to provide a back play option.*
- *Defenders can take possession of the ball and attempt to score on the two small goals placed on the outside near midfield.*
- *Defenders become comfortable in playing and defending in front of their goal area.*
- *Defenders learn to take the ball outside and attack.*
- *The attackers in 7v7 play consist of one forward and two midfielders.*
- *Keeping shape of the formation.*

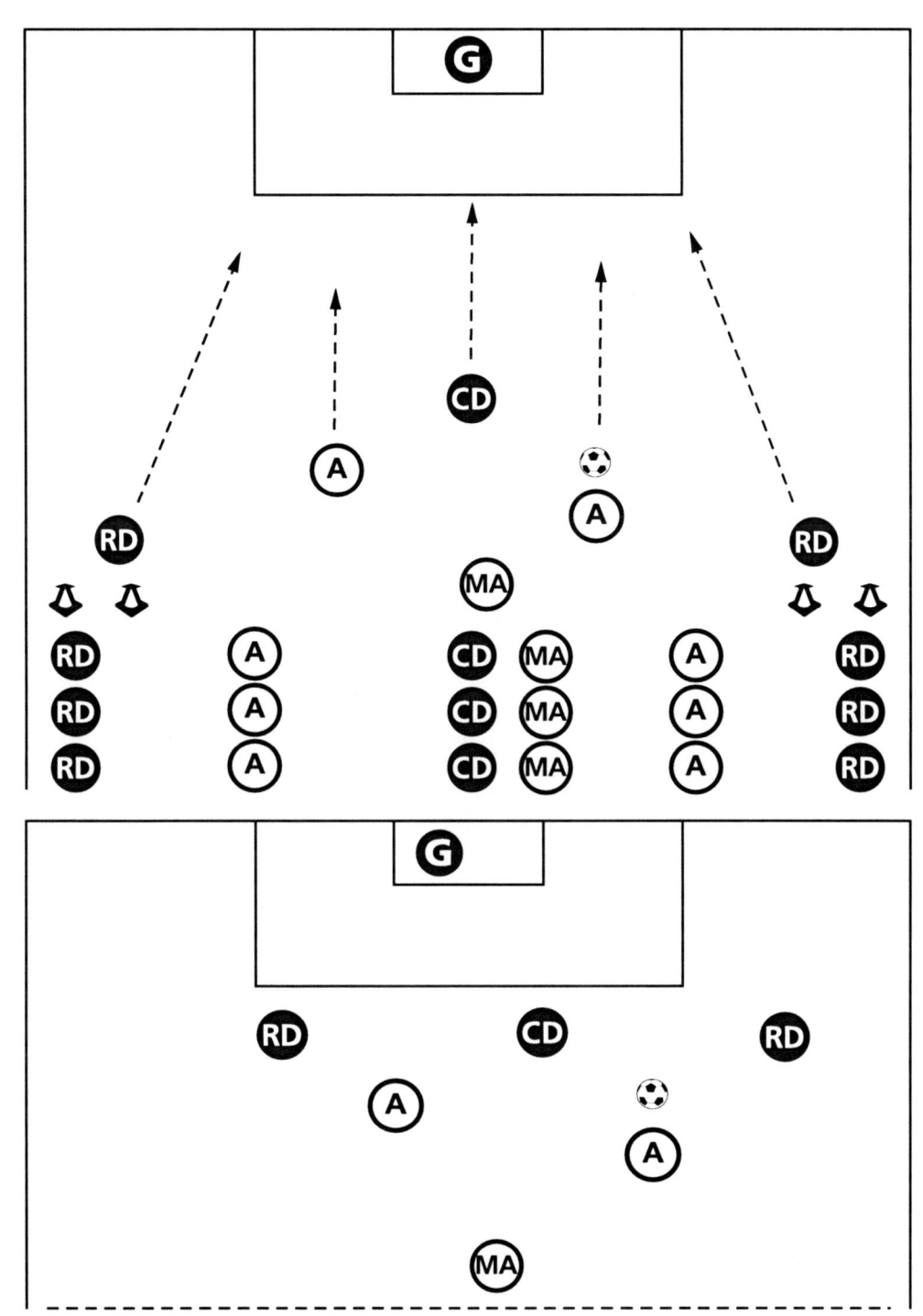

Approximate position of players once play starts

CD Center Contain Defender **RD** Recovery Defender **A** Attacker **MA** Midfield Attacker **G** Goalie ⚽ Ball

VIII. ADD TWO RECOVERING DEFENSIVE MIDFIELDERS:

A. TEACH AND DEMONSTRATE:

Players needed: One center contain defender, two recovery outside defenders, two recovering defensive midfielders, two attackers with one ball, one goalie

1. Set up the play as described above in section VII. A.
b. In the 3-2-1 alignment, the two recovering midfielders will now make their recovery runs into the defensive third to support the defenders.

2. As the recovering midfielders make their recovery runs into the defense, they must see where the spaces are that have been created between the three defenders and proceed to take up position between the outside defenders and the contain defender.
   • This will create a defensive wall.
   • This will make it difficult for the attackers to penetrate.

3. The coach must give a third go for the defensive midfielders to proceed to make their recovery runs.

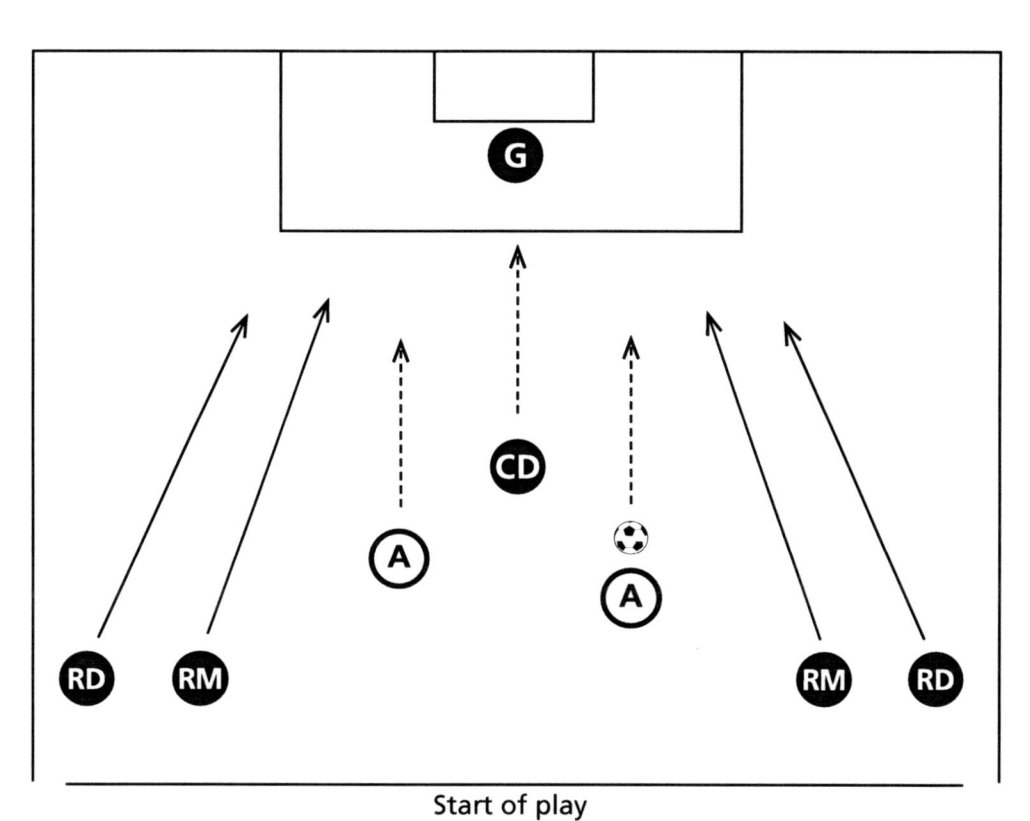

Start of play

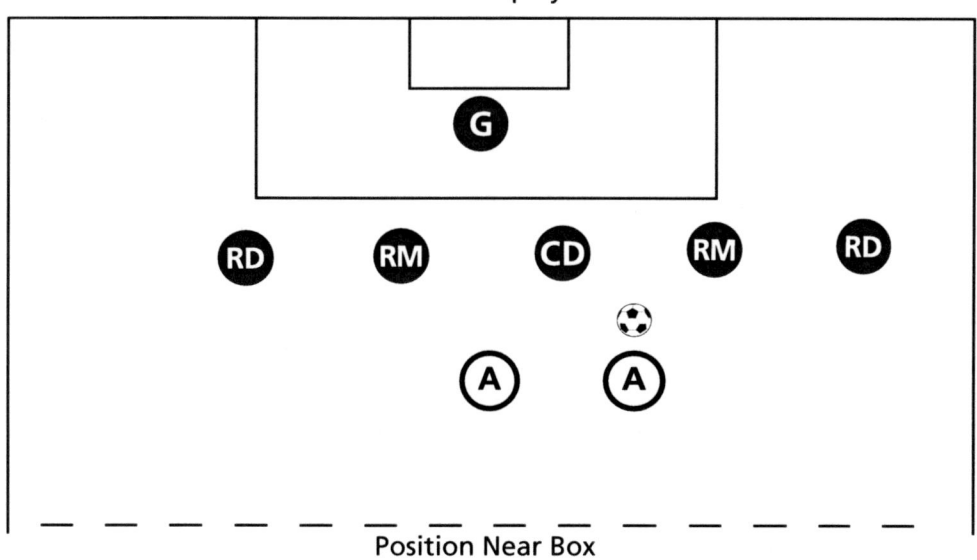

Position Near Box

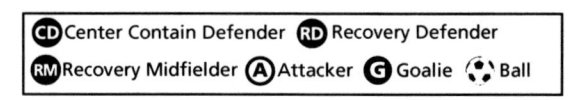

CD Center Contain Defender **RD** Recovery Defender
RM Recovery Midfielder **A** Attacker **G** Goalie ⚽ Ball

B. SET UP THE RECOVERING DEFENSIVE MIDFIELDER PLAY FOR TEAM PRACTICE:

1. Set up this recovery play as described in section VII. B.

2. Set up two additional lines:

a. One line on the left side and to the right of the outside defender.

b. One line to the right side and to the left of the outside defender.

3. It is imperative that the players rotate clockwise into the next line after each run through of this Recovery Defensive Play. Players must learn how to play each position.

4. To play all the players through at a much faster pace and eliminate players standing, the team should be divided into two groups with each group playing towards the opposite goal.

5. Use three goes to signal the start of the play.

a. First go the original three players start play

b. Delay a few seconds before calling the second go to give the contain defender and the two attackers time to advance.

c. On the second go the recovery defenders begin their runs.

d. On the third go the recovering defensive midfielders begin their runs.

Emphasize:

a. All items emphasized in previous section VII. B.

b. As the recovering midfielders make their recovery runs into the defense, they must see where the spaces are that have been created between the three defenders and proceed to take up position between the outside defenders and the contain defender.

- *This will create a defensive wall.*
- *This will make it difficult for the attackers to penetrate.*

c. Keeping shape of the formation.

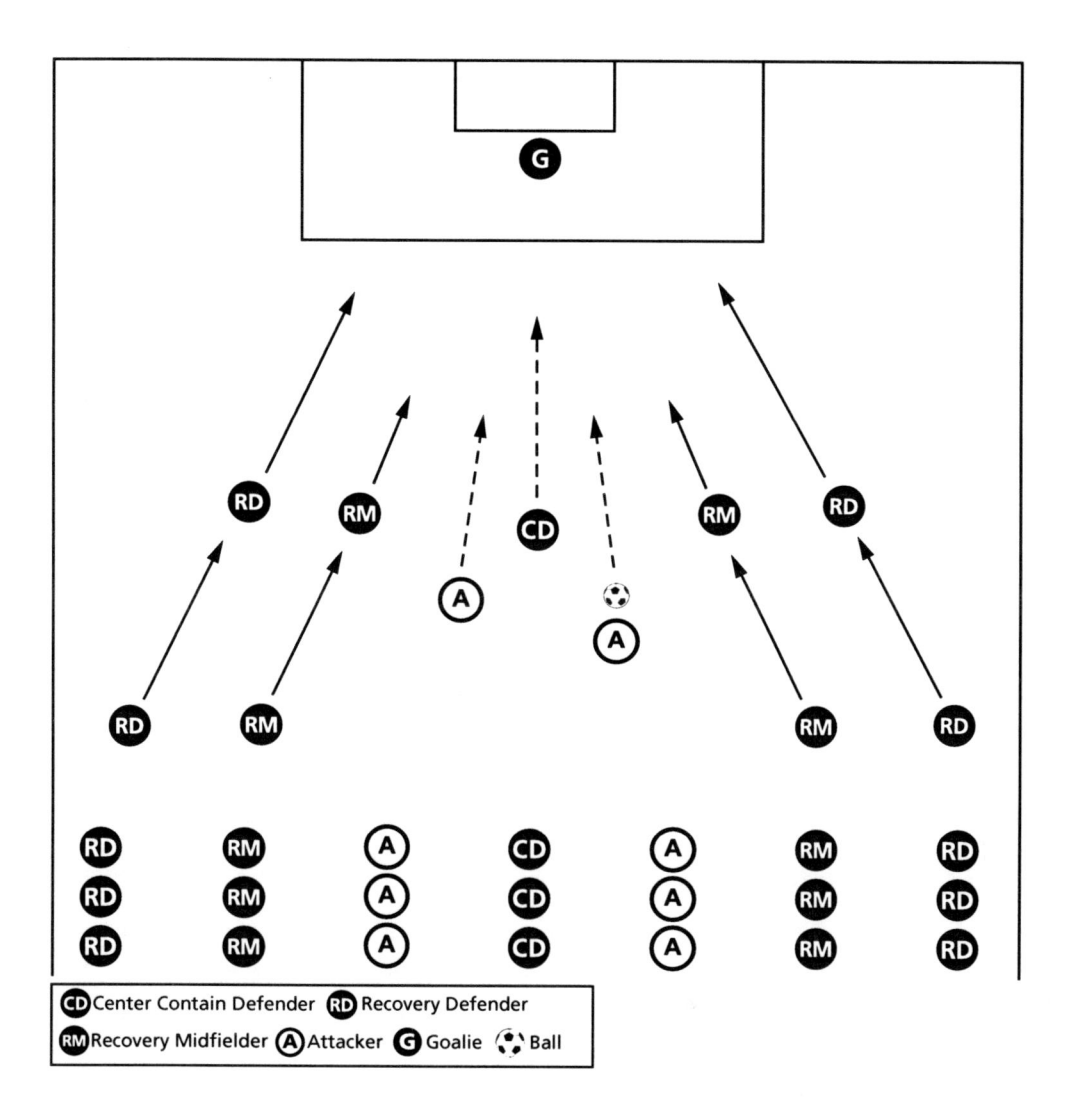

CD Center Contain Defender **RD** Recovery Defender
RM Recovery Midfielder **A** Attacker **G** Goalie ⚽ Ball

IX. 9V9 AND 11V11 PLAY—ADDING SWEEPER CENTER BACK DEFENDER:

A. TEACH AND DEMONSTRATE:

Simulate a situation where the defense is caught on the attack and must recover goal-side to prevent a dangerous situation that could result in a goal by now adding a Sweeper Central Defender.

Players needed: One center contain defender, one "sweeper" center recovery defender, two recovering outside defenders, two attackers with one ball, one goalie

1. Set up this play as described in previous section VII. A. 1 &2.

2. Add the fourth defender to establish the full four back defense.

a. This fourth defender will be called the sweeper back.

b. In the defensive third of the field the sweeper back will be the last man back and takes up the position in front of the goalie.

c. The sweeper back organizes the defense and all other defenders must obey the instructions of the sweeper back.

d. The sweeper back is free to move in any direction necessary to block the attack.

e. The sweeper back will be used as an extra attacker when the team advances into the attacking third of the field.

- To simulate the sweeper back having advanced into the attack and now must recover, we position this player into the center behind the two attackers.
- The coach must now call out a third go which signals the sweeper back to make the recovery run towards the own goal.
- The sweeper back must make this recovery run down the middle of the field with the penalty spot as the guiding line.

f. Once the sweeper back has reached the position behind the contain defender, this sweeper back must face the attackers and:

- Be in position to support the contain defender.
- Direct the contain defender to either continue to contain the attackers or attack the ball.
- Instruct the outside recovering defenders to be in possession of the goal-side territory and be prepared to challenge any attacker coming into that territory.
- The sweeper back must be free to defend wherever play has broken down.

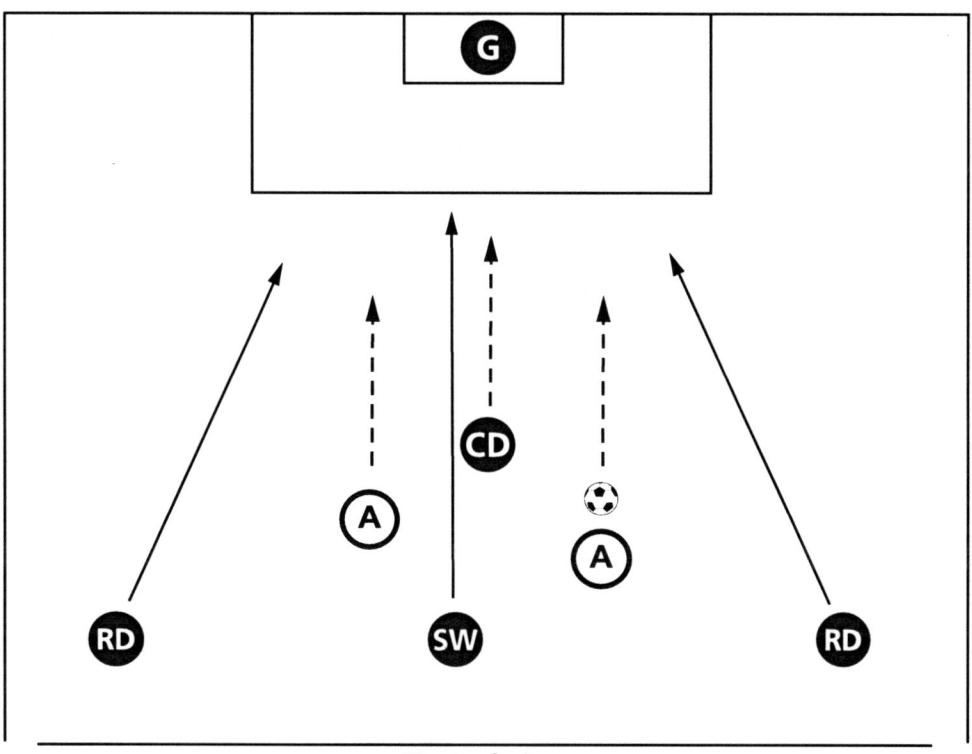

Start of play

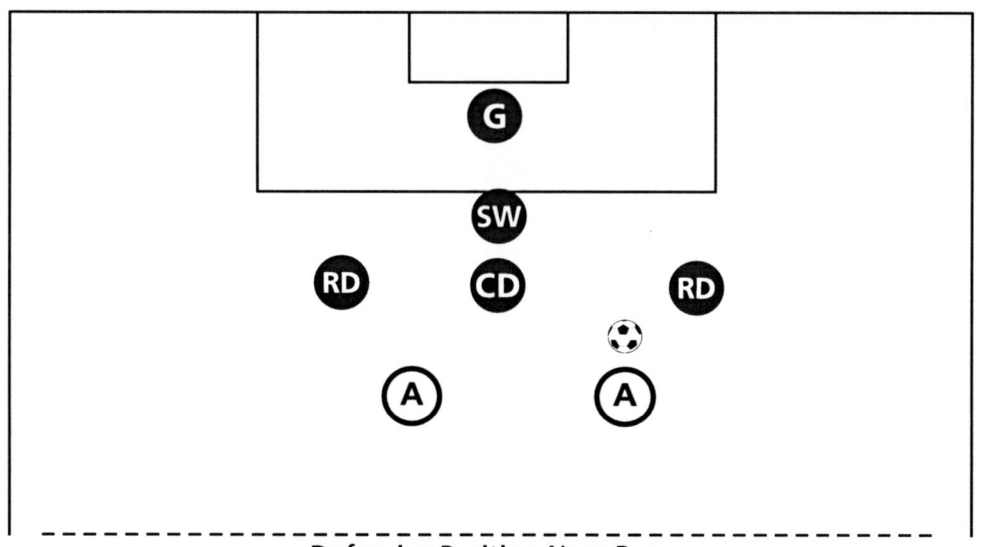

Defensive Position Near Box

CD Center Contain Defender **RD** Recovery Defender **SW** Sweeper Defender **A** Attacker **G** Goalie ⚽ Ball

B. SET UP THE RECOVER SWEEPER DEFENDER PLAY FOR TEAM PRACTICE:

1. Set up the team play as described in previous section VII. B. 1-4

5. Use three goes to signal the start of the play.
    - First go the original three players start play
    - Delay a few moments before calling the second go to give the contain defender and the two attackers time to advance.
    - On the second go the recovery defenders begin their runs.
    - On the third go the recovering center sweeper back starts the recovery run which finishes behind the contain defender.

6. The center contain defender will also be called the "stopper back" defender whose main responsibility is to hold the center ground consisting of the area approximately between the goal posts.

7. When dealing with youth teams it is best to give the two center backs specific responsibilities otherwise both center backs may be found out of position.

Emphasize:
- *All points in the EMPHASIZE section found in section VII. B.*
- *Points from previous section IX. A. 2 a–f.*
- *Keeping shape of the formation.*

NOTE:
The defense for 9v9 and 11v11 Team Play has now been set in a 4–3–1 for 9v9 and 4–4–2 for 11v11 alignments. The four defenders now know and understand how to organize themselves.

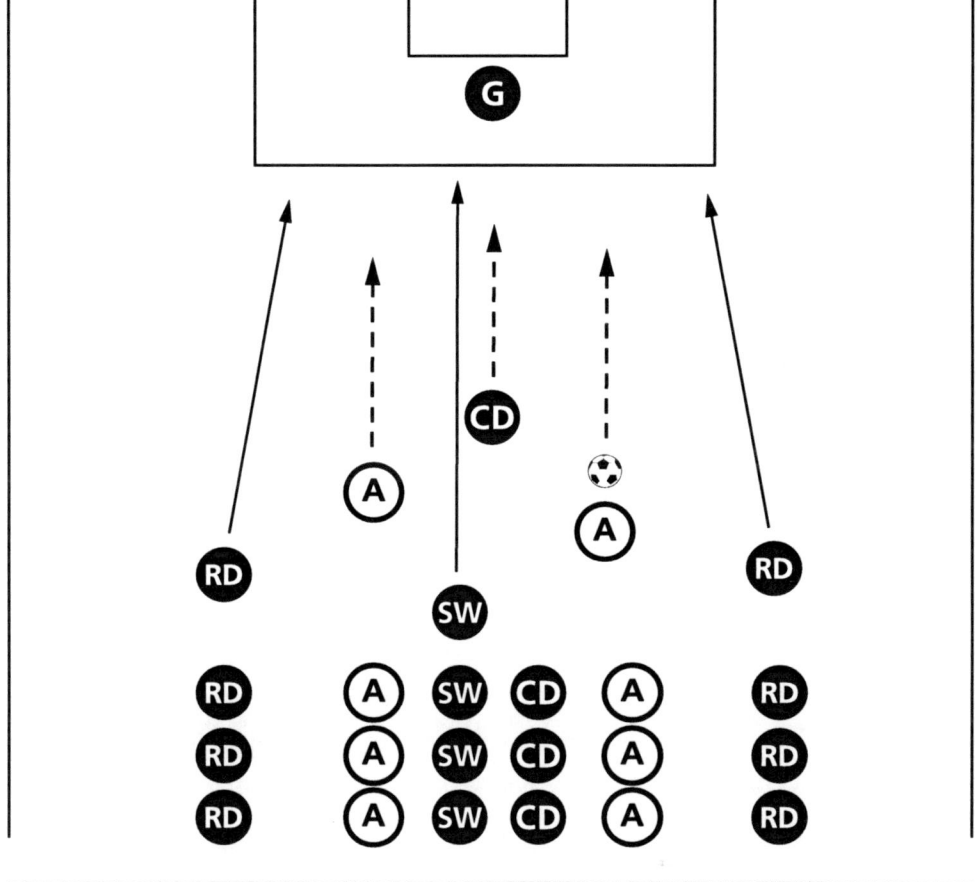

CD Center Contain Defender **RD** Recovery Defender **SW** Sweeper Defender **A** Attacker **G** Goalie ⚽ Ball

C. ADD TWO ATTACKING MIFIELDERS TO THE PLAY:

1. Set up team play as described in section IX. A & B.
   - In 9v9 the attackers consist of one forward and one mid-fielder.
   - In 11v11 the attackers consist of two attacking forwards.

2. Add the two midfielders to the attackers.
   - These two attacking midfielders will be positioned behind the two forward attackers.
   - These two midfield attackers provide the two attackers the option to play the ball back when facing defensive pressure.

3. These two additional midfield attackers will begin play on the third go along with the recovering sweeper defender.
4. A scrimmage game is now played in the defensive third near the goal.
   - Defenders now must defend under pressure in the most dangerous area of the field.
   - This scrimmage will build the defenders confidence to defend in the most dangerous area of the field.
5. Near the midfield area of the field, set up one small goal on the right outside and one small goal on the left outside.
   - If the defense takes possession of the ball they are now able to go on a counter attack and score on either of those small goals.
   - This will teach the defense to go on a counter attack to the outside which will be worked on in year number two when actual transition from defense to attack will be taught.
6. A 4v4 game has now been created in the defensive third.

EMPHASIZE:
- *All items from EMPHASIZE in previous section VII. B & IX.*
- *Midfield Attackers must remain behind first two attackers to provide a back play option.*
- *Defenders can take possession of the ball and attempt to score on the two small goals placed on the outside near midfield.*
- *Defenders become comfortable in playing and defending in front of their goal area.*
- *Defenders learn to take the ball outside and attack.*
- *The attackers in 9v9 play consist of one forward and one midfielder with two midfielders added as support attackers.*
- *The attackers in 11v11 play consist of two forwards and two attacking midfielders who are added as support attackers.*
- *Keeping shape of the formation.*

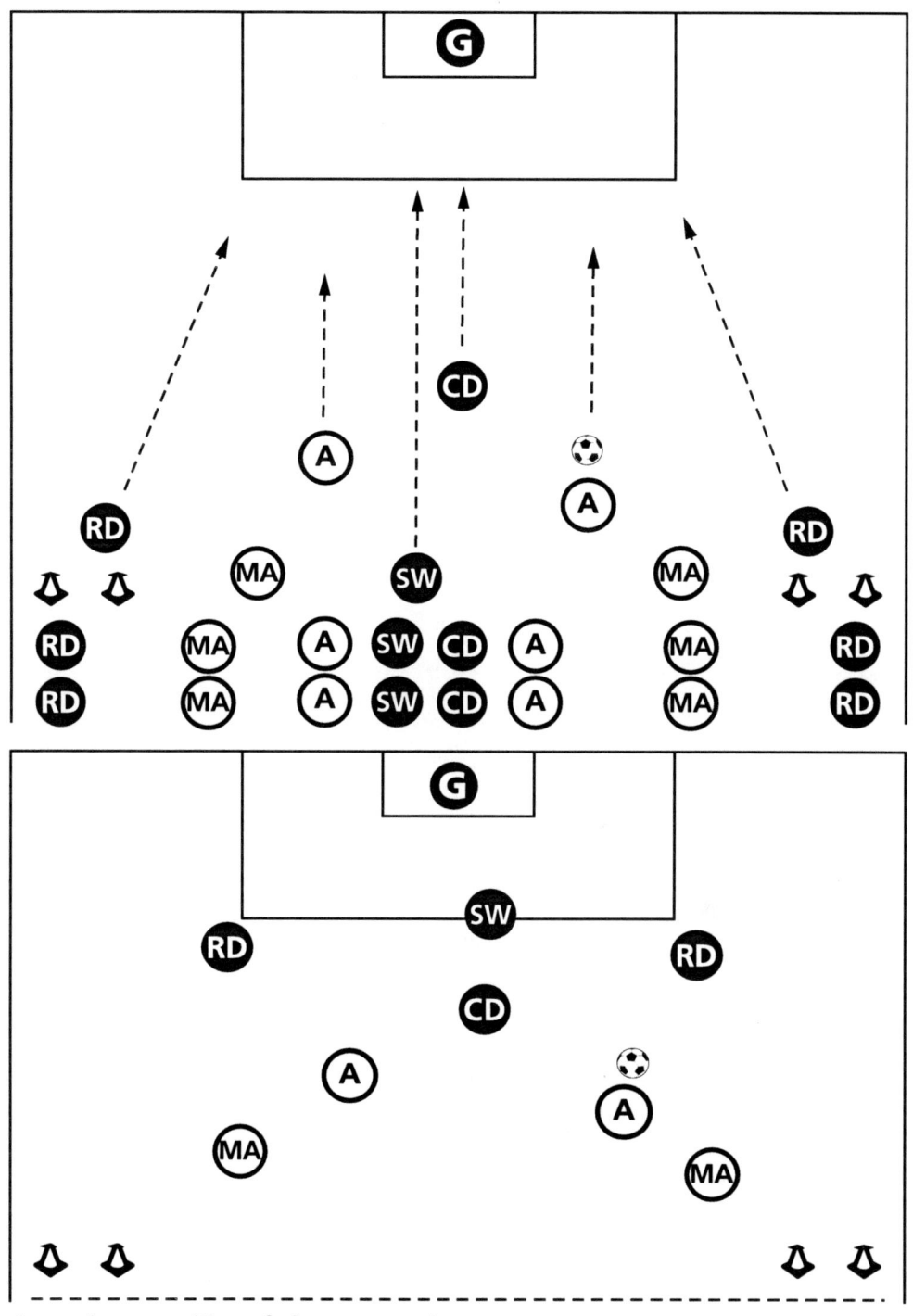

Approximate position of players once play starts

CD Center Contain Defender **RD** Recovery Defender **SW** Sweeper Defender
MA Midfield Attacker **A** Attacker **G** Goalie ⚽ Ball

D. ADD TWO RECOVERING DEFENSIVE MIDFIELDERS TO THE PLAY:

Players needed for recovering defensive midfielders: One center contain defender, one sweeper defender, two recovering outside defenders, two recovering midfielders, two attackers with one ball, two attacking midfielders, One goalie

1. Set up play as described in previous sections VIII. A and IX. A.

2. Use four goes to signal the start of the play.
   - First go the original three players start play
   - Delay a few moments before calling the second go to give the contain defender and the two attackers time to advance.
   - On the second go the recovery defenders begin their runs.
   - On the third go the recovering center sweeper back starts the recovery run which finishes behind the contain defender.
   - On the fourth go the two recovery defensive midfielders go.

3. A 6v4 game is created with play in the defensive third.

EMPHASIZE:
- *All items of EMPHASIZE in previous sections VIII. and IX.*
- *A defensive wall has been created around the goalie box.*

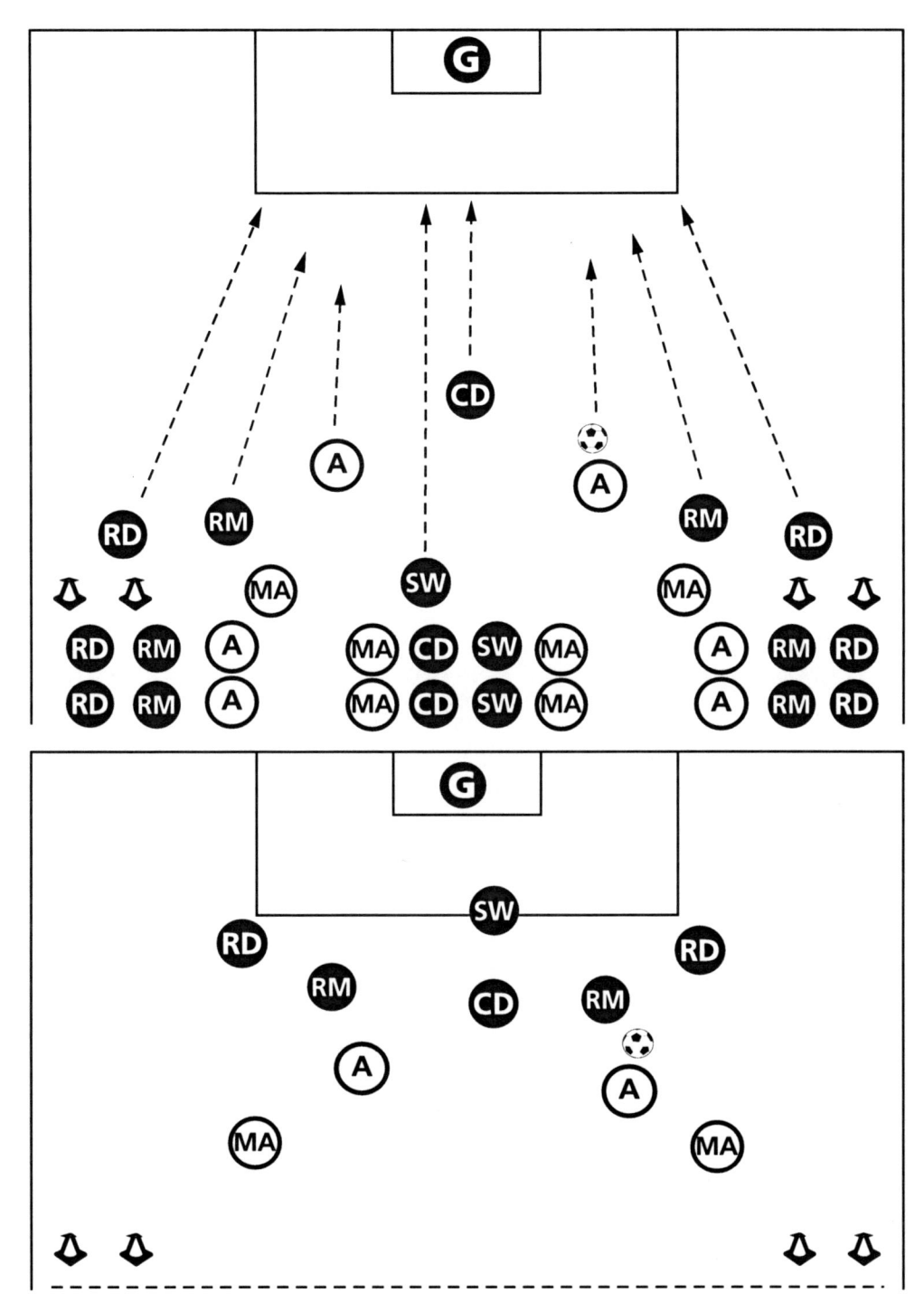

Approximate position of players once play starts

CD Center Contain Defender **RD** Recovery Defender **SW** Sweeper Defender
RM Recovery Midfielder **MA** Midfield Attacker **A** Attacker **G** Goalie ⚽ Ball

X. DIVIDE PLAYING FIELD INTO THIRDS:

To minimize the player's decision making process on the field during a game, the player must learn that the decisions are dictated by the area of the playing field the player is playing in.

The playing field is divided into three sections:

1. The DEFENSIVE THIRD is the section of the field closest to the own goal area.

When players are defending in their own defensive third of the field, the decisions must be very conservative.

a. Mark each opposing player very tightly.
b. Create superior defensive numbers by bringing the midfielders back into the defense for support of the defenders while at the same time closing all open lanes which the opponent could exploit.
c. Forwards retreat into the upper part of the defensive third.
d. All balls played by the opposing team must be won by the own team.
- Any mistakes by the own team in this defensive third of the field can be very costly and result in a goal.
- All balls must be cleared: Quickly, high, to the outside
- If the pressure is heavy, clear the ball downfield as far as possible and then quickly pull up field and defend as far from the own goal as the opportunity allows.
- It may take several clearances before a team can re-establish itself away from the own defensive third of the field.
- The defenders must always remain patient and contain the danger rather than committing to the ball until the defender has support.

2. The MIDDLE THIRD of the field:

When players have re-established control of the game in the middle third of the field the focus changes from defense to attack.

a. Players do not have to be marked very tightly.
b. The attacking team can now begin to become creative and look to play the ball into the open spaces on the field.
c. The attacking team should remain patient regarding their penetration towards the opponents goal.

d. The team that dominates the middle third of the field generally will dominate the game since the penetration into the own defensive third by the opponent is minimized while the attack into the own attacking third of the field can be developed and carried through.

e. Once again superior numbers must be created with
- The own forwards now positioned at the top of the middle third and penetrate into the own attacking third.
- The own midfielders in control of this entire middle third of the field and in support of the developing attack.
- The own defenders must push forward to the back end of the middle third of the field to be in support of the developing attack while preventing the opponent to play towards the own goal area.

3. The ATTACKING THIRD of the field:

When the players have penetrated into the attacking third of the field, the play of the own team must become very creative.

a. The opposing defenders must now mark tightly.
b. Own forwards and midfielders have the freedom to move into the available spaces and attack from there.
c. The play must be very quick in the attacking third of the field.
d. Every moment lost before a shot or threat on the opponents goal buys time for their defenders to gain superior numbers and close any passing or shooting lanes.
e. The alignment must once again change in the attacking third of the field.
- Midfielders must push forward and be in a position to be in immediate support of the attackers or become attackers.
- Defenders must push forward and be in position to support the entire attack as well as prevent the opponent from playing the ball out of their defensive third creating a quick counter attack.
f. The pressure from the attacking team must be: Quick, Constant, Creative
g. The attacking team must recognize what the defense has failed to cover and then develop the thrust on goal from that weakness.

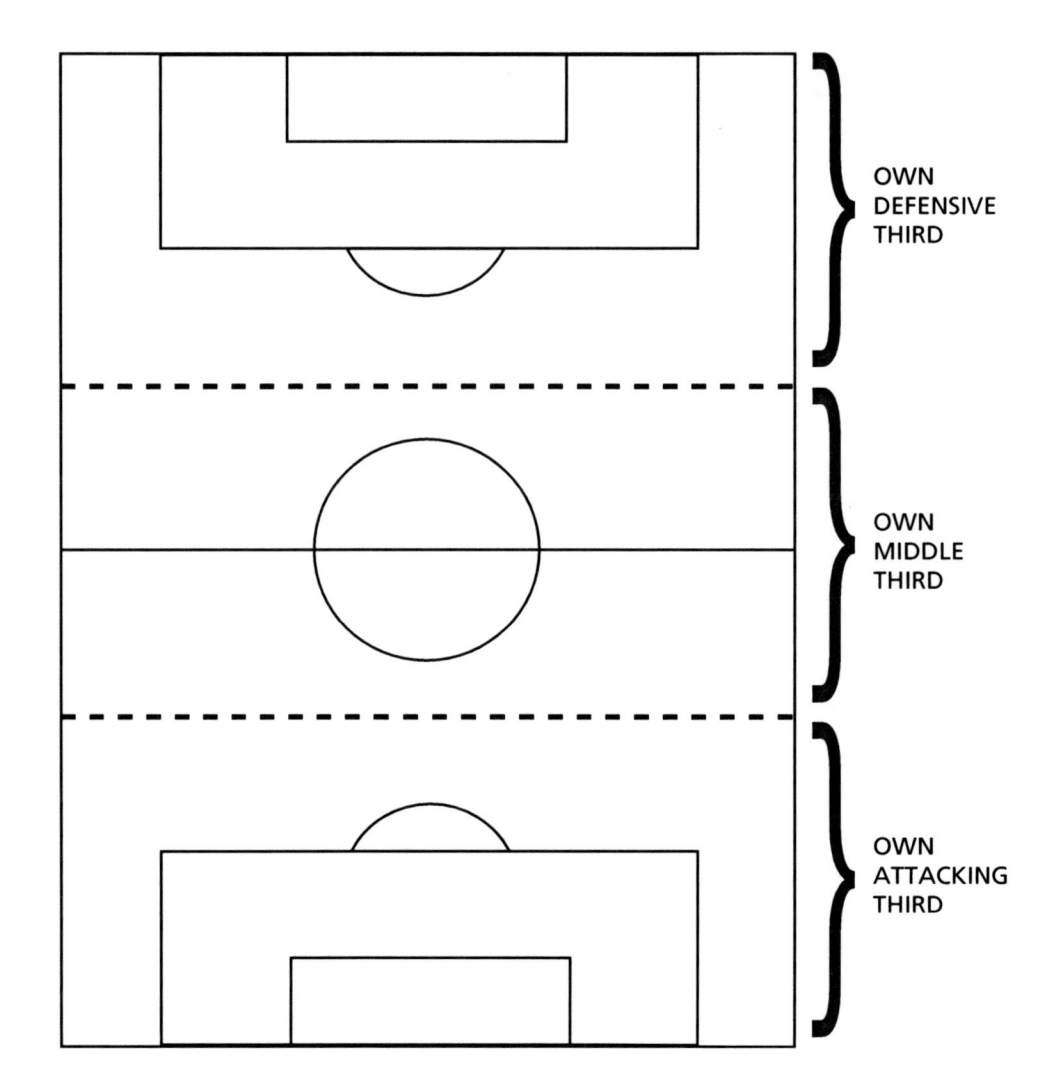

XI: TEAM FORMATIONS:

A. 7v7 TEAM PLAY:

1. The formation in the 7v7 team play should be 3–2–1: Three defenders, two midfielders, one forward

a. By playing with a 3–2–1 alignment the players learn from the beginning that there are three elements.

- A defensive element
- A midfield element
- An attacking element

b. Although a 3–3 alignment works with 7v7 play, the fact that there are three elements in a game will not be taught when using only two lines of three defenders and three forwards.

c. Since we always begin with building the defense when developing a team, it is important that a three defender alignment is established.

2. The 3–2–1 alignment changes in each third of the field.

a. In the defensive third the two midfielders are drawn back into the defense and create a 5–1 alignment:
   - To support the defenders.
   - To fill in any open gaps of territory into which the opponent can attack.
   - Superior numbers have been created in the defensive section of the playing field.

b. When advancing into the middle third of the field this 5–1 alignment changes to a 3–2–1 alignment:
   - Three defenders are held at the top of the defensive third.
   - Two midfielders have pushed forward into the middle third of the playing field to support the attack.
   - The forward has taken a position that threatens the opposing team's goal.
   - With midfielders pushing forward superior numbers are created in the middle third of the field.

c. When reaching the attacking third of the field this 3–2–1 alignment changes to a 2–2–2 or a 2-1-3 alignment:
   - The two outside defenders pinch into the middle of the field.
   - The central defender whom we have titled the stopper-sweeper back pushes forward to become a midfielder alongside the right midfielder or becomes the lone midfielder in a 2–1–3 alignment.
   - The left midfielder pushes forward and becomes an attacker alongside the forward or both midfielders become forwards.
   - Superior numbers are now achieved in the attacking third.
   - Repeatedly walk the team through each third to show how the formation changes.

5-1 ALIGNMENT

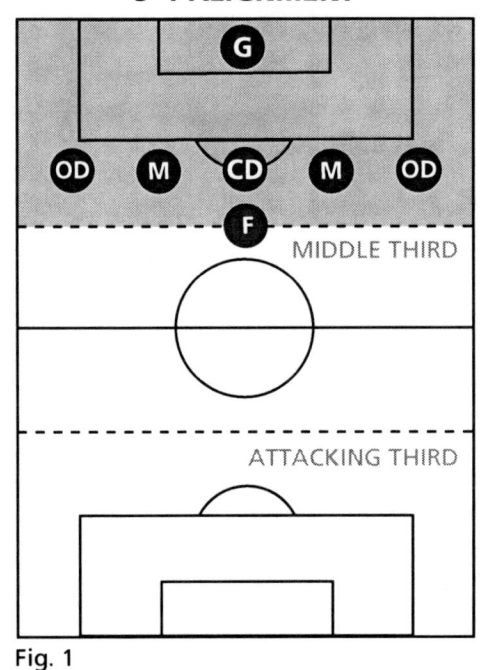

Fig. 1

3-2-1 ALIGNMENT

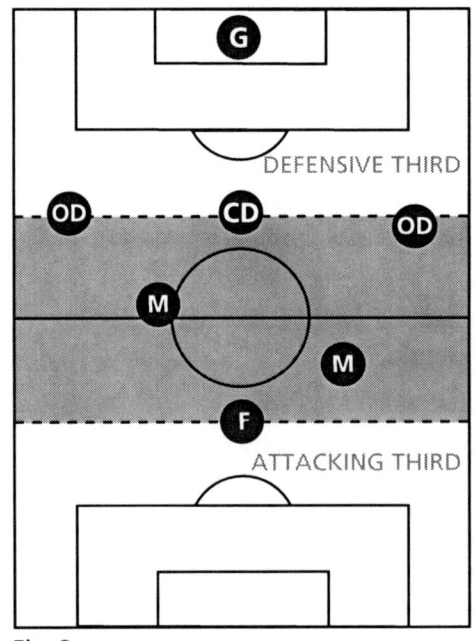

Fig. 2

**2-2-2 ALIGNMENT OR
2-1-3 ALIGNMENT**
Two Outside Defenders,
One Central Defender, Three Attackers

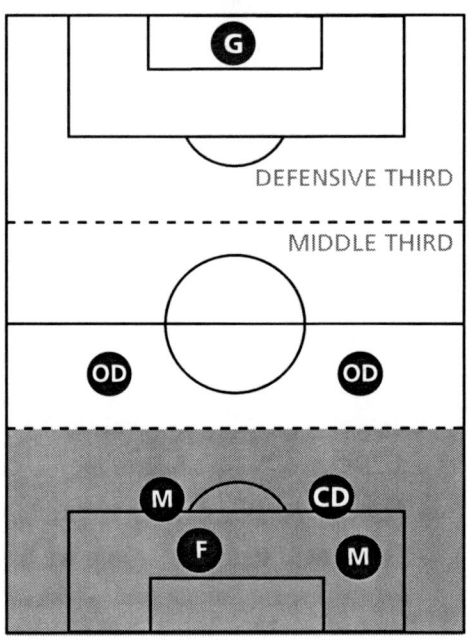

Fig. 3

CD Center Defender **OD** Outside Defender
M Midfielder **F** Forward **G** Goalie

3. Teach the players how a 3–2–1 in the 7v7 play formation is cut out of the 4–4–2 formation when playing 11v11.
a. Players must understand that the actual game of soccer is played by 11 players versus 11 players.
b. Players must understand that their game of 7 players versus 7 players is related to the actual game of 11v11.

This diagram shows a standard 4–4–2 Alignment from the 11v11 play. The players **highlighted in black** shows how the 3–2–1 in 7v7 play is derived from the 4–4–2 in 11v11 play.

The game of soccer is always 11v11.

4-4-2 ALIGNMENT FROM 11V11

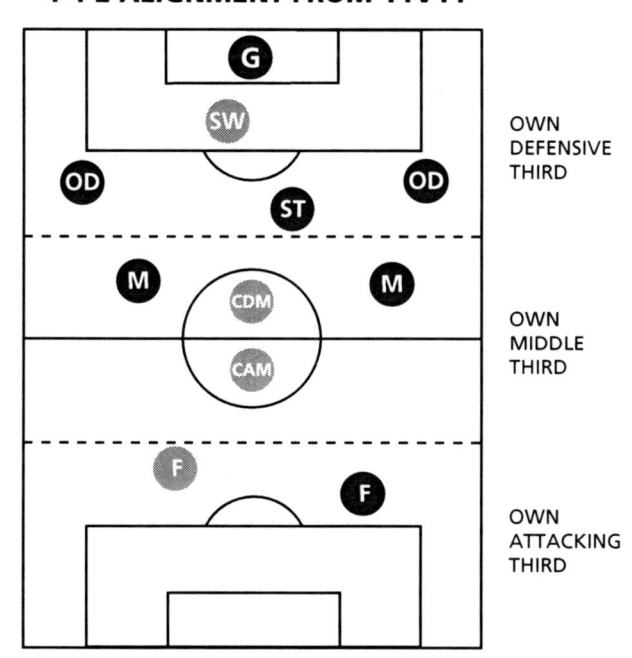

OWN DEFENSIVE THIRD

OWN MIDDLE THIRD

OWN ATTACKING THIRD

ST Stopper Defender **OD** Outside Defender **M** Midfielder
F Forward **G** Goalie **SW** Sweeper Defender
CDM Center Defensive Midfielder **CAM** Center Attacking Midfielder

B. 9v9 TEAM PLAY:

1. The formation in the 9v9 team play should be 4–3–1: Four defenders, three midfielders, one forward

a. By playing with a 4–3–1 alignment the players learn from the beginning that there are three elements.
   - A defensive element
   - A midfield element
   - An attacking element

b. Since we always begin with building the defense when developing a team, it is important that the full four defender alignment is now established.
   - The defensive element is now completely established.
   - The stopper-sweeper position for the center back defender is now broken into two separate positions.
   - The sweeper defender is the last defender behind the ball who has the freedom to roam to any point on the field to support the defense.
   - The stopper defender is responsible to defended the center of the field which is considered the most dangerous ground.
   - The modern game has two central defenders without the sweeper and stopper labels.
   - Dealing with youth developing players it is best to give the two central defenders specific duties thereby using the terms sweeper and stopper.
   - If the two developing youth center defenders do not have specific duties then there will be occasions when both defenders have roamed out of the center leaving the most dangerous ground exposed to the opponent.

2. The 4–3–1 alignment changes in each third of the field.

a. In the defensive third the three midfielders are drawn back into the defense and create a 6–1–1 alignment:
   - To support the defenders.
   - To fill in any open gaps of territory into which the opponent can attack.
   - Superior numbers have been created in the defensive section of the playing field.

b. When advancing into the middle third of the field this 6–1–1 alignment changes to a 4–3–1 alignment:
   - Four defenders are held at the top of the defensive third.
   - Three midfielders have pushed forward into the middle third of the playing field to support the attack.

- The forward has taken a position that threatens the opposing team's goal.
- With midfielders pushing forward superior numbers are created in the middle third of the field.

c. When reaching the attacking third of the field this 4–3–1 alignment changes to a 3–3–2 or a 3–2–3 alignment:
  - The two outside defenders pinch into the middle of the field.
  - The stopper back holds the middle of the field.
  - The central defender whom we have titled the sweeper back pushes forward to become the center midfielder alongside the two outside midfielders in a 3–3–2 alignment or becomes a second midfielder in a 3–3–2 alignment with one of the outside midfielders pushing into the attack.
  - The center midfielder pushes forward and becomes an attacker alongside the forward in a 3-3-2 alignment or the sweeper back pushes further to the front to become a forward (3-2-3 alignment).
  - Superior numbers are now achieved in the attacking third of the playing field.
  - Repeatedly walk the team through each third to show how the formation changes.

6–1–1 ALIGNMENT

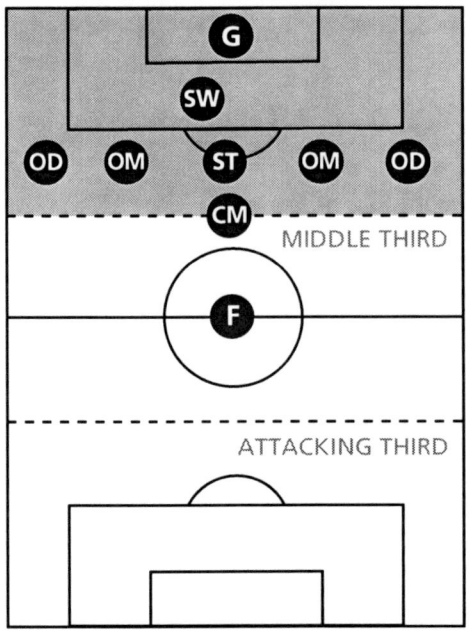

Fig. 1

4–3–1 ALIGNMENT

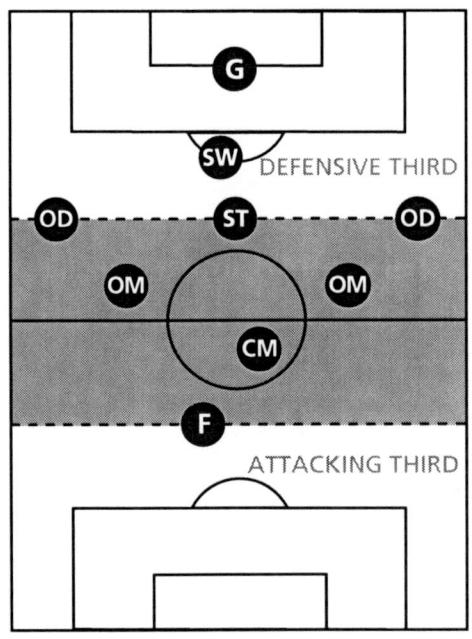

Fig. 2

**3–3–2 ALIGNMENT OR
3–2–3 ALIGNMENT**

- Two Outside Defenders and Stopper,
- Sweeper Back and one Outside Midfielder,
- Forward, Center Midfielder and one Outside Midfielder

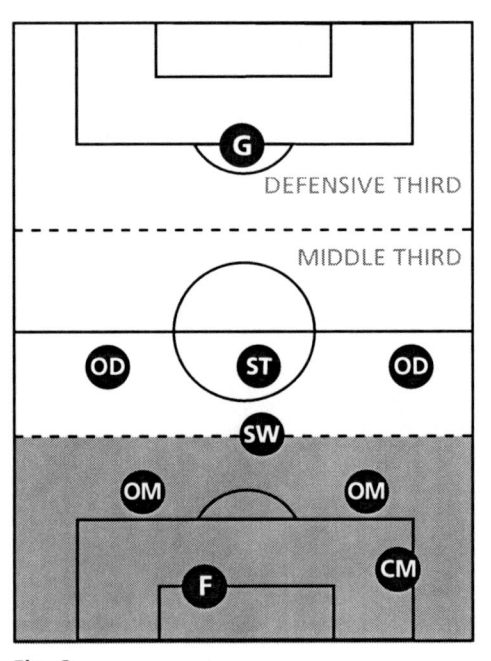

Fig. 3

ST Stopper Defender **SW** Sweeper Defender
OD Outside Defender **OM** Outside Midfielder
CM Center Midfielder **F** Forward **G** Goalie

3. Teach the players how a 4–3–1 in the 9v9 play formation is cut out of the 4–4–2 formation when playing 11v11.

a. Players must understand that the actual game of soccer is played by 11 players versus 11 players.

b. Players must understand that their game of 9 players versus 9 players is related to the actual game of 11v11.

This diagram shows a standard 4–4–2 Alignment from the 11v11 play. The players highlighted in black shows how the 4–3–1 in 9v9 play is derived from the 4–4–2 in 11v11 play.

4-4-2 ALIGNMENT FROM 11V11

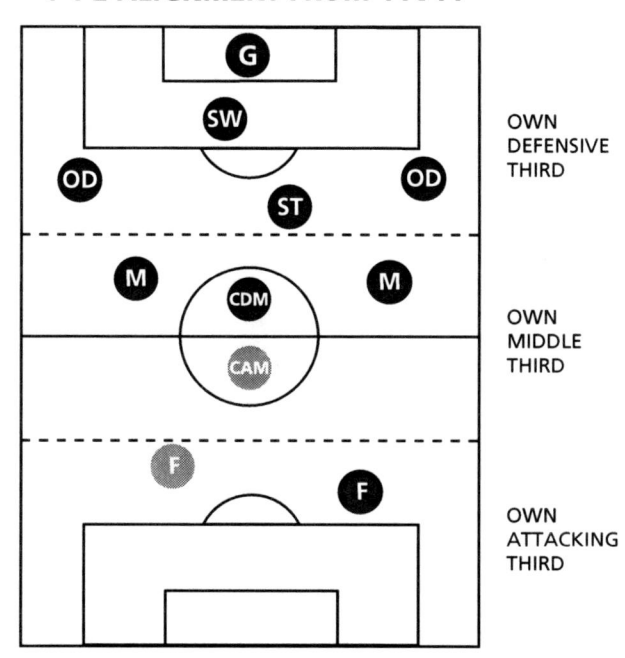

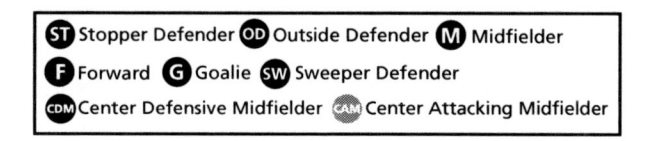

OWN DEFENSIVE THIRD

OWN MIDDLE THIRD

OWN ATTACKING THIRD

(ST) Stopper Defender (OD) Outside Defender (M) Midfielder
(F) Forward (G) Goalie (SW) Sweeper Defender
(CDM) Center Defensive Midfielder (CAM) Center Attacking Midfielder

C. 11v11 TEAM PLAY:

1. The formation in the 11v11 team play should be 4-4-2: Four defenders, four midfielders, two forwards. This 4-4-2 formation is a standard formation and is the easiest formation from which to teach the game of soccer.

2. The 4-4-2 alignment changes in each third of the field.

a. In the defensive third the three midfielders are drawn back into the defense and create a 7-2-1 alignment:
   - To support the defenders.
   - To fill in any open gaps of territory into which the opponent can attack.
   - Superior numbers have been created in the defensive section of the playing field.

b. When advancing into the middle third of the field this 7-2-1 alignment changes to a 4-4-2 alignment:
   - Four defenders are held at the top of the defensive third.
   - Four midfielders have pushed forward into the middle third of the playing field to support the attack.
   - Two forwards have taken a position that threatens the opposing team's goal.
   - With midfielders pushing forward superior numbers are created in the middle third of the field.

c. When reaching the attacking third of the field this 4-4-2 alignment changes to a 3-4-3 or a 3-3-4 alignment:
   - The two outside defenders pinch into the middle of the field.
   - The stopper back holds the middle of the field.
   - The central defender whom we have titled the sweeper back pushes forward alongside the defensive center midfielder and the two outside midfielders while the attacking center midfielder pushes forward into the attack in a 3-4-3 alignment.
   - The sweeper back pushes forward and becomes an attacker alongside the forwards and attacking center midfielder in a 3-3-4 alignment.
   - Once 11v11 play is reached, numerous attacking formations can be developed.
   - Superior numbers are now achieved in the attacking third of the playing field.
   - Repeatedly walk the team through each third to show how the formation changes from the defensive third to the attacking third and back to the defensive third.

7–2–1 ALIGNMENT

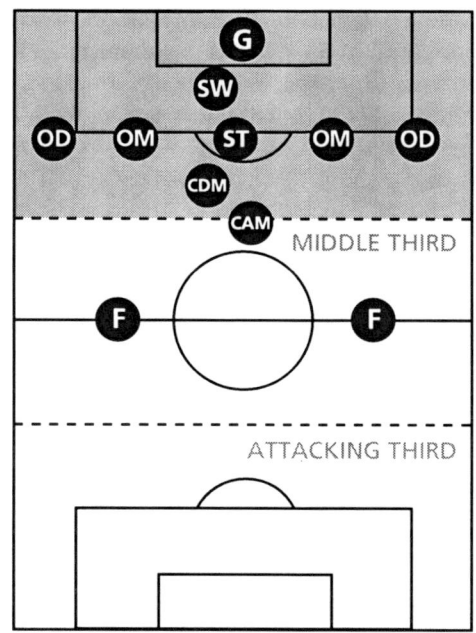

Fig. 1

4–4–2 ALIGNMENT

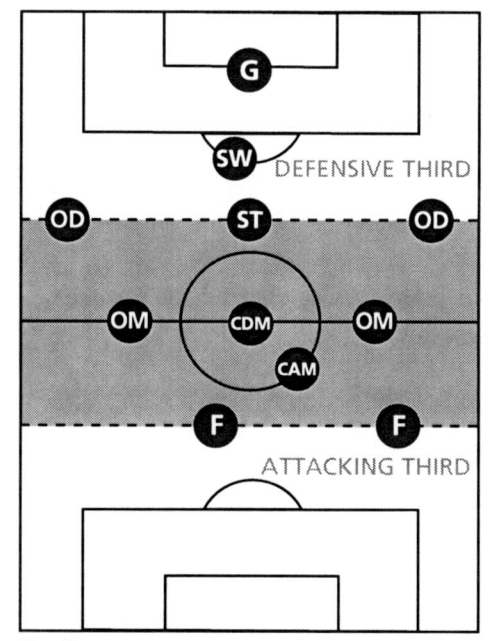

Fig. 2

3–4–3 ALIGNMENT

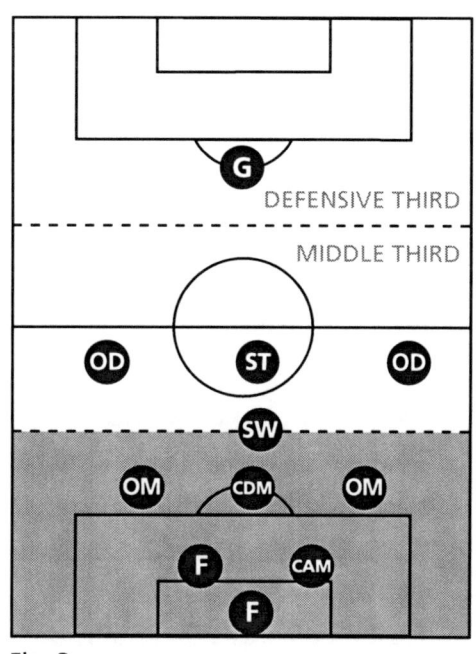

Fig. 3

ST Stopper Defender		SW Sweeper Defender	
OD Outside Defender		OM Outside Midfielder	
CDM Center Defensive Midfielder		F Forward	
CAM Center Attacking Midfielder		G Goalie	

NOTE:

Player positioning is a constant changing situation during the flow of the game. The previously mentioned scenarios of alignment changes in each third of the field are mere examples to teach players that the changes in each third must result in superior numbers of own players. The positioning of players must always result in the ability to defend the own goal while at the same time provide strength in the number of players to successfully attack the opponents goal. The positioning of players can result in any configuration that meets this end result.

XII. CRITERIA FOR POSITIONS:

In YEAR ONE of the team development, the coach must look for players who will eventually play particular positions. When choosing the players for positions, work with the criteria that players play their best when they are placed into a position that is natural and comfortable for them.

A. PLAYER QUALITIES:

1. Study the players from the beginning:

a. How does each player think?

b. What is each player's mental and physical toughness?

c. What is the player's speed and quickness?

d. What is each player's creativity?

e. What is each player's individual ball skills?

f. What is the focus and attention span of each player?

g. Where does the player like to line up when given a choice, in the defense or in the attack?

h. What is each player's attitude towards the game, fellow players, the coaches, and the openness to new learning experiences?

NOTE: This criteria listed in XII. A. #1 will determine the most suitable position for each player.

2. At the early ages players must be exposed to every position.

a. The players must understand that their final position can and probably will be different.

b. The player must learn that in order to have a good technical understanding of the game, each player must understand the requirements of each position on a team.

c. The player must learn that to be able to recognize a developing attacking or defensive situation, each player must understand the decision making process required of each position on a team.

3. As the player matures:

a. Each player will settle into a permanent position.

b. The ability to play a position is enhanced by having played each position on a team and thereby understanding the requirements of each position on a team.

4. Exposing players to every position should **only** be done at practice and **never** in a game.

a. In a game young players face an opposing team that is out to beat them, the parents are all lined up on both sides of the field screaming, and a referee is there like a policeman. The pressures are too high on the child to now also have to deal with an unfamiliar and new position.

b. Identify players who have an interest in being goalies as early as possible. Very young players should never be forced to play goalie in a game if they do not wish to play this position. I have seen children cry when told to play goalie. This will not make the game enjoyable for that child and therefore is a counter productive policy that youth leagues have as their rule.

B. POSITION CRITERIA:

1. When building a team, we must always start with the defense since a good defense keeps the game manageable and sets up the attack.

a. The SWEEPER position is a free position requiring the ability:
- to direct the teammates in their positioning in the defensive third.
- to direct teammates to cover opposing players.
- to possess ball skills in order to develop a counter attack.
- to remain confident in pressure situations.
- to make attacking runs forward and finish on the opposing goal.
- to read attacking and defending plays and adjust to the continuous developments.
- to play without having one specific assignment while constantly adjusting to developing situations.
- to roam anywhere on the field of play.
- to be the last man back on defense.

Emphasize:

The sweeper must be very quick, skilled, confident, intelligent, and be an all around player who can not only defend but has the ability to move into the attack.

b. The STOPPER position requires the player to possess the ability:
- to defend the center of the field from goalpost to goalpost.
- to mark the main attacker from the opposing team.
- to be tenacious when marking an opposing player.
- to win the ball especially in the own goal box.
- to counter attack and set up the penetration into the attacking third of the playing field.
- to have patience to contain opposing players thereby buying time for the other defenders to make their recovery runs.

Emphasize:

The stopper must have very quick reactions, patience, and must be able to defend the middle ground which is the most dangerous area of the playing field.

c. The OUTSIDE DEFENDER positions will mark the opposing wing attackers which requires the player to possess the ability:
- to have good foot speed.
- to prevent the wing attackers from playing the ball to the inside.
- to clear all balls forward towards the attacking third and to the outside.
- to make weak side runs into the attack and thereby creating superior numbers in the attacking third of the field.
- to make recovery runs into the defensive third from the middle third or attacking third when having advanced as part of the attack.

2. Once the defensive players have been identified, the midfield will receive the next focus. Without a solid midfield the control of the game will become difficult since the team will be unable to develop a strong attack while at the same time be unable to develop support for the defense and support for the attackers. A strong midfield is required to create superior numbers in each third of the playing field.

a. The CENTER MIDFIELDER should be one of the best all encompassing player on the team which requires the ability:
   - to have complete field vision.
   - to direct the players into the defensive support.
   - to direct the players into the attack.
   - to mark the opposing midfielder.
   - to distribute the ball accurately in any direction.
   - to handle the ball with skill.
   - to penetrate and finish in the attacking third of the playing field.

b. The OUTSIDE MIDFIELDERS must possess the ability to play the length of the field which requires the ability:
   - to recover into the defensive third and support the outside defense.
   - to give support to the attack.
   - to penetrate and finish on the opposing goal from the outside.
   - to distribute the ball with quality passes and crosses.
   - to cover the opposing outside midfielder.
   - to stretch the defense thereby creating the necessary spaces in the middle section of the field and in front of the opposing goal area.

c. If the team formation is 11v11 play, the center midfield will be split between a DEFENSIVE MIDFIELDER and an ATTACKING MIDFIELDER.

   DEFENSIVE MIDFIELDER:
   - Must mark the opposing team's Attacking Midfielder in a four midfielder alignment.
   - The primary responsibility of this midfielder is defensive.
   - Must communicate with teammates and give instructions.

   ATTACKING MIDFIELDER:
   - Must adjust to any part of the field that enables the player to become a danger for the opposing defense.
   - Must mark the opposing sweeper or opposing attacking center midfielder when own team is on defense.
   - Must possess individual ball skills, field vision, and decision making ability.
   - The primary responsibility of this midfielder is to penetrate towards to opponents goal and finish an attack.

Emphasize:

Midfielder must:

- *possess quickness.*
- *possess individual ball handling skills.*
- *possess touch on the ball.*
- *possess the ability to defend as well as attack.*
- *possess field vision.*
- *possess creativity.*
- *possess the ability to control the territory from the defensive third to the attacking third of the playing field.*
- *possess endurance.*

3. The FORWARDS position is the final area of emphasis.

a. All forwards require the ability:

- to control the ball with skill.
- to penetrate the opponents goal against superior numbers.
- to finish on goal with a quick shot.
- to shoot within limited space.
- to have touch on the ball that determines the speed, power, and placement of the ball.
- to attack players 1v1 with confidence and decisiveness.
- to mark opposing defenders when they make attacking runs into own defensive third.
- to prevent the opposing defense from developing an attack.
- to possess speed and quickness.

b. Forwards play in the attacking third of the field and must establish dominance in this territory in order to create fear in the defense thereby creating a reluctance by the defenders to go on the attack. Forwards only retreat when the opposing defense goes on the attack.

4. Primary and Secondary Responsibility:

Each player must learn that every position has a primary responsibility as well as a secondary responsibility. The decisions that a player makes will be based on these responsibilities. Players must understand that both responsibilities make the decision by a player automatic.

a. If the primary responsibility for one player is to pressure the ball then the secondary responsibility for the second player is take position in support of the pressure player.
b. For defenders the primary responsibility is to defend with the secondary responsibility being to attack.
c. For midfielders the primary or secondary responsibility will depend on whether the own team is attacking or defending.
d. For forwards the primary responsibility is to attack and finish on the opponent's goal while their secondary responsibility is to defend.

5. Qualities a Player Possesses:

The qualities each player possesses will determine the position a player will play during a game.

a. How well does a player's communicate with teammates?
b. How well does a player support the teammates?
c. How good are the individual ball skills of a player?
d. How well does the player play without the ball and gives balance to an attack or the defense?
e. How well does the player counterattack?
f. How well does the player recover into the defense?
g. How well does the player move from each third of the field?
h. How quickly does the player recognize developing situations?
i. How well does the player transition from defense to attack?
j. What is the player's distribution ability?
k. What is the player's field vision?
l. What is the player's passing ability?
m. What is the player's touch on the ball?
n. What is the player's endurance and mental toughness?

C. POSITIONS AND ALIGMENTS:

1. The formation of a team will change constantly as players attack and defend with the purpose of always creating superior numbers in each third of the playing field.

2. All players are defenders and attackers.

a. The forwards are the first line of defense that prevent the opponent from penetrating into the own territory.

b. The defenders are the first line of the attack who develop the attack when they repossess the ball.

3. Formation should be creative.

Example 1:
If the team has a player who possesses speed, ball skills, endurance, and field vision, then that player can be hidden in the defense as a second sweeper or stopper. Once the opportunity is created, then that player quickly moves forward to play in the attacking third of the field. This player recovers back into the defensive third of the field once the opponent takes repossession of the ball. This hidden player will generally advance unmarked by the opposing team.

Example 2:
If a strong and fast left footed player is available, the alignment can be overloaded to the own right side of the field. This left footed player can then penetrate into the left side of the field, where little pressure exists, with the ball then being sent into this left space for this player to finish on the opponent's goal.

4. In the defensive third and middle third of the field always first develop those players who will need to possess the center part of the field before focusing on the outside positions.

EMPHASIZE:

- *Soccer has set plays.*
- *A player's decisions are based in relationship to the location of the ball and what open spaces have been created.*
- *A player must read the developing play and make the decision where to best take up position in order to support the player with the ball.*
- *As an attack develops, a player must learn to ask, "Am I in the best position of support to receive the ball?"*
- *The difference with set plays in soccer from other sports is that in soccer the players must recognize the developing play without being able to first talk about it.*

XIII. SHOOTING PLAY:

During the First Year Development the players must work on shooting to develop the proper shooting mechanics. It is up to the coach to find the appropriate time when to introduce this Shooting Play.

A. SHOOTING MECHANICS:

1. TEACH and DEMONSTRATE the mechanics of taking a shot:

a. Players must learn to time their steps in the approach to the ball.
- The sequence of steps when approaching the ball must all be even steps until the ball is reached in order to maintain power when striking the ball.
- The player must not include small studder steps before reaching the ball since those steps will slow the shooting player and thereby limiting the power of the shot.

b. For a driven ball that has power, the plant foot must be directly next to the ball in order that the player's weight is over the ball.

c. The plant foot must be at such a distance from the ball to allow the kicking foot to swing through the ball with ease. If the plant foot is too close to the ball the power of the shot will diminish.

d. The kicking leg must not be stiff thereby striking the ball with the whole straight leg.
- Do not allow the kicking player to strike the ball from the hip since the power of the shot will be diminished.
- The kicking leg must bend at the knee when bringing the leg back for the kick.
- When bringing the leg forward to strike the ball, the leg from the knee down straightens at the moment of impact on the ball thereby creating a snap which will increase the power of the shot.
- The foot must be locked at the ankle when striking the ball.
- The type of shot will depend on where the kicking foot makes contact with the ball.
- Let the kicking leg follow through with the swing.

e. The hips must face the direction of the kick.

f. Keep the eyes on the ball until the ball is struck.

B. SET UP TEAM PRACTICE FOR SHOOTING MECHANICS:

1. All players with a ball form a line across the goal area approximately fifteen feet away from the top of the goal area.

2. At the coach's command each player plays the ball forward to the line at the top of the goal area:

a. Players run onto their played ball with the focus of learning the timing of the approaching run by making even steps to the ball.

b. When reaching the ball, each player must then focus on the proper placement of the plant foot.

c. Prepare the kicking foot and make the shot on goal.

3. This sequence must then be repeated until each player has acquired the proper shooting mechanics.

4. In the beginning the coach should stop at each part of the shooting sequences and call out the next part thereby walking the players through the entire shooting mechanics.

5. Practice this shooting mechanics with both the right foot and the left foot.

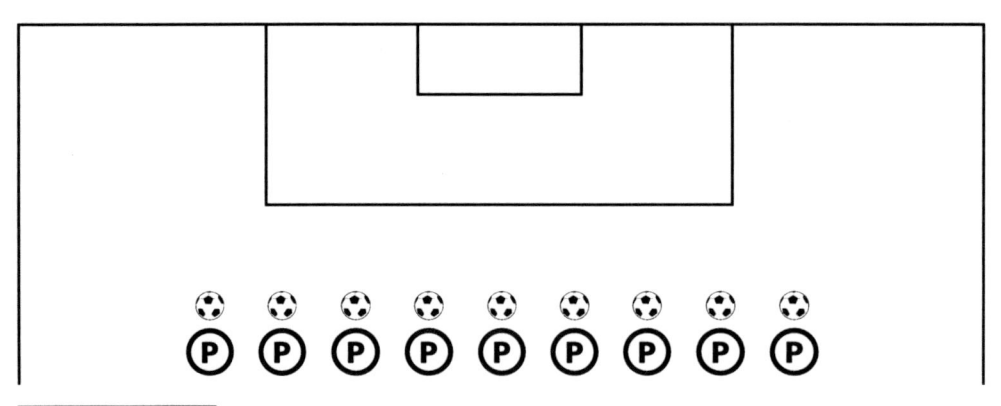

Ⓟ Players � Ball

C. SHOOTING PLAY:

1. Standing in the center at the top of the goal line place anywhere from three to six balls directly onto the goal line to the right of the center and the same amount of balls to the left of the center.

NOTE:
The amount of balls placed on each side of the center will depend on the age of the players, their shooting ability, and the number of available balls.

2. A cone is placed in the center between the two rows of balls and approximately two feet in front of the row of balls.

3. A cone is placed in the center between the two rows of balls and approximately five feet behind the row of balls.

4. Each player will work through this play one at a time:
   - Each shooter starts at the front cone, runs around the back cone, approaches the first ball on the left side and shoots the ball towards the goal.
   - After each shot, the player must run in front of the balls towards the front cone, go around the front cone, go around the back cone, approach the next ball and shoot it towards the goal.
   - This sequence of runs and shots repeats itself until all the balls have been shot on both the left side as well as the right side.
   - The shooting player never stops running.
   - The players not shooting: must gather the balls from behind the goal and throw the balls to the players who are positioned behind the balls. The players behind the ball must reset the balls for the next shooter.
   - With all players working together, each player can shoot as soon as the previous shooter is finished and no time will be lost.

5. Begin the shooting play by allowing the players to approach each ball slowly.
   - Players must build towards executing this shooting play under full speed.
   - Players must learn to drive harder when they become tired.
   - Players will thereby build a mental toughness.

6. Using numerous available goals:
   - The team of players can be split into several groups.
   - The smaller number of players each group consists of, the more chances each players will have to practice their shooting.
   - The smaller number of players each group consists of, the faster the players will be able to go through their rotation.
   - Breaking up in the number of groups will depend on the amount of available soccer balls. This shooting play requires enough balls to tire the player while the player is shooting.

Emphasize:

The purpose of this shooting play is to simulate shooting under game conditions. By the time the player shoots the last ball they will be very tired if they have executed under full speed. Most of the game is played under fatigue and the players must learn to shoot while being tired.

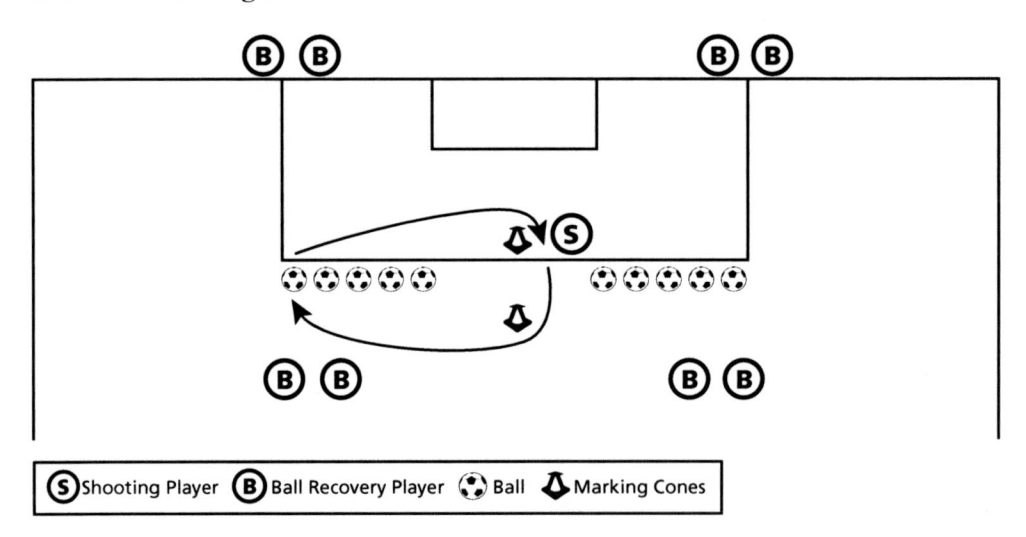

S Shooting Player **B** Ball Recovery Player ⚽ Ball ⬥ Marking Cones

XIV. INDIRECT AND DIRECT KICKS:

A. INDERECT DEFENSIVE:

1. The decision as to the number of players in a wall is based on:
a. The location of the direct or indirect kick.
b. Whether a team is playing 7v7 or 9v9 or 11v11.

2. Location of the kick and the number of team players:
a. If the kick is directly in front of the goal the most number of players will be required in the defensive wall.
   - In 7v7 team play place four players into the defending wall.
   - In 9v9 team play place five players into the defending wall.
   - In 11v11 team play place six players into the defending wall.
   - The wall must be placed to cover one side of the goal.
   - The goalie is to cover the open side of the goal.

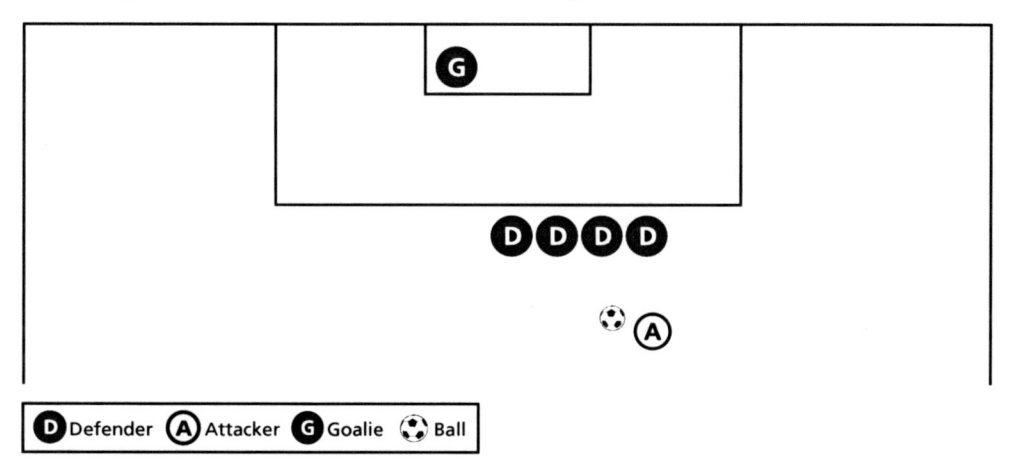

b. If the kick is further to the right side or left side from the center then fewer number of players will be required in the defensive wall.
   - In 7v7 team play place three players into the defending wall.
   - In 9v9 team play place four players into the defending wall.
   - In 11v11 team play place either four or five players into the defensive wall.
   - The number of players in the defensive wall will depend on how close the kick being taken is to the center of the goal.
   - The wall is placed to cover the near goal post area of the goal.
   - The goalie is to cover the open back side of the goal.

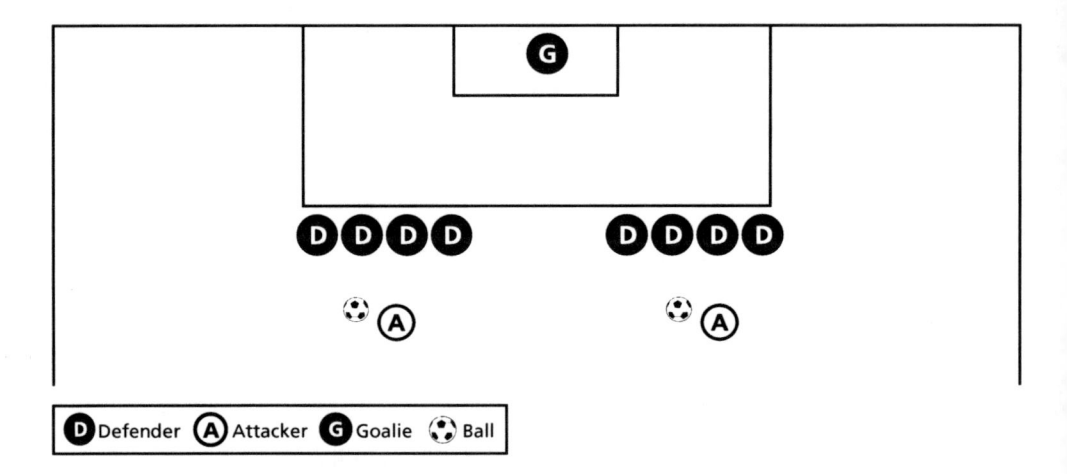

| D | Defender | A | Attacker | G | Goalie | ⚽ | Ball |

c. If the kick is further to the right side or left side from the center and is shot from the corner of the penalty box, then the number players required in the defensive wall is further reduced.
   - In 7v7 team play place two players into the defending wall.
   - In 9v9 team play place tree players into the defending wall.
   - In 11v11 team play place three players into the defending wall.
   - The wall is placed to cover the near goal post area of the goal.
   - The goalie is to cover the open back side of the goal.

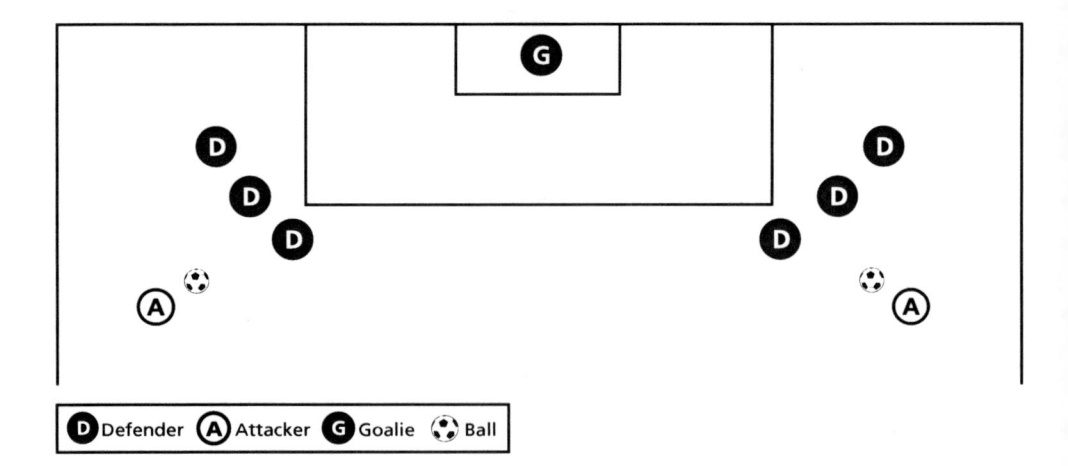

| D | Defender | A | Attacker | G | Goalie | ⚽ | Ball |

d. If the kick is from the left or the right side of the penalty area the number of players required in the defensive wall is further reduced.
  - In 7v7 team play place one player as a defending wall.
  - In 9v9 team play place two players into the defending wall.
  - In 11v11 team play place two players into the defending wall.
  - The wall is placed to cover the near goal post area of the goal.
  - The goalie is to cover the open back side of the goal.

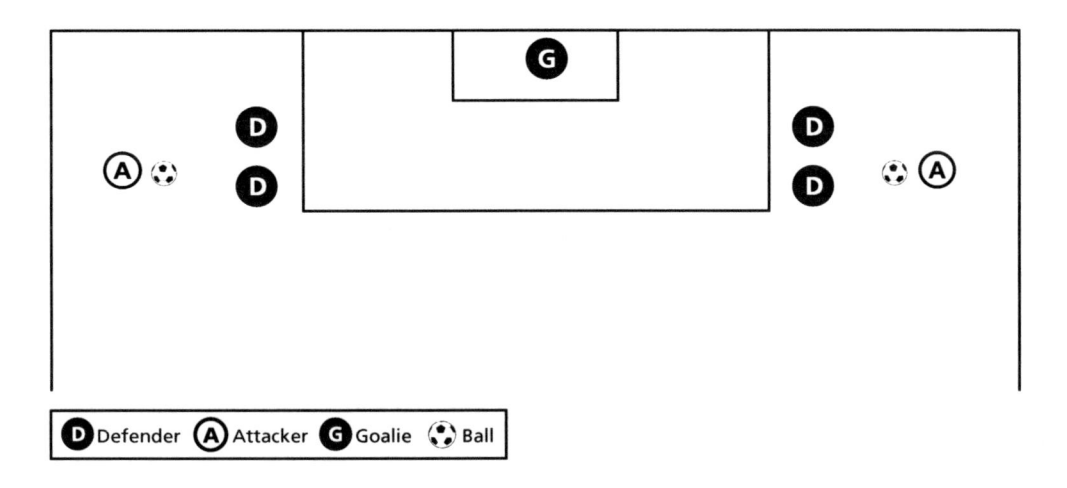

D Defender A Attacker G Goalie Ball

e. If the kick is from near to top of the defensive third in 7v7 or 9v9 or 11v11 play:
  - One player is required to be positioned in front of the shooter if the kick comes from the right or left side of the goal.
  - Two defensive players are required to form a defensive wall if the kick comes from the center towards the goal.

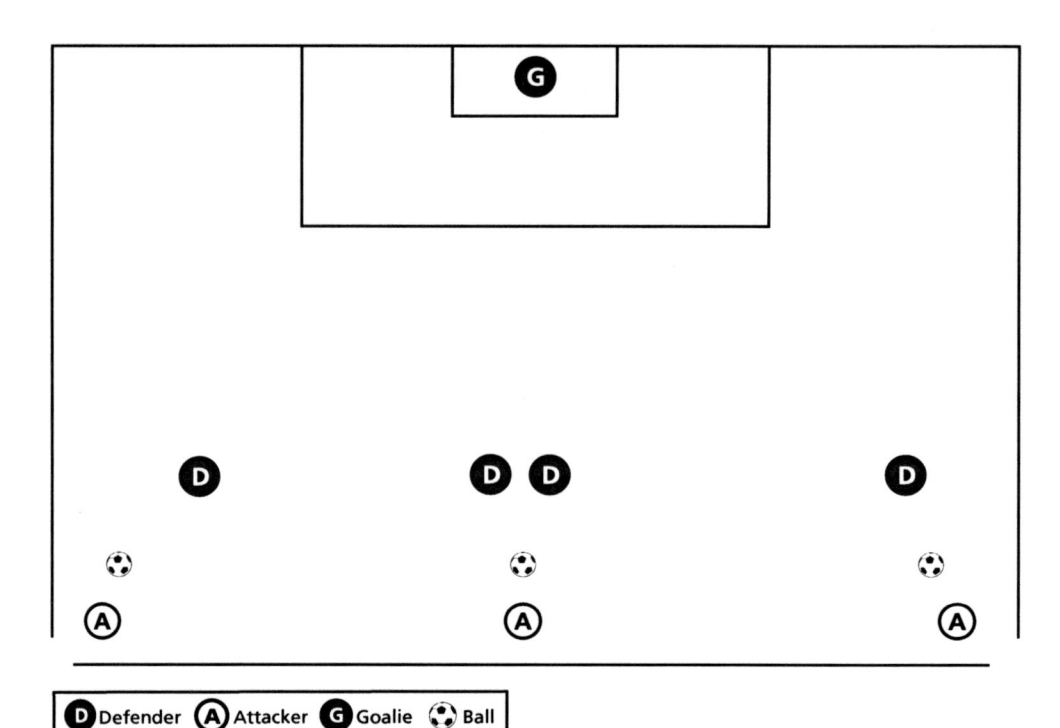

3. The player positioning in the wall:

a. The area where the direct or indirect kick will come from will dictate that the nearest defensive players to the ball will form the wall.

b. The tallest player must line up to be in line with the near goal post and with each shorter player positioned towards the open area of the goal.

c. The goalie will defend the open area of the goal which is not covered by the defensive wall.

d. The purpose of the wall is to make the area smaller which the gaoalie needs to defend.

e. In the event that the kick is shot over the wall it will most likely be shot over the shorter players. The ball will still be savable by the goalie since the shorter players are positioned nearer to the area defended by the goalie.

f. The players on the wall must stand tightly next to each other and not allow any space between each other through which a shot can be placed onto the goal.

g. The goalie is responsible for setting up the wall:
   - All players must listen to the goalie's instructions at all times.
   - The goalie must go near post and instruct the tallest end defensive player where to position in order that this player is in line with the near goalpost.
   - The goalie decides how many players are to be in the defensive wall.
   - The goalie will direct the wall to move either further to the right or further to the left.

4. The defensive wall should line up ten yards from the ball and not allow the referee to step the line further away from the ball.
a. If the referee moves the wall further back from the ball the angles of the wall to the near post will change with openings being created for the attacker to shoot through.
b. Once the wall is moved back there may not be enough time to re-align the defensive wall with the near post.

EMPHASIZE:

- *Defensive players must form the defensive wall quickly in order to prevent a shot on a wide open goal.*
- *One player on the defense must be designated to attack the ball on an indirect kick as soon as the first attacking shooter touches the ball.*
- *Forwards from the defending team must recover towards the own goal in order to mark the free opponent attackers.*
- *The tallest player is positioned in line with the near post.*
- *The goalie organizes the defensive wall and defending players must listen to the goalie's instructions.*
- *Players in the defensive wall must press together tightly to eliminate any spaces for the attacking shooter to place the ball.*

B. INDIRECT OFFENSIVE:

Direct or Indirect Kicks are an important part in a game because it is the only time that an attack on an opponent's goal is organized and executed without the defense being able to pressure the ball before it is kicked.

1. Quick Kick or Set-Play:

a. The decision whether to take a quick kick or take the time to set up a set-play will depend on:
   - The referee's decision for a second whistle.
   - The number of defenders in the area.
   - The position of the defenders.
   - The number of attackers who have moved quickly into an attacking position.

b. In most circumstances the decision for the attacking team should be to take the time to set up the play in order to execute the attack properly.
   - This will give the defensive team time to organize their defense.
   - The defense is still at a disadvantage since the defense can only react to the attack.

c. When setting up for a direct or indirect shot, the attacking team should always designate one attacker who will attempt to force entry into the defensive wall.
   - This will throw off the attention and the focus of the defensive players in the wall.
   - A hole could be created in the defensive wall through which the shooter could place the shot on goal.
   - The attacker in the wall could suddenly pull out of the wall and penetrate further towards goal to:
     – Act as a decoy
     – Create confusion in the defense
     – Finish an attack

d. The attack on the opponent must be creative.
   - When a set-play becomes complicated, it will give the defenders time to break up the attacking play.
   - The outcome will be poor execution with negative results.
   - The simpler and the more direct the attack is, the better the chance for a positive result

2. Indirect kicks:

a. The ball has to be touched by one other attacking player before it can be shot at the opponent's goal.

b. If the ball is played from one attacker to the shooter, the ball should be played back to the shooter thereby away from the defenders.

c. Attacking players should make runs towards the goal to be in position to redirect the ball into the goal or handle any rebounds.

d. The greater the confusion the attackers can create for the defense, the better the chance of scoring a goal.

e. The decision of which indirect set-play to use will depend on where the ball is placed.
- If the ball is near the goal area, then the shot should be directly on goal after the second touch.
- If the ball is near the beginning of the attacking third or in the middle third of the playing field, then the ball should be kicked into the penalty area on the first touch and then sent towards the goal on the second touch by the attacking team's best finisher.

f. The timing and execution are what makes indirect kicks successful.

INDIRECT SET-UP PLAY SITUATION ONE:

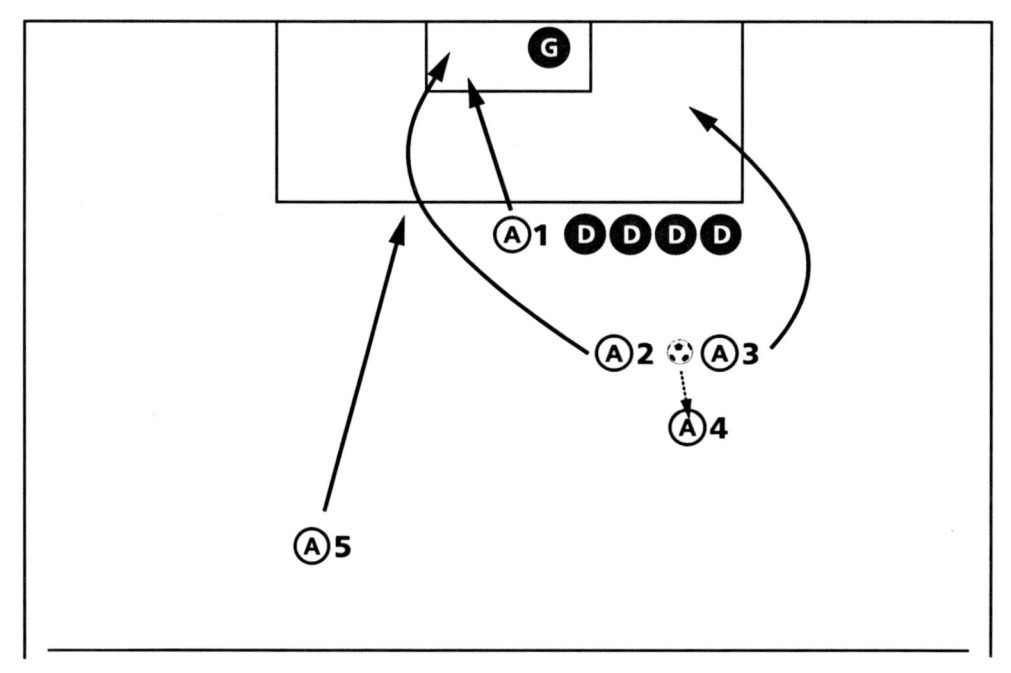

D Defender **A** Attacker **G** Goalie ⚽ Ball

- The two best attacking finishers are placed on either side of the ball with the attacking shooter placed several feet behind the ball.
- Attacker 3 on the right of the ball suddenly plays the ball back to Attacker 4, the shooter, who in turn places the ball on goal.
- As soon as the ball is played back to Attacker 4, Attackers 2 and 3 must make their sprint runs into the goal area.
- Attacker 1 is positioned in the defensive wall and sprints away from the wall as soon as the shot is placed toward the goal taking up a position in the center of the goal area.
- Attacker 5 can be a weak-side defender who will make a run to the top of the goal area.
- From this one formation many varied attacking runs and shot combinations can be developed.
- The number of attacking players used will depend on 7v7 or 9v9 or 11v11 team play.

7V7 TEAM PLAY: Eliminate Attacker A1 and/or A5 for example.

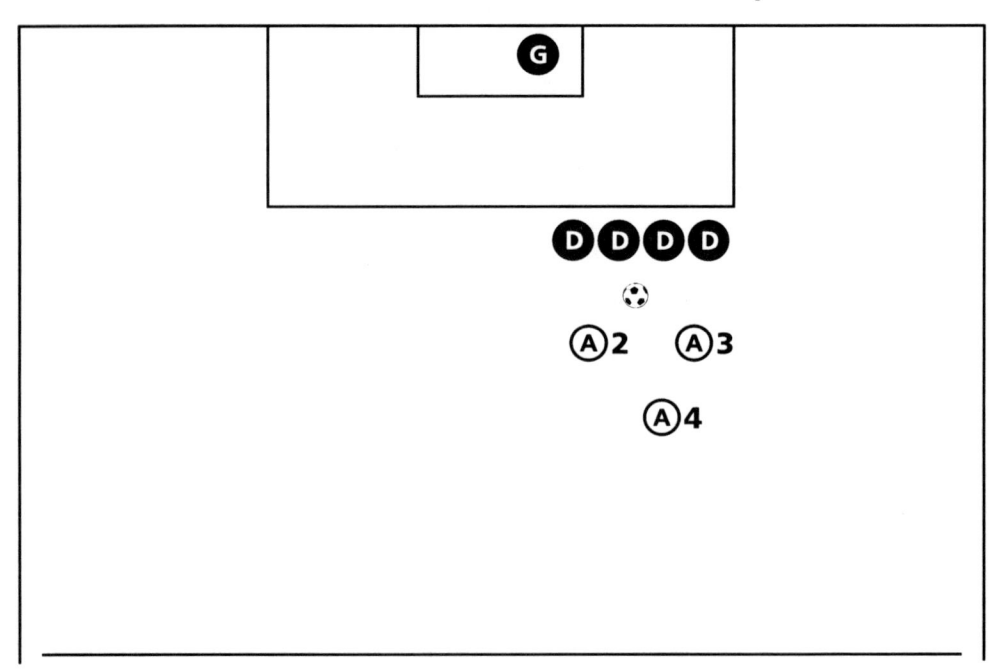

D Defender A Attacker G Goalie Ball

9V9 TEAM PLAY: Eliminate Attacker A1 for example.

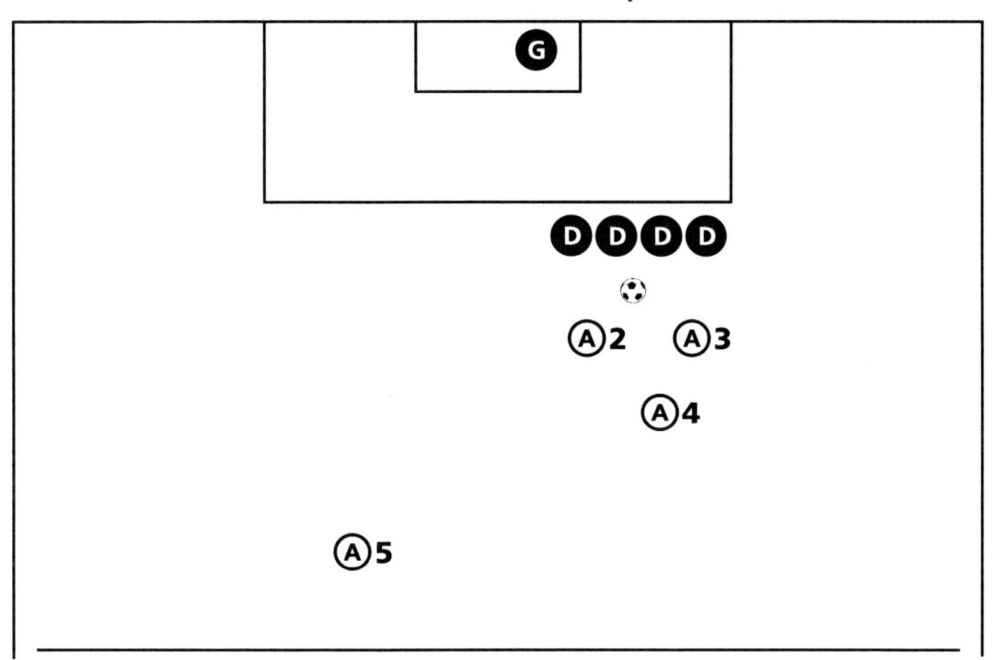

INDIRECT SET-UP PLAY SITUATION TWO:

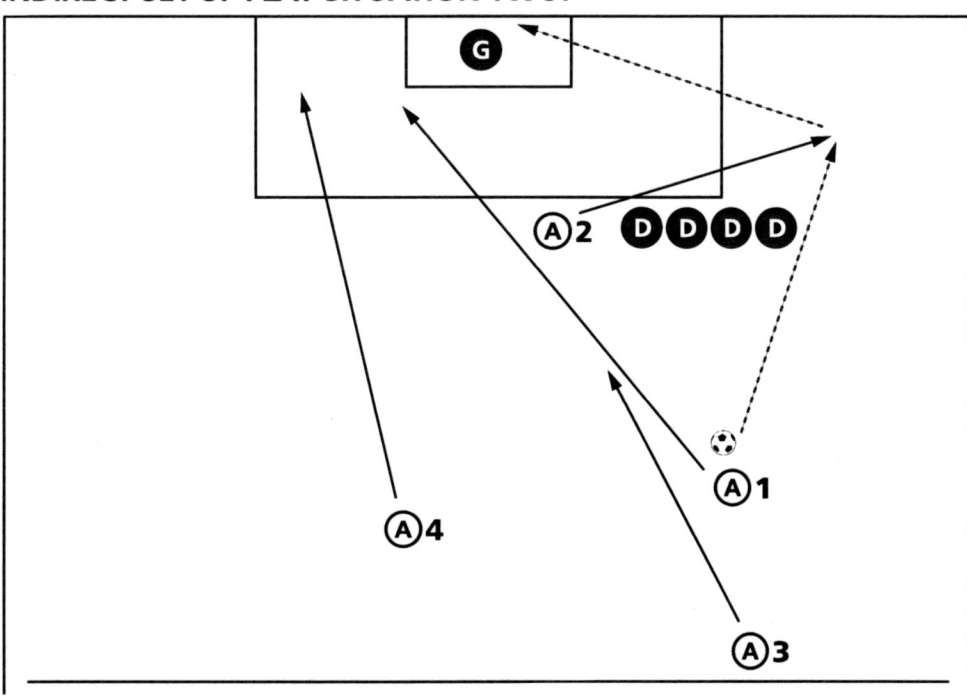

D Defender **A** Attacker **G** Goalie ⚽ Ball
→ Direction of attacking runs   --→ Direction of the ball

- Attacker 1 is the shooter who will play the ball to the far side of the defensive wall.
- Attacker 2 breaks from the wall at the time the ball is played and meets the ball behind the defensive wall.
- Attacker 2 takes a quick shot on goal.
- Attacker 1 makes a run to the center of the goal area.
- Other attackers, such as Attackers 3 and 4, must make runs to create confusion and be in position to make a rebound shot.
- The number of attackers used will depend on 7v7 or 9v9 or 11v11 team play.

INDIRECT SET-UP PLAY SITUATION THREE:

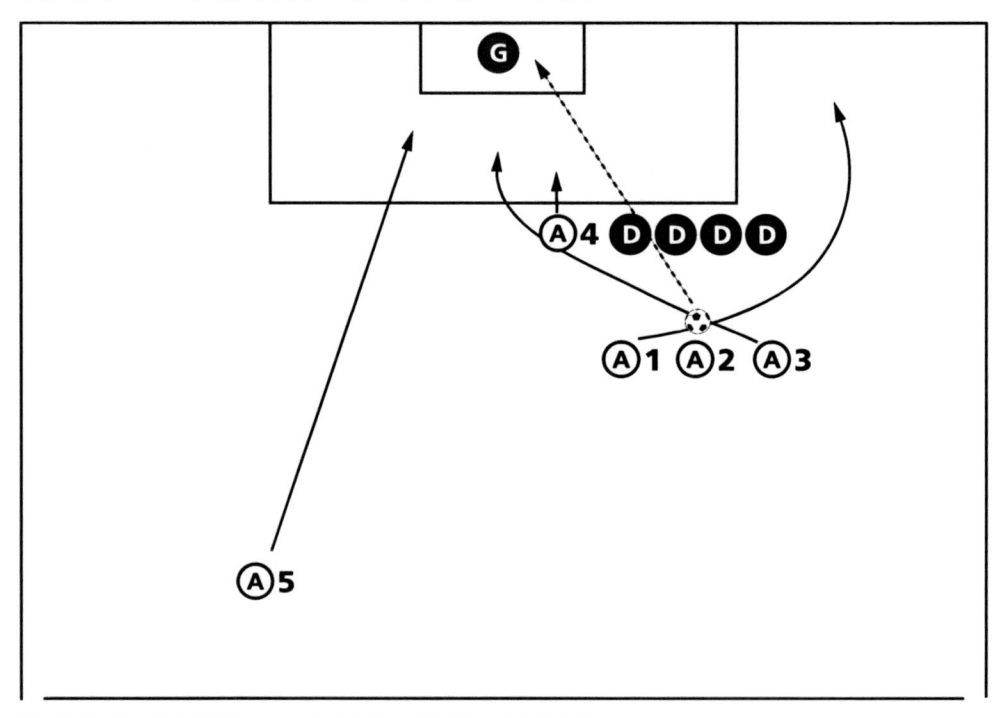

D Defender **A** Attacker **G** Goalie ● Ball
⟶ Direction of attacking runs ⇢ Direction of the ball

- Attacker 1 steps over the ball, but does not touch the ball, and continues to make the arching run around the outside of the defensive wall into the goalie box.
- Attacker 3 steps over the ball, plays the ball with the bottom of the foot or heel back to Attacker 2 and continues to make an arching run around the near side of the defensive wall into the center of the goalie box.

- Attacker 4 breaks from the wall at the time the ball is played and takes up a position on the top of the goalie box.
- Attacker 2 takes a direct shot on goal.
- Other attackers, such as Attacker 5, must make runs on goal to create confusion and be in position to make a rebound shot.
- This shooting sequence can be altered with different players touching the ball, running over the ball, and playing to a different shooter.
- The number of attackers used will depend on 7v7 or 9v9 or 11v11 team play. Attacker A1 and/or Attacker 5 and/or Attacker 4 can be eliminated.

INDIRECT SET-UP PLAY SITUATION FOUR:

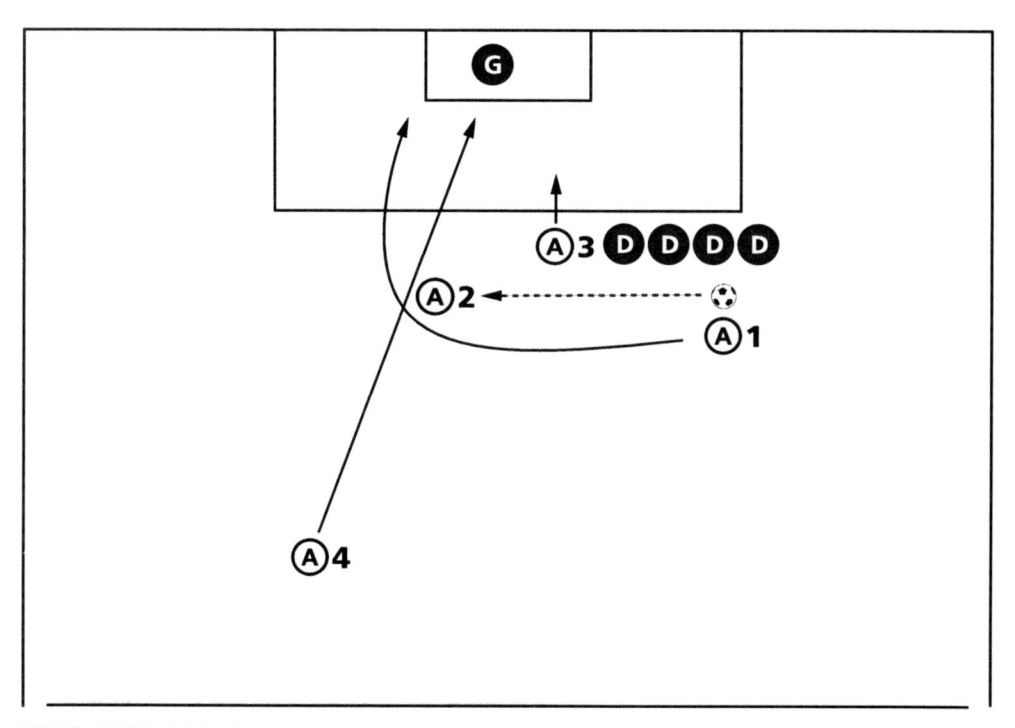

D Defender **A** Attacker **G** Goalie ⚽ Ball
→ Direction of attacking runs   --▶ Direction of the ball

- Attacker 1 plays the ball to Attacker A2 and immediately make a run around the far side of the defensive wall and into the goalie area to create confusion and be ready for a rebound shot.
- Attacker 2 takes a quick shot on goal.

- Attacker 3 breaks from the wall at the time the ball is played and takes up a position on the top of the goalie box.
- Other attackers, such as Attacker 4, must make runs on goal to create confusion and be in position to make a rebound shot.
- This attack is a simple and direct attack that depends on a very quick execution.
- The number of attackers used will depend on 7v7 or 9v9 or 11v11 team play. Attacker A3 and/or Attacker 4 can be eliminated.

INDIRECT SET-UP PLAY SITUATION FIVE:

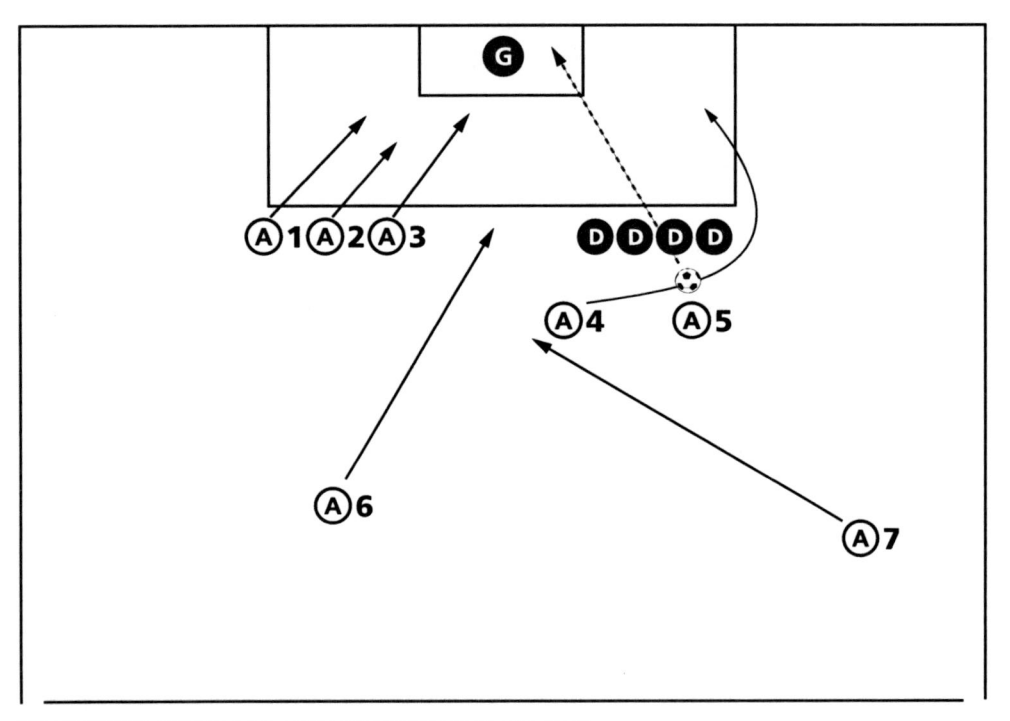

D Defender **A** Attacker **G** Goalie Ball
→ Direction of attacking runs   ---▶ Direction of the ball

- Attacker 4 runs over the ball, with the bottom of the shoe plays it back to Attacking Shooter 5 and continues with an arching run to the outside of the defensive wall and into the goalie box to create confusion.
- Attacking Shooter 5 shoots on goal.
- When the ball is touched by Attacker 4, it is at that time that Attackers 1, 2, 3, 6 and 7 will make their runs into the goalie area taking up positions to create confusion.

- This attacking situation is best designed for 11v11 play since it uses numerous players but can be modified for 7v7 or 9v9 team play by eliminating players who participate in this attacking play.

EMPHASIZE:

- *All indirect set-up play situations must be practiced prior to each game.*
- *The team captain makes the call as to which set-up play is executed.*

C. DIRECT KICKS:

1. As with the indirect kicks, the decision as to whether to shoot directly on goal or to play the ball to another attacker will depend on:
a. The location from where the direct kick will take place.
b. The accuracy of the shooter.
c. Attacker's ability to finish on goal.

2. With an accurate shooter and with the ball near the goal area, the shot should be directly on goal.

3. If the team's most accurate shooter is near the ball at the time the penalty is called, the shooter should have the freedom to take a very quick shot to catch the defense and goalkeeper out of position and by surprise.

4. If the shooter is not that accurate or as a change of pace, the attacking team can play the ball as if it were an indirect kick.
a. Shoot the ball to the far post and have attackers come to the ball.
b. Create confusion in the defense by overloading one area of the field with attackers yet sending an attacking finisher to another area where the ball is played.
c. Any one of the indirect set-up plays described previously in Section XIV. B. 2 can be utilized with direct kicks.
d. The shooter can directly shoot on goal while the additional attackers make runs as described in the indirect set-up plays to create confusion and be in position for rebound shots.

5. The captain must decide which direct kick is to be used.

EMPHASIZE:

- *TEACH and DEMONSTRATE each separate indirect and direct kick combinations.*
- *Each player on the team must REPEATEDLY practice each attacking position from being the feeder, the shooter, the wall attacker, and the attacking runners.*

- *Through REPETITION, players will not only learn the complete attacking combinations, but the best attackers for each specific task will be identified.*
- *THE YOUNGER THE TEAM, THE FEWER INDIRECT OR DIRECT SET-UP PLAYS SHOULD BE TAUGHT.*
- *KEEP IT SIMPLE!*

XV. CORNER KICKS:

Corner Kicks along with direct and indirect kicks provide the attacking team with an opportunity to score since the game is stopped and a play can be set up.

A. ATTACKING:

1. The attacking team must create confusion for the defense in the defending goalie area.
a. Attackers must be organized and know exactly what their duties are on each corner kick.
b. Attackers must take possession of the territory in front of the goal.
2. The attack must be sudden and the ball played to goal as quickly as possible. The type of corner kick to be taken will depend on:
a. The accuracy and ability of the shooter to place the ball near the penalty spot or to the weak side of the goal.
b. The ability of the attackers to finish.
c. The type of corner kicks set-up play that had already been taken during the game.
3. The captain of the team will call the type of set-up corner kick play that is to be taken.
a. Each set-up corner kick play should be given a number.
b. Attackers are signaled into motion when the shooter signals by raising the hand into the air.
   - The distant attackers make attacking runs into designated positions upon the shooter's signal.
   - The close attackers will momentarily delay their attacking runs but must be in position at the point when the ball is struck.
c. Timing and execution will increase the chance for the attackers to be successful.

4. CORNER KICK SET-UP PLAYS:

a. Attacking players positioning prior to the corner kick:

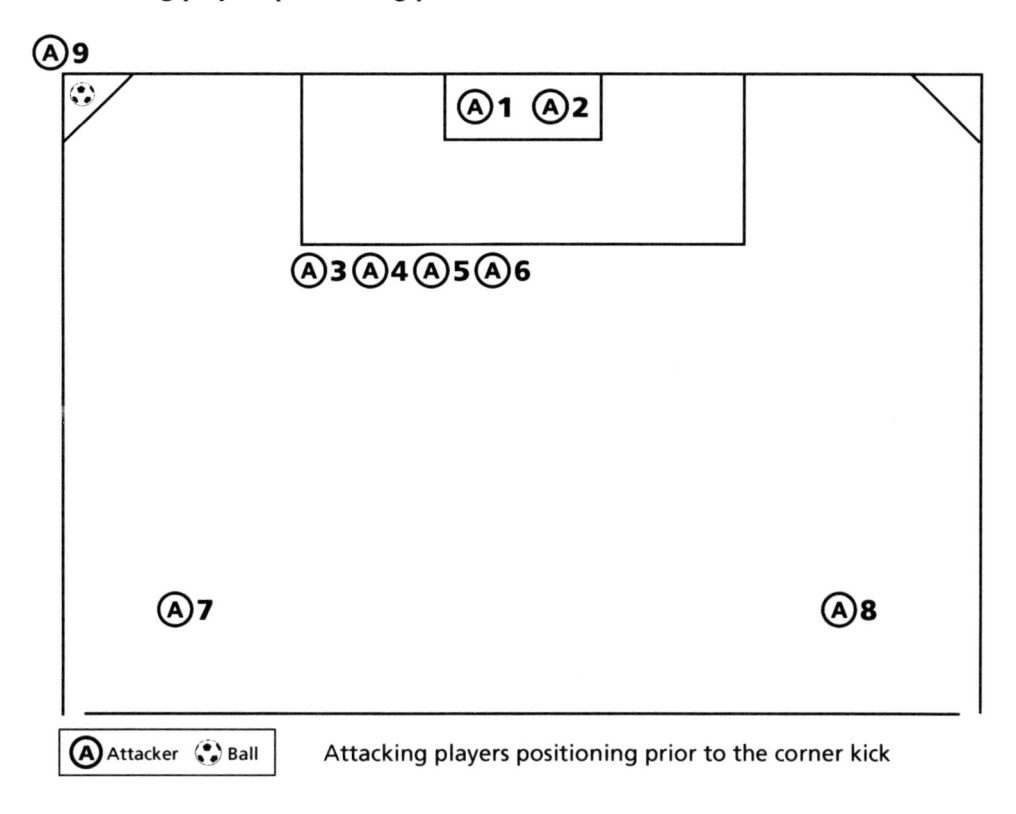

Attacking players positioning prior to the corner kick

- Attacking forwards 1 and 2 will line up on the goal line to create a problem for the opposing team's goalie and defenders.
- Midfield attackers 3, 4, 5, and 6 will line up together at the top of the goal box. The center midfielder will decide to which spot in the penalty area each attacking midfielder will make the attacking run.
- Defensive attackers 7 and 8 will make runs into support from the midfield area.
- The taller defenders should be pulled into the attack as midfielders while the shorter midfielders are moved to the defender attacking positions.

b. CORNER KICK SET-UP PLAY—SITUATION ONE:

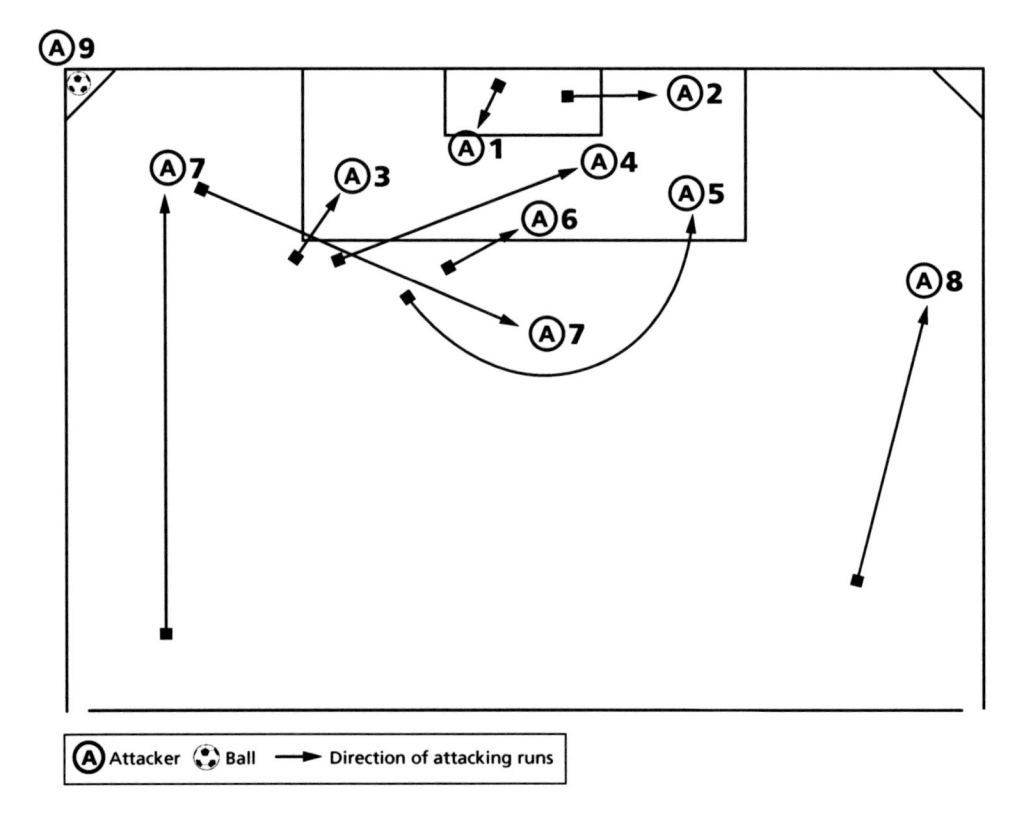

- As attacking shooter 9 raises the arm as the signal, attacker 7 makes the run to the area where it will appear that a short corner kick is in progress thereby drawing a defender from the goal area.
- Attacker 8 makes the run to the weak backside area to be in a support position.
- As the attacking shooter 9 drops the raised arm, midfield attacker 6 runs to the penalty spot area.
- Midfield attacker 5 makes an arching run to the area beyond the backside post and takes up the position inside but near the top of the penalty box.
- Midfield attacker 4 moves to a position between the penalty spot and the six yard line.
- As shooter 9 approaches the ball, attacker 3 moves forward into the penalty box and takes a position slightly beyond the penalty box line and towards the shooter side of the penalty box.
- Attacker 1 moves out of the goal area and takes a position near post and on the six yard box line.

- Attacker 2 moves out of the goal area to take a position backside of the six yard box.
- Attacker 7 makes an arching run and takes a position in the center and outside the penalty box.
- To which attacker the ball is played should vary with each corner kick.
- With each corner kick, the attacking players making runs to areas of the field should vary their particular runs to other territorial positions with the purpose of creating confusion for the defenders.
- The control midfielder will inform each attacker to what part of the territory each run will be made. For example, attackers 7 and 8 can make diagonal runs with attacker 7 going to the weak side of the corner kick while attacker 8 will go to the strong side of the corner kick.
- In 7v7 and 9v9 team play, players must be removed from the attacking runs.

Example:
- In 7v7 team play attackers 2, 3, 4, 8 are non existent.
- In 9v9 team play attackers 2, 3, 8 are non existent.

c. CORNER KICK SET-UP PLAY—SITUATION TWO:

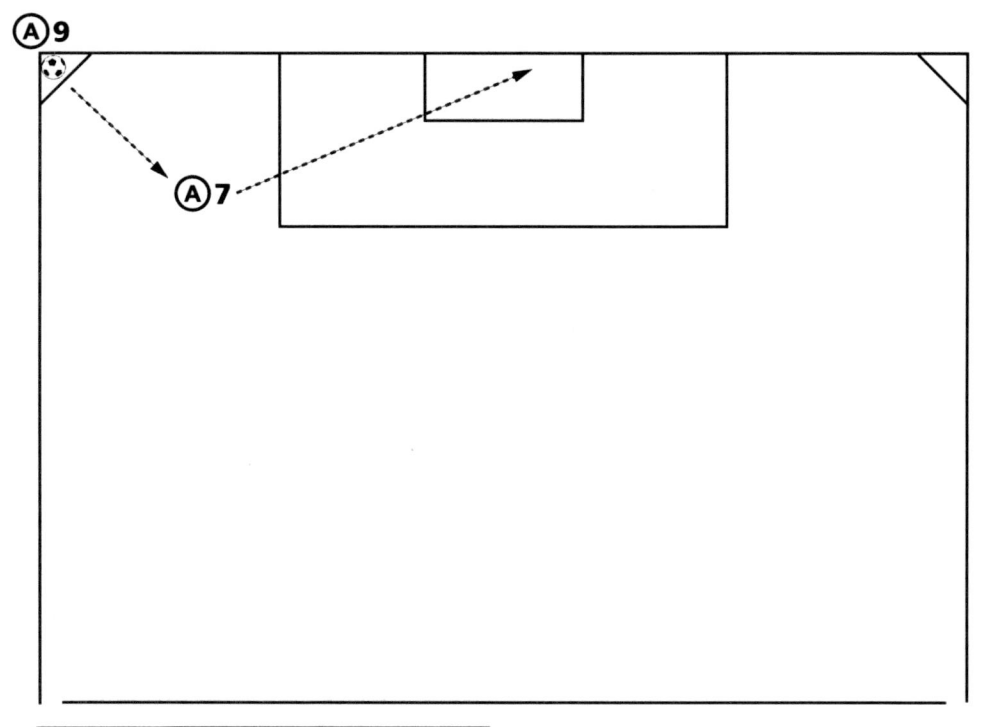

- Set up the same formation as described in previous section XV. 4. b. Situation One.
- The attacking shooter 9 plays the ball short and directly to attacker 7 who either shoots on goal or plays the ball to the weak side attackers.
- The most accurate shooter must be in position as attacker 7.
- With 7v7 or 9v9 team play this short corner kick set-up play should be used if the team does not possess an attacking shooter who has the ability to get the ball into the air and into the penalty box in front of the goal.

d. CORNER KICK SET-UP PLAY—SITUATION THREE:

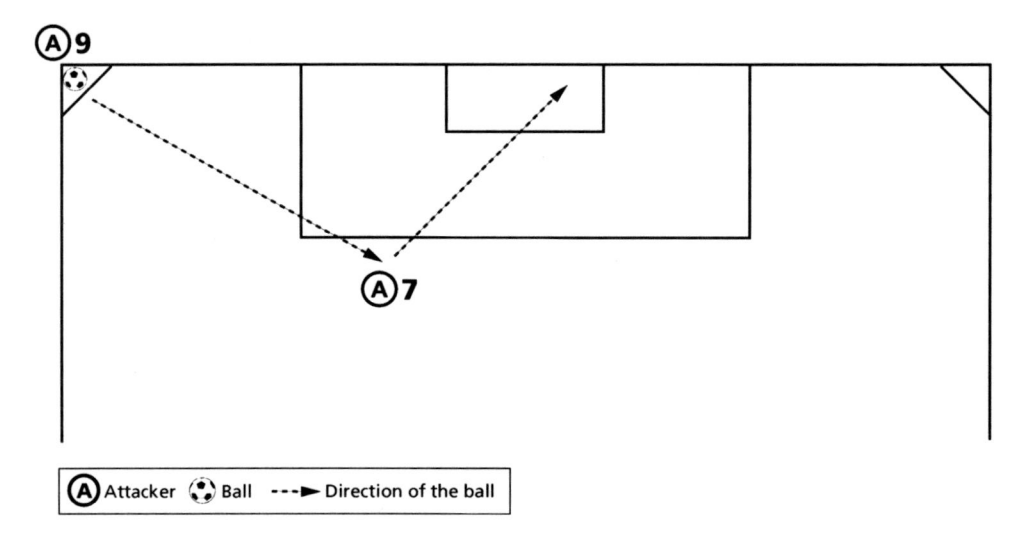

- Set up the same formation as described in previous section XV. 4. b. Situation One and Two.
- The attacking shooter 9 plays the ball short and directly to attacker 7 who in turn plays the ball to the attackers in the penalty box area who must then shoot on goal.
- The most accurate shooter must be in position as attacker 7.
- With 7v7 or 9v9 team play this short corner kick set-up play should be used if the team does not possess an attacking shooter who has the ability to get the ball into the air and into the penalty box in front of the goal.

B. DEFENSE:

1. Defenders must pick the attacker they will be marking no matter the appearance of the attacking alignment.

a. Defenders must pick their mark immediately.

b. Defenders should line up next to their mark.

2. Defenders must be aware of any attacker moving into the attack from a distant defender/attacker position.

3. Defenders must win the ball in their own penalty area.

a. Clear the ball as high and as far as possible away from the goal.

b. Clear the ball to the outside.

c. The primary decision is to clear the ball and not to attempt to develop an attack from this part of the field.

d. Once possession of the ball has been re-established, defenders must immediately push out of their defensive third of the field.

e. The forwards from the defending team must chase the cleared ball, gain possession of the ball and go on a quick counter attack while the opposing team players are still up field attacking the own goal.

EMPHASIZE:

The defensive players cannot come in second when defending a corner kick in the own area of the field. They must drive hard and decisively to the ball.

XVI: KICK OFF:

A. 7v7 TEAM PLAY

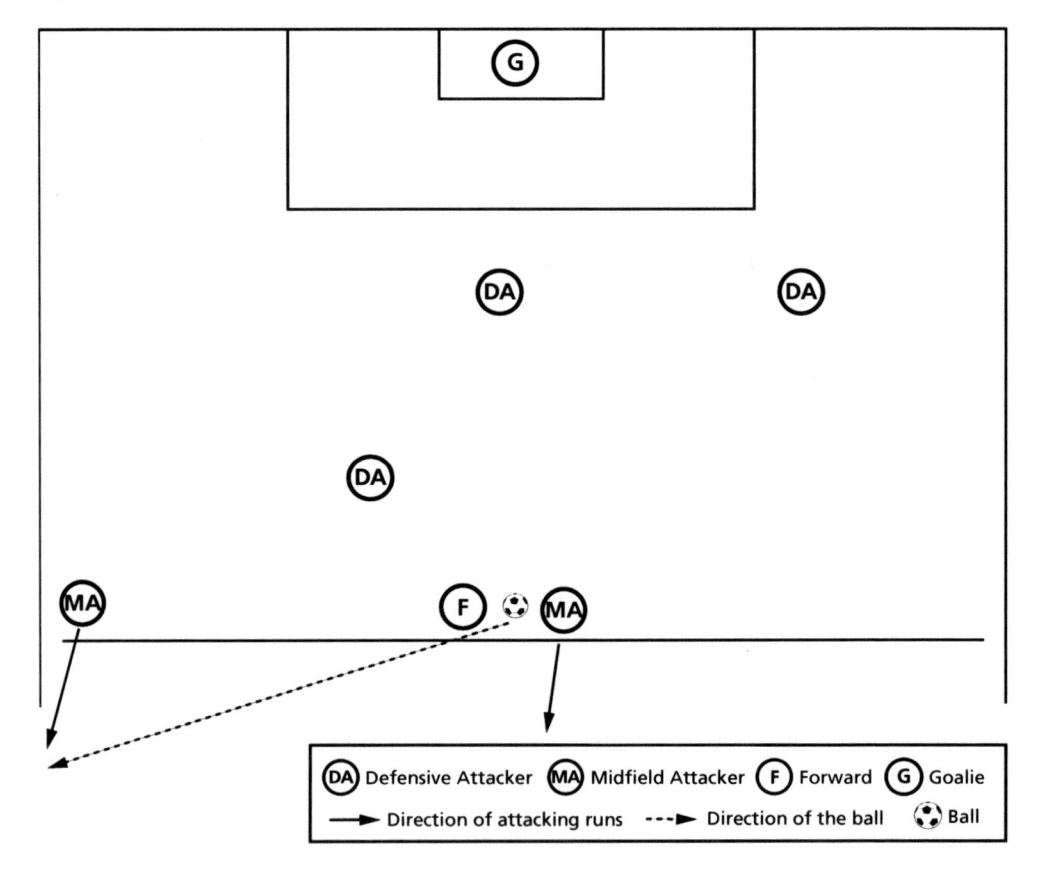

1. The lone forward must line up at the center spot with one of the outside midfielders who must be positioned not more than two feet alongside of the forward.

2. The second outside midfielder to whose side the ball is played must be positioned close to the sideline at midfield.

3. The outside defender to whose side the ball is played must be positioned just outside the circle.

a. This will fill the gap created by the midfielder moving out towards the sideline.

b. The outside defender will be in position to defend the area if the play should break down.

4. Kicking-Off the ball:

a. If the ball will be played to the right sideline then the ball will be kicked off by the right forward to the left forward who then passes the ball wide to the right outside midfielder who is positioned near the right sideline.

b. If the ball will be played to the left sideline then the ball will be kicked off by the left forward to the right forward who then passes the ball wide to the left outside midfielder who is positioned near the left sideline.

c. It is important that the ball is played to the outside quickly
   - to prevent the surging opponents from gaining possession of the ball in the middle ground.
   - until such time when the own team has developed players with a strong enough kick to be able to play the ball first backwards to the center midfielder and then to the outside players.

d. Speed of play is most important since the sooner the ball is played out of the middle the sooner the danger is decreased in the event that the opponent gains possession of the ball.

e. With each Kick-Off, the side to which the ball is played should alternate.

f. On a kick-off, the ball must first cross the midfield line completely before it can be played by the second attacker.

B. 9v9 TEAM PLAY

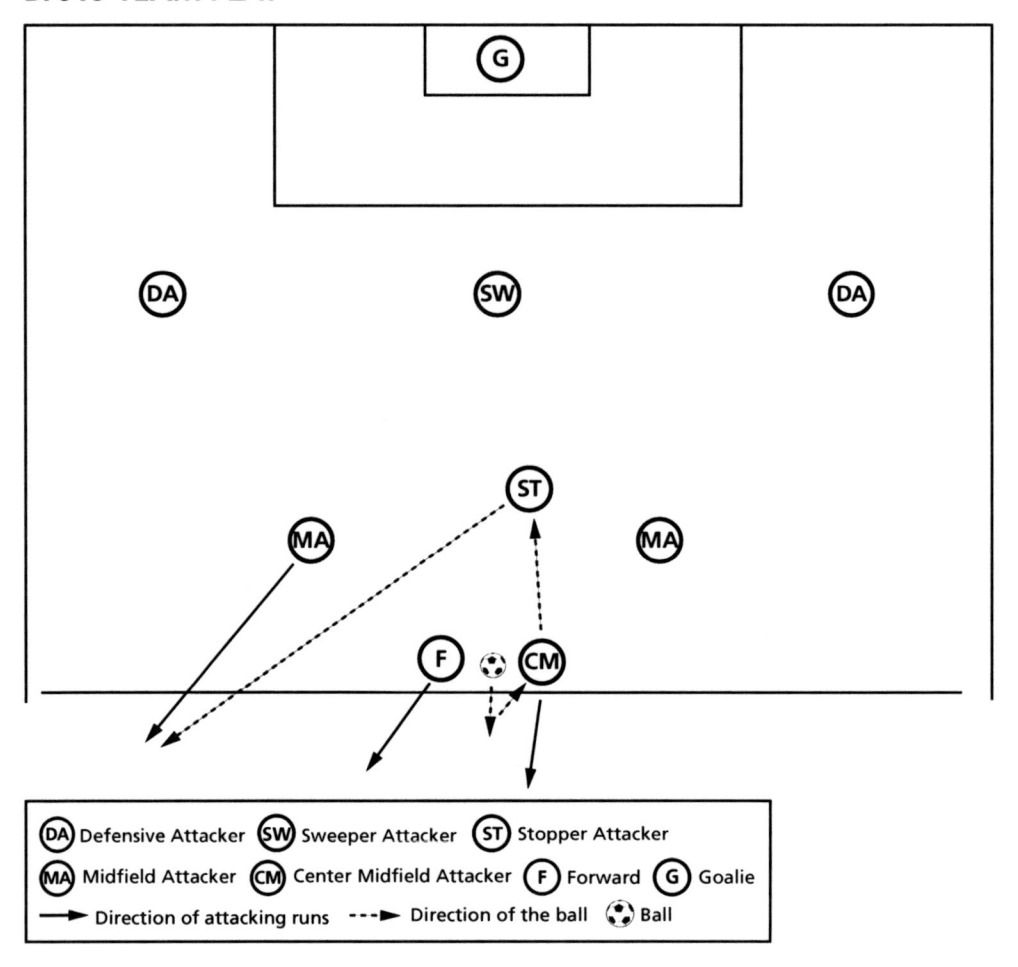

(DA) Defensive Attacker **(SW)** Sweeper Attacker **(ST)** Stopper Attacker
(MA) Midfield Attacker **(CM)** Center Midfield Attacker **(F)** Forward **(G)** Goalie
→ Direction of attacking runs   --▶ Direction of the ball   ⚽ Ball

1. The lone forward must line up at the center spot with the center midfielder who must be positioned not more than two feet alongside of the forward.

2. The stopper back takes a position just outside the circle in the center of the field.

3. The sweeper back takes the position in the center area of the field vacated by the stopper who has moved forward into the area normally controlled by the center midfielder.

4. Kicking-Off the ball:

a. The ball is played by one forward to the second attacker who in turn plays the ball quickly back to the stopper back.

b. The stopper back plays the ball to either one of the outside midfielders.

c. As soon as the ball has been played back to the stopper back, the opposing players will move forward towards the ball which will create space in the opponent's part of the field.

d. As soon as the two forwards kick off the ball they must advance into the opponent's part of the field and into the space that has been created by the advancing opponents.

e. Once the ball has been played by the stopper back to the outside midfielder, the outside midfielder can then play the ball up to the forward.

f. On a kick-off, the ball must first cross the midfield line completely before it can be played by the second attacker.

C. 11v11 TEAM PLAY

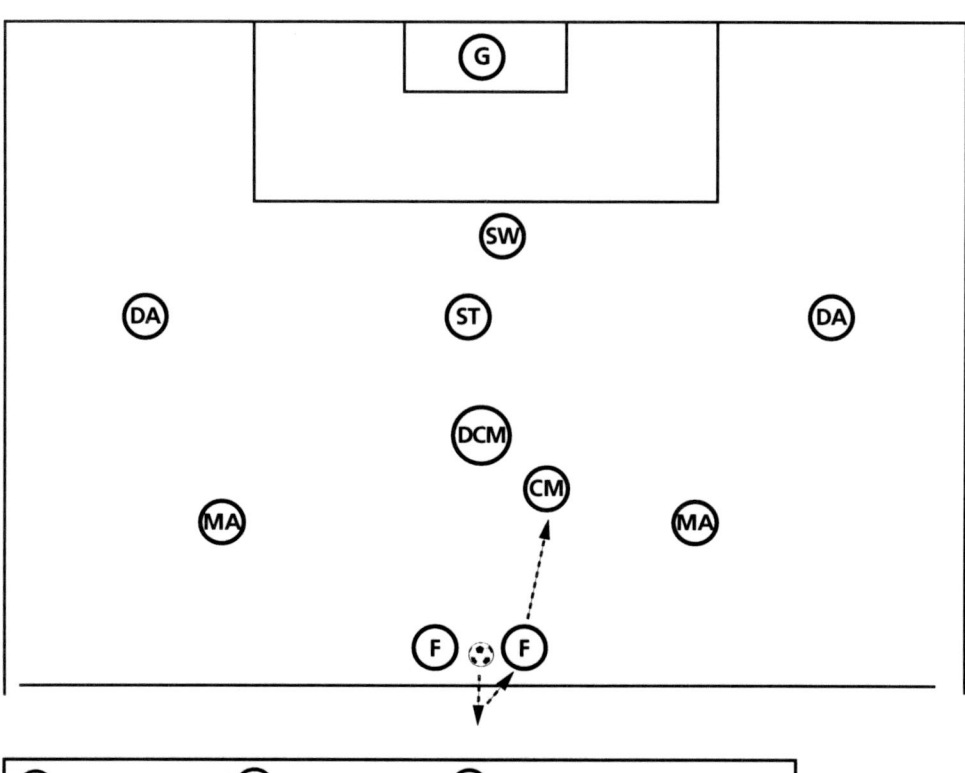

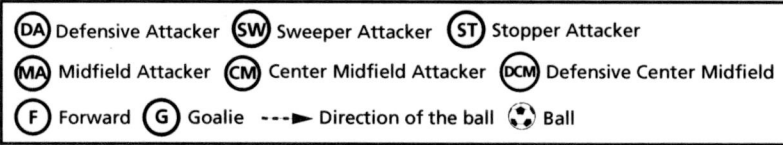

(DA) Defensive Attacker **(SW)** Sweeper Attacker **(ST)** Stopper Attacker
(MA) Midfield Attacker **(CM)** Center Midfield Attacker **(DCM)** Defensive Center Midfield
(F) Forward **(G)** Goalie ---▶ Direction of the ball ⚽ Ball

1. The two forwards must be close together in order that the ball can be played quickly.
2. The ball is played from one forward the other forward but must advance across the midfield line.
3. The forward with the ball plays the ball back to either one of the center midfielders.
4. Space should have been created in the opponent's territory as soon as the opposing players advance to attack the ball. The own forwards must take advantage of this space.
5. The ball can be played by the center midfielders in many ways and will depend on what pressure and space has been provided by the opponent.
a. the ball can be played back to the stopper and then to the outside defender.
b. The ball can be played back and directly to the outside defender.
c. The ball can be played to the outside midfielder.
d. The ball can be played immediately to the forward.

EMPHASIZE:

When DEFENDING against a Kick-Off, the players must attack the ball immediately after the ball has been played forward over the midfield line. Immediate pressure is necessary to eliminate the time the kicking-off team has to develop the attack.

YEAR TWO

In the second year of the team development the focus of the program is on learning the roles of the pressure defender and the second or support defender. Once the players understand their roles when defending, the attention of the program shifts to transitioning as a team from the defensive third of the field of play into the middle third. The second year of learning finishes by having transitioned as a team all the way into the attacking third of the field of play.

Transition from one third of the field of play to another third is always about a full team transition. Success of a team in their transition play will depend on how organized the players are as a team. It should be easier in the second year to learn these principals of the game of soccer since the players have learned what it means to organize in the first year.

Repetition of a limited number of plays per practice is the key to success. Always stay with the new play until the coach is certain that the players understand the material that is being taught.

I. REVIEW YEAR ONE:

It is imperative that all the material taught in Year One be reviewed in the initial practices of the new year of development. The younger the team, the more the players will have forgotten from one year to the next. As the coach, one can take nothing for granted. Do not attempt to rush through the material from Year One.

II. WEAVE PLAY:

1. This Weave Play is learned in Year Two with six players in a group. Four players are positioned to make up a square and two players are positioned in the middle of the square.

Fig. 1   Fig. 2   Fig. 3

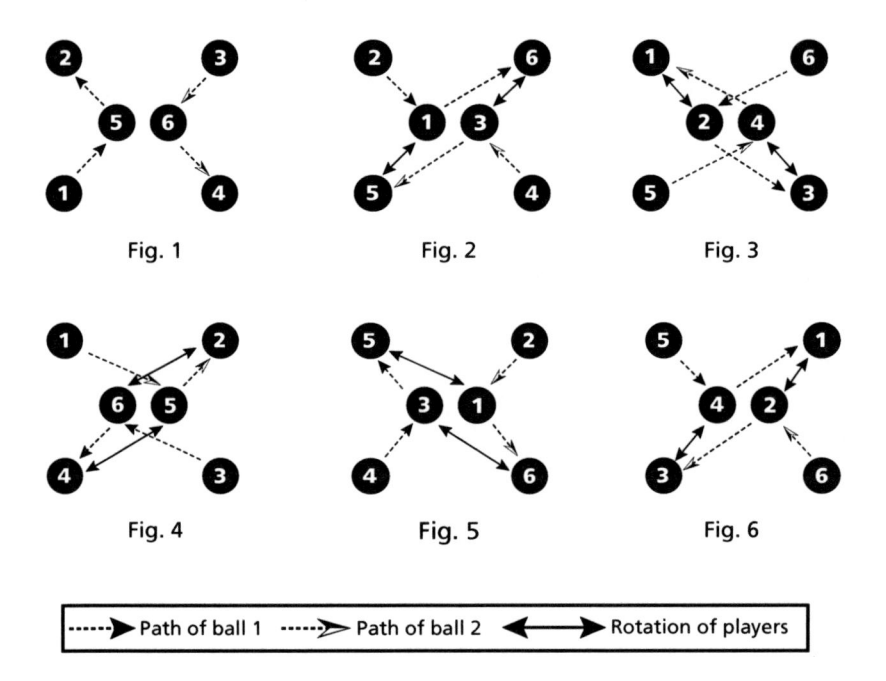

Fig. 4   Fig. 5   Fig. 6

┄┄▶ Path of ball 1   ┄┄▶ Path of ball 2   ◀━━▶ Rotation of players

- Two balls are used in this Weave Play
- The ball is always first played from the outside player to the middle player. Any re-start always is played from the outside into the middle
- The balls are played by the outside players positioned directly opposite each other

FIGURE 1:
- Player 1 plays the ball #1 from the outside to the middle player 5
- At the same time Player 3 plays ball #2 from the outside to middle player 6
- Player 5 plays the ball #1 from the middle to the outside player 2
- Player 6 plays the ball #2 from the middle to the outside player 4

FIGURE 2:
- Player 5 moves to the outside to where player 1 was positioned while player 1 moves into the middle
- Player 6 moves to the outside to where player 3 was positioned while player 3 moves into the middle
- Player 2 plays the ball #1 from the outside to the middle player 1
- Player 1 plays the ball #1 from the middle to the outside player 6
- Player 4 plays the ball #2 from the outside to the middle player 3
- Player 3 plays the ball #2 from the middle to the outside player 5

FIGURE 3:
- Player 1 moves to the outside to where player 2 was positioned while player 2 moves into the middle
- Player 3 moves to the outside to where player 4 was positioned while player 4 moves into the middle
- Player 6 plays the ball #1 from the outside to the middle player 2
- Player 2 plays the ball #1 from the middle to the outside player 3
- Player 5 plays the ball #2 from the outside to the middle player 4
- Player 4 plays the ball #2 from the middle to the outside player 1

FIGURE 4:
- Player 2 moves to the outside to where player 6 was positioned while player 6 moves into the middle
- Player 4 moves to the outside to where player 5 was positioned while player 5 moves into the middle
- Player 3 plays the ball #1 from the outside to the middle player 6
- Player 6 plays the ball #1 from the middle to the outside player 4
- Player 1 plays the ball #2 from the outside to the middle player 5
- Player 5 plays the ball #2 from the middle to the outside player 2

FIGURE 5:
- Player 6 moves to the outside to where player 3 was positioned while player 3 moves into the middle
- Player 5 moves to the outside to where player 1 was positioned while player 1 moves into the middle
- Player 4 plays the ball #1 from the outside to the middle player 3
- Player 3 plays the ball #1 from the middle to the outside player 5
- Player 2 plays the ball #2 from the outside to the middle player 1
- Player 1 plays the ball #2 from the middle to the outside player 6

FIGURE 6:
- Player 3 moves to the outside to where player 4 was positioned while player 4 moves into the middle
- Player 1 moves to the outside to where player 2 was positioned while player 2 moves into the middle

- Player 5 plays the ball #1 from the outside to the middle player 4
- Player 4 plays the ball #1 from the middle to the outside player 1
- Player 6 plays the ball #2 from the outside to the middle player 2
- Player 2 plays the ball #2 from the middle to the outside player 3

The whole sequence continuous to repeat itself.

2. BUILDING ONTO THE WEAVE PLAY IN YEAR TWO:

a. Using the RIGHT foot, the player prepares the ball to the right of the player with the outside of the right foot then makes a pass to the next player in the rotation. To make an accurate pass the player's body position must be facing the player being passed to.

b. Execute the weave as stated in item #a while using the outside of the LEFT foot for the outside ball preparation and then pass.

c. Touch-On-The-Ball: Learn to touch the ball with proper power that will cover the correct distance between players. Players usually kick everything with the same power on the ball regardless of distance.
   - Bring the players close together approximately three feet from the center players.
   - Begin the weave sequence using the right foot. The passes must be soft because the players are close together.
   - After each pass the passing player takes a step back.
   - The touch on the ball is harder with each increase of distance.
   - The distance is increased until the players have to cover a longer distance with their pass.
   - Once the furthest point is reach, the players must take one step forward after each pass thereby decreasing the distance and the touch on the ball.
   - The weave passing space increase or decrease is continuous.

d. Execute the weave as stated in item #c while using the LEFT foot for the soft or hard pass.

e. Each outside player picks the ball up with the hands and throws the ball to the center player.
   - The center player chest traps the ball and prepares the ball with the chest to the right side.

- The ball is prepared to the right side by turning the chest to the right at the point of impact with the ball.
- The center player then makes a right footed pass to the next outside player.
- The player switch then takes place.

f. Execute the weave as stated in item #e while preparing the ball to the left side then using the LEFT foot for the pass.

g. Using one ball but two players:
  - One of the two center players is designated as the shadow defender.
  - This shadow defender will stay in the middle for several rotation before being substituted by another player.
  - The shadow defender does not put any actual pressure on the rotating center players.
  - The shadow defender remains close to the center passing player to teach the center passing player to control the ball, shield the shadow defender, and make the proper pass to the outside player.

h. Execute this shadow defender as described in item #g while the passing players use their left foot to execute the passes.

i. Using this weave play, heading can be practiced. Players can learn to pass with their head and still rotate players.

III. PRESSURE AND SUPPORT DEFENDER:

A. REVIEW

Review the material regarding the pressure defender and the support defender as taught in Year One, Item IV. Defensive Technique 2v1 Situation # 1–4.

1. TEACH—DEMONSTRATE RESPONSIBILITY CHANGE:

Fig. 1

As the pressure defender moves to meet the attacker, the support defender move forward with the pressure defender. Both defenders move in unison when channeling the attacker keeping the same distance between them.

Fig. 2

Pressure defender allows the attacker with the ball to get past on purpose.

Fig. 3

Support defender moves up to meet the attacker and thereby becomes the new pressure defender.

Fig. 4

Pressure defender moves to support thereby becomes the new support defender.

SD Support Defender   **PD** Pressure Defender   **A** Attacker   ⚽ Ball

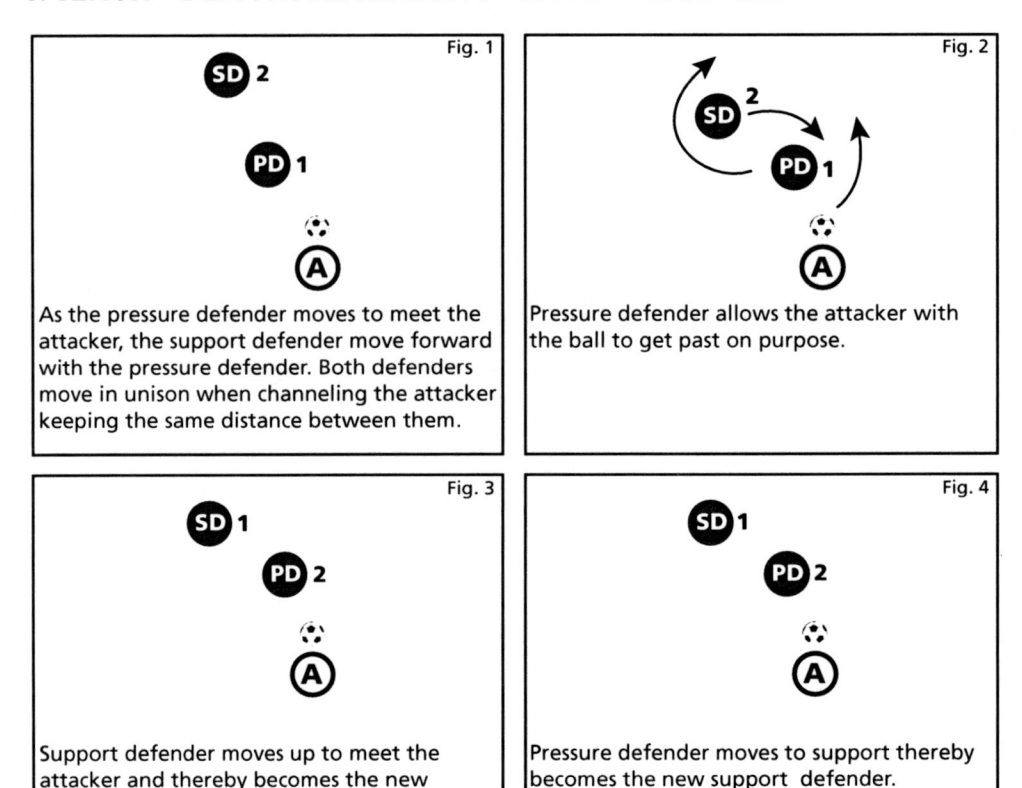

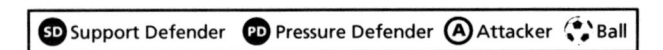

FIGURE 1:

a. The first defensive player to the ball is designated as the pressure defender.

b. How to play as the pressure defender is described in YEAR ONE Item #III #1.

c. A second defender must move into position approximately five feet goal-side and inside of the pressure defender and this defender is designated as the support defender.

d. Both players must back up in unison and keep their distance as the attacker advance with the ball.

FIGURE 2:

e. After the attacker has advanced a few steps, the pressure defender must permit the attacker to advance past the pressure defender. This action on the part of the pressure defender is on purpose.

FIGURE 3:

f. Once the attacker is past the original pressure defender, The support defender moves up and becomes the new pressure defender.

FIGURE 4:

g. At the same time the original pressure defender moves back and becomes the support defender. This recovery run by the original pressure defender to the support defender position must always be goal-side and inside of the attacker.

2. SET UP PLAY FOR TEAM PRACTICE:

a. Split team into groups of threes.
b. In each group one player will be the support defender and form a line across the goal area with the goal behind them.
c. In each group one player will be the pressure defender and form a line across the goal area approximately five feet in front of the support defender.
d. In each group one player will be the attacker with the ball and form a line across the goal area approximately twenty or more feet outside the penalty area.
e. Each attacker must be opposite two defenders.
f. Players must be spread out for each set of defenders and attackers to have room to play.
g. Play now begins as described above in item #2.

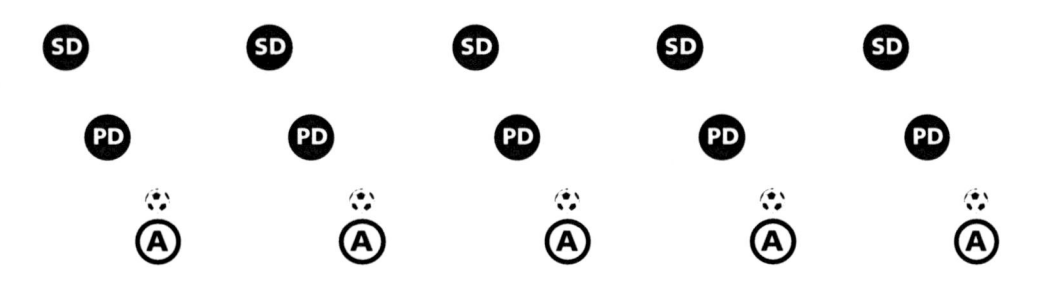

SD Support Defender **PD** Pressure Defender **A** Attacker **Ball**

B. TEACH AND DEMONSTRATE RESPONSIBILITY CHANGE USING TWO ATTACKERS:

Fig. 1

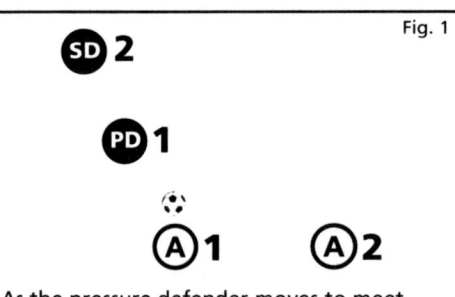

As the pressure defender moves to meet attacker 1, the support defender moves forward with the pressure defender. Both defenders move in unison when channeling attacker 1, keeping the same distance between them.

Fig. 2

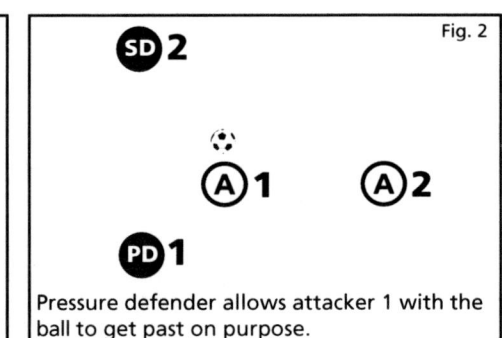

Pressure defender allows attacker 1 with the ball to get past on purpose.

Fig. 3

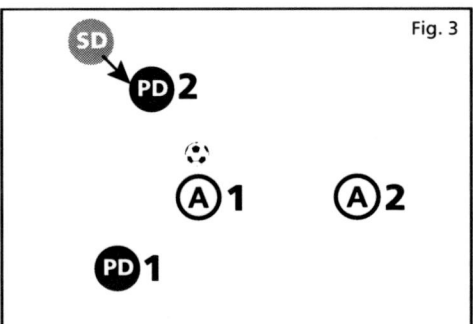

Support defender moves up to meet attacker 1 and thereby becomes the new pressure defender.

Fig. 4

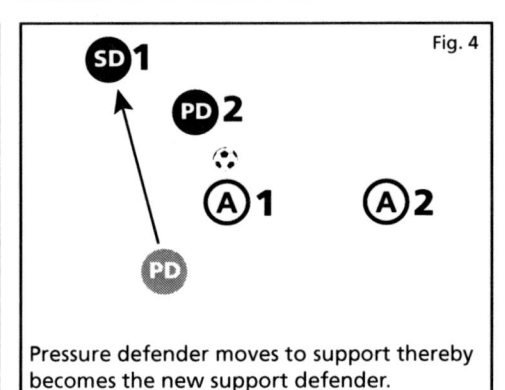

Pressure defender moves to support thereby becomes the new support defender.

Fig. 5

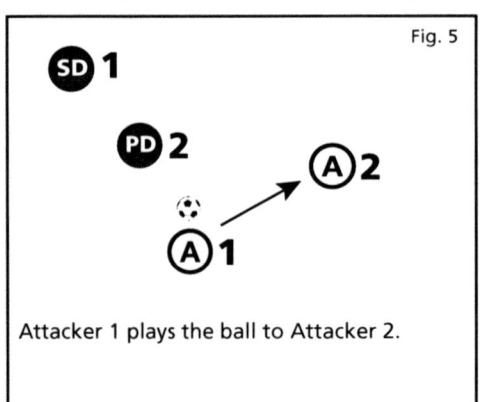

Attacker 1 plays the ball to Attacker 2.

Fig. 6

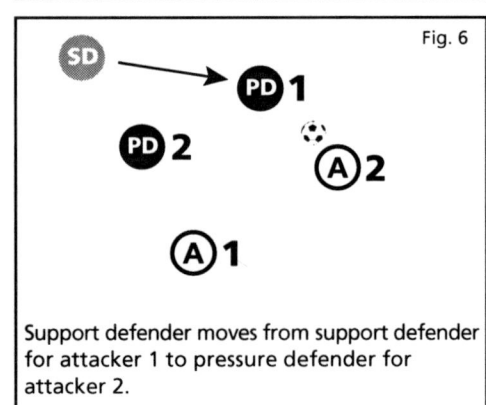

Support defender moves from support defender for attacker 1 to pressure defender for attacker 2.

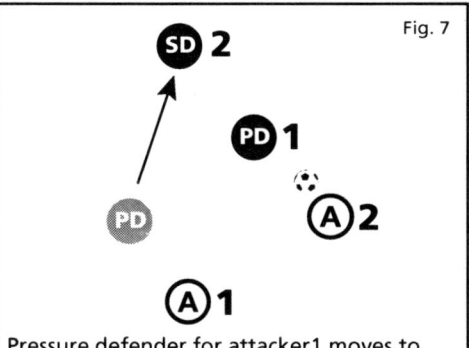

Fig. 7: Pressure defender for attacker1 moves to support defender for attacker 2.

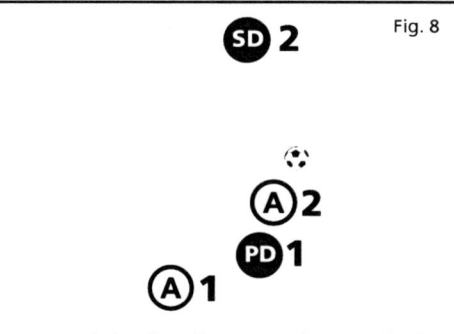

Fig. 8: Pressure defender allows attacker 2 with the ball to get past on purpose after attacker 2 has advanced forward a few steps.

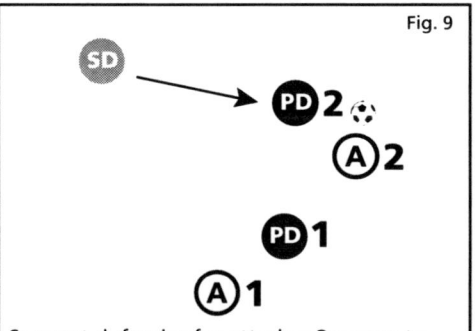

Fig. 9: Support defender for attacker 2 moves to pressure for attacker 2.

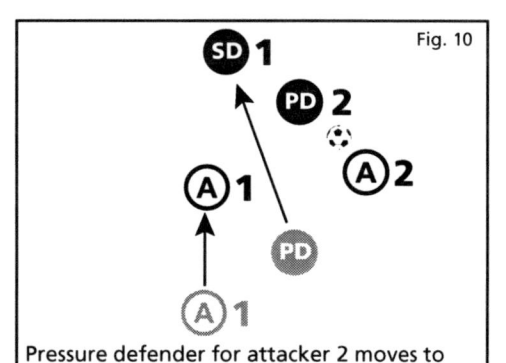

Fig. 10: Pressure defender for attacker 2 moves to support defender for attacker 2. Attacker 1 advances.

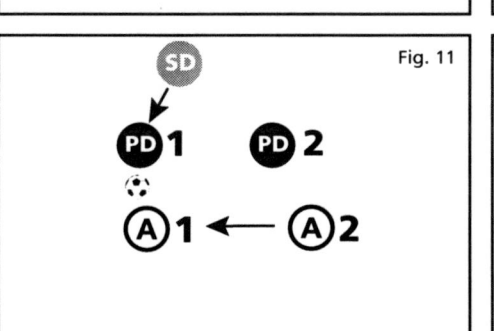

Fig. 11: Attacker 2 plays the ball to attacker 1 at that point support for attacker 2 moves to pressure for attacker1.

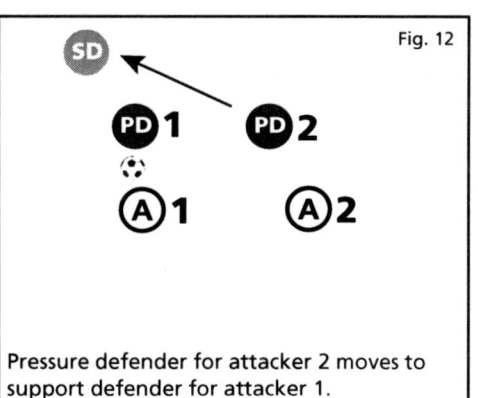

Fig. 12: Pressure defender for attacker 2 moves to support defender for attacker 1.

SD Support Defender **PD** Pressure Defender **A** Attacker ⚽ Ball

1. Review Section III items #1 a - d. Section VI. Items #1,2,3 described in YEAR ONE.
2. TEACH and DEMONSTRATE:
a. Players required:
   - Two defensive players with the first defender being the pressure defender an the second defender being the support defender.
   - Two attacking players with the ball.
b. Both defenders are synchronized in their movement while channeling the attacker to the outside.
c. In this segment the defenders not only learn pressure and support but also how the roles of each defender changes from being a pressure defender to being a support defender and back again.
d. The first four moves by all players is described above in Section III item #2 in Figures 1,2,3,4.

FIGURE 5:
e. Attacker 1 plays the ball to attacker 2.

FIGURE 6:
f. It is the support defender for attacker 1 who now moves and becomes the pressure defender for attacker 2.

FIGURE 7:
g. The pressure defender moves back and changes the pressure role into a support role for attacker 2.

FIGURE 8:
h. While attacker 2 advances with the ball for a few moments, the two defenders must contain by backing up while keeping their proper distance.
i. The support defender must send instructions.
j. The attacker 1 advances with attacker 2 but must not get ahead of attacker 2.

NOTE:
This play is for the benefit of the defenders for the purpose of learning to work in unison. The attackers are merely there as actors.

k. After the attacker 2 has advanced a few steps, the pressure defender allows the attacker 2 to advance past the pressure defender.

NOTE:

The purpose is for the role change of the two defenders.

FIGURE 9:

l. The support defender for attacker 2 now changes by moving into position to become the pressure defender for attacker 2.

FIGURE 10:

m. The pressure defender who had just allowed attacker 2 to get past now moves back and changes the role to a support defender for attacker 2.

FIGURE 11:

n. The attacker 2 plays the ball back to attacker 1.

o. The role of the support defender for attacker 2 instantly changes by moving towards attacker 1 and becoming the pressure defender for attacker 1.

FIGURE 12:

p. The role of the pressure defender for attacker 2 instantly changes by moving back to a position of becoming the support defender for attacker 1.

EMPHASIZE:

a. *The attackers continue to make the passes back and forth with the defenders changing their roles from player to player and pass to pass as demonstrated in the above Figures 1–12.*

b. *Review Sections III and IV, items #3—EMPHASIZE in YEAR ONE.*

c. *The roles of the defenders change instantly from pressure to support on a continuous basis throughout a game.*

3. SET UP PLAY FOR TEAM PRACTICE:

a. Set up the players on the field as described above in item A #2.

b. Each group players must now be split into groups of four by adding a second attacker.

c. Players will advance from one end of the field to the other as described in the previous Items #A and B.

d. Players should change positions in order that they are able to learn to play each one.

4. RELATING PRESSURE and SUPPORT DEFENDER IN 7v7 DEFENSIVE TEAM PLAY:

a. Review Recovery Runs in Section VII and VIII of YEAR ONE.

b. TEACH and DEMONSTRATE:

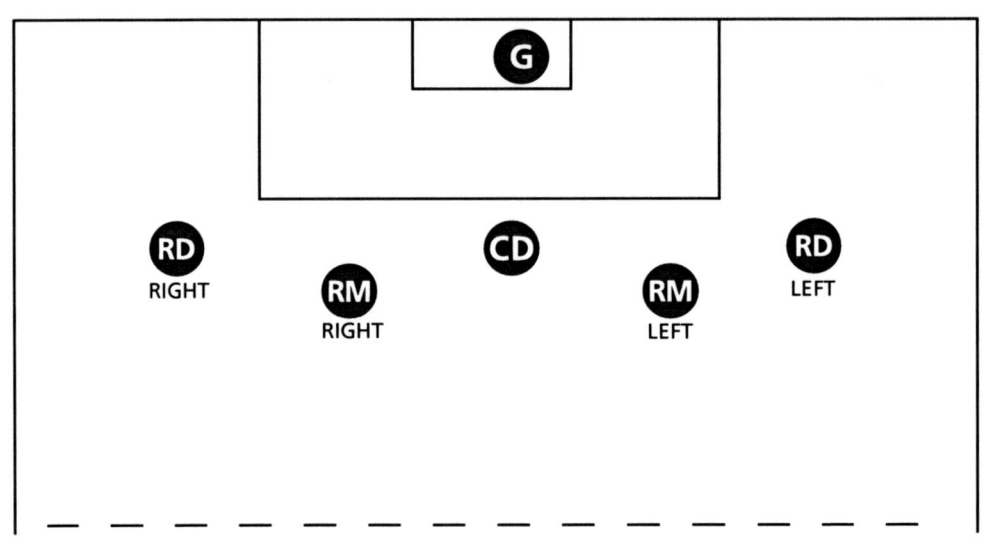

Fig. 1 — Defensive player positions after defensive players have made their recovery runs.

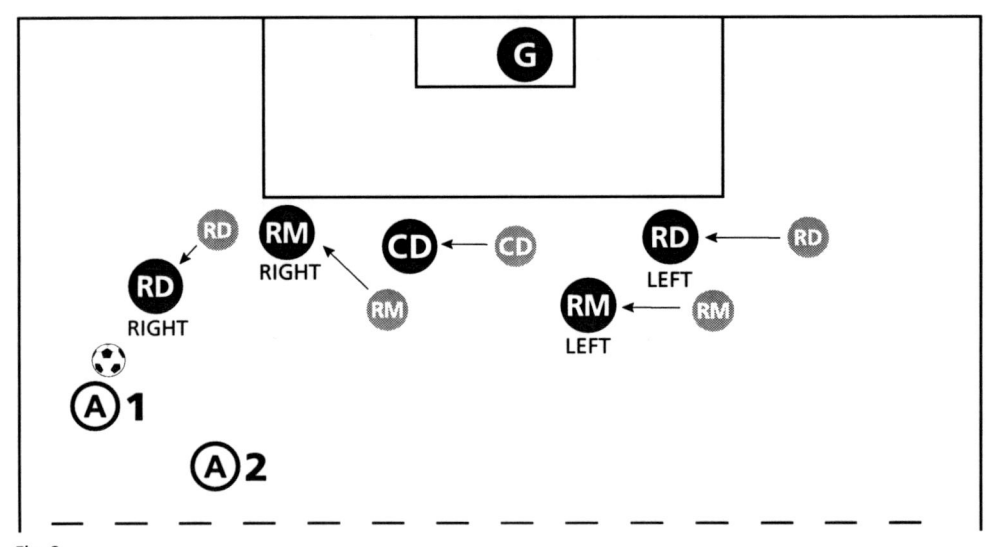

Fig. 2

CD Center Contain Defender **RD** Recovery Defender **RM** Recovery Midfielder **A** Attacker **G** Goalie ⚽ Ball

FIGURE 2:

- Two attackers with the ball are introduced.
- The right outside recovery defender becomes the pressure defender for attacker 1.
- The right recovery midfielder retreats and takes position inside and behind the outside defender thereby becoming the support defender for attacker one.

160

- The central recovery defender, the left recovery midfielder, and left recovery outside defender all move to the right and take position in the spaces that had been created.

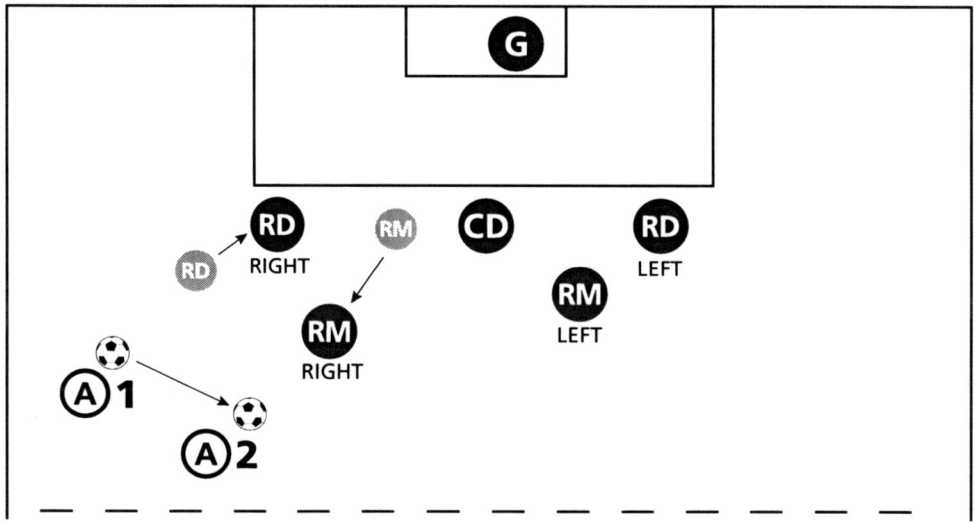

Fig. 3

FIGURE 3:

- Ball is played from attacker 1 to attacker 2.
- Right recovery midfielder moves forward to take position goal-side and inside thereby changing role from support defender for attacker 1 to pressure defender for attacker 2.
- Right outside recovery defender moves back and takes position behind right recovery midfielder thereby changing role from pressure defender for attacker 1 to outside support defender for attacker 2.
- Right outside recovery defender holds position on the outside to cover attacker 1 or any other attacker who potentially will make an outside attacking run.
- Central defender becomes the primary inside support defender for attack 2.

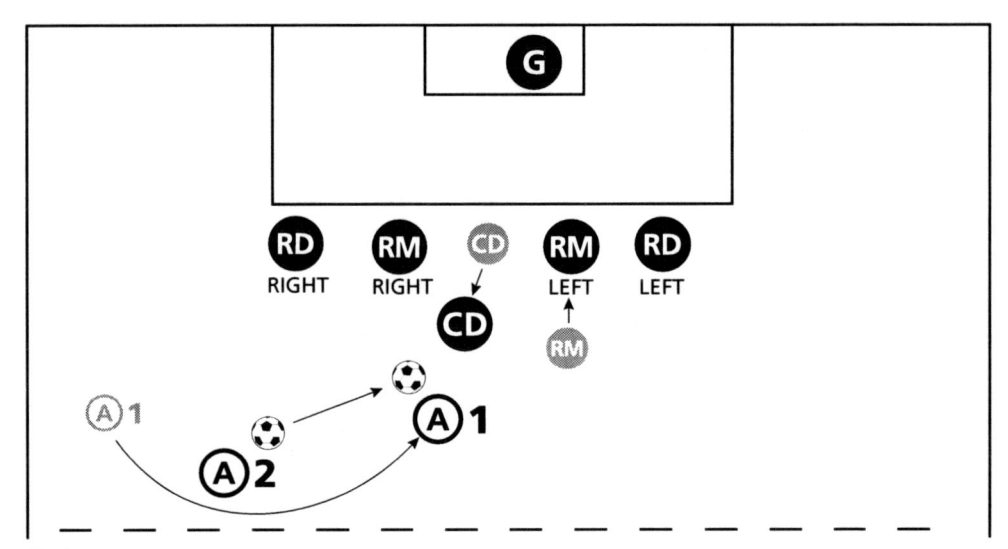

Fig. 4

FIGURE 4:

- Attacker 1 makes a run into the center of the field.
- Attacker 2 plays the ball to attacker 1.
- Central defender moves forward and takes position in front of attacker 1 thereby changes role from support defender for attacker 2 to pressure defender for attacker 1.
- Right recovery midfielder moves back to take position behind central defender thereby changing role from pressure defender for attacker 2 to right outside support defender for attacker 1.
- Left recovery midfielder moves back to take position behind central defender thereby remaining left outside support defender for attacker 1.

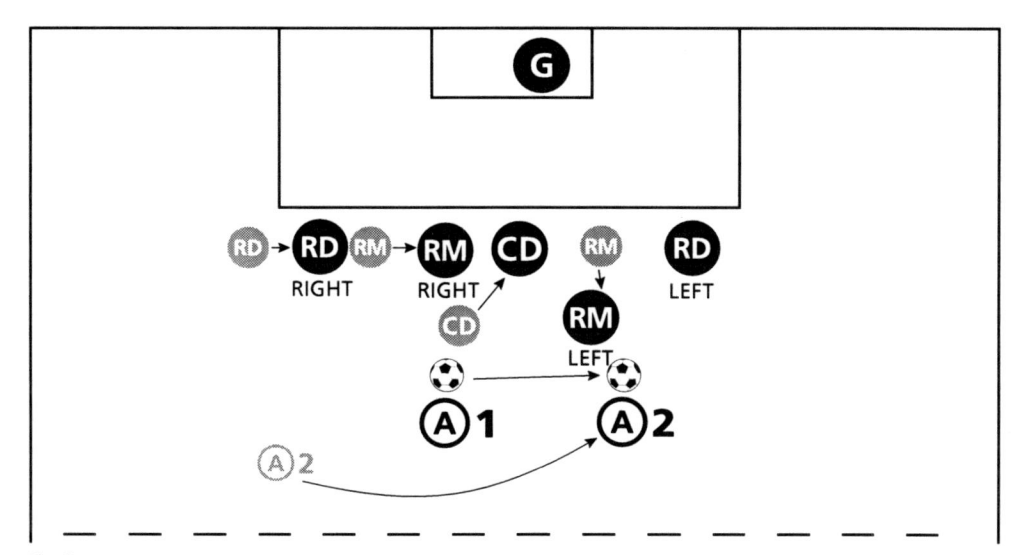

Fig. 5

FIGURE 5 :

- Attacker 2 makes a run into the left side of the field.
- Attacker 1 plays the ball to attacker 2.
- Left recovery midfielder moves forward and takes position in front of attacker 2 thereby changes role from left outside support defender for attacker 1 to pressure defender for attacker 2.
- Central defender moves back to take position behind left recovery midfielder thereby changing role from pressure defender for attacker 1 to central support defender for attacker 2.
- The central recovery defender, the right recovery midfielder, and right recovery outside defender all move to the left and take position in the spaces that had been created.
- The left outside recovery defender holds the outside position but should have remained positioned towards the center of the field.
- Left outside recovery defender remains in the role of a support defender whose purpose is to prevent an outside attacking run by attacker 2 or any other advancing attacker.

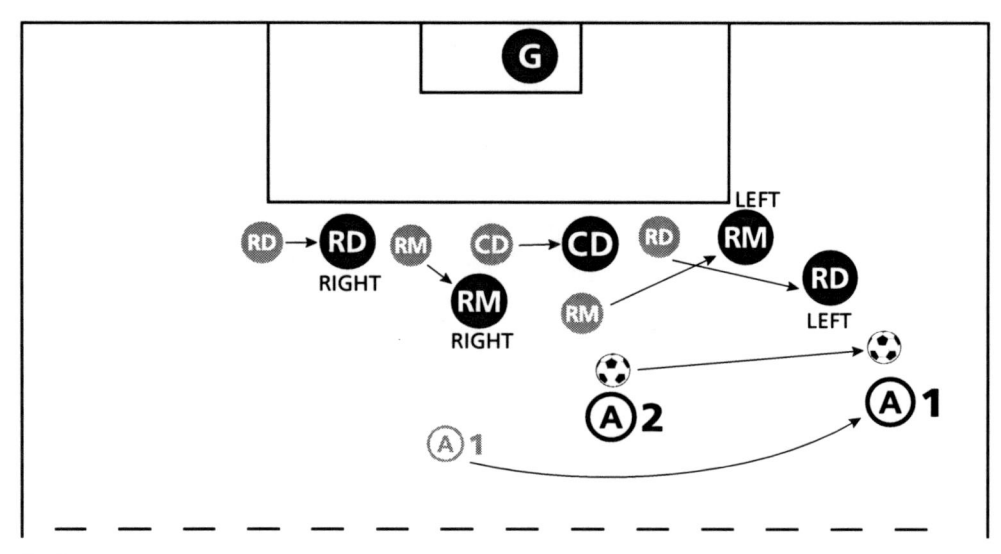

Fig. 6

FIGURE 6 :

- Attacker 1 makes a run out to the left side of the field.
- Attacker 2 plays the ball to attacker 1.
- The left outside recovery defender becomes the pressure defender for attacker 1.
- The left recovery midfielder retreats and takes position inside and behind the outside defender thereby becoming the support defender for attacker 1.
- The central recovery defender, the right recovery midfielder, and right recovery outside defender all move to the left and take position in the spaces that had been created.

5. **RELATING PRESSURE and SUPPORT DEFENDER IN 9v9 and 11v11 DEFENSIVE TEAM PLAY:**

a. Review Recovery Runs in Section IX of YEAR ONE.

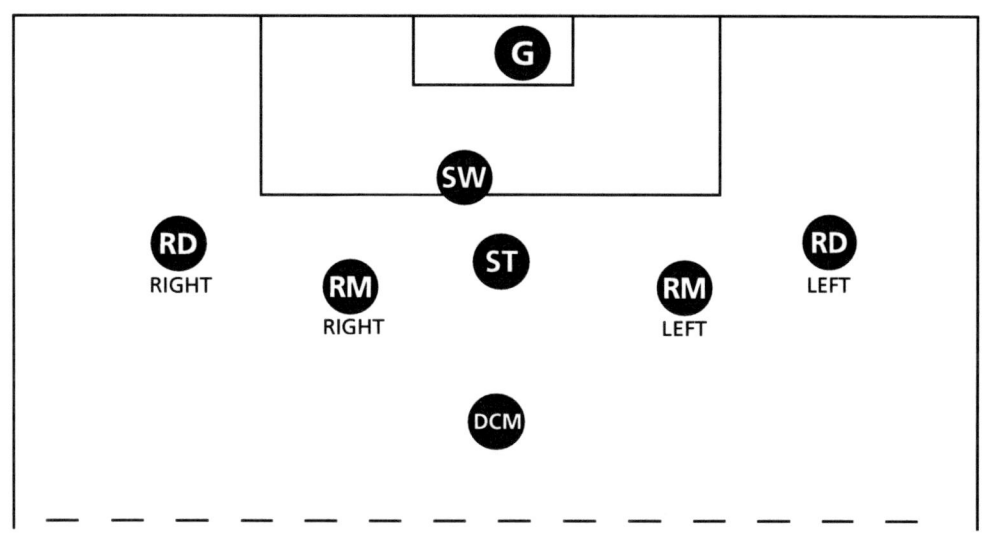

Fig. 1 Defensive player positions after defensive players have made their recovery runs.

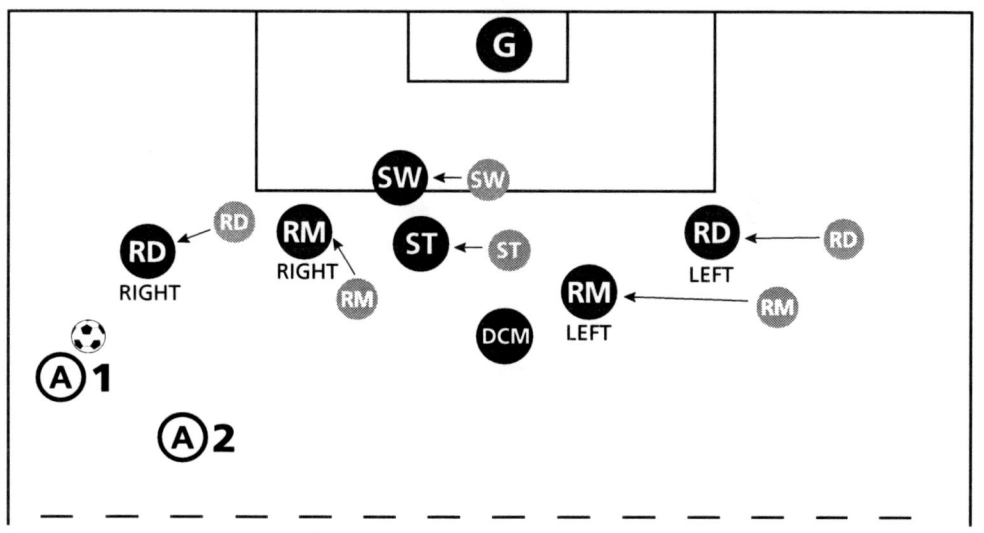

Fig. 2

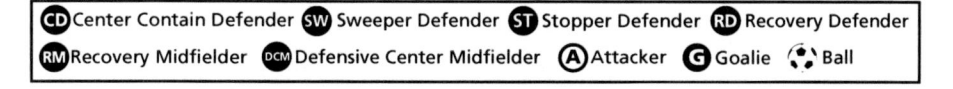

CD Center Contain Defender **SW** Sweeper Defender **ST** Stopper Defender **RD** Recovery Defender
RM Recovery Midfielder **DCM** Defensive Center Midfielder **A** Attacker **G** Goalie ⚽ Ball

165

FIGURE 2:

- Two attackers with the ball are introduced.
- The right outside recovery defender becomes the pressure defender for attacker 1.
- The right recovery midfielder retreats and takes position inside and behind the outside defender thereby becoming the support defender for attacker one.
- The stopper recovery defender, the left recovery midfielder, and left recovery outside defender all move to the right and take position in the spaces that had been created.
- Sweeper defender moves slightly to the right and is in position to defend the center or support the right side in the event of a breakdown.
- Defensive center midfielder holds the center ground.

FIGURE 3:

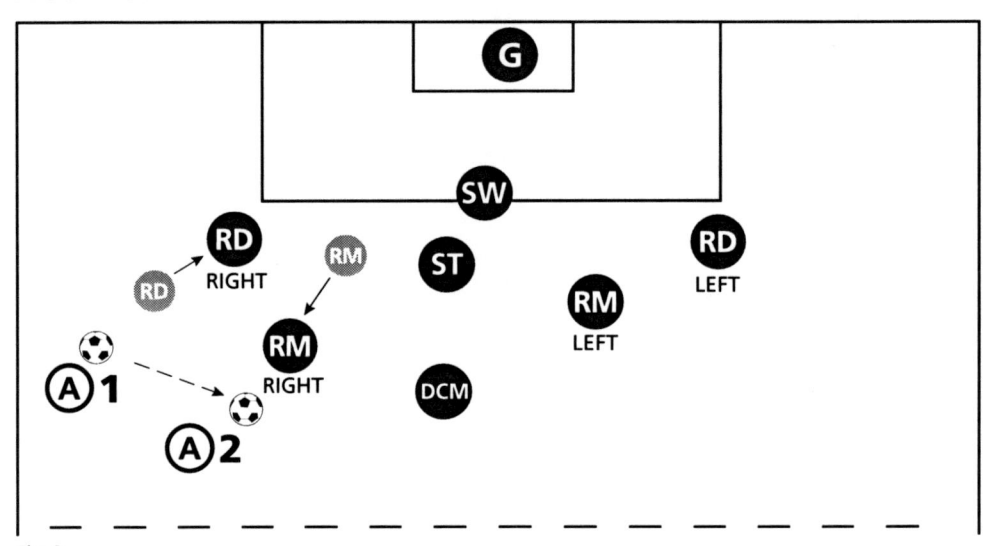

Fig. 3

- Ball is played from attacker 1 to attacker 2.
- Right recovery midfielder moves forward to take position goal-side and inside thereby changing role from support defender for attacker 1 to pressure defender for attacker 2.
- Right outside recovery defender moves back and takes position behind right recovery midfielder thereby changing role from pressure defender for attacker 1 to outside support defender for attacker 2.
- Right outside recovery defender holds position on the outside to cover attacker 1 or any other attacker who potentially will make an outside attacking run.

- Stopper defender becomes the primary inside support defender for attacker 2.
- Sweeper remains positioned behind defense and in the center thereby is in position to defend the center or support the right side in the event of a breakdown.
- Defensive center midfielder holds the center ground and is a support defender in the event the attacker suddenly attacks towards the center.
- Defensive center midfielder is in position to cover any attacker advancing from the rear into the center.

FIGURE 4:

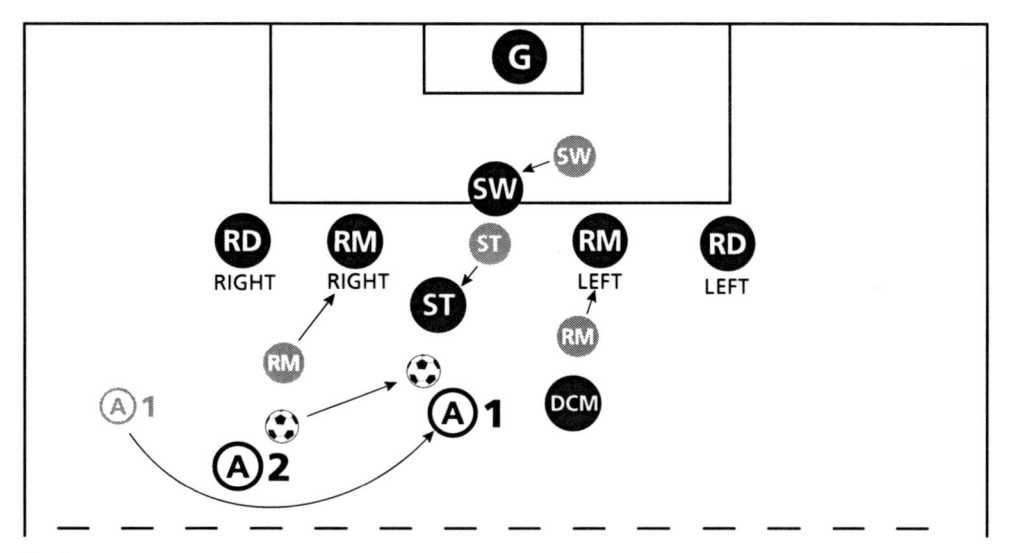

Fig. 4

- Attacker 1 makes a run into the center of the field.
- Attacker 2 plays the ball to attacker 1.
- Stopper defender moves forward and takes position in front of attacker 1 thereby changing role from support defender for attacker 2 to pressure defender for attacker 1.
- Right recovery midfielder moves back to take position behind stopper defender thereby changing role from pressure defender for attacker 2 to right outside support defender for attacker 1.
- Left recovery midfielder moves back to take position behind stopper defender thereby remaining left outside support defender for attacker 1.
- Sweeper remains positioned behind defense and in the center thereby is in position to defend the center or support either outside side in the event of a breakdown.

- Defensive center midfielder holds the center ground and is a support defender in the event the attacker suddenly attacks towards the center or left side.
- Defensive center midfielder is in position to cover any attacker advancing from the rear into the center.

FIGURE 5:

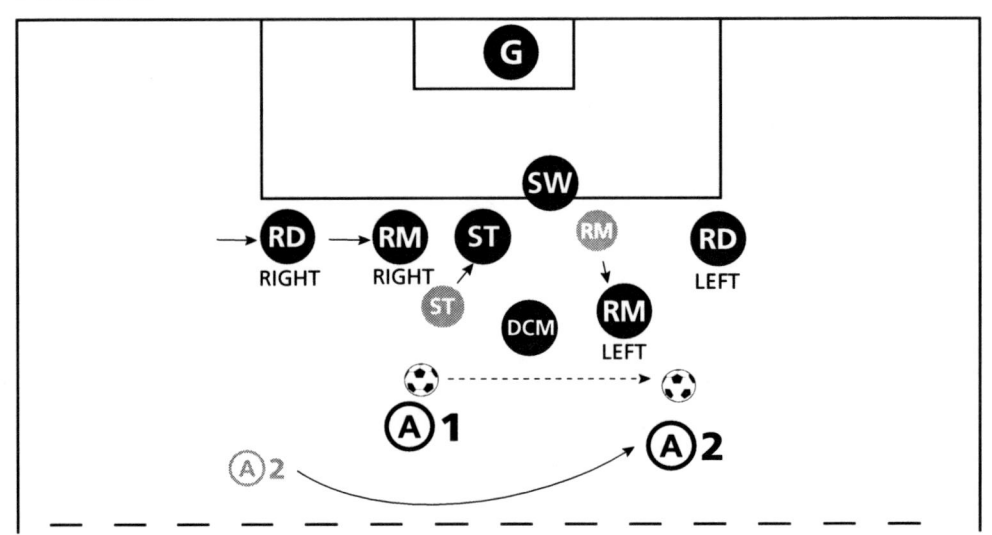

Fig. 5

- Attacker 2 makes a run into the left side of the field.
- Attacker 1 plays the ball to attacker 2.
- Left recovery midfielder moves forward and takes position in front of attacker 2 thereby changing role from left outside support defender for attacker 1 to pressure defender for attacker 2.
- Stopper defender moves back to take position behind left recovery midfielder thereby changing role from pressure defender for attacker 1 to central support defender for attacker 2.
- The stopper recovery defender, the right recovery midfielder, and right recovery outside defender all move to the left and take position in the spaces that had been created.
- The left outside recovery defender holds the outside position but should have remained positioned towards the center of the field.
- Left outside recovery defender remains in the role of a support defender whose purpose is to prevent an outside attacking run by attacker 2 or any other advancing attacker.

- Sweeper remains positioned behind defense and moves slightly to the left of the center thereby is in position to defend the center or support the left side in the event of a breakdown.
- Defensive center midfielder holds the center ground and is a support defender in the event the attacker suddenly attacks towards the center or left side.
- Defensive center midfielder is in position to cover any attacker advancing from the rear into the center.

FIGURE 6:

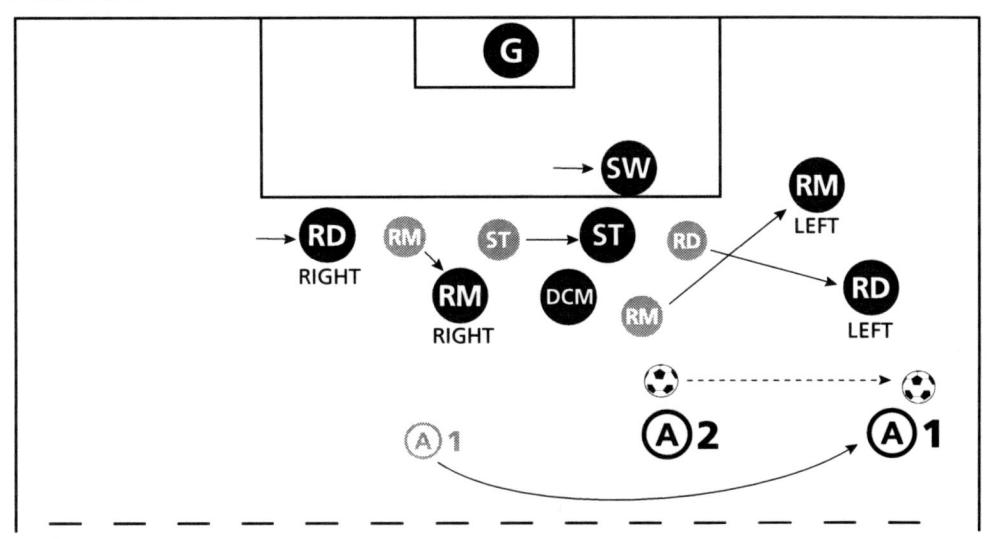

Fig. 6

- Attacker 1 makes a run out to the left side of the field.
- Attacker 2 plays the ball to attacker 1.
- The left outside recovery defender becomes the pressure defender for attacker 1.
- The left recovery midfielder retreats and takes position inside and behind the outside defender thereby becoming the support defender for attacker 1.
- The stopper recovery defender, the right recovery midfielder, and right recovery outside defender all move to the left and take position in the spaces that had been created.
- Sweeper remains positioned behind defense and moves slightly to the left of the center thereby is in position to defend the center or support the left side in the event of a breakdown.
- Defensive center midfielder holds the center ground and is a support defender in the event the attacker suddenly attacks towards the center or left side.
- Defensive center midfielder is in position to cover any attacker advancing from the rear into the center.

NOTE:

By using only two attackers and a full 7v7 or 9v9 or 11v11 defense, the pressure and support defender concept is demonstrated. This team play must be repeated by having the two attackers go across the entire defense from the defensive left side to the defensive right side and then back and forth. This is a very sophisticated defensive style of play so the benefits of it may not become evident for some time in the future. If enough players are available several attackers can be placed across the defense thereby eliminating attacker movement with only the ball being played across the defense.

Additional attackers can also advance forward with the ball being played from one side to another with a quick long pass.

TRANSITION PLAY FOR 7v7, 9v9, 11v11:

1. Sections IV, V, VI, and VII will teach the transition game.
2. Players must learn how to attack as a team and how to defend as a team.
3. The transitions from each third of the field must be learned by the players to execute on instinct.
4. This transition on the outside of the field teaches the players to play the ball wide and that the game can actually be played on the outside and not only in the middle of the field.
5. The defenders are taught that they can advance all the way into the attack thereby becoming part of the attack.

IV. 7V7 TRANSITION PLAY FROM DEFENSIVE THIRD INTO MIDDLE THIRD ENDING AT MIDFIELD:

In the second year of development, teams must learn to transition from the defensive third forward in an organized method of play. Instead of simply kicking the ball out and up the middle, players must understand keeping possession of the ball and developing an attack from the defensive third.

A. TRANSITION TO THE RIGHT DEFENSIVE SIDE:

1. Review Recovery Runs in Section VII and VIII of YEAR ONE. Start this transition segment to the defensive right side with the recovery run.

2. TEACH and DEMONSTRATE:

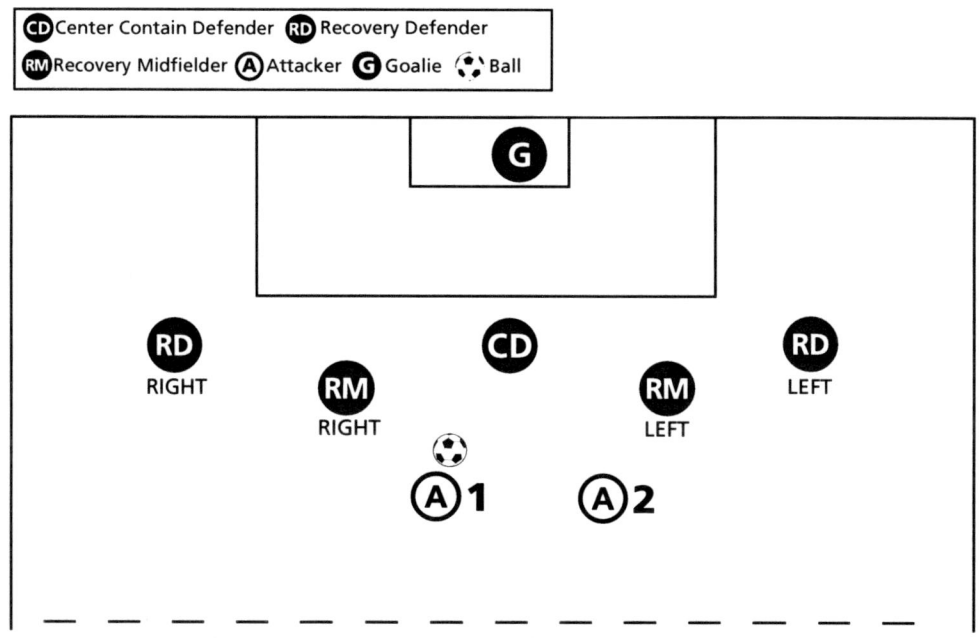

CD Center Contain Defender **RD** Recovery Defender
RM Recovery Midfielder **A** Attacker **G** Goalie ⚽ Ball

Fig. 1 Defensive player positions after defensive players have made their recovery runs.

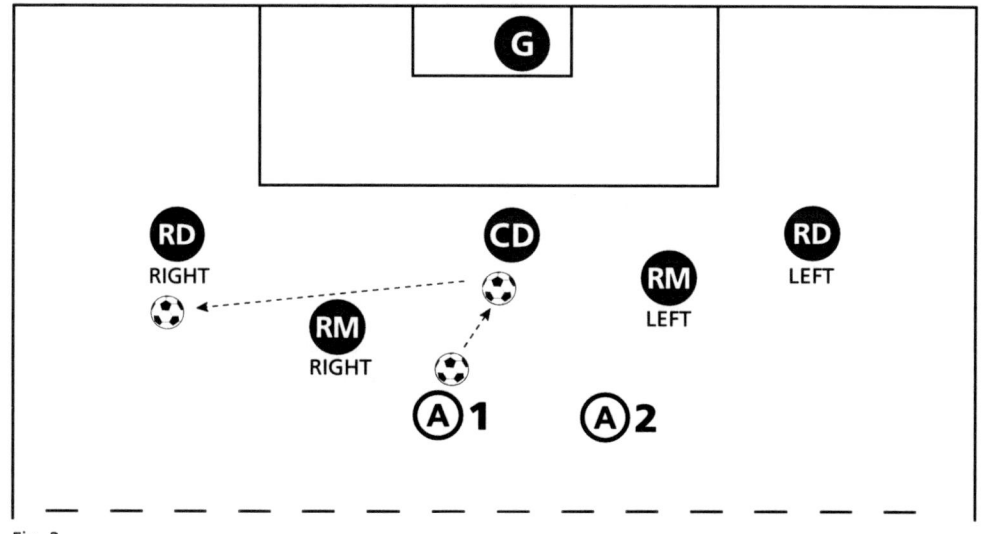

Fig. 2

- Attacker with the ball pretends to have the ball taken away by the center defender by passing it to the center defender.
- Center defender turns and passes the ball to the right outside recovery defender.
- This is a play for the midfielders and defenders to learn how to transition.

- The attackers are merely there to simulate an attack by an opponent and therefore the play is not for the attackers.

FIGURE 3:

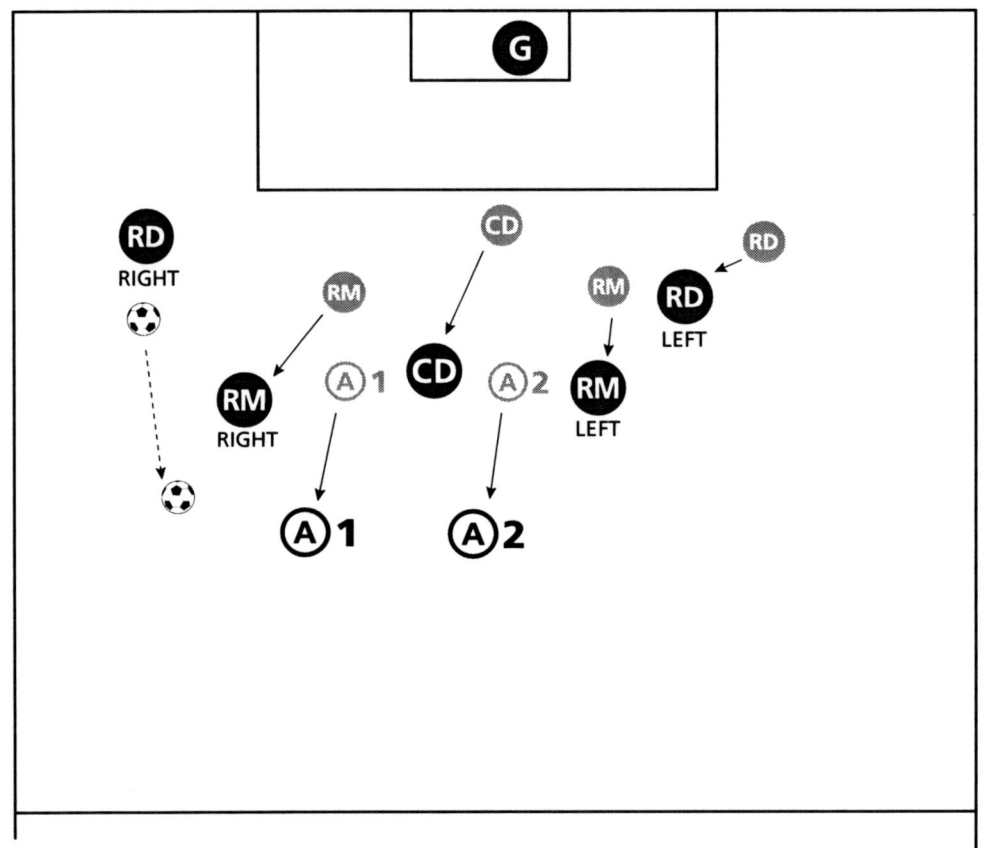

Fig. 3

- As soon as the ball is played by the center defender to the right outside recovery defender, the right recovery midfielder makes a sprint up field and to the outside.
- The right outside recovery defender passes the ball forward to the sprinting right recovery midfielder. This pass must lead the midfielder.
- The central defender follows the play forward and also moves into position toward the right defensive side,
- The left recovery midfielder and the left outside recovery defender move forward and into position toward the right defensive side.
- As the play moves forward on the right defensive outside, the space that is being left open by the forward attacking progress of the defending team is now being filled by the center defender, the left recovery outside midfielder, and the left recovery outside defender.

- This defensive adjustments by the center defender, the left recovery outside midfielder, and the left recovery outside defender is most important and must be demonstrated and thoroughly taught to the team.
- Without this defensive adjustment a wide open center will exist for the opponent to play into and exploit your team.
- The two attackers are simply actors in this play and move their position all the way to midfield and to the defensive right outside.

FIGURE 4:

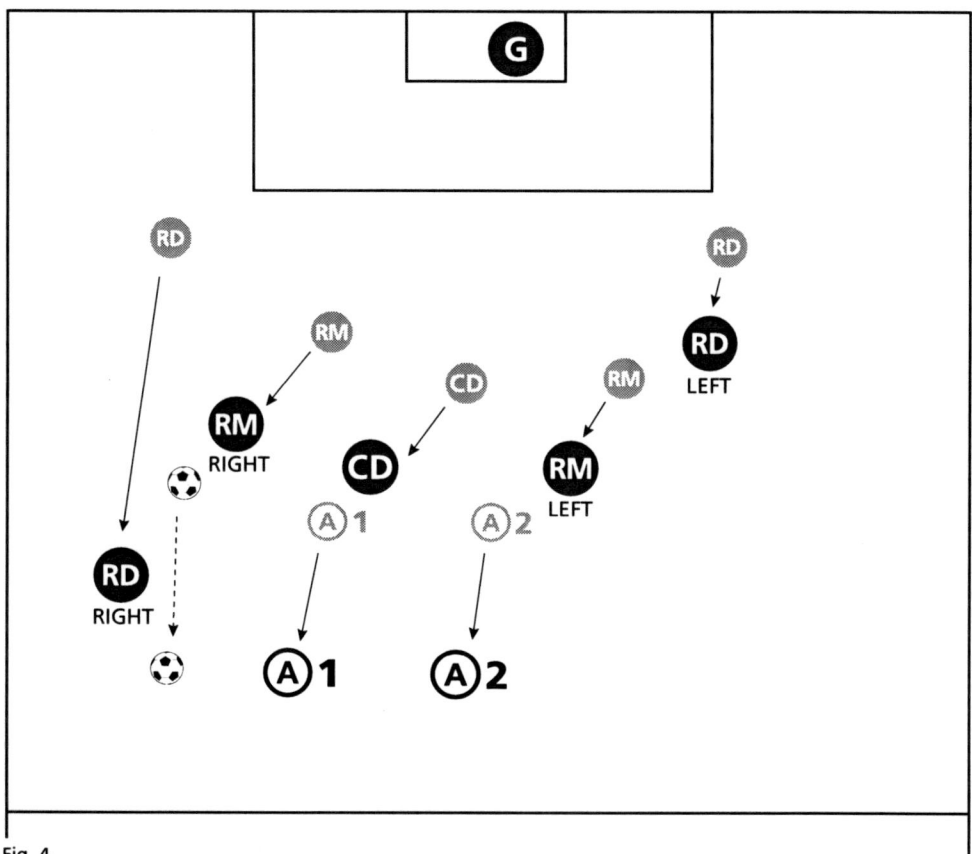

Fig. 4

- As soon as the ball is played by the right outside recovery defender to the right recovery midfielder, the right outside recovery defender makes a sprint up field and to the outside.
- The right recovery midfielder then passes the ball forward to the sprinting right outside recovery defender. This pass must lead the defender.
- The central defender follows the play forward and also moves into position toward the right defensive side,

- The left recovery midfielder and the left outside recovery defender move forward and into position toward the right defensive side.
- The center defender, the left recovery outside midfielder, and the left recovery outside defender must continue to fill the spaces created by the forward progress by the right outside defender and midfielder.
- The center defender gradually slides into position behind the attacking right outside recovery defender and right outside recovery midfielder.
- This defensive adjustments by the center defender, the left recovery outside midfielder, and the left recovery outside defender is most important and must continually be stressed to the team.
- Without this defensive adjustment there will exist a wide open center for the opponent to play into and exploit your team.
- The two attackers are simply actors in this play and continue to move their position all the way to midfield and to the defensive right outside.

FIGURE 5:

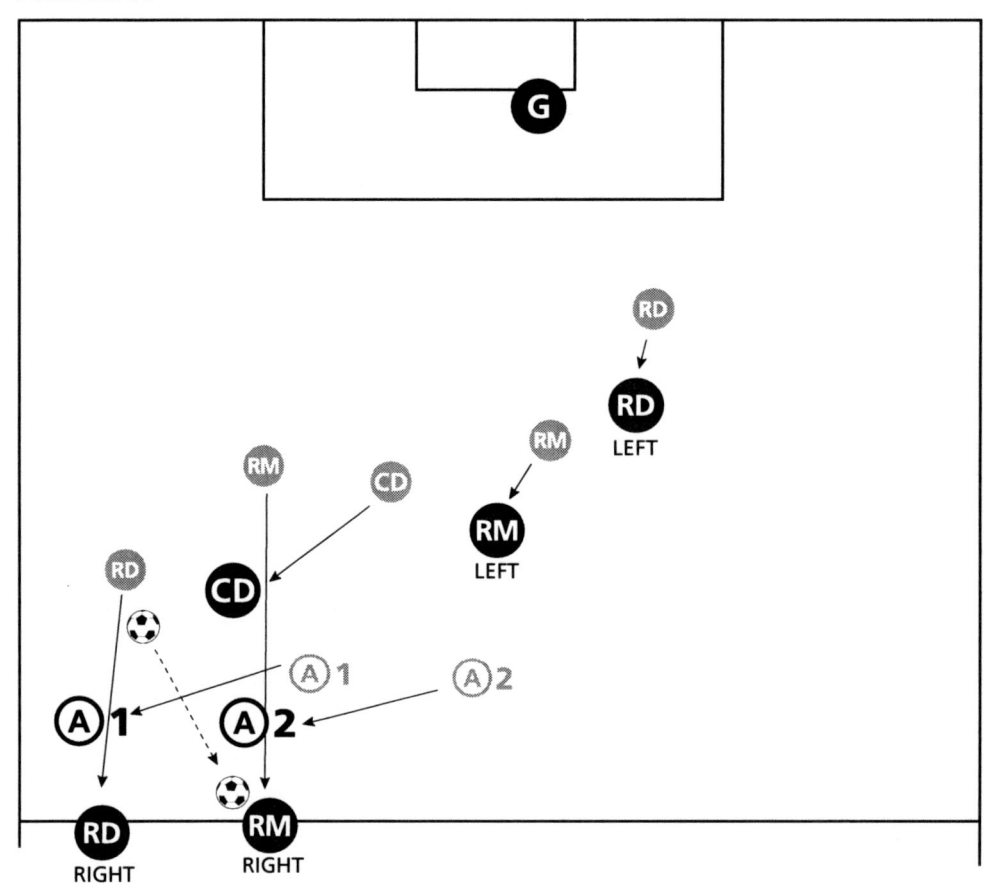

Fig. 5

- As soon as the ball is played by the right recovery midfielder to the right outside recovery defender, the right recovery midfielder makes a sprint up field but halts the forward progress at midfield.
- The right outside recovery defender then passes the ball forward to the sprinting right recovery midfielder who is stopped at midfield.
- The right outside recovery defender sprints forward as soon as the ball is played to the right recovery midfielder but stops at midfield.
- The central defender follows the play forward and also moves into position toward the right outside defensive side.
- The central defender should now be in position to contain any counter attack on the right outside.
- The left recovery midfielder moves forward and into the center position and the left outside recovery defender move forward and toward the right defensive side to be in position to support the center or contain any threat on the left defensive side.
- This defensive adjustments by the center defender, the left recovery outside midfielder, and the left recovery outside defender is most important and must continually be stressed to the team.
- Without this defensive adjustment there will exist a wide open center for the opponent to play into and exploit your team.
- The two attackers are simply actors in this play and continue to move their position all the way to midfield and to the defensive right outside. They will finish this stage of transition play on the right defensive outside. Their position is between the right outside recovery defender—right recovery midfielder and the central defender.

FIGURE 6:

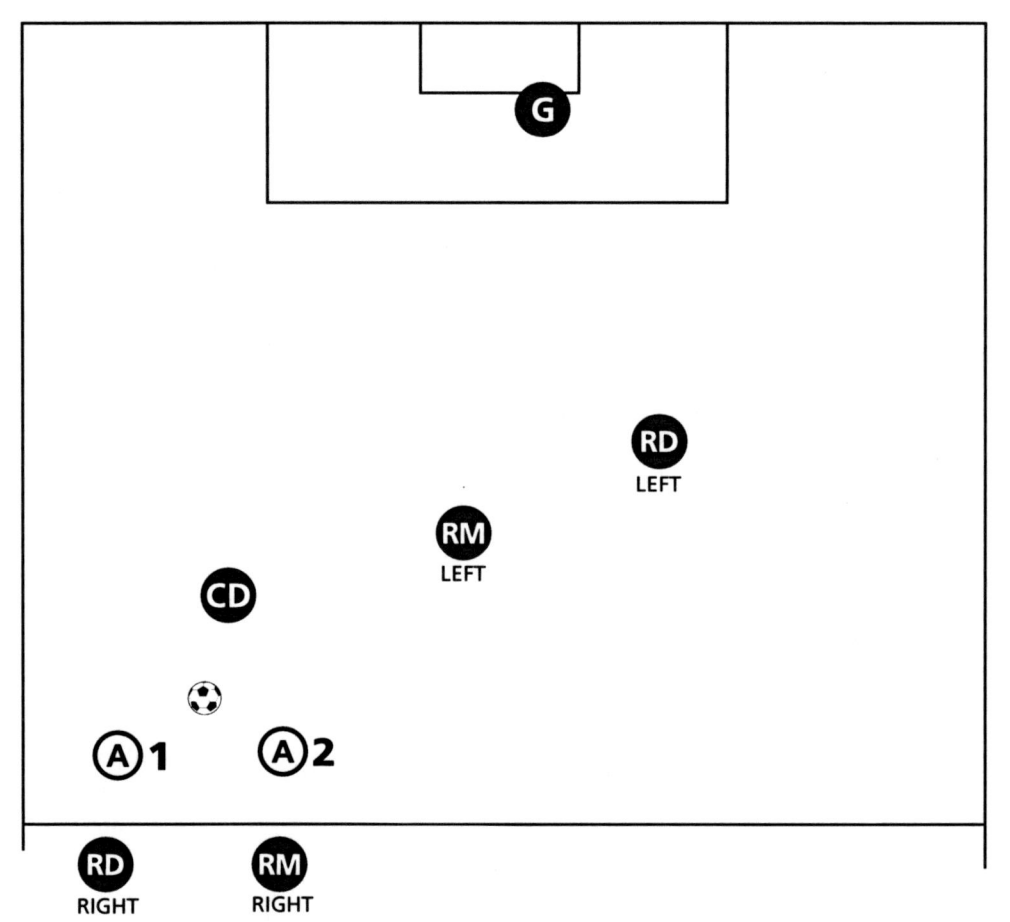

- Formation after the defensive team has transitioned forward and to the outside from the defensive third into the middle third and finishing this segment at midfield.
- The attack will now be created by the attackers on the right outside.
- The defense will now learn that the recovery run sequence learned in section VII and VIII in YEAR ONE develops exactly the same way on the outside of the playing field as it did in the middle area of the playing field.
- The attackers must keep their attack on the outside so that the outside recovery run can be learned and understood by the players.

FIGURE 7:

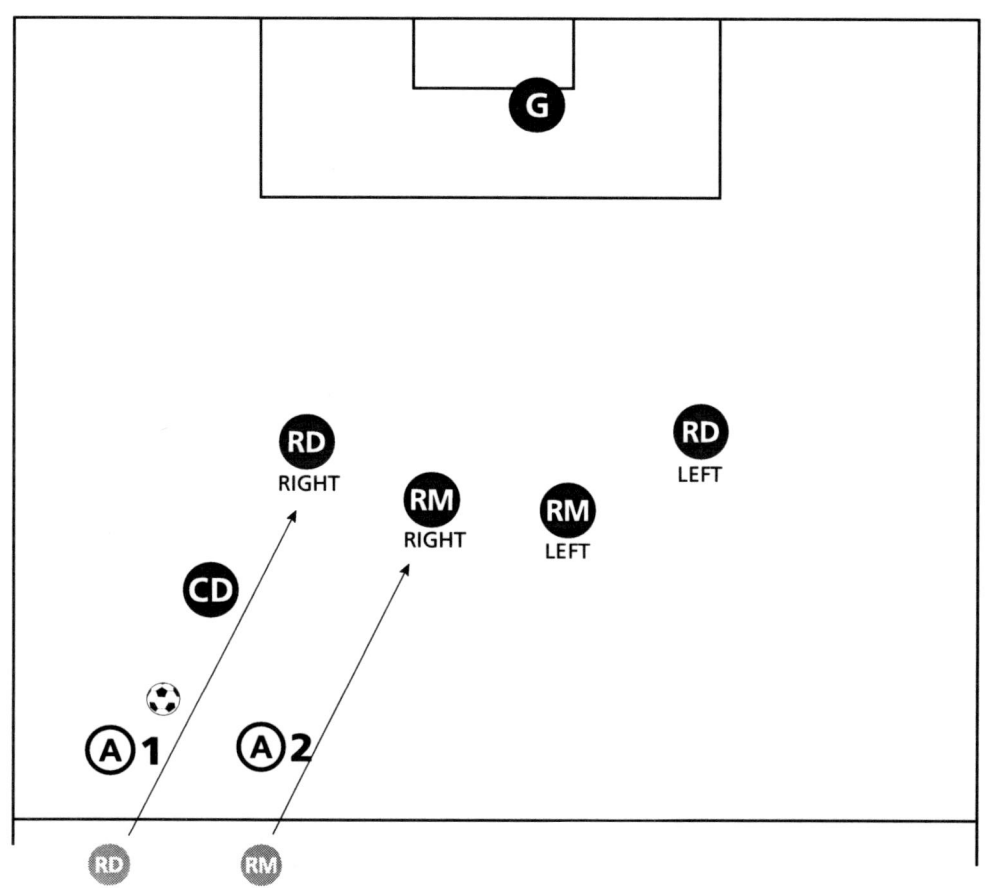

Fig. 7

- The right outside recovery defender and the right recovery midfielder pretend that they have lost the ball to the attackers at midfield.
- The attackers now go on a counter attack on the right outside by passing the ball back and forth between them.
- The center midfielder has been positioned to cover the right defensive outside when the right outside recovery defender and the right recovery midfielder pushed forward and attacked up the right outside.
- The center midfielder will now contain the two attackers by retreating and not attacking the ball.
- The right outside recovery defender and right recovery midfielder make their recovery runs back into a defensive support position behind the containing center midfielder.

FIGURE 8:

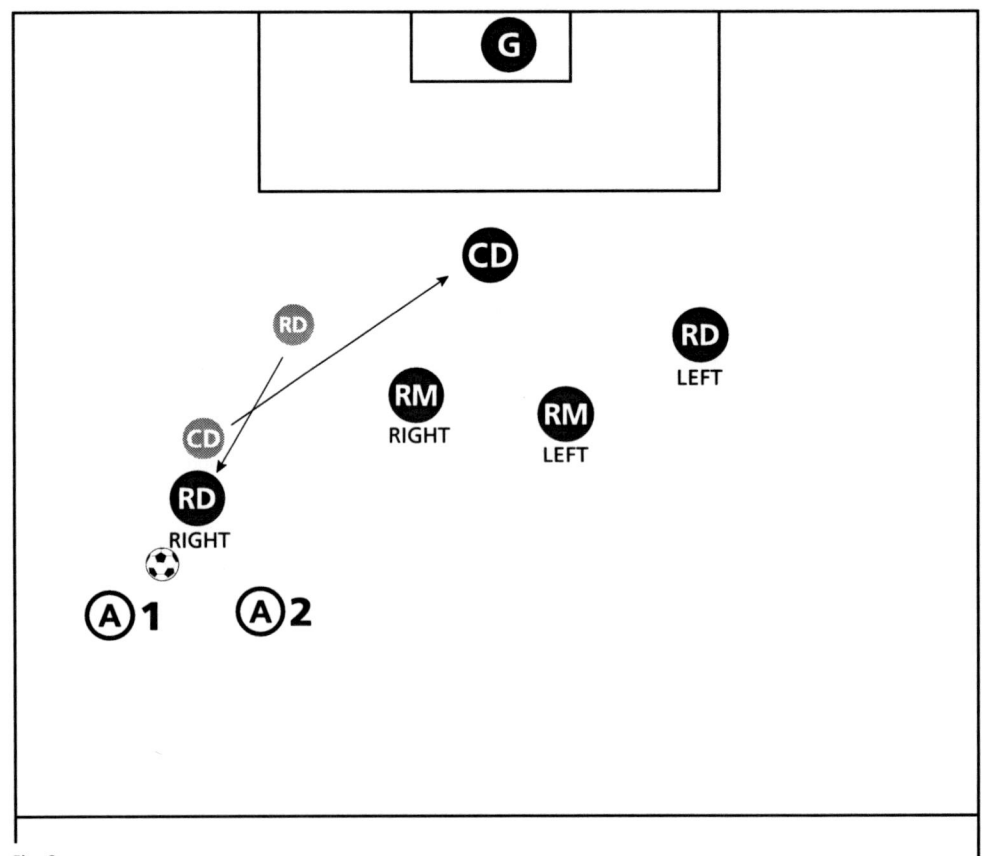

Fig. 8

- Once the right outside recovering defender is in the support position, this defender must release the central defender and take the position between the attacker as the contain defender.
- The central defender, once freed by the right outside recovery defender, retreats to take a position in the center of the field.
- The right outside recovery defender keeps containment of the attackers by retreating until the entire defense is once again set in the defensive part of the playing field thereby creating support for the containing defender.
- The left recovery midfielder and the left outside recovery defender can now begin to move towards the left defensive outside.

FIGURE 9:

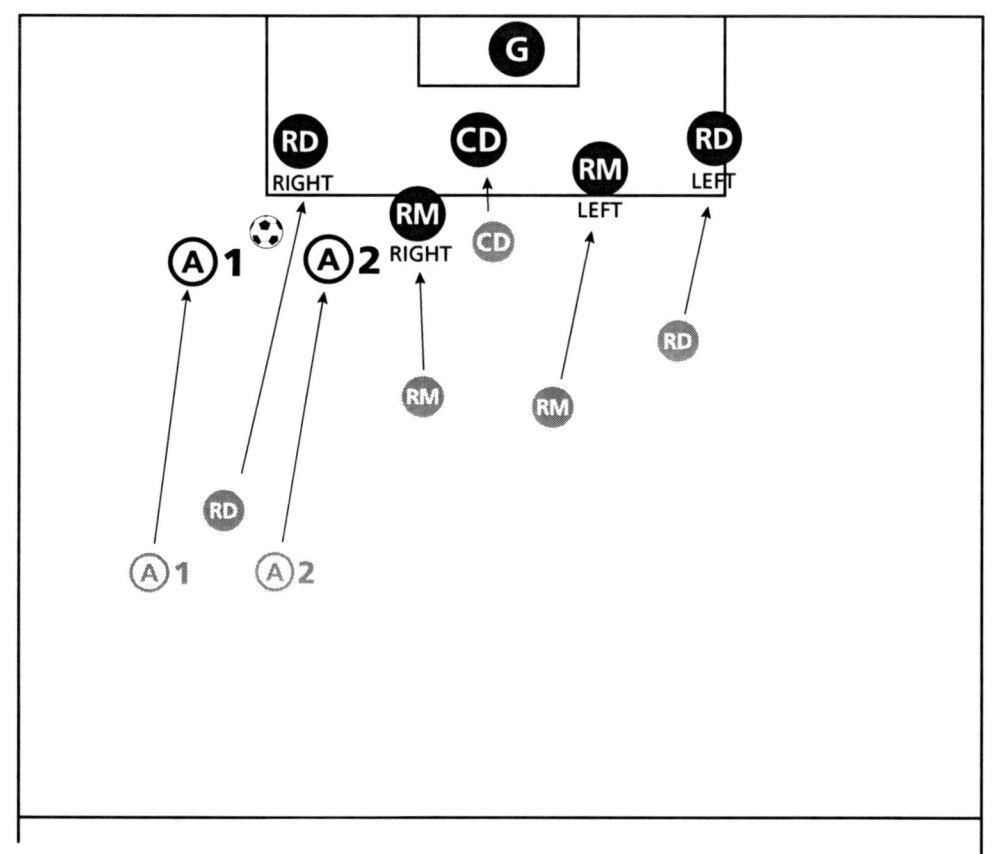

Fig. 9

- Once the attack and the recovery have reached all the way back into defense, the play is ended.
- **This sequence from the recovery run to transitioning to the right defensive side all the way to midfield, must now be repeated until the players on the team understand how to execute this transition segment.**

B. TRANSITION TO THE LEFT DEFENSIVE SIDE

Start this transition segment to the defensive left side with the recovery run.
FIGURE 10:

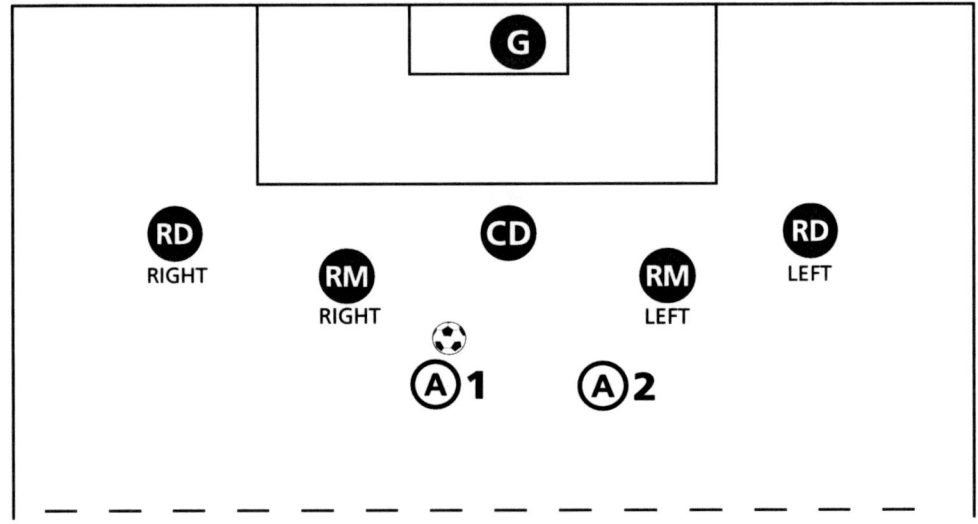

Fig. 10   Defensive player positions after defensive players have made their recovery runs.

FIGURE 11:

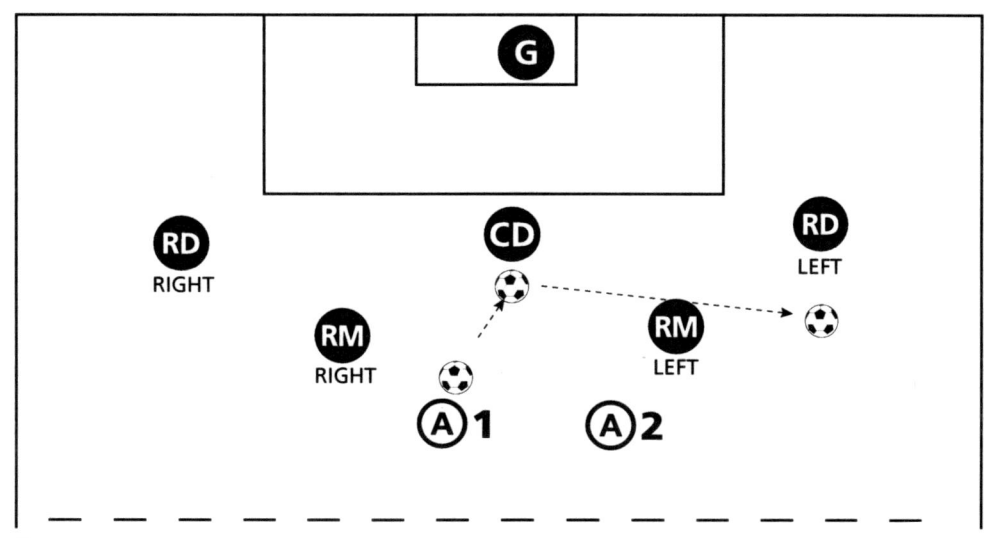

Fig. 11

- Attacker with the ball pretends to have the ball taken away by the center defender by passing it to the center defender.
- Center defender turns and passes the ball to the left outside recovery defender.
- The midfielder and defender learn how to transition up the left defensive side.
- The attackers are merely there to simulate an attack by an opponent and therefore this play is not for the attackers.

FIGURE 12:

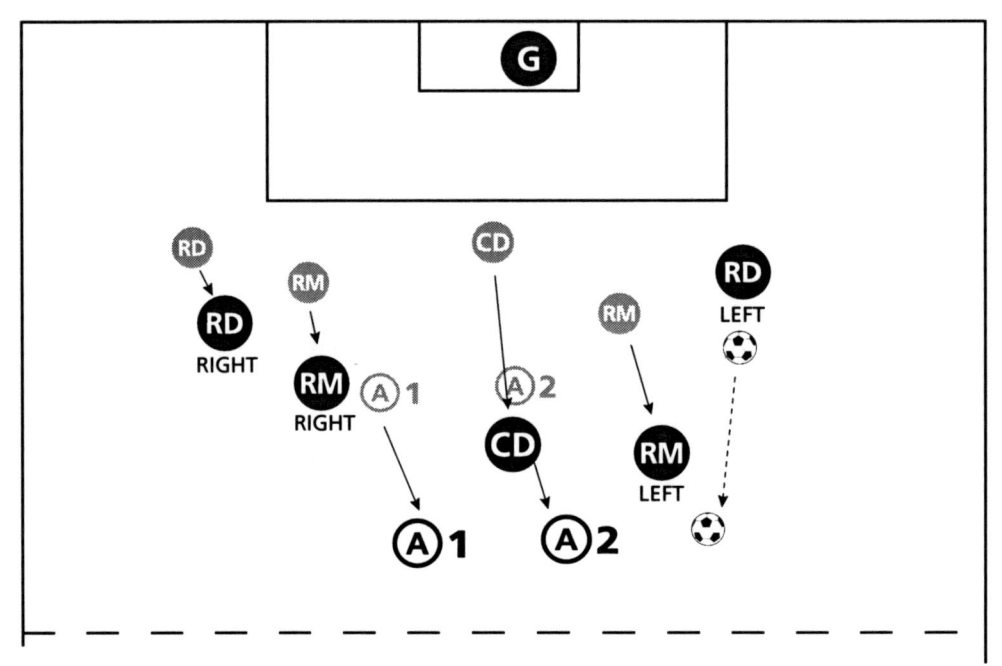

Fig. 12

- As soon as the ball is played by the center defender to the left outside recovery defender, the left recovery midfielder makes a sprint up field and to the outside.
- The left outside recovery defender passes the ball forward to the sprinting left recovery midfielder. This pass must lead the midfielder.
- The central defender follows the play forward and also moves into position toward the left defensive side.
- The right recovery midfielder and the right outside recovery defender move forward and into position toward the left defensive side.
- As the play moves forward on the left defensive outside, the space that is being left open by the forward attacking progress of the defending team is now being filled by the center defender, the right recovery outside midfielder, and the right recovery outside defender.
- This defensive adjustments by the center defender, the right recovery outside midfielder, and the right recovery outside defender is most important and must be demonstrated and thoroughly taught to the team.

- Without this defensive adjustment there will exist a wide open center for the opponent to play into and exploit your team.
- The two attackers are simply actors in this play and move their position all the way to midfield and to the defensive left outside.

FIGURE 13:

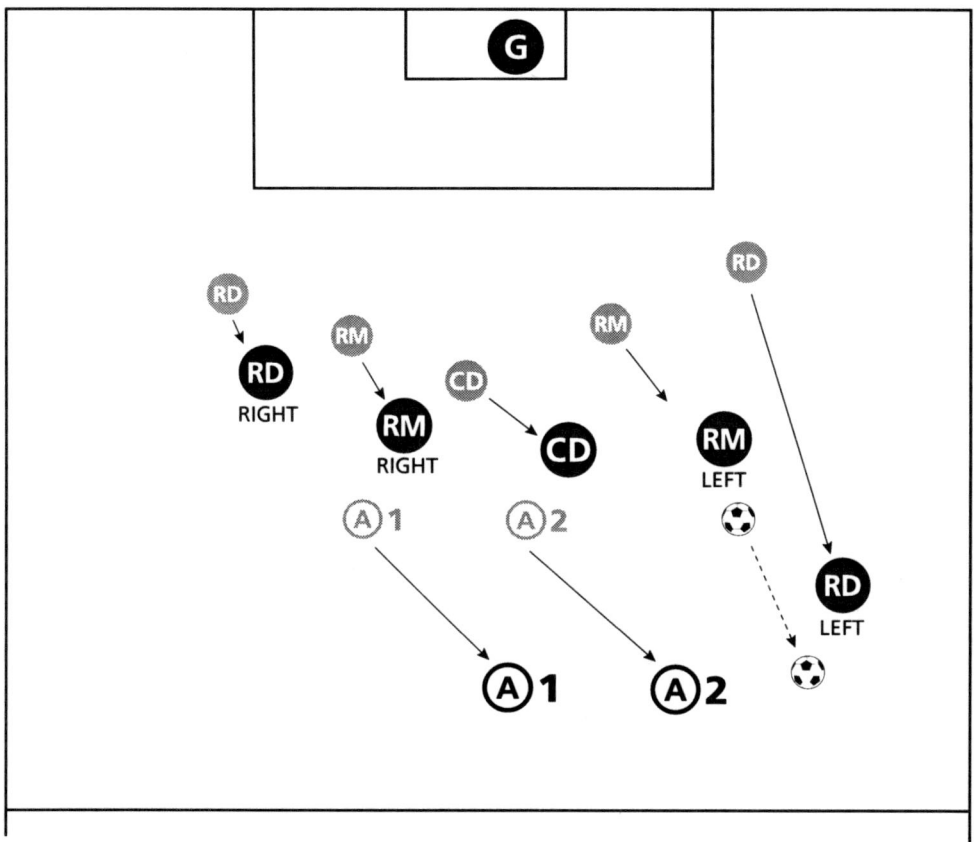

Fig. 13

- As soon as the ball is played by the left outside recovery defender to the left recovery midfielder, the left outside recovery defender makes a sprint up field and to the outside.
- The left recovery midfielder then passes the ball forward to the sprinting left outside recovery defender. This pass must lead the defender.
- The central defender follows the play forward and also moves into position toward the left defensive side,
- The right recovery midfielder and the right outside recovery defender move forward and into position toward the left defensive side.

- The center defender, the right recovery outside midfielder, and the right recovery outside defender must continue to fill the spaces created by the forward progress of the left outside recovery defender and midfielder.
- The center defender gradually slides into position behind the attacking left outside recovery defender and left outside recovery midfielder.
- This defensive adjustments by the center defender, the right recovery outside midfielder, and the right recovery outside defender is most important and must continually be stressed to the team.
- Without this defensive adjustment there will exist a wide open center for the opponent to play into and exploit your team.
- The two attackers are simply actors in this play and continue move their position all the way to midfield and to the defensive left outside.

FIGURE 14:

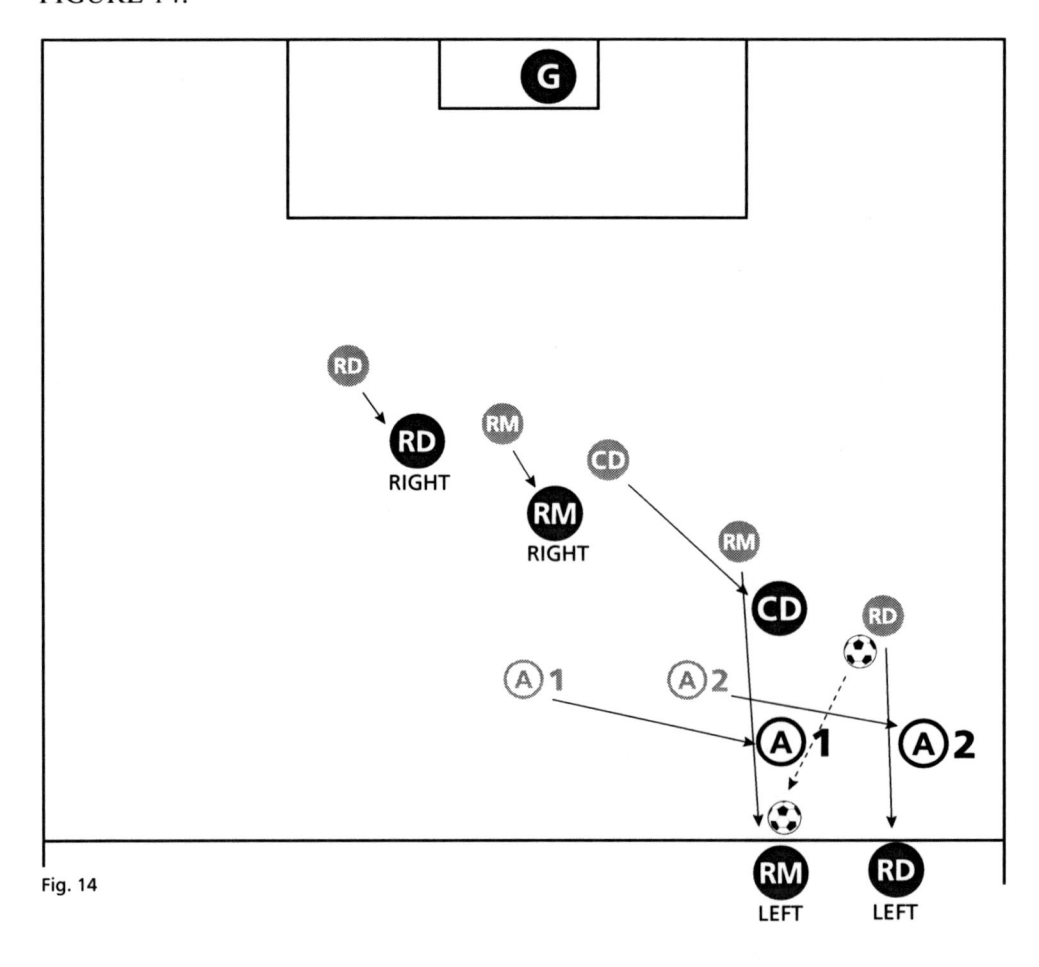

Fig. 14

- As soon as the ball is played by the left recovery midfielder to the left outside recovery defender, the left recovery midfielder makes a sprint up field but halts the forward progress at midfield.
- The left outside recovery defender then passes the ball forward to the sprinting left recovery midfielder who is stopped at midfield.
- The left outside recovery defender sprints forward as soon as the ball is played to the left recovery midfielder but stops at midfield.
- The central defender follows the play forward and also moves into position toward the left outside defensive side.
- The central defender should now be in position to contain any counter attack on the left outside.
- The right recovery midfielder moves forward and into the center position and the right outside recovery defender move forward and toward the left defensive side to be in position to support the center or contain any threat on the right defensive side.
- This defensive adjustments by the center defender, the right recovery outside midfielder, and the right recovery outside defender is most important and must continually be stressed to the team.
- Without this defensive adjustment there will exist a wide open center for the opponent to play into and exploit your team.
- The two attackers are simply actors in this play and continue to move their position all the way to midfield and to the defensive left outside. They will finish this stage of transition play on the left defensive outside. Their position is between the left outside recovery defender—left recovery midfielder and the central defender.

FIGURE 15:

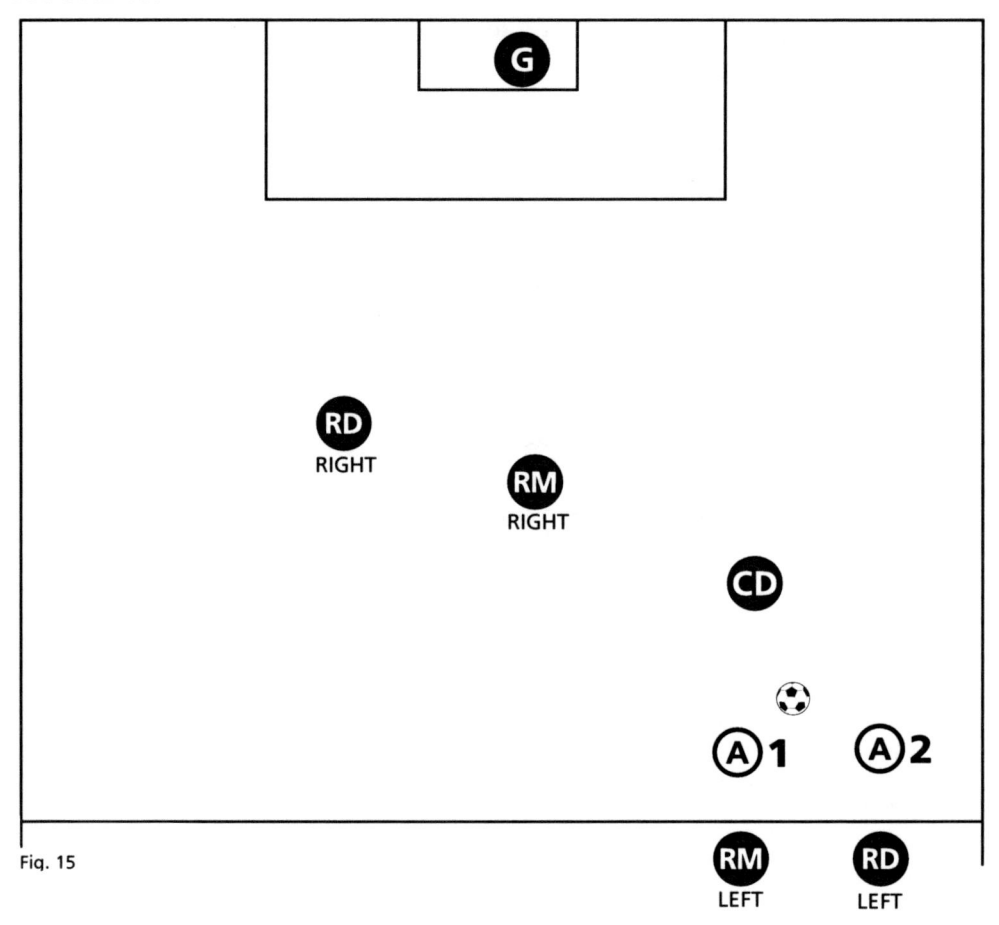

Fig. 15

- Formation after the defensive team has transitioned forward and to the outside from the defensive third into the middle third and finishing this segment at midfield.
- The attack will now be created by the attackers on the left outside.
- The defense will now learn that the recovery run sequence learned in section VII and VIII in YEAR ONE develops exactly the same way on the outside of the playing field as it did in the middle area of the playing field.
- The attackers must keep their attack on the outside so that the outside recovery run can be learned and understood by the players.

FIGURE 16:

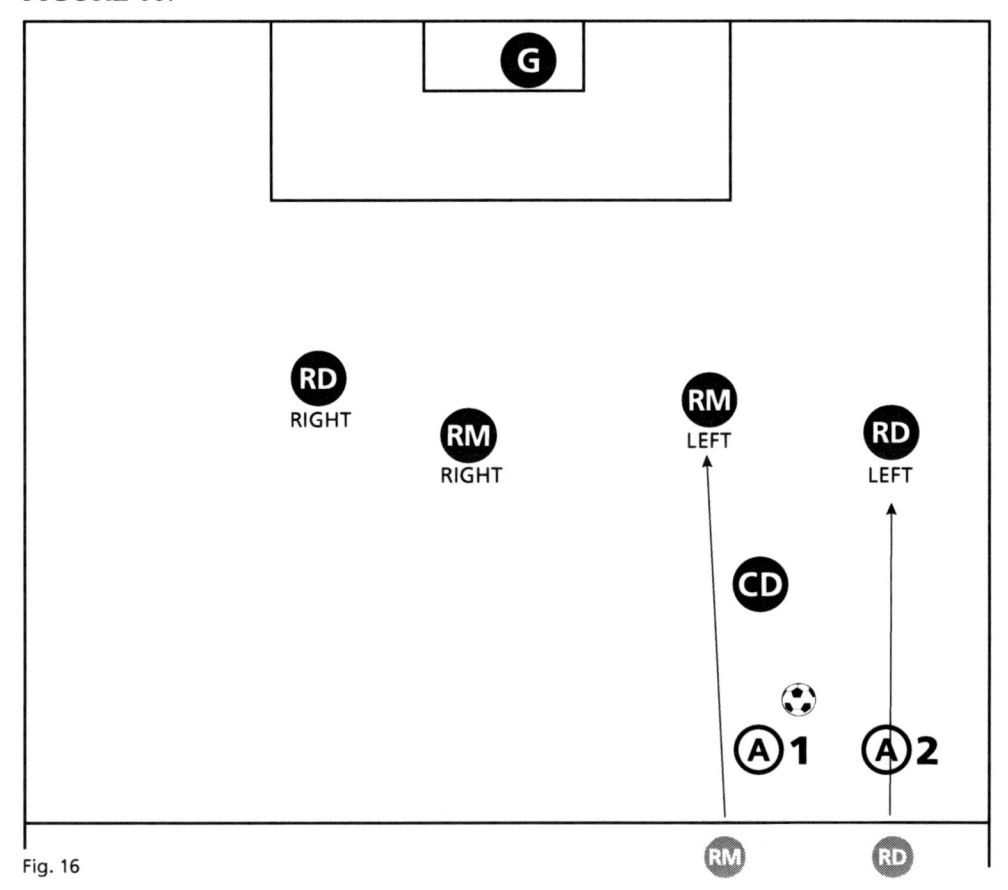

Fig. 16

- The left outside recovery defender and the left recovery midfielder pretend that they have lost the ball to the attackers at midfield.
- The attackers now go on a counter attack on the left outside by passing the ball back and forth between them.
- The center midfielder has been positioned to cover the left defensive outside when the left outside recovery defender and the left recovery midfielder pushed forward and attacked up the left outside.
- The center midfielder will now contain the two attackers by retreating and not attacking the ball.
- The left outside recovery defender and left recovery midfielder make their recovery runs back into a defensive support position behind the containing center midfielder.

FIGURE 17:

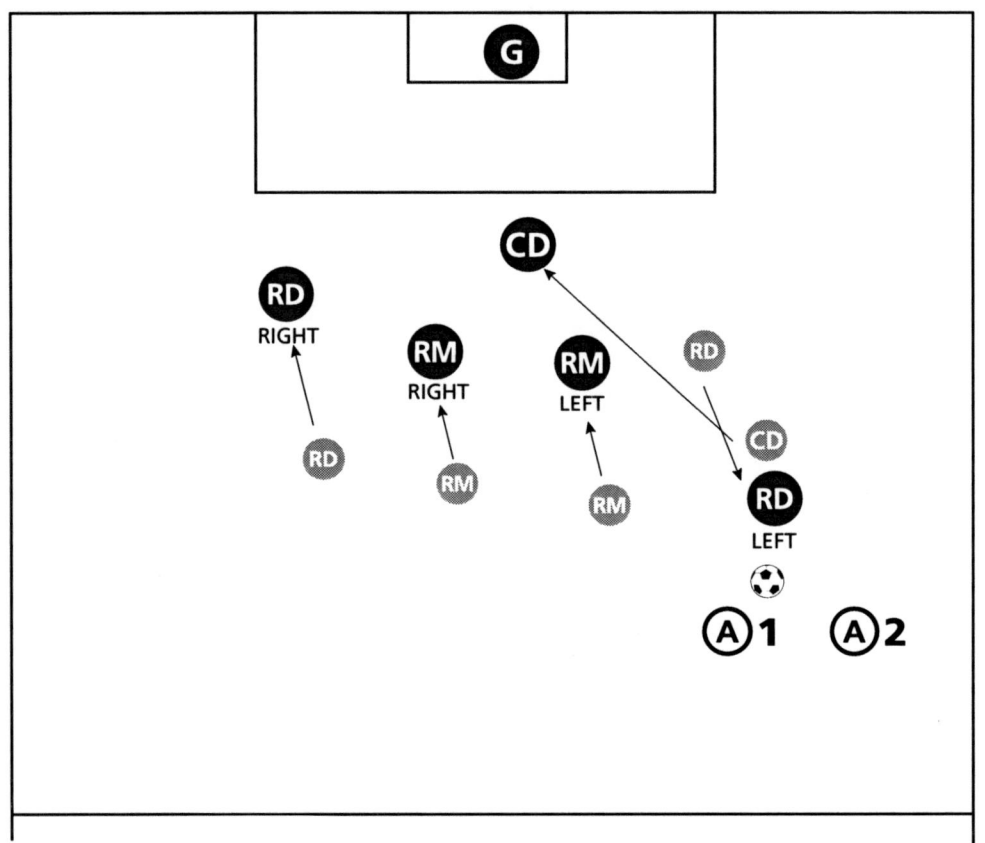

Fig. 17

- Once the left outside recovering defender is in the support position, this defender must release the central defender and take the position between the attacker as the contain defender.
- The central defender, once freed by the left outside recovery defender, retreats to take a position in the center of the field.
- The left outside recovery defender keeps containment of the attackers by retreating until the entire defense is once again set in the defensive part of the playing field thereby creating support for the containing defender.
- The right recovery midfielder and the right outside recover defender can now begin to move towards the right defensive outside.

FIGURE 18:

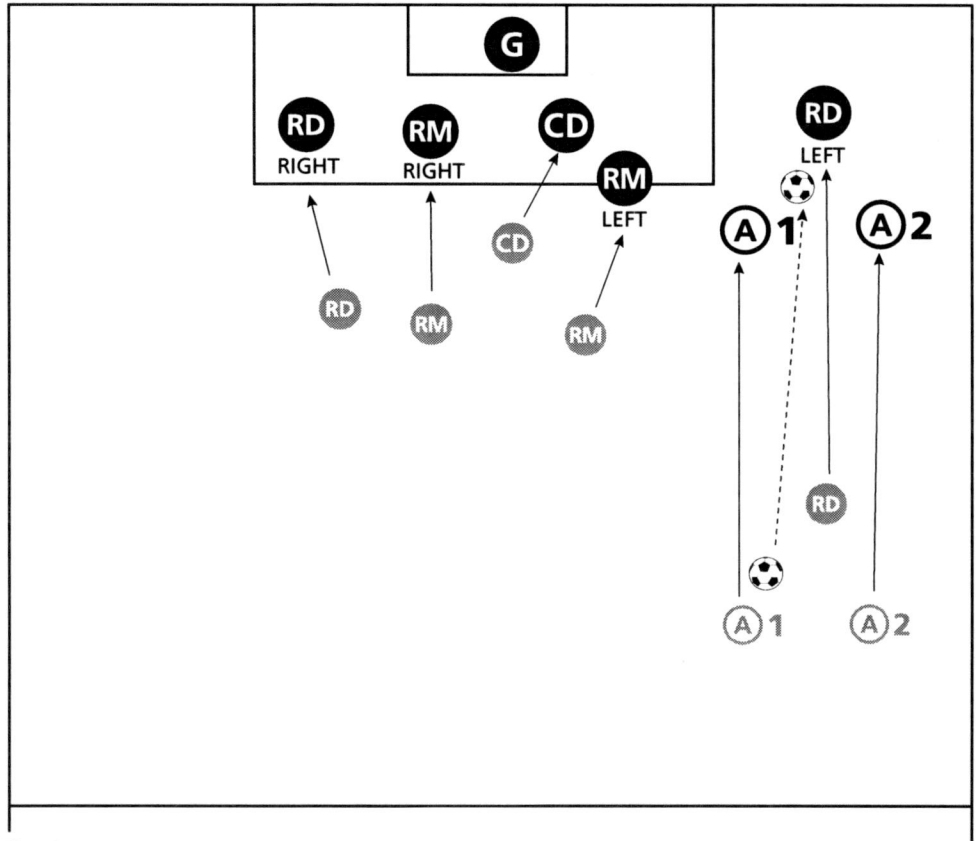

Fig. 18

- Once the attack and the recovery have reached all the way back into defense, the play is ended.

NOTE:

The players have now been taught how:
- Recovery from the attack coming up the middle of the playing field.
- Take possession of the ball.
- Begin a counter attack by playing the ball to the outside with the outside recovery defender and midfielder attacking forward with give-and-go passes.
- The remaining defenders move forward cautiously and towards the outside thereby defending the empty areas created by the attacking outside recovery defender and recovery midfielder.
- Contain the counter attack by the attackers.
- Recovery runs on the outside by the outside recovery defender and recovery midfielder.

- Outside recovery defender takes over the role of containment thereby releasing the central defender to take position back in the center of the playing field.
- **This sequence from the recovery run to transitioning to the LEFT defensive side all the way to midfield, must now be repeated until the players on the team understand how to execute this transition segment.**

C. TRANSITION PLAY UNINTERRUPTED TO THE RIGHT THEN TO LEFT DEFENSIVE SIDES:

1. The team plays the transition sequence beginning with the center recovery run, to the right defensive side, and recovers on the right defensive side as described in the previous section A. Figures 1 through 8.

2. Once the sequence has reached back to the right defensive side of the penalty area, instead of beginning left side transition with the center recovery run, the attackers pretend that they have lost possession of the ball and pass the ball back to the center defender.

3. The center defender begins the transition sequence to the left defensive side of the field by passing the ball to the left outside recovery defender as described in the previous section B. Figures 9 through 17.

4. Once the sequence has reached back to the left defensive side of the penalty area, instead of beginning right side transition with the center recovery run, the attackers pretend that they have lost possession of the ball and pass the ball back to the center defender.

5. The center defender begins the transition sequence to the right defensive side of the field by passing the ball to the right outside recovery defender as described in the previous section A. Figures 1 through 8.

6. The transition is now played uninterrupted between the right defensive side and the left defensive side.

EMPHASIZE:
- *Recovery runs are an important element of the sport of soccer.*
- *Players learn to organize recovery runs on the outside of the playing area and not just in the middle of the field.*
- *Defenses learn to adjust their positioning while under constant motion.*
- *In the defensive third of the field it is most important to play the ball out of the center thereby avoiding problems in the event of a breakdown.*

V. 7V7 TRANSITION PLAY FROM THE MIDDLE THIRD INTO THE ATTACKING THIRD OF THE FIELD:

1. Once the players can transition fluidly between the right and the left defensive side, the transition from the middle third into the attacking third of the field is now demonstrated and taught.

2. To finish on the opponent's goal, it is necessary for a team to know how to bring superior numbers forward. Relying on one or two forwards to handle the scoring is not a good tactical approach. Youth teams have a tendency to believe that they only need to train forwards to score. To have a better chance to score on an opponent the whole team must be brought into the attack.

FIGURE 1:

Using the previous section IV. Figures 1 through 5, start with the recovery run sequence, play ball to the right defensive outside, begin attack by the recovery defensive team with a give and go play between the right out side recovery defender and the right recovery midfielder, and move forward to midfield.

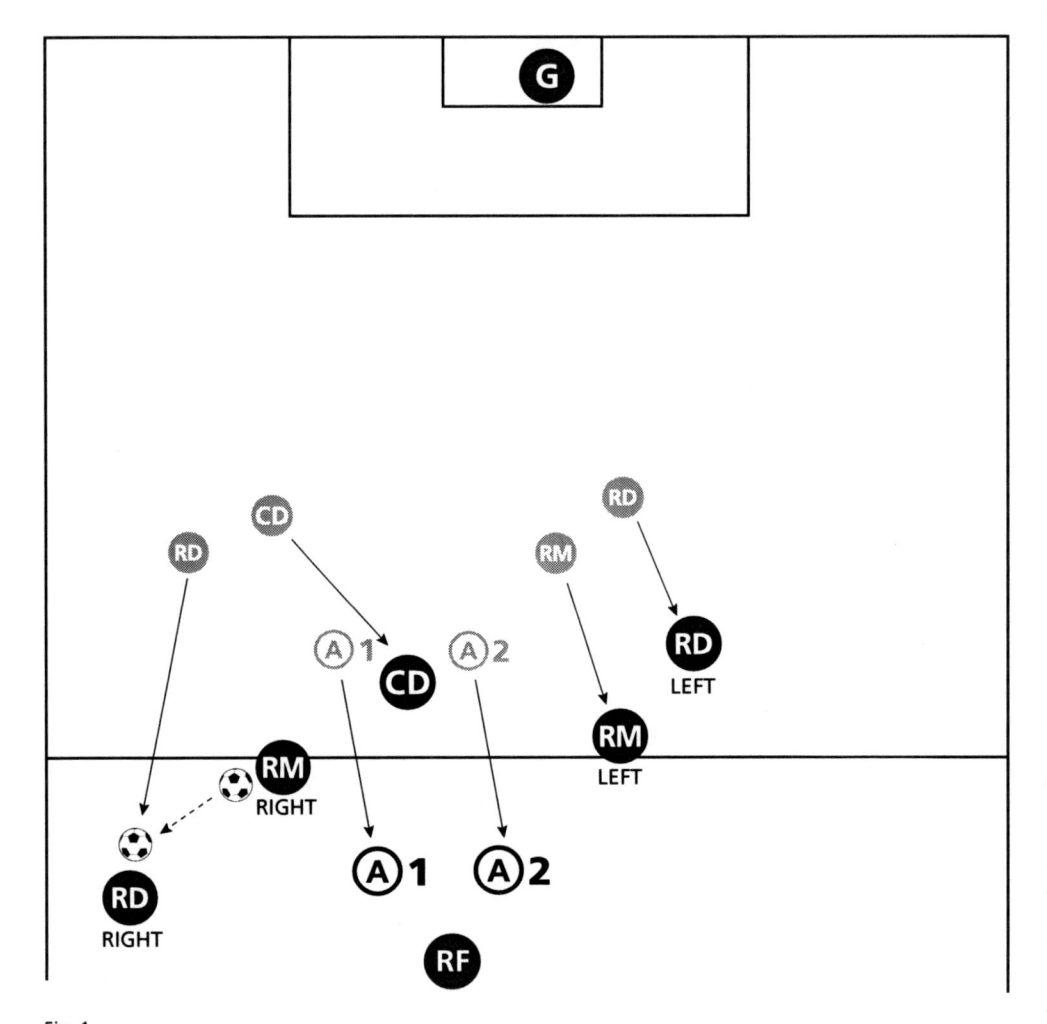

Fig. 1

- As soon as the ball is played by the right outside recovery defender to the right recovery midfielder, the right outside recovery defender makes a sprint up field, to the outside, and across midfield.
- The central defender and left recovery outside defender move towards midfield and adjust towards the right defensive side.
- The left recovery midfielder adjusts to midfield and towards the right defensive side
- The recovery forward has now advanced to the top of middle third of the field.
- The attack by the recovery defense has now crossed midfield and is moving forward towards the opponent's goal.
- The opposing attackers keep moving back, to the right defensive side, and all the way to the opponent's box area.

FIGURE 2:

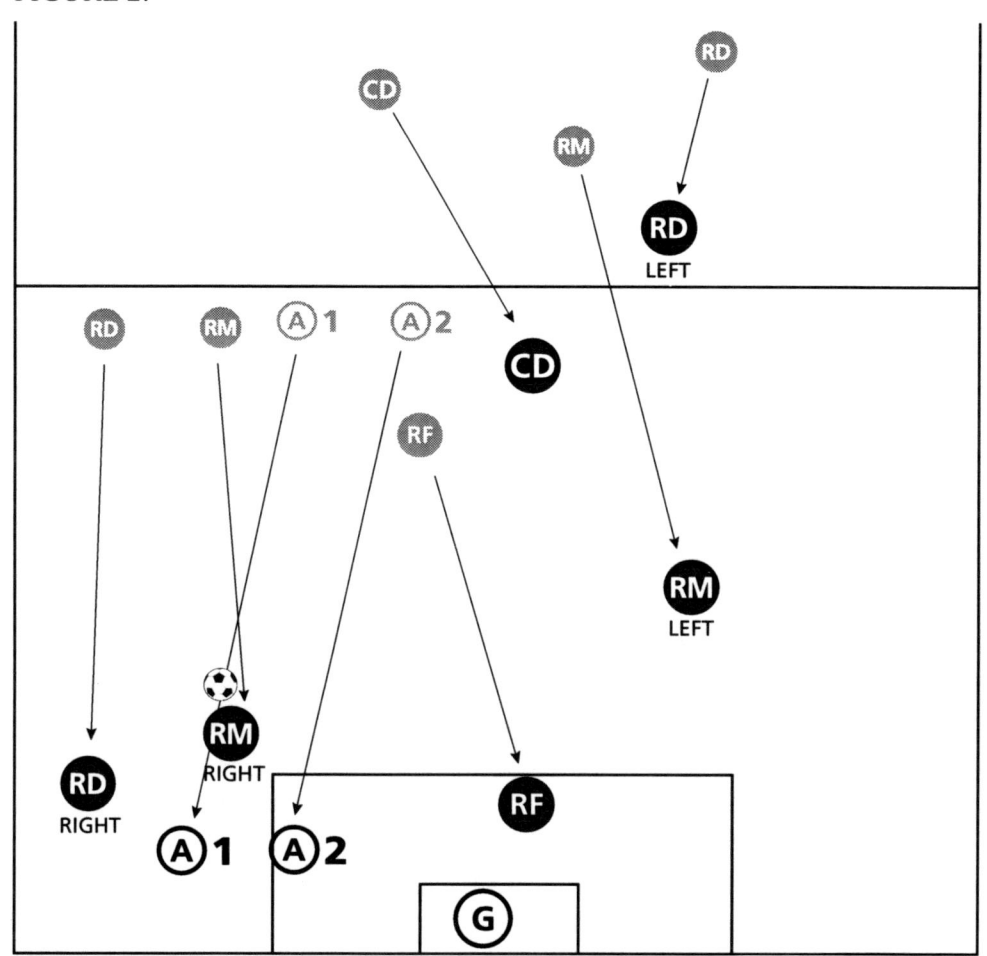

Fig. 2

- As soon as the ball is played by the right outside recovery defender to the right recovery midfielder, the right outside recovery defender makes a sprint forward to receive the ball from the right recovery midfielder.
- The right outside recovery defender and the right midfielder continue this give-and-go passing play until the right outside recovery defender has reached the position outside the penalty area and almost to the goal line.
- Once the right outside recovery defender has reached this desired position, the right outside midfielder passes the ball to the right outside recovery defender then moves inside to take a position on top of the box and near the corner of the box.
- The center defender moves across midfield and takes up a position towards the center of the field between the top of the opponent's box and the midfield line.
- The left midfielder moves forward to take up a position near the top of the opponent's box and left from the center of the field.
- The left outside recovery defender takes up a position at the midfield line but to the left of the center of the field.
- The right outside recovery defender has been taught to go onto the attack and thereby the attacking recovery defensive team has now brought numbers into the attack.
- The midfielders are in position to attack the goal with the left recovery midfielder in position to pick up any ball played into the backside or be the first to contain any counter attack.
- The recovery forward has advanced into the goal area to threaten any ball played into the center of the goal.
- The central defender is brought forward enough to become a scoring threat yet is in position to defend a counter attack.
- The left outside defender is in position to be the last defender back to contain any counter attack and buy time for the rest of the defenders to make their recovery runs back into defensive positions as was taught in YEAR ONE with the recovery runs.
- The two attackers move forward and take up an outside position.

FIGURE 3:

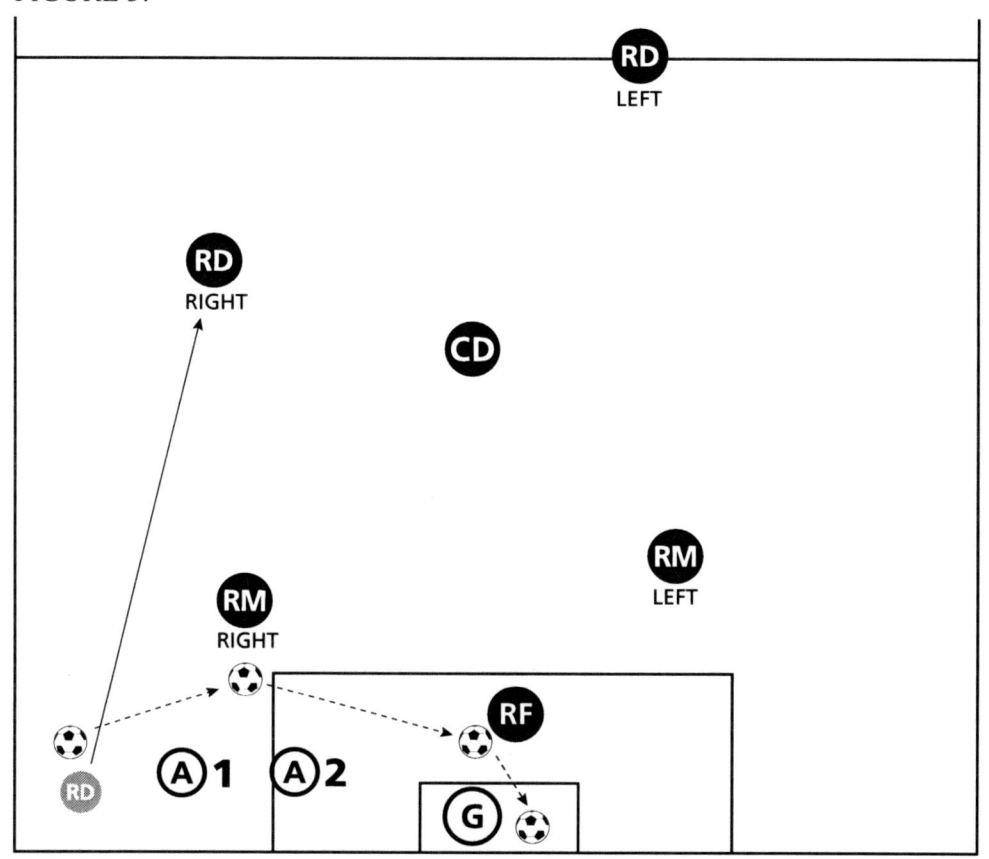

Fig. 3

- The right outside recovery defender plays the ball back to the right recovery midfielder who is positioned on top of the box near the corner of the box.
- Once the right outside recovery defender has made the pass back to the right outside midfielder, the right outside recovery defender must make a recovery run and take position near midfield.
- The right recovery midfielder makes a pass to the recovery forward who takes a shot on goal.

EMPHASIZE:

- *The players have executed a set attacking play by transitioning on the defensive right side from the defensive third of the field, through the middle third of the field, and all the way to the attacking third of the field then finishing with a shot on the opponent's goal.*
- *The players have learned how to overload every third of the field with their own players on the defensive right side.*

- *The players have learned how to have a player in position in every part of the field on the defensive right side to either advance the attack or contain a counter attack.*

FIGURE 4:

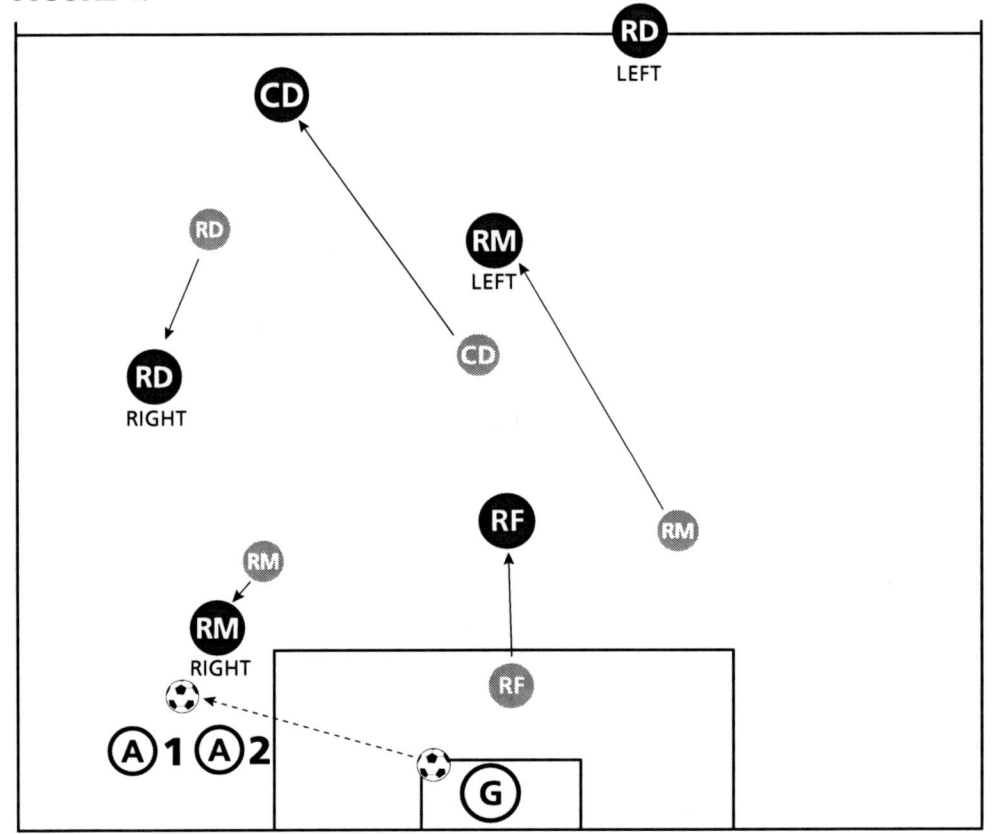

Fig. 4

- The attacking team will begin a counter attack on the right defensive side.
- The goalie plays the ball to the attackers who had taken a position on the outside.
- The attackers are there to teach the recovery defense how to recover the full length of the field.
- The attacker will advance by passing the ball back and forth.
- The right recovery midfielder will advance and contain the two attackers.
- The outside right recovery defender will advance to move into position to be in support of the right recovery midfielder.
- The central defender recovers to a position near midfield and to the defensive right outside.
- The left recovery midfielder recovers to a position near midfield and to the center of the field.

- The recovery forward recovers up the middle.
- The defense does not take the ball from the attackers but works only on learning how to retreat and recover into their defensive third of the field.

FIGURE 5:

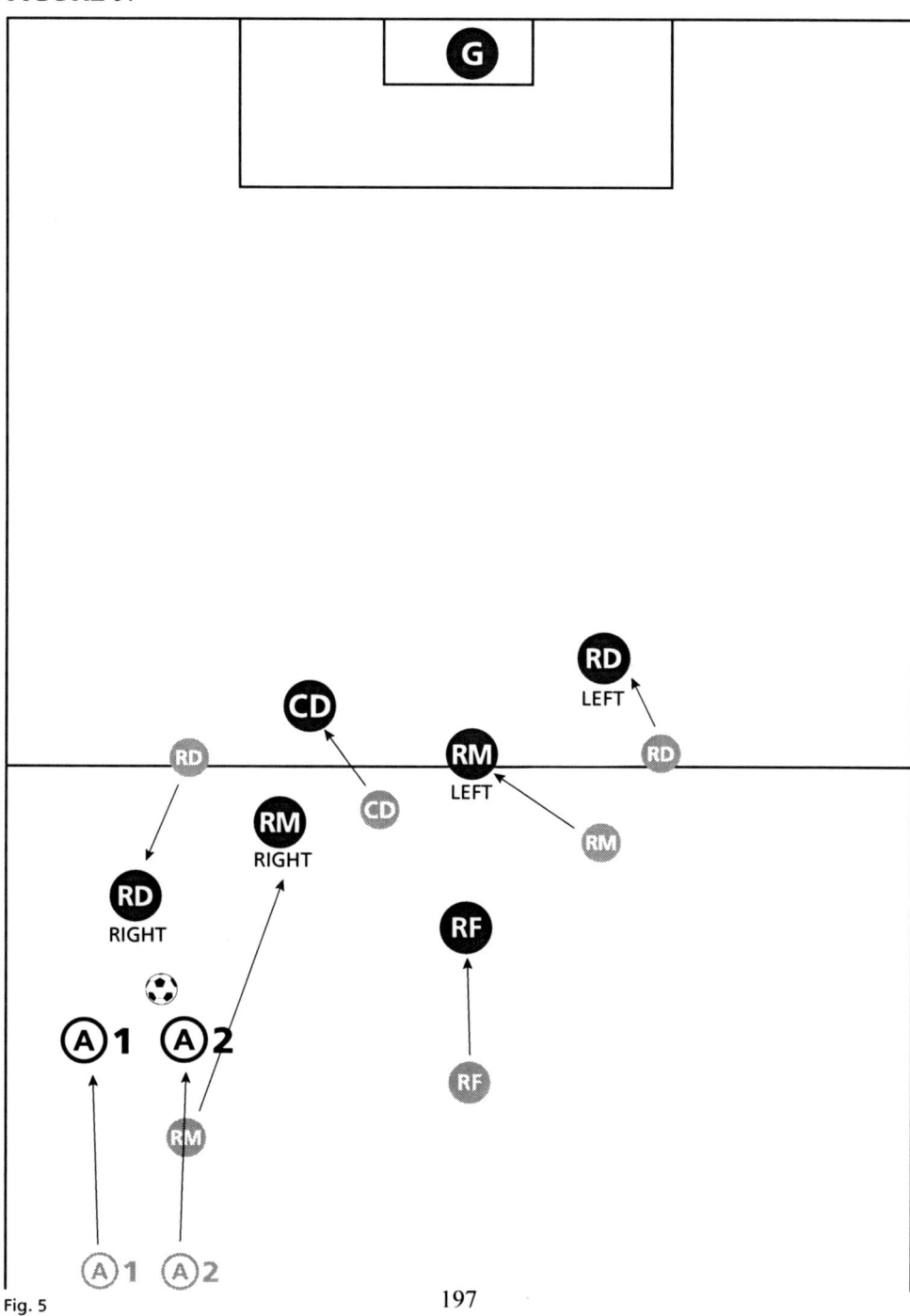

Fig. 5

- As the attackers 1 & 2 advance forward, the right recovery midfielder pretends to have been beaten by the two attackers and allows them to advance past.
- The right recovery midfielder then recovers to midfield.
- The right outside recovery defender now contains the attackers.
- The central defender, the left recovery midfielder, and the left outside recovery defender recover past midfield.

FIGURE 6:

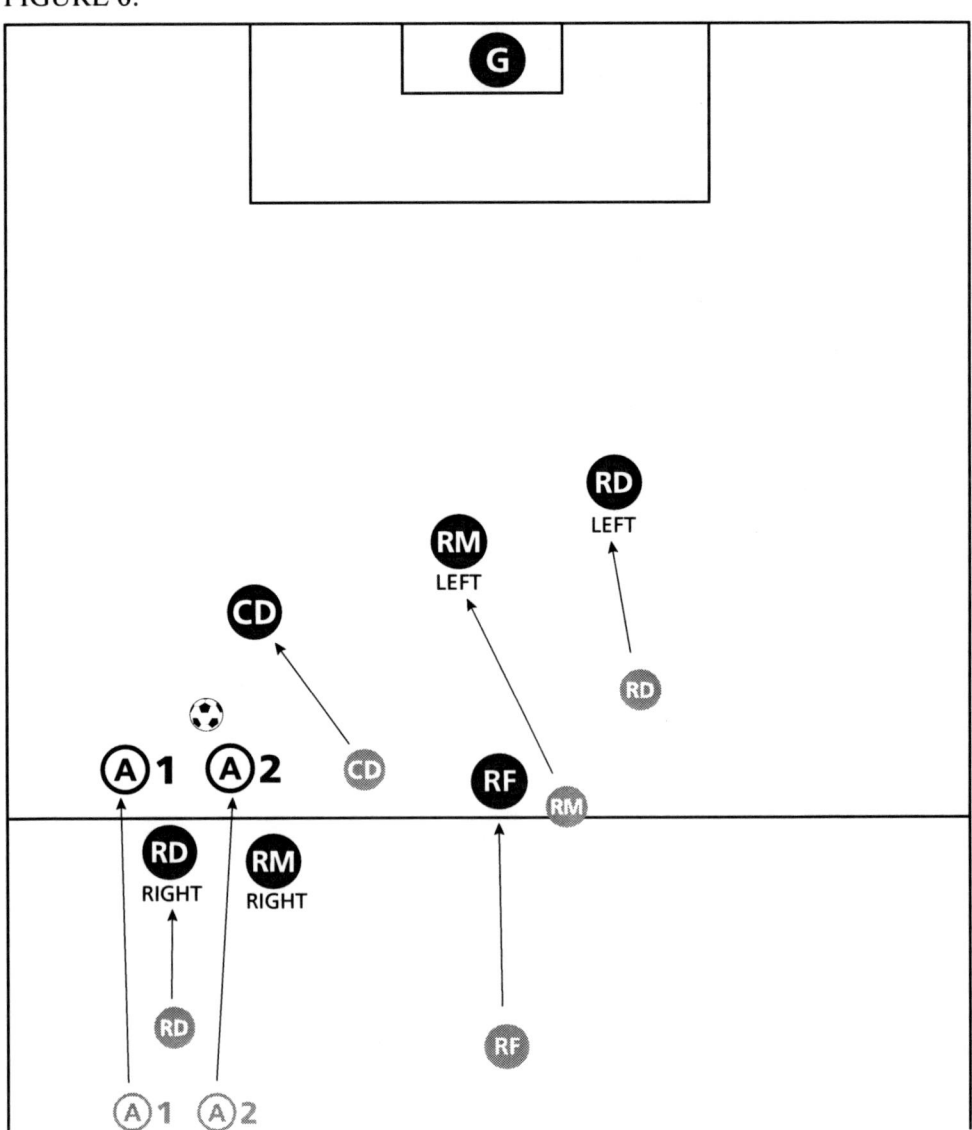

Fig. 6

- As the attackers 1 & 2 advance forward, the right outside recovery defender pretends to have been beaten by the two attackers and allows them to advance past.
- The right outside recovery defender then recovers to midfield.
- The central defender will recover and take up the position as the contain defender in front of the attackers.
- The left recovery midfielder recovers back and to the center.
- The left outside recovery defender recovers back and slightly to the left defensive outside.
- The recovery forward recovers to the center and near the edge of the center circle.
- The remaining recovery will be as previously described in YEAR TWO section IV. A. Figures 6–9.
- Once the sequence has reached back to the right defensive side of the penalty area, instead of beginning the left side transition with the center recovery run, the attackers pretend that they have lost possession of the ball and pass the ball back to the center defender.
- The center defender begins the transition sequence to the left defensive side of the field by passing the ball to the left outside recovery defender as described in YEAR TWO in the previous segment IV. Section B. Figures 9 through 17 and continues the play forward to midfield on the left defensive side.

FIGURE 7:

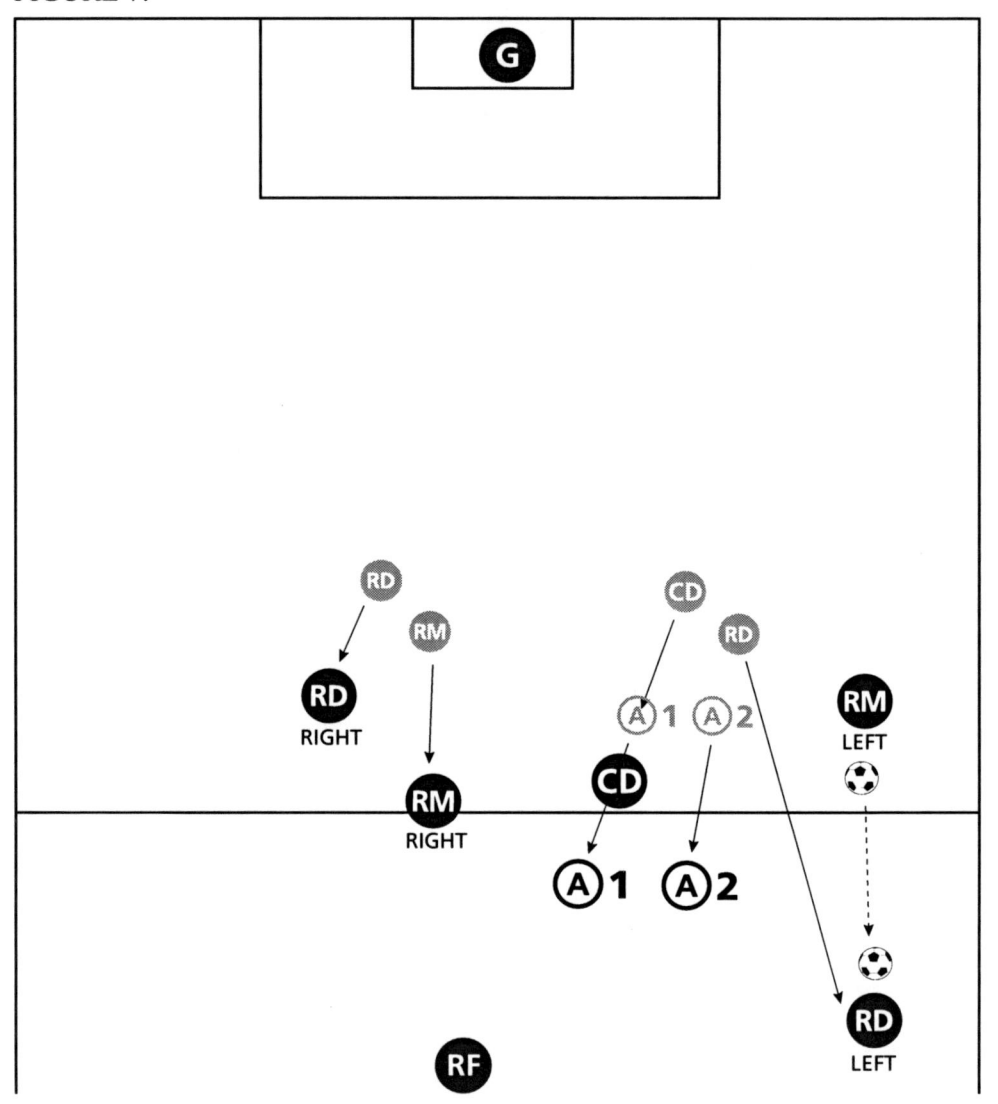

Fig. 7

- As soon as the ball is played by the left outside recovery defender to the left recovery midfielder, the left outside recovery defender makes a sprint up field, to the outside, and across midfield.
- The central defender and right recovery outside defender move towards midfield and adjust towards the left defensive side.
- The right recovery midfielder adjusts to midfield and towards the left defensive side
- The recovery forward has now advanced to the top of the middle third of the field.

200

- The attack by the recovery defense has now crossed midfield and is moving forward towards the opponent's goal.
- The opposing attackers keep moving forward, to the left defensive side, and all the way to the opponent's box area.

FIGURE 8:

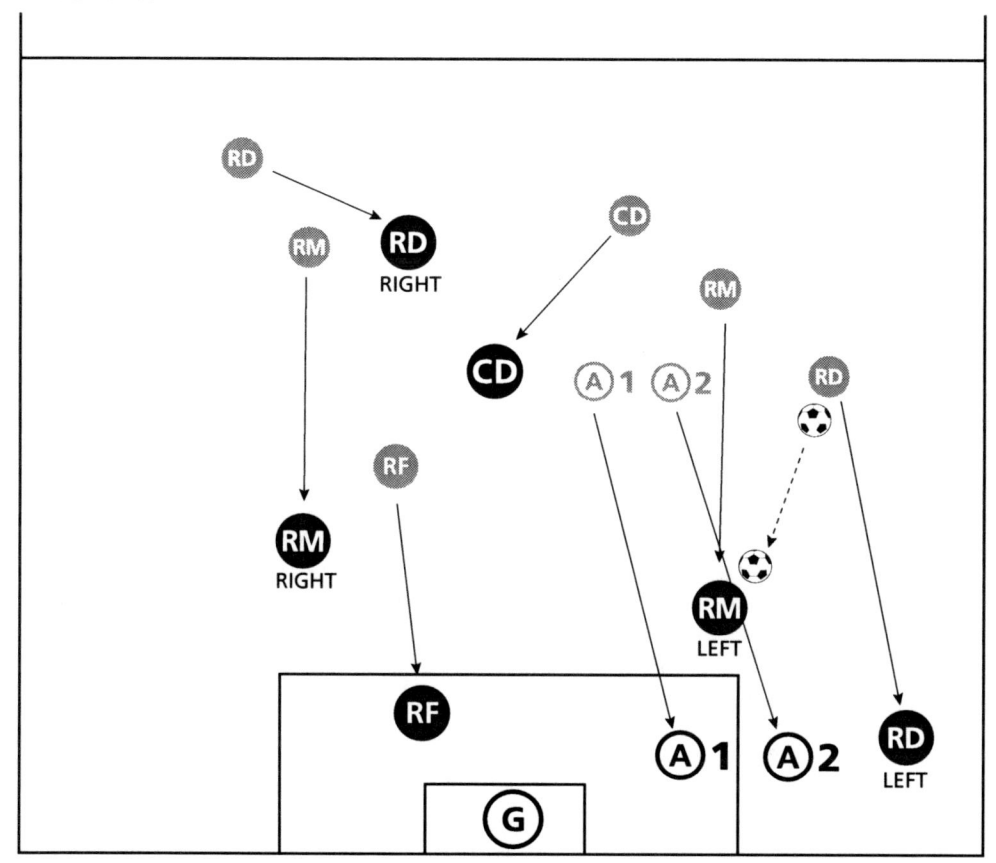

Fig. 8

- As soon as the ball is played by the left outside recovery defender to the left recovery midfielder, the left outside recovery defender makes a sprint forward to receive the ball from the left recovery midfielder.
- The left outside recovery defender and the left midfielder continue this give-and-go passing play until the left outside recovery defender has reached the position outside the penalty area and almost to the goal line.
- Once the left outside recovery defender has reached this desired position, the left outside midfielder passes the ball to the left outside recovery defender then moves inside to take a position on top of the box and near the corner of the box.
- The center defender moves across midfield and takes up a position towards the center of the field between the top of the opponent's box and the midfield line.
- The right midfielder moves forward to take up a position near the top of the opponent's box and right from the center of the field.
- The right outside recovery defender takes up a position at the midfield line but to the right of the center of the field.
- The left outside recovery defender has been taught to go onto the attack and thereby the attacking recovery defensive team has now brought numbers into the attack.
- The midfielders are in position to attack the goal with the right recovery midfielder in position to pick up any ball played into the backside or be the first to contain any counter attack.
- The recovery forward has advanced into the goal area to threaten any ball played into the center of the goal.
- The central defender is brought forward enough to become a scoring threat yet is in position to defend a counter attack.
- The right outside defender is in position to be the last defender back to contain any counter attack and buy time for the rest of the defenders to make their recovery runs back into defensive positions as was taught in YEAR ONE with the recovery runs.
- The two attackers move forward and take up an outside position.

FIGURE 9:

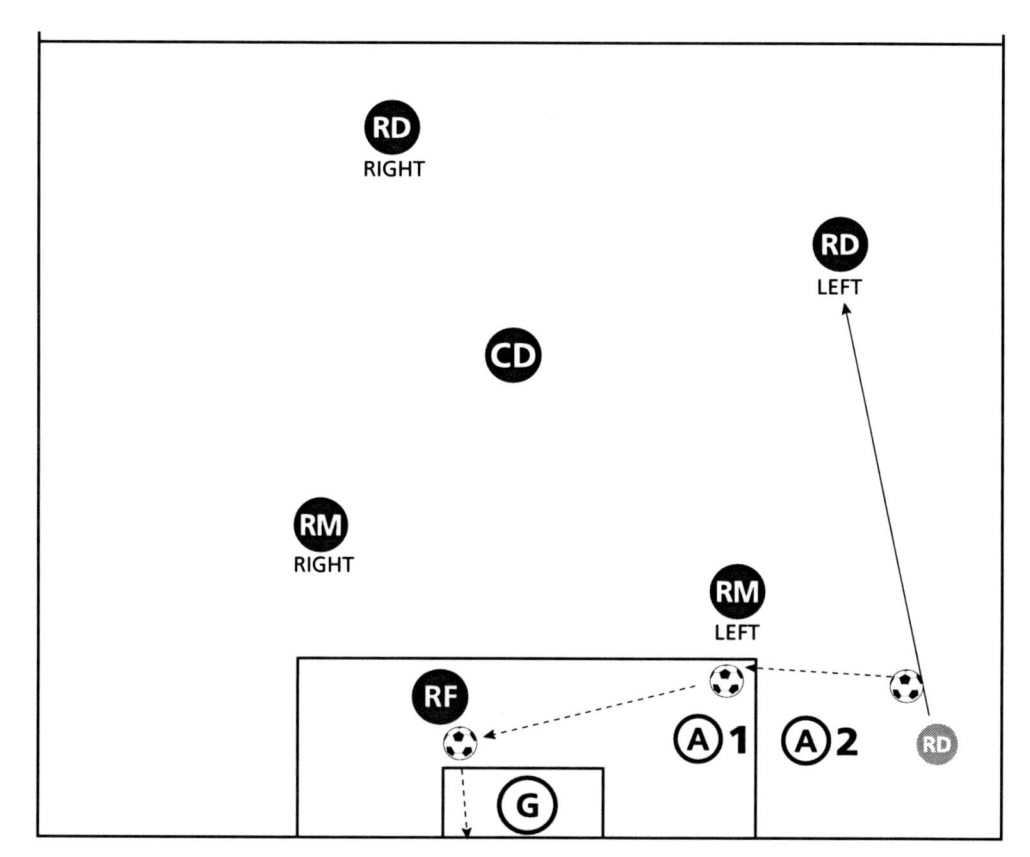

Fig. 9

- The left outside recovery defender plays the ball back to the left recovery midfielder who is positioned on top of the box near the corner of the box.
- Once the left outside recovery defender has made the pass back to the left outside midfielder, the left outside recovery defender must make a recovery run and take position near midfield.
- The left recovery midfielder makes a pass to the recovery forward who takes a shot on goal.

EMPHASIZE:

- *The players have executed a set attacking play by transitioning on the defensive left side from the defensive third of the field, through the middle third of the field, and all the way to the attacking third of the field then finishing with a shot on the opponent's goal.*

- *The players have learned how to overload every third of the field with their own players on the defensive left side.*
- *The players have learned how to have a player in position in every part of the field on the defensive left side to either advance the attack or contain a counter attack.*

FIGURE 10:

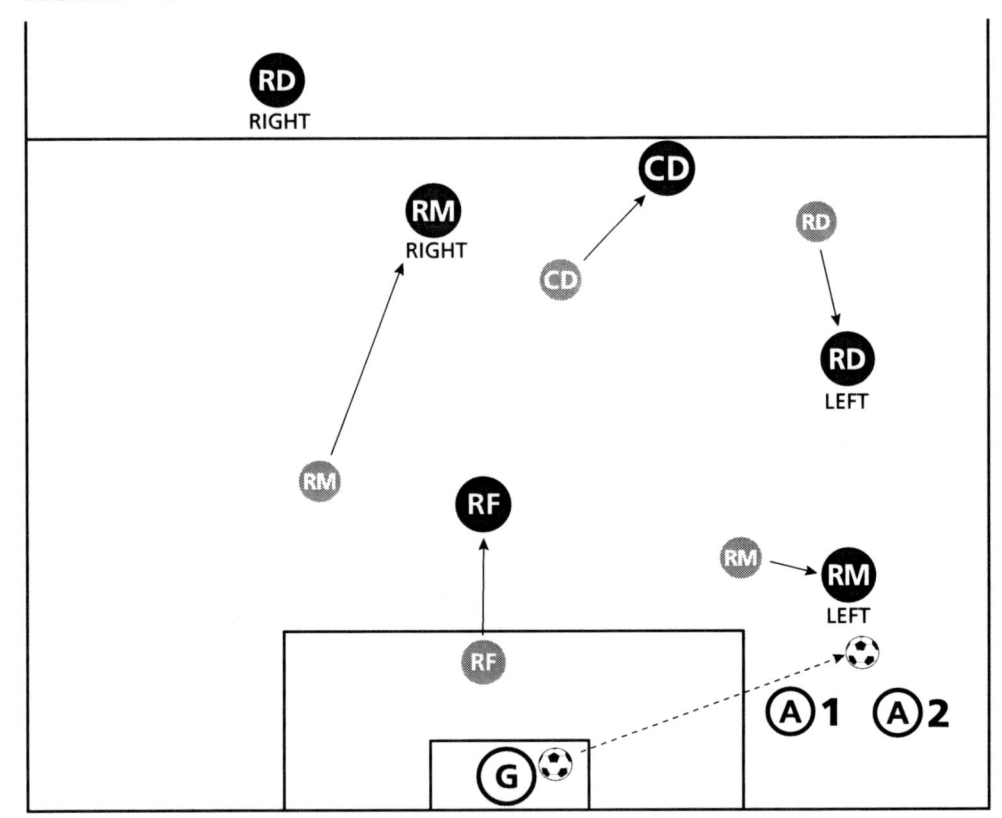

Fig. 10

- The attacking opposing team will begin a counter attack on the left defensive side.
- The goalie plays the ball to the attackers who had taken a position on the outside.
- The attackers are there to teach the recovery defense how to recover the full length of the field.
- The attacker will advance by passing the ball back and forth.
- The left recovery midfielder will advance and contain the two attackers.
- The outside left recovery defender will advance to move into position to be in support of the left recovery midfielder.
- The central defender recovers to a position near midfield and to the defensive left outside.

- The right recovery midfielder recovers to a position near midfield and to the center of the field.
- The recovery forward recovers up the middle.
- The defense does not take the ball from the attackers but works only on learning how to retreat and recover into their defensive third of the field.

FIGURE 11:

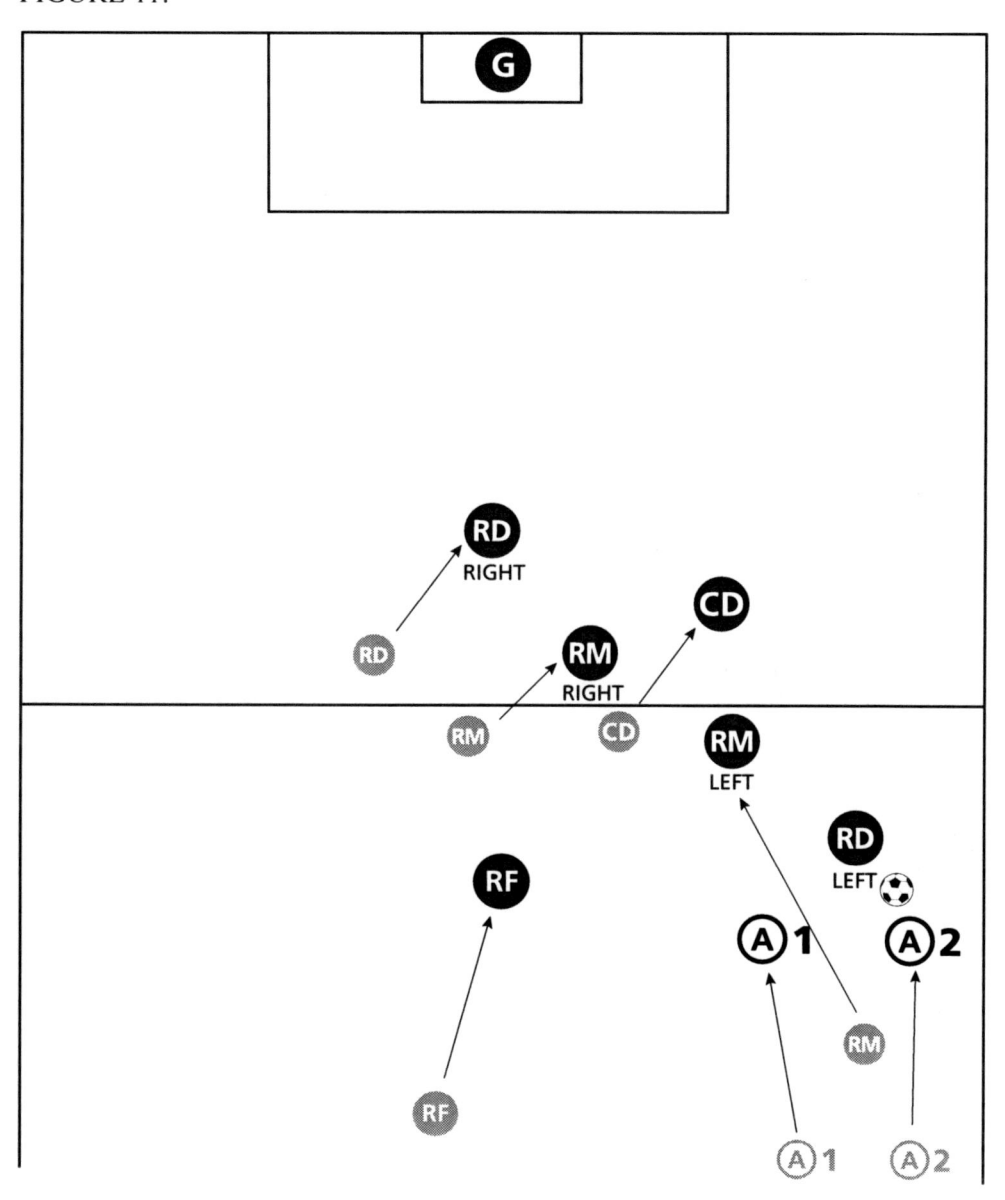

Fig. 11

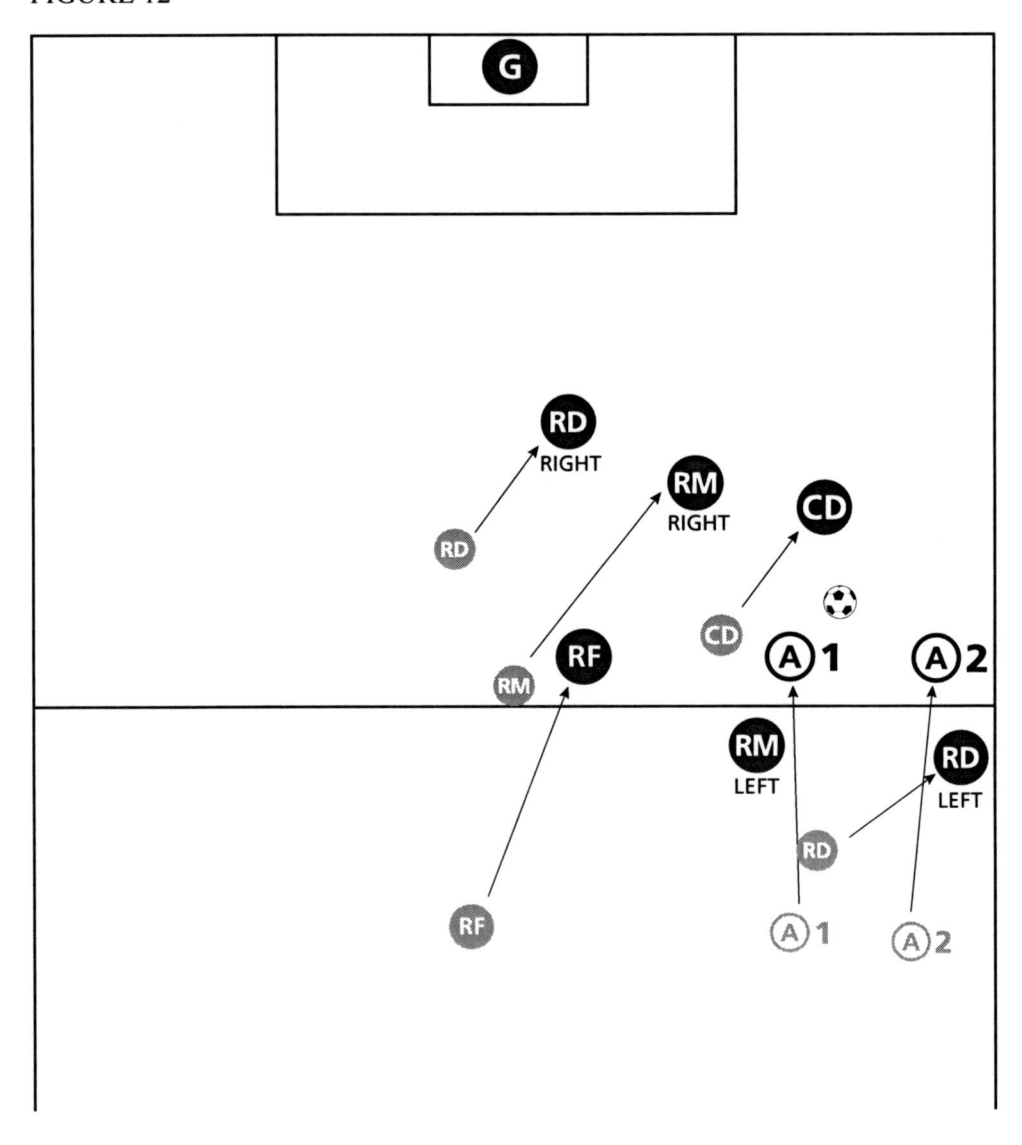

- As the attackers 1 & 2 advance forward, the left recovery midfielder pretends to have been beaten by the two attackers and allows them to advance past.
- The left recovery midfielder then recovers to midfield.
- The left outside recovery defender now contains the attackers.
- The central defender, the right recovery midfielder, and the right outside recovery defender recover past midfield.

FIGURE 12

Fig. 12

- As the attackers 1 & 2 advance forward, the left outside recovery defender pretends to have been beaten by the two attackers and allows them to advance past.
- The left outside recovery defender then recovers to midfield.
- The central defender will recover and take up the position as the contain defender in front of the attackers.
- The right recovery midfielder recovers back and to the center.
- The right outside recovery defender recovers back and slightly to the right defensive outside.
- The recovery forward recovers to the center and near the edge of the center circle.
- The remaining recovery will be as previously described in YEAR TWO section IV. B. Figures 16–18.
- Once the sequence has reached back to the left defensive side of the penalty area, instead of beginning the right side transition with the center recovery run, the attackers pretend that they have lost possession of the ball and pass the ball back to the center defender.
- The center defender begins the transition sequence to the right defensive side of the field by passing the ball to the right outside recovery defender as described in YEAR TWO in the previous segment IV. Section A. Figures 2 through 5 and continues the play forward to midfield on the right defensive side.

NOTE:
1. **The transition is now practiced uninterrupted between the right defensive side and the left defensive side of the field, from the defensive third of the field through the middle third of the field and into the attacking third of the field.**
2. **Once the players know the transition on the outside between the defender and the midfielder, other attacking sequences can be taught to the players such as:**
a. **Playing the ball from one outside of the field to the other outside of the field by passing it through the center midfielder.**

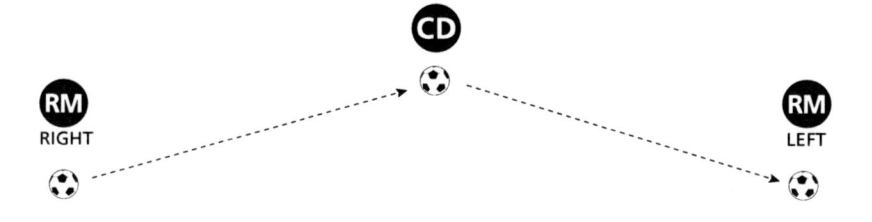

b. A give-and-go sequence can be developed between an outside player and the center defender and the ball can be advanced that way.

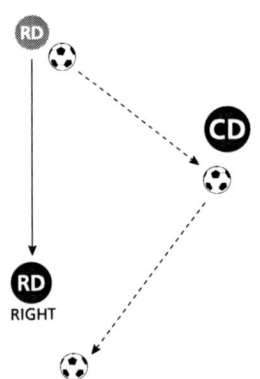

c. A ball can be played to the center defender by an outside player and the center defender can play the ball forward and back outside to an overlapping defender who has move forward into the attack.

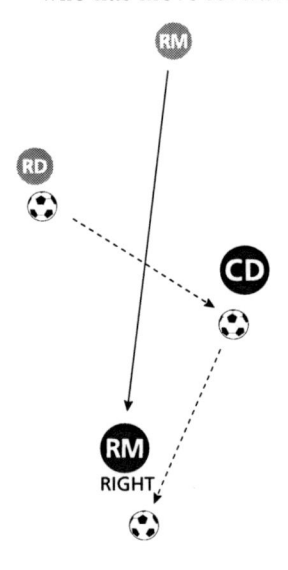

d. Any number of other combinations of playing the ball forward in the transition can be designed and practiced by the team.

e. Whenever a new combination of passing is taught to the team, it must be practiced by the full team who must learn how to advance together as a team.

VI. 9V9 AND 11V11 TRANSITION PLAY FROM DEFENSIVE THIRD INTO MIDDLE THIRD ENDING AT MIDFIELD:

In the second year of development, teams must learn to transition from the defensive third forward in an organized method of play. Instead of simply kicking the ball out and up the middle, players must understand the concept of keeping possession of the ball and developing an attack from the defensive third.

A. TRANSITION TO THE RIGHT DEFENSIVE SIDE:

1. Review Recovery Runs in Section IX of YEAR ONE. Start this transition segment to the defensive right side with the recovery run.

2. TEACH and DEMONSTRATE:

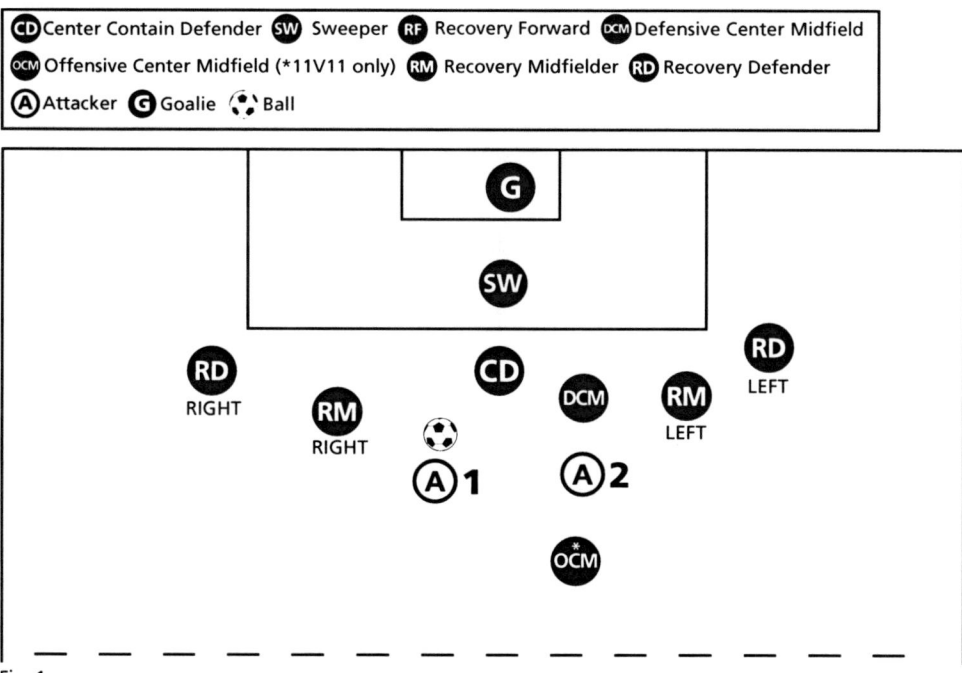

CD Center Contain Defender **SW** Sweeper **RF** Recovery Forward **DCM** Defensive Center Midfield
OCM Offensive Center Midfield (*11V11 only) **RM** Recovery Midfielder **RD** Recovery Defender
A Attacker **G** Goalie ⚽ Ball

Fig. 1 Defensive player positions after defensive players have made their recovery runs.

FIGURE 2:

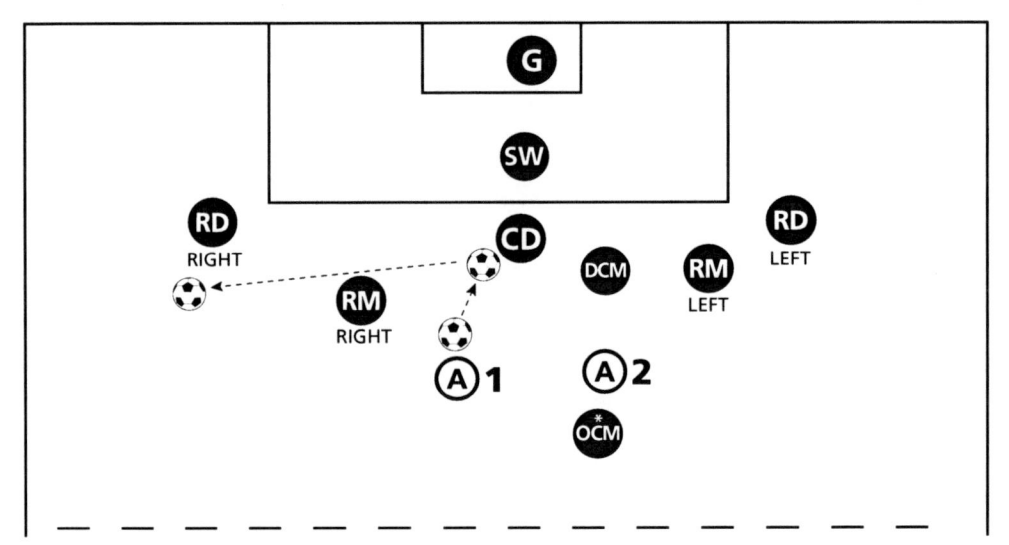

Fig. 2

- Attacker with the ball pretends to have the ball taken away by the center defender by passing it to the center defender.
- Center defender turns and passes the ball to the right outside recovery defender.
- This is a play for the midfielders and defenders to learn how to transition.
- The attackers are merely there to simulate an attack by an opponent and therefore the play is not for the attackers.

FIGURE 3:

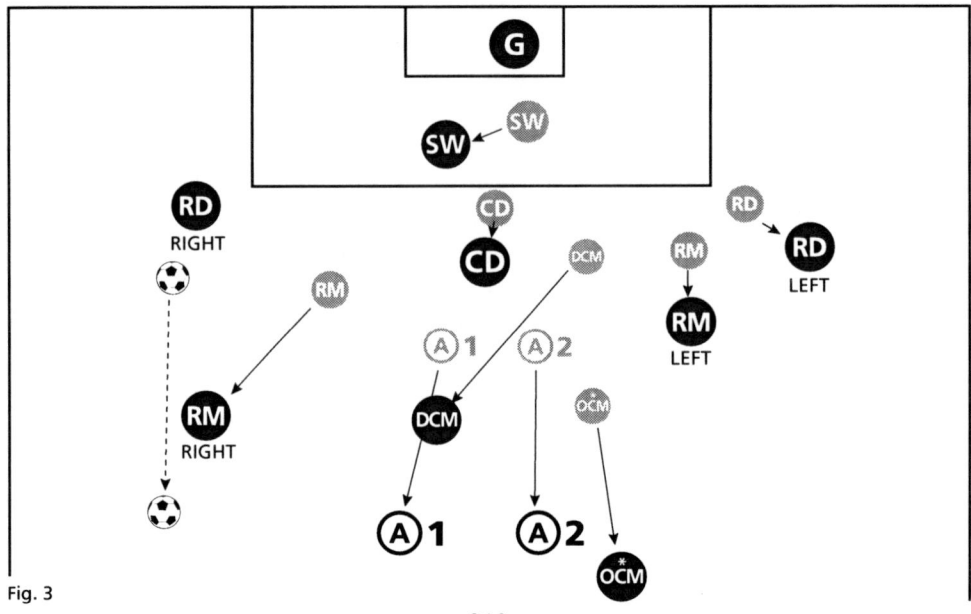

Fig. 3

210

- As soon as the ball is played by the center defender to the right outside recovery defender, the right outside recovery midfielder makes a sprint up field and to the outside.
- The right outside recovery defender passes the ball forward to the sprinting right outside recovery midfielder. This pass must lead the midfielder.
- The central defensive midfielder follows the play forward and also moves into position toward the right defensive side.
- The sweeper moves forward and to the right defensive side
- The central defender holds back to defend the center.
- The left outside recovery midfielder and the left outside recovery defender move forward and into position slightly toward the right defensive side.
- In 11v11 play, the center offensive midfielder moves forward into the middle third of the field.
- The two attackers are simply actors in this play and move their position all the way to midfield and to the defensive right outside.

FIGURE 4

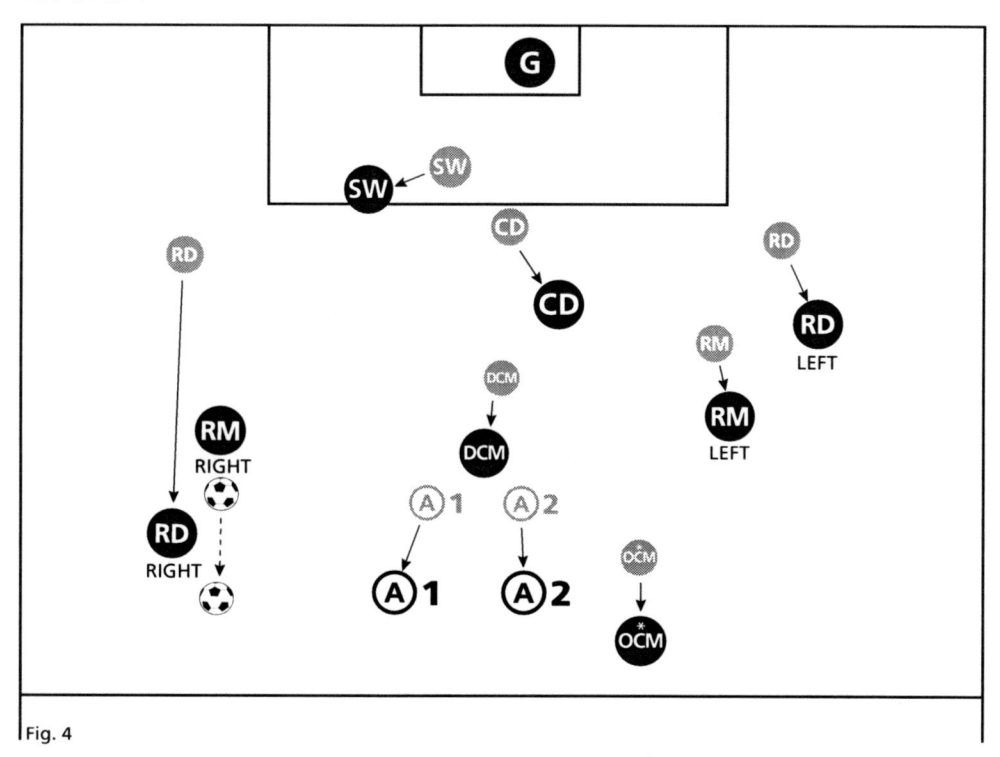

Fig. 4

- As soon as the ball is played by the right outside recovery defender to the right outside recovery midfielder, the right outside recovery defender makes a sprint up field and to the outside.
- The right outside recovery midfielder then passes the ball forward to the sprinting right outside recovery defender. This pass must lead the defender.
- The central defensive midfielder follows the play forward and also moves into position toward the right defensive side.
- The sweeper adjusts to the defensive right and takes up position at the top of the goalie box.
- The central defender continues to hold back to defend the center.
- The left outside recovery midfielder and the left outside recovery defender move forward.
- In 11v11 play, the center offensive midfielder moves forward to midfield.
- The center defensive midfielder gradually slides into position behind the attacking right outside recovery defender and right outside recovery midfielder.
- The two attackers are simply actors in this play and continue to move their position all the way to midfield and to the defensive right outside.

FIGURE 5

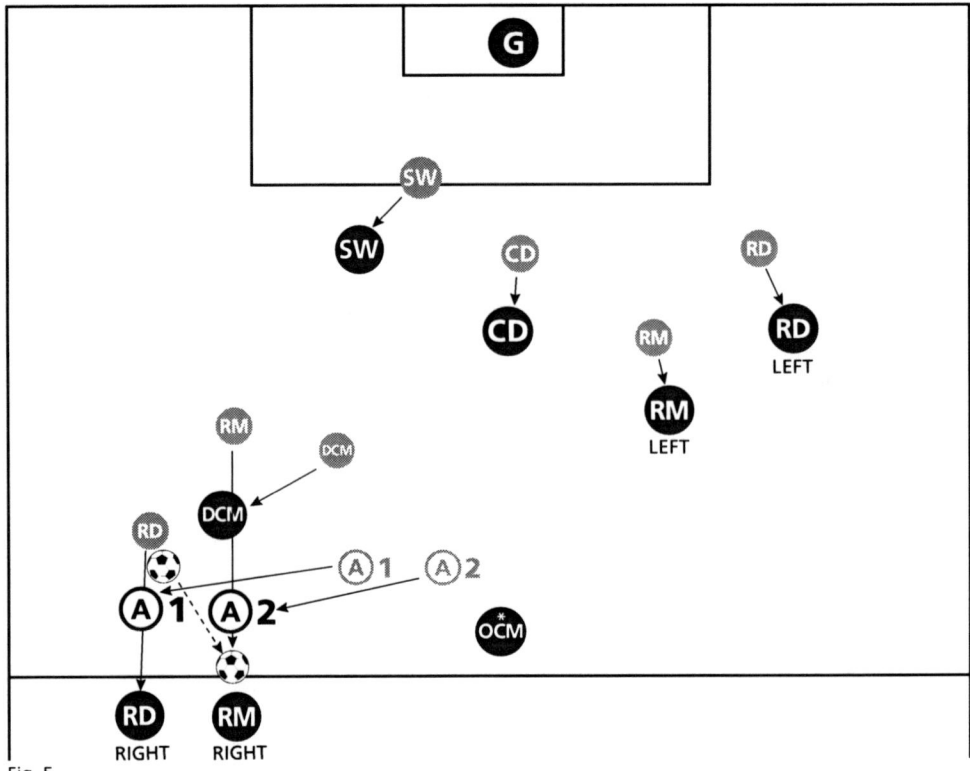

Fig. 5

212

- As soon as the ball is played by the right outside recovery midfielder to the right outside recovery defender, the right outside recovering midfielder makes a sprint up field but halts the forward progress at midfield.
- The right outside recovery defender then passes the ball forward to the sprinting right outside recovery midfielder who is stopped at midfield.
- The right outside recovery defender sprints forward as soon as the ball is played to the right outside recovery midfielder but stops at midfield.
- The center defensive midfielder follows the play forward and also moves into position toward the right outside defensive side.
- The central defensive midfielder should now be in position to contain any counter attack on the right outside.
- The sweeper adjusts to the defensive right and takes up position outside of the goalie box.
- The central defender continues to holds back to defend the center.
- The left recovery midfielder and the left outside recovery defender move forward.
- In 11v11 play, the center offensive midfielder remains positioned at midfield.
- The two attackers are simply actors in this play and continue to move their position all the way to midfield and to the defensive right outside. They will finish this stage of transition play on the right defensive outside. Their position is between the right outside recovery defender—right recovery midfielder and the center defensive midfielder.

FIGURE 6:

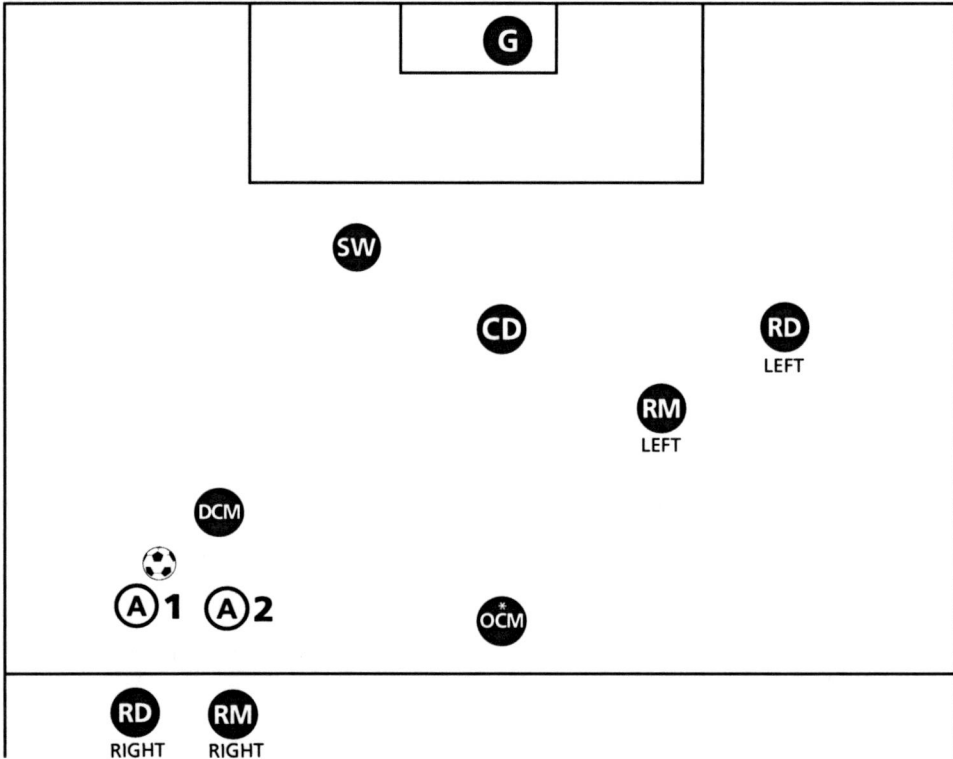

Fig. 6

- Formation after the defensive team has transitioned forward and to the outside from the defensive third into the middle third and finishing this segment at midfield.
- The attack will now be created by the attackers on the right outside.
- The defense will now learn that the recovery run sequence learned in section IX in YEAR ONE develops exactly the same way on the outside of the playing field as it did in the middle area of the playing field.
- The attackers must keep their attack on the outside so that the outside recovery run can be learned and understood by the players.

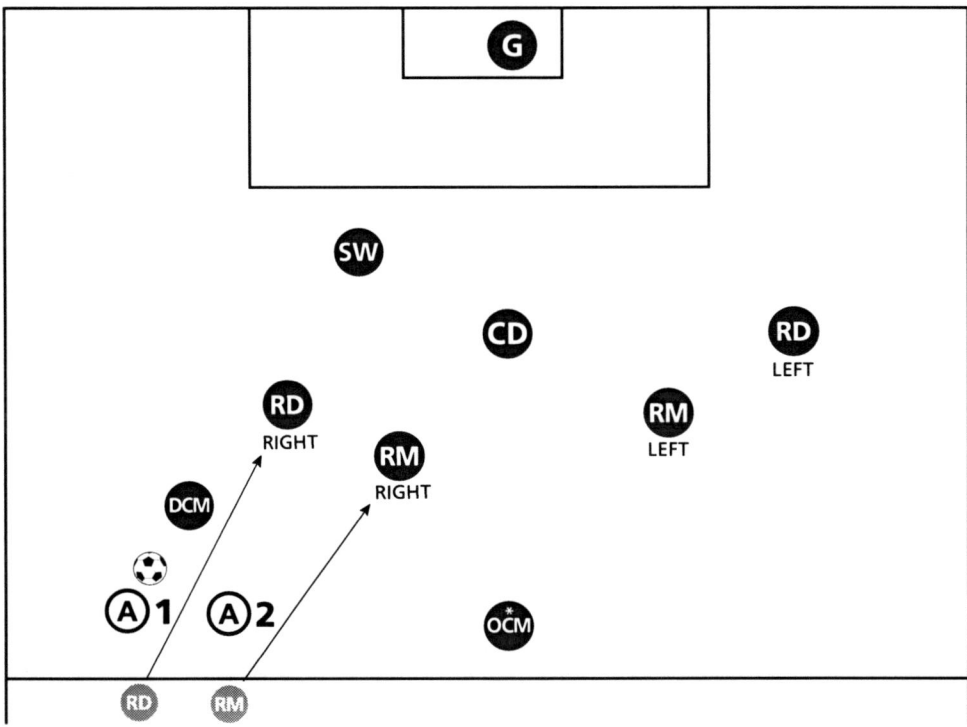

FIGURE 7:

- The right outside recovery defender and the right outside recovery midfielder pretend that they have lost the ball to the attackers at midfield.
- The attackers now go on a counter attack on the right outside by passing the ball back and forth between them.
- The center defensive midfielder has been positioned to cover the right defensive outside when the right outside recovery defender and the right recovery midfielder had pushed forward and had attacked up the right outside.
- The center defensive midfielder will now contain the two attackers by retreating and not attacking the ball.
- The right outside recovery defender and right outside recovery midfielder make their recovery runs back into a defensive support position behind the containing center midfielder.

FIGURE 8:

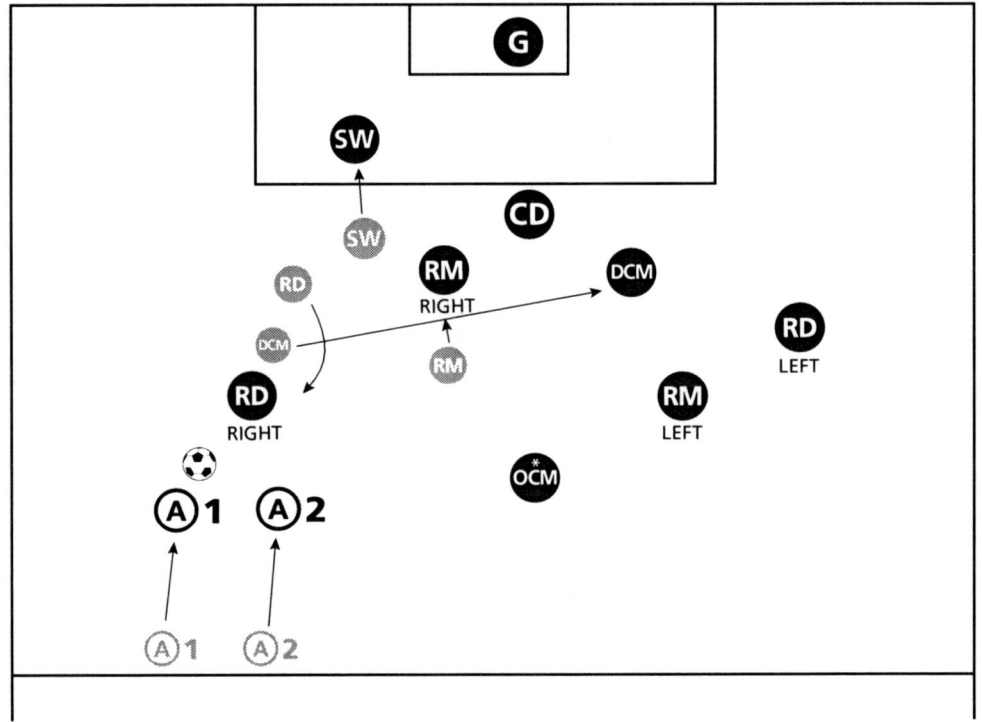

Fig. 8

- Once the right outside recovering defender is in the support position, this defender must release the central defensive midfielder and take the position between the attacker as the contain defender.
- The center defensive midfielder, once freed by the right outside recovery defender, retreats to take a position in the center of the field near the penalty box.
- The right outside recovery defender keeps containment of the attackers by retreating until the entire defense is once again set in the defensive part of the playing field thereby creating support for the containing defender.
- The sweeper adjusts back into the penalty box but keeps position on the right defensive side.
- In 11v11 play, the center offensive midfielder adjusts back into the defensive third but maintains position in the center of the playing field.
- The left outside recovery midfielder and the left outside recover defender can now begin to move towards the left defensive outside while retreating.

FIGURE 9:

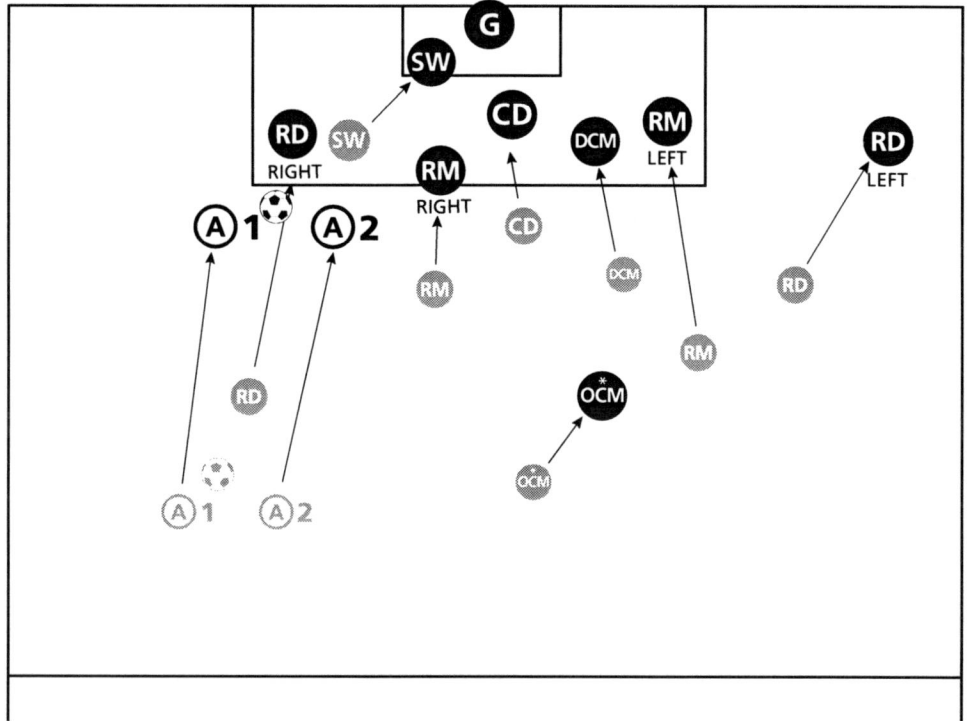

Fig. 9

- Once the attack and the recovery have reached all the way back into defense, the play is ended.

- **This sequence from the recovery run to transitioning to the right defensive side all the way to midfield, must now be repeated until the players on the team understand how to execute this transition segment.**

B. TRANSITION TO THE LEFT DEFENSIVE SIDE;

FIGURE 10:
Start this transition segment to the defensive left side with the recovery run.

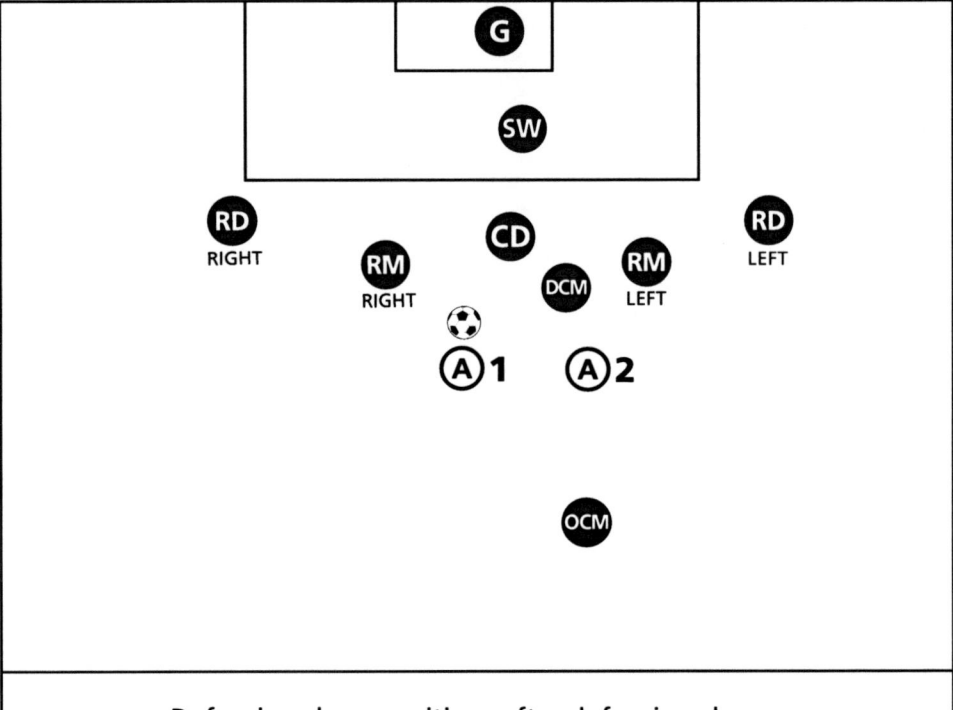

Fig. 10

Defensive player positions after defensive players have made their recovery runs.

FIGURE 11:

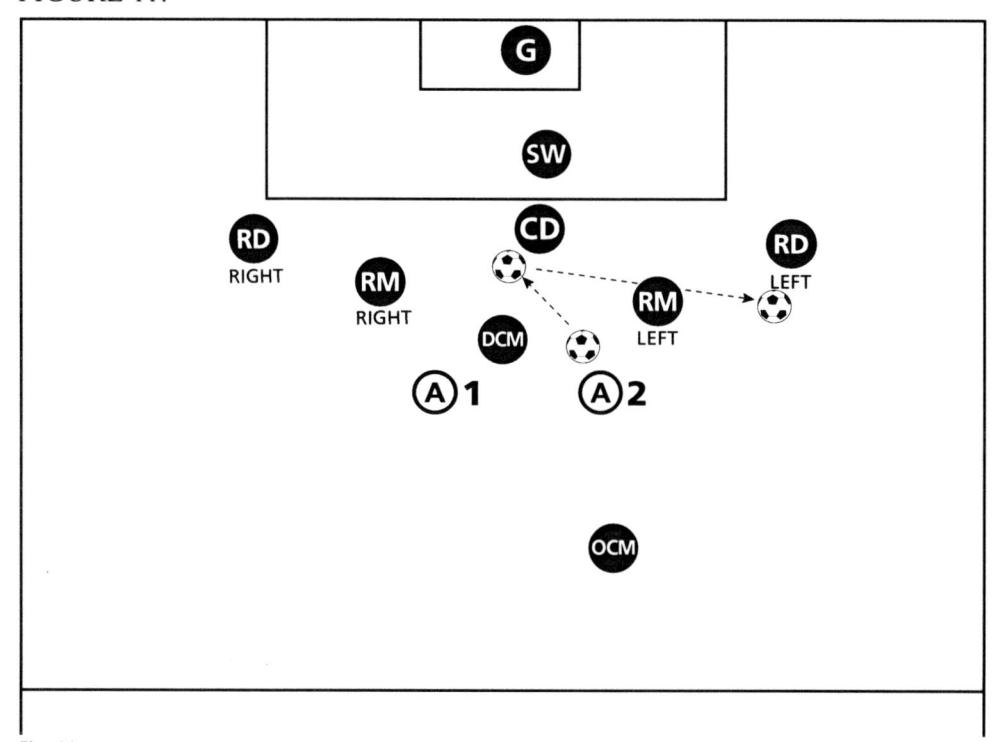

Fig. 11

- Attacker with the ball pretends to have the ball taken away by the center defender by passing it to the center defender.
- Center defender turns and passes the ball to the left outside recovery defender.
- The midfielder and defender learn how to transition up the left defensive side.
- The attackers are merely there to simulate an attack by an opponent and therefore the play is not for the attackers.

FIGURE 12:

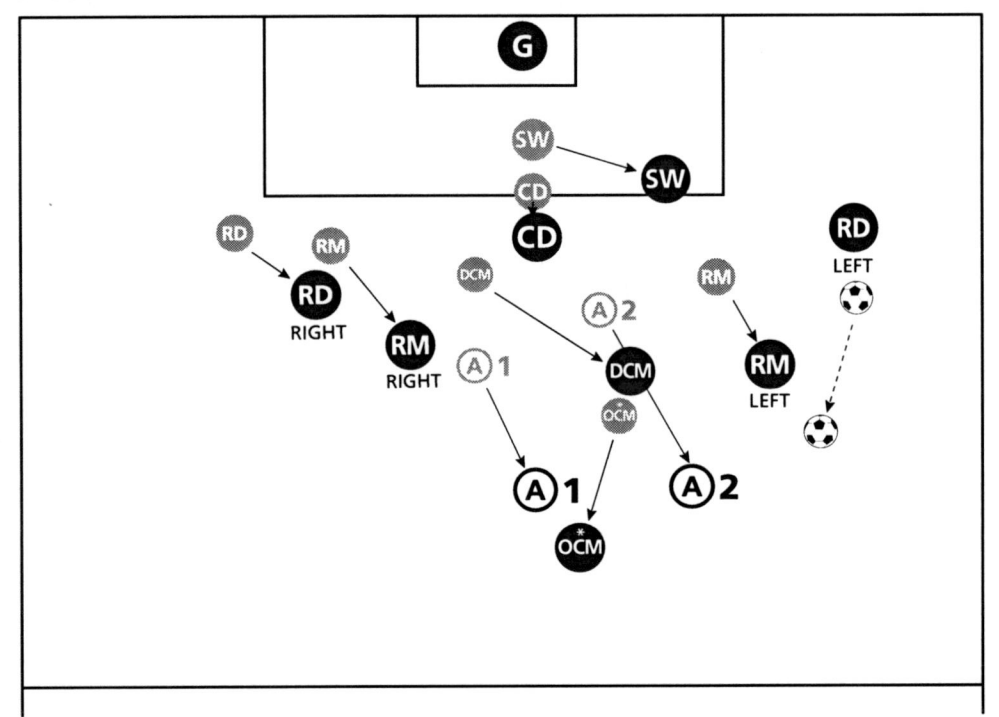

Fig. 12

- As soon as the ball is played by the center defender to the left outside recovery defender, the left outside recovery midfielder makes a sprint up field and to the outside.
- The left outside recovery defender passes the ball forward to the sprinting left outside recovery midfielder. This pass must lead the midfielder.
- The central defensive midfielder follows the play forward and also moves into position toward the left defensive side.
- The sweeper moves forward and to the left defensive side
- The central defender holds back to defend the center.
- In 11v11 play, the center offensive midfielder moves forward into the middle third of the field.
- The right outside recovery midfielder and the right outside recovery defender move forward and into position slightly toward the left defensive side.
- The two attackers are simply actors in this play and move their position all the way to midfield and to the defensive right outside.

220

FIGURE 13

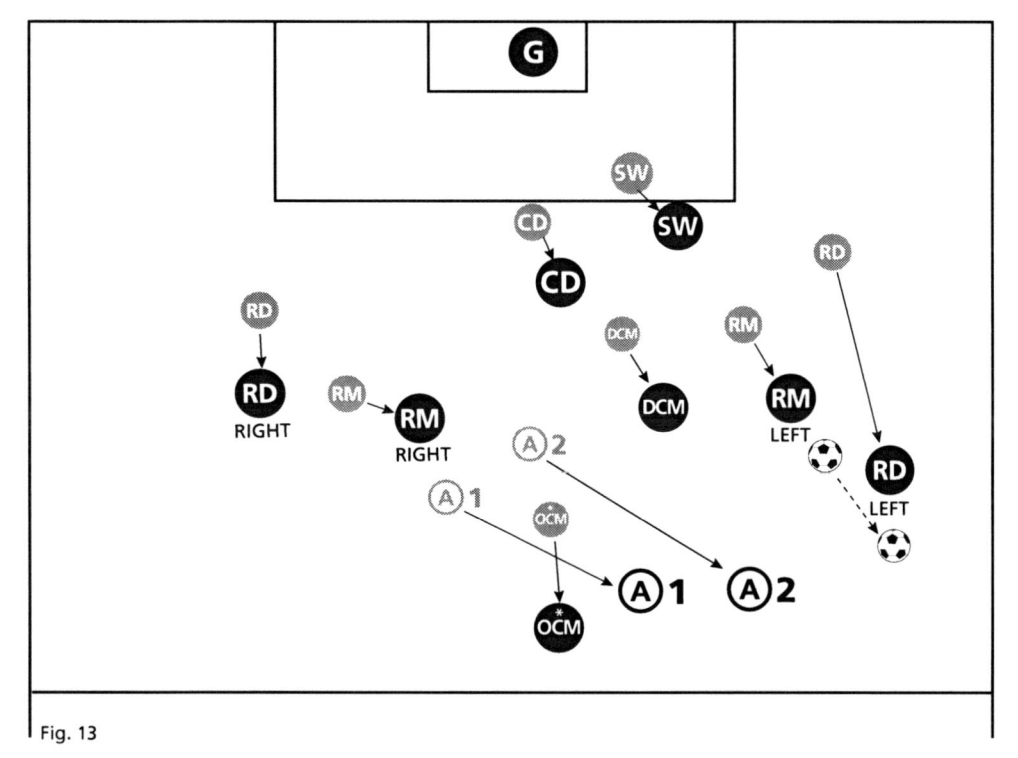

Fig. 13

- As soon as the ball is played by the left outside recovery defender to the left outside recovery midfielder, the left outside recovery defender makes a sprint up field and to the outside.
- The left outside recovery midfielder then passes the ball forward to the sprinting left outside recovery defender. This pass must lead the defender.
- The central defensive midfielder follows the play forward and also moves into position toward the left defensive side.
- The sweeper adjusts to the defensive left and takes up position at the top of the goalie box.
- The central defender continues to hold back to defend the center.
- The right outside recovery midfielder and the right outside recovery defender move forward.
- In 11v11 play, the center offensive midfielder moves forward to midfield.
- The center defensive midfielder gradually slides into position behind the attacking left outside recovery defender and left outside recovery midfielder.
- The two attackers are simply actors in this play and continue to move their position all the way to midfield and to the defensive right outside.

FIGURE 14

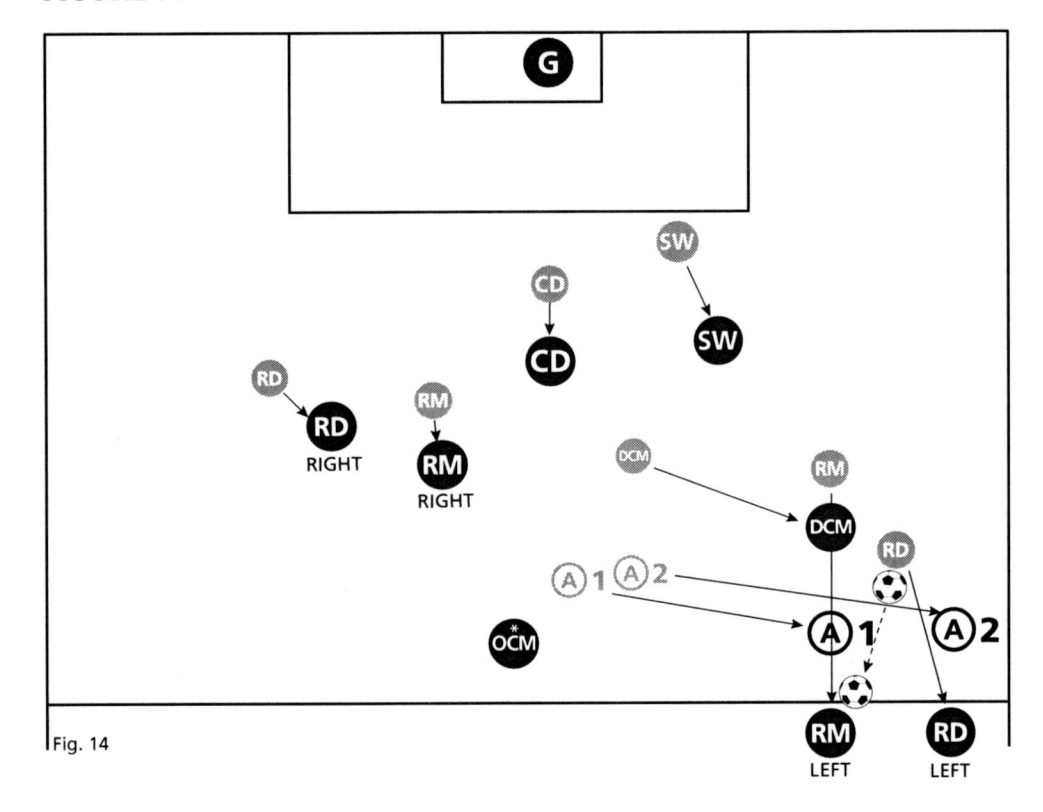

- As soon as the ball is played by the left outside recovery midfielder to the left outside recovery defender, the left outside recovery midfielder makes a sprint up field but halts the forward progress at midfield.
- The left outside recovery defender then passes the ball forward to the sprinting left outside recovery midfielder who is stopped at midfield.
- The left outside recovery defender sprints forward as soon as the ball is played to the left outside recovery midfielder but stops at the midfield.
- The center defensive midfielder follows the play forward and moves into position toward the left outside defensive side.
- The central defensive midfielder should now be in position to contain any counter attack on the left outside.
- The sweeper adjusts to the defensive left and takes up position outside of the goalie box.
- The central defender continues to hold back to defend the center.
- The right outside recovery midfielder and the right outside recovery defender move forward.

222

- In 11v11 play, the center offensive midfielder remains positioned at midfield.
- The two attackers are simply actors in this play and continue to move their position all the way to midfield and to the defensive left outside. They will finish this stage of transition play on the left defensive outside. Their position is between the left outside recovery defender—left recovery midfielder and the central defender.

FIGURE 15:

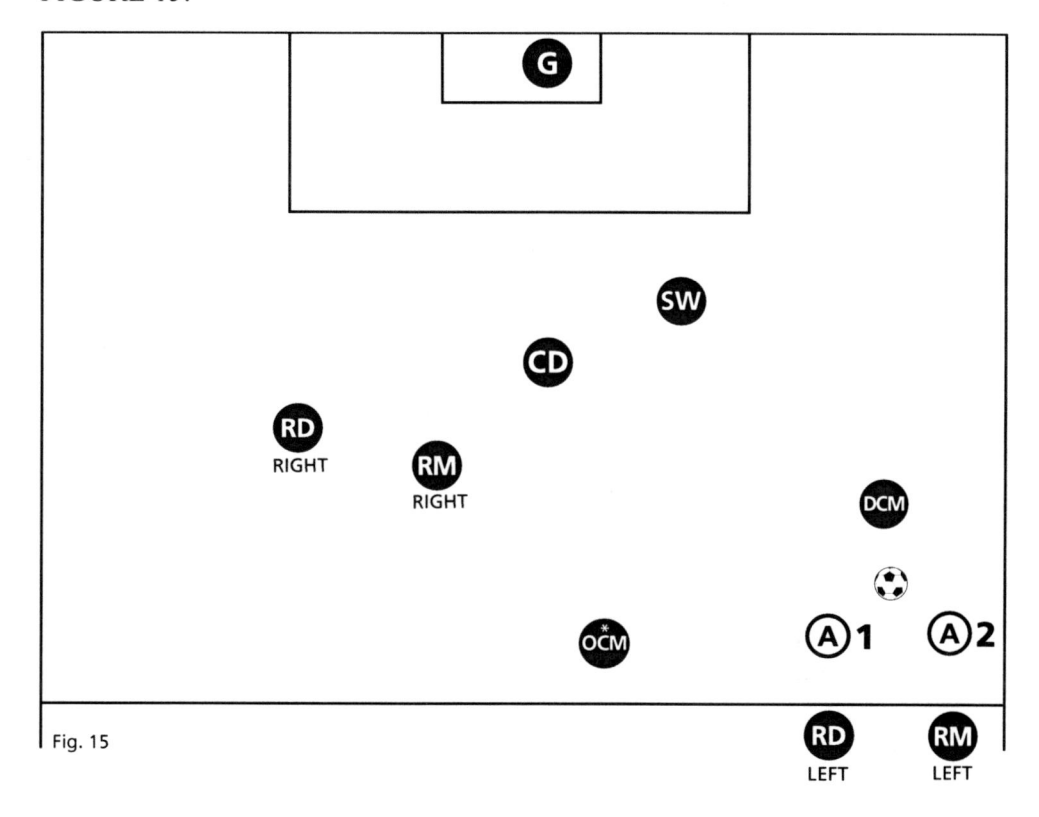

Fig. 15

- Formation after the defensive team has transitioned forward and to the outside from the defensive third into the middle third and finishing this segment at midfield.
- The attack will now be created by the attackers on the left outside.
- The defense will now learn that the recovery run sequence learned in section IX in YEAR ONE develops exactly the same way on the outside of the playing field as it did in the middle area of the playing field.
- The attackers must keep their attack on the outside so that the outside recovery run can be learned and understood by the players.

FIGURE 16

Fig. 16

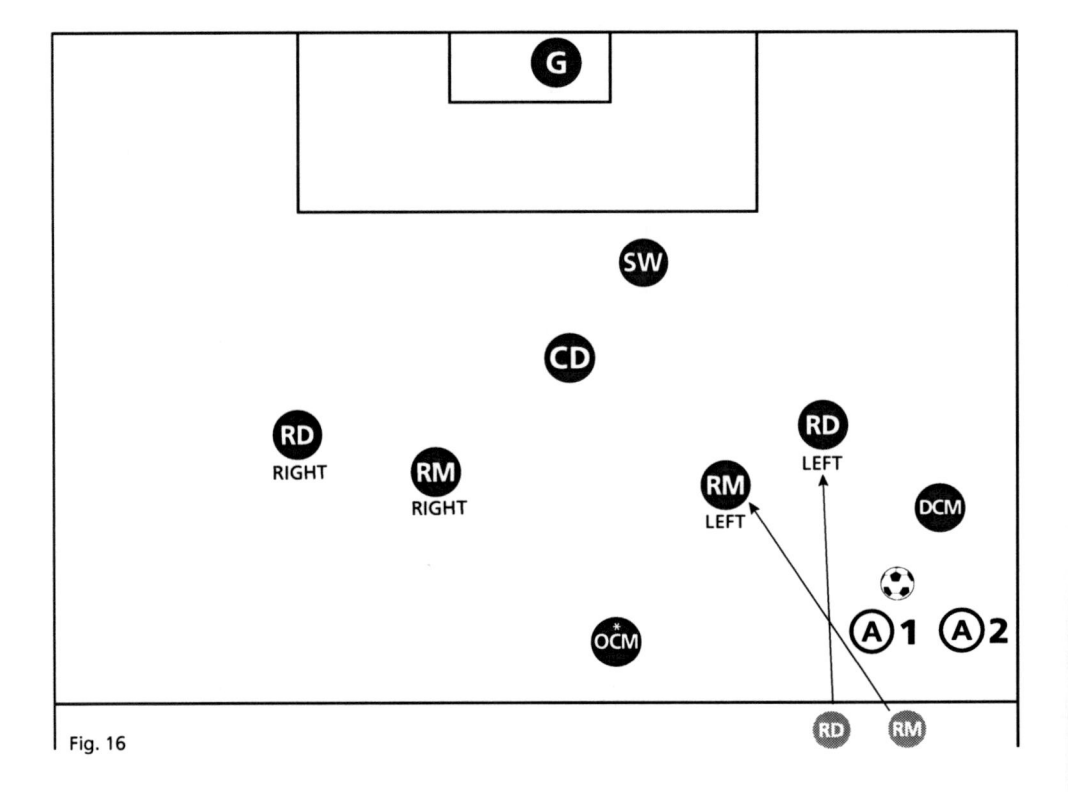

- The left outside recovery defender and the left outside recovery midfielder pretend that they have lost the ball to the attackers at midfield.
- The attackers now go on a counter attack on the left outside by passing the ball back and forth between them.
- The center defensive midfielder has been positioned to cover the left defensive outside when the left outside recovery defender and the left outside recovery midfielder had pushed forward and had attacked up the left outside.
- The center defensive midfielder will now contain the two attackers by retreating and not attacking the ball.
- The left outside recovery defender and left outside recovery midfielder make their recovery runs back into a defensive support position behind the containing center midfielder.

FIGURE 17:

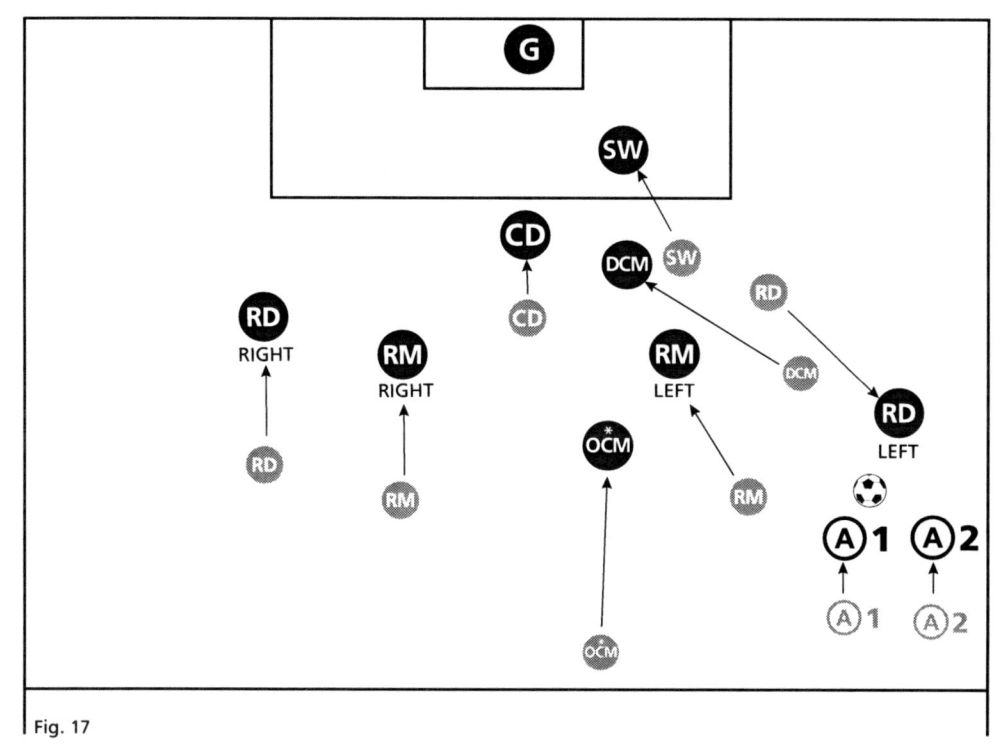

Fig. 17

- Once the left outside recovering defender is in the support position, this defender must release the central defensive midfielder and take the position between the attacker as the contain center defensive midfielder.
- The center defensive midfielder, once freed by the left outside recovery defender, retreats to take a position in the center of the field near the penalty box.
- The left outside recovery defender keeps containment of the attackers by retreating until the entire defense is once again set in the defensive part of the playing field thereby creating support for the containing defender.
- The sweeper adjusts back into the penalty box but keeps position on left defensive side.
- In 11v11 play, the center offensive midfielder adjusts back into the defensive third but maintains position in the center of the playing field.
- The right outside recovery midfielder and the right outside recover defender can now begin to move towards the right defensive outside while retreating.

FIGURE 18:

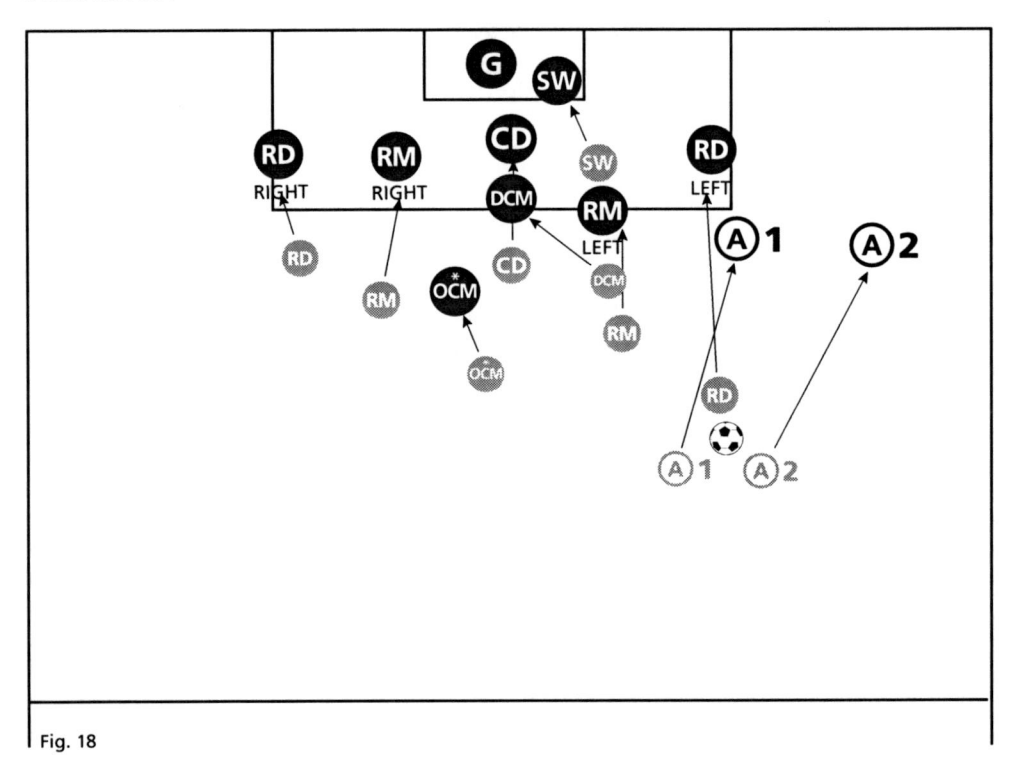

Fig. 18

- Once the attack and the recovery have reached all the way back into defense, the play is ended.

NOTE:

The players have now been taught how:

- Recover from the attack coming up the middle of the playing field.
- Take possession of the ball.
- Begin a counter attack by playing the ball to the outside with the outside recovery defender and midfielder attacking forward with give-and-go passes.
- The remaining defenders move forward cautiously and towards the outside thereby defending the empty areas created by the attacking outside recovery defender and recovery midfielder.
- Contain the counter attack by the attackers.
- Recovery runs on the outside by the outside recovery defender and recovery midfielder.
- Outside recovery defender takes over the role of containment thereby releasing the center defensive midfielder to take position back in the center of the playing field.
- **This sequence from the recovery run to transitioning to the LEFT defensive side all the way to midfield, must now be repeated until the players on the team understand how to execute this transition segment.**

C. TRANSITION PLAY UNINTERRUPTED TO THE RIGHT THEN TO LEFT DEFENSIVE SIDES:

1. The team plays the transition sequence beginning with the center recovery run, to the right defensive side, and recovers on the right defensive side as described in the previous section A. Figures 1 through 8.

2. Once the sequence has reached back to the right defensive side of the penalty area, instead of beginning left side transition with the center recovery run, the attackers pretend that they have lost possession of the ball and pass the ball back to the center defender.

3. The center defender begins the transition sequence to the left defensive side of the field by passing the ball to the left outside recovery defender as described in the previous section A. Figures 1 through 8.

4. Once the sequence has reached back to the left defensive side of the penalty area, instead of beginning right side transition with the center recovery run, the attackers pretend that they have lost possession of the ball and pass the ball back to the center defender.

5. The center defender begins the transition sequence to the right defensive side of the field by passing the ball to the right outside recovery defender as described in the previous section A. Figures 1 through 8.

6. The transition is now played uninterrupted between the right defensive side and the left defensive side.

EMPHASIZE:
- *Recovery runs are an important element of the sport of soccer.*
- *Players learn to organize recovery runs on the outside of the playing area and not just in the middle of the field.*
- *Defenses learn to adjust their positioning while under constant motion.*
- *In the defensive third of the field it is most important to play the ball out of the center thereby avoiding problems in the event of a breakdown.*

VII. 9V9 AND 11V11 TRANSITION PLAY FROM THE MIDDLE THIRD INTO THE ATTACKING THIRD OF THE FIELD:

1. Once the players can transition fluidly between the right and the left defensive side, the transition from the middle third into the attacking third of the field is now demonstrated and taught.

2. To finish on the opponent's goal, it is necessary for a team to know how to bring superior numbers forward. Relying on one or two forwards to handle the scoring is not a good tactical approach. Youth teams have a tendency to believe that they only need to train forwards to score. To have a better chance to score on an opponent the whole team must be brought into the attack.

FIGURE 1:
Using the previous section VI. Figures 1 through 5, start with the recovery run sequence, play the ball to the right defensive outside, begin attack by the recovery defensive team with a give and go play between the right out side recovery defender and the right recovery midfielder, and move forward to midfield.

CD Center Contain Defender **SW** Sweeper **RF** Recovery Forward **DCM** Defensive Center Midfield
OCM Offensive Center Midfield (*11V11 only) **RM** Recovery Midfielder **RD** Recovery Defender
A Attacker **G** Goalie ⚽ Ball

Fig. 1

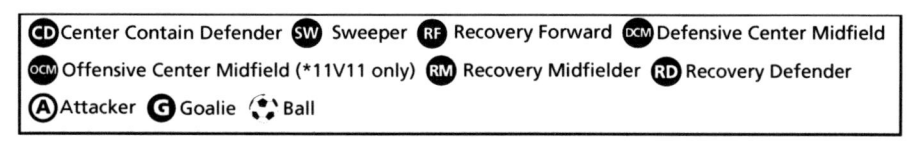

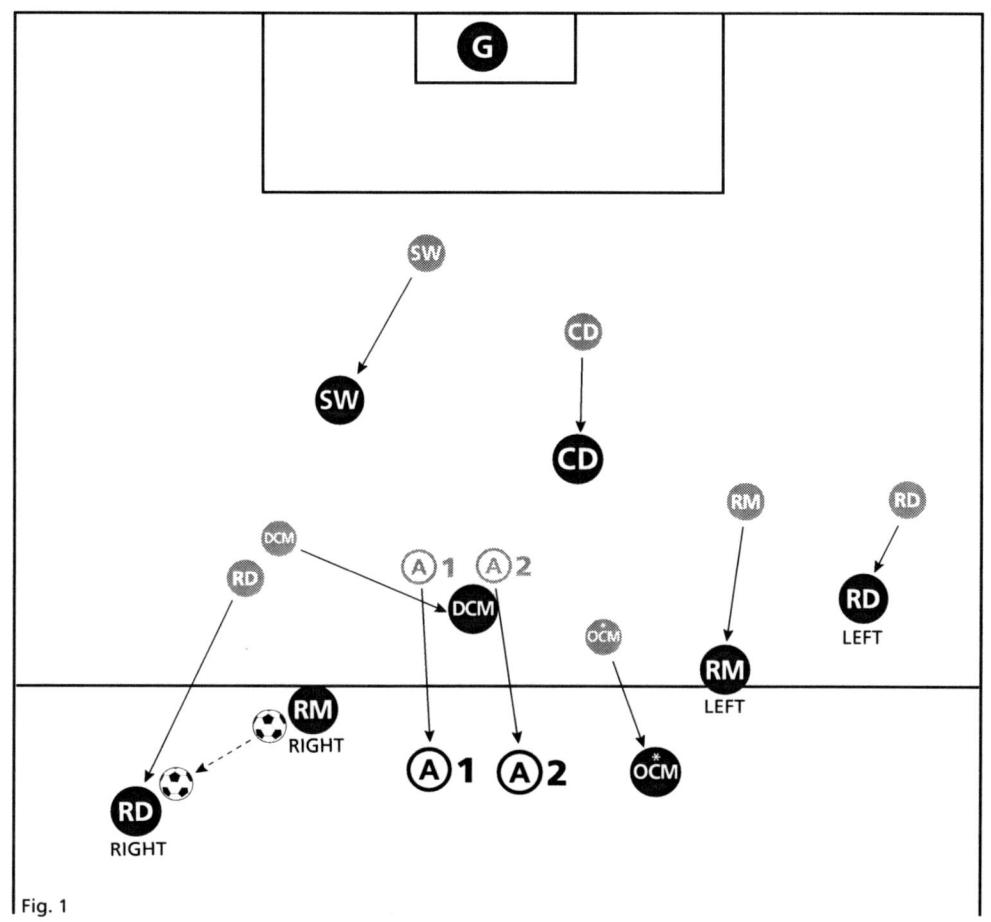

- As soon as the ball is played by the right outside recovery defender to the right outside recovery midfielder, the right outside recovery defender makes a sprint up field, to the outside, and across midfield.
- The center defensive midfielder moves towards midfield and adjust towards the center but still somewhat on the right defensive side.
- The center defender adjusts forward and continues to defend the center.
- The sweeper adjusts forward but somewhat to the right defensive side.
- The left outside recovery midfielder adjusts to midfield.
- The left outside recovery defender adjusts forward.

- In 11v11 play, the center offensive midfielder crosses midfield.
- The recovery forward has now advanced to the top of middle third of the field.
- In 11v11 play, a second recovery forward is introduced.
- The attack by the recovery defense has now crossed midfield and is moving forward towards the opponent's goal.
- The opposing attackers keep moving forward, to the right defensive side, and all the way to the opponent's box area.

FIGURE 2:

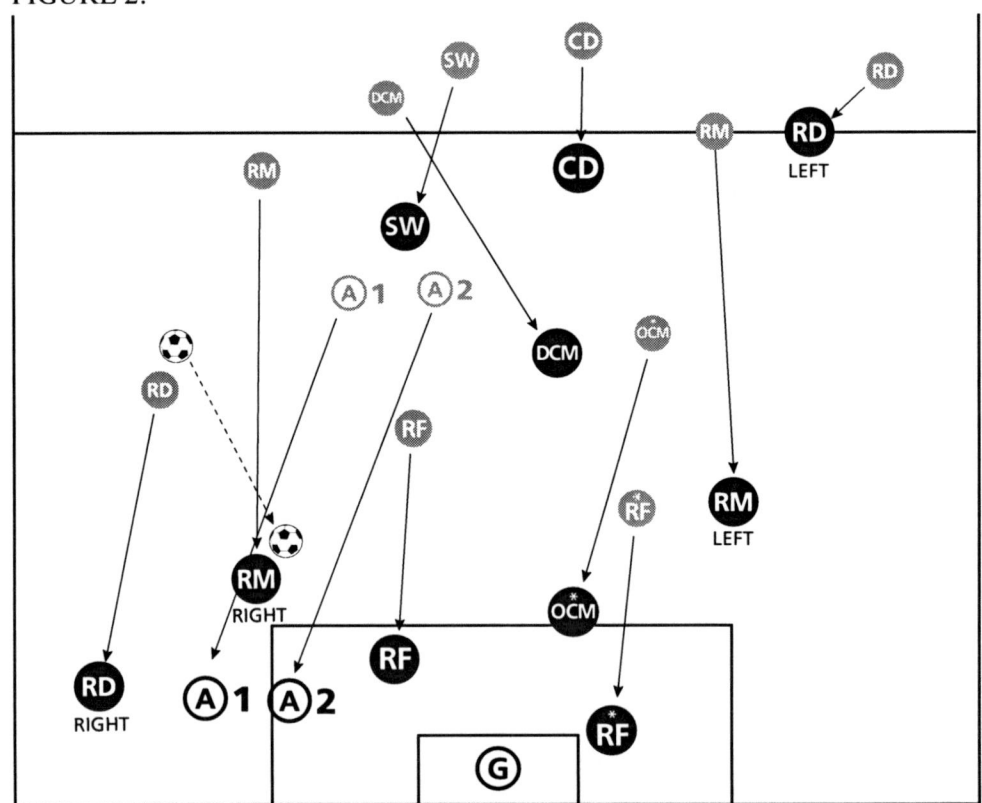

Fig. 2

- As soon as the ball is played by the right outside recovery defender to the right outside recovery midfielder, the right outside recovery defender makes a sprint forward to receive the ball from the right outside recovery midfielder.
- The right outside recovery defender and the right outside recovery midfielder continue this give-and-go passing play until the right outside recovery defender has reached the position outside the penalty area and almost to the goal line.

- Once the right outside recovery defender has reached this desired position, the right outside recovery midfielder passes the ball to the right outside recovery defender and then moves inside to take a position on top of the box and near the corner of the box.
- The center defensive midfielder moves across midfield and takes up a position towards the center of the field between the top of the opponent's box and the midfield line.
- The center defender adjusts forward to the midfield spot.
- The sweeper adjusts forward, across the midfield line, ahead of the center defender, and takes position towards the right defensive side of the field.
- The left outside midfielder moves forward to take up a position near the top of the opponent's box and left from the center of the field.
- The left outside recovery defender takes up a position at the midfield line but to the left of the center of the field.
- In 11v11 play, the center offensive midfielder moves forward to take a position on top of the opponents goalie box and in the center.
- The right outside recovery defender has been taught to go onto the attack and thereby the attacking recovery defensive team has now brought numbers into the attack.
- The midfielders are in position to attack the goal with the left recovery midfielder in position to pick up any ball played into the backside or be the first to contain any counter attack.
- The recovery forward has advanced into the goal area to threaten any ball played into the center of the goal.
- In 11v11 play, a second recovery forward takes up a position on the six yard box.
- The sweeper is brought forward enough to become a scoring threat yet is in position to defend a counter attack.
- The two attackers move forward and take up an outside position.

FIGURE 3:

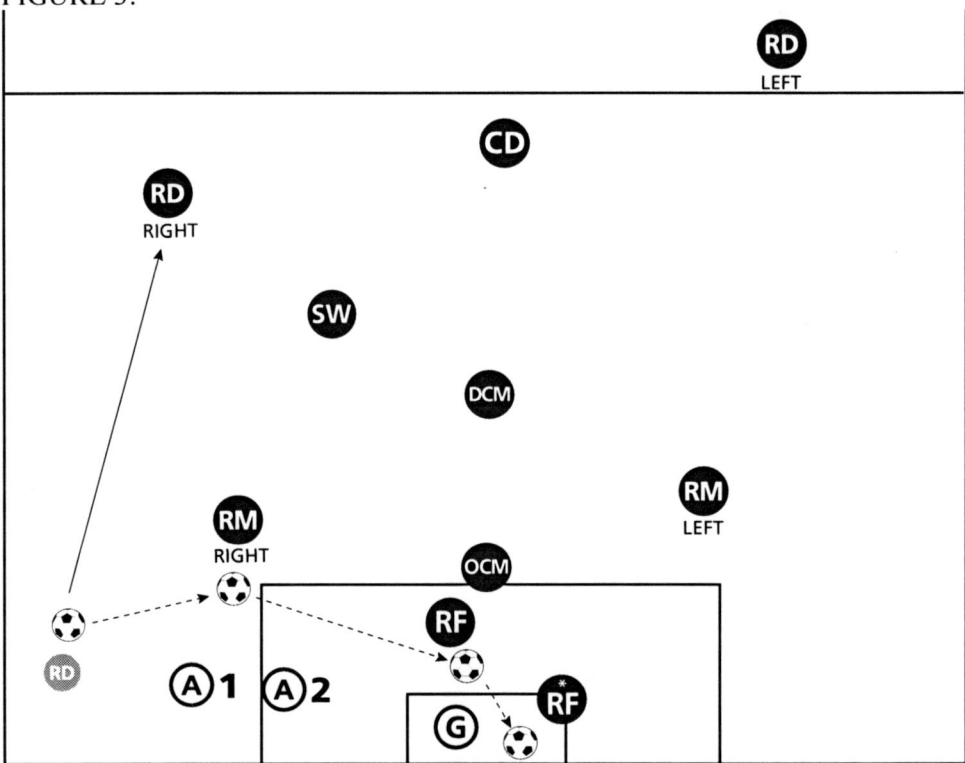

Fig. 3

- The right outside recovery defender plays the ball back to the right outside recovery midfielder who is positioned on top of the box near the corner of the box.
- Once the right outside recovery defender has made the pass back to the right outside recovery midfielder, the right outside recovery defender must make a recovery run and take position near midfield.
- The right outside recovery midfielder makes a pass to the recovery forward who takes a shot on goal.

EMPHASIZE:

- *The players have executed a set attacking play by transitioning on the defensive right side from the defensive third of the field, through the middle third of the field, and all the way to the attacking third of the field then finishing with a shot on the opponent's goal.*
- *The players have learned how to overload every third of the field with their own players on the defensive right side.*
- *The players have learned how to have a player in position in every part of the field on the defensive right side to either advance the attack or contain a counter attack.*

FIGURE 4:

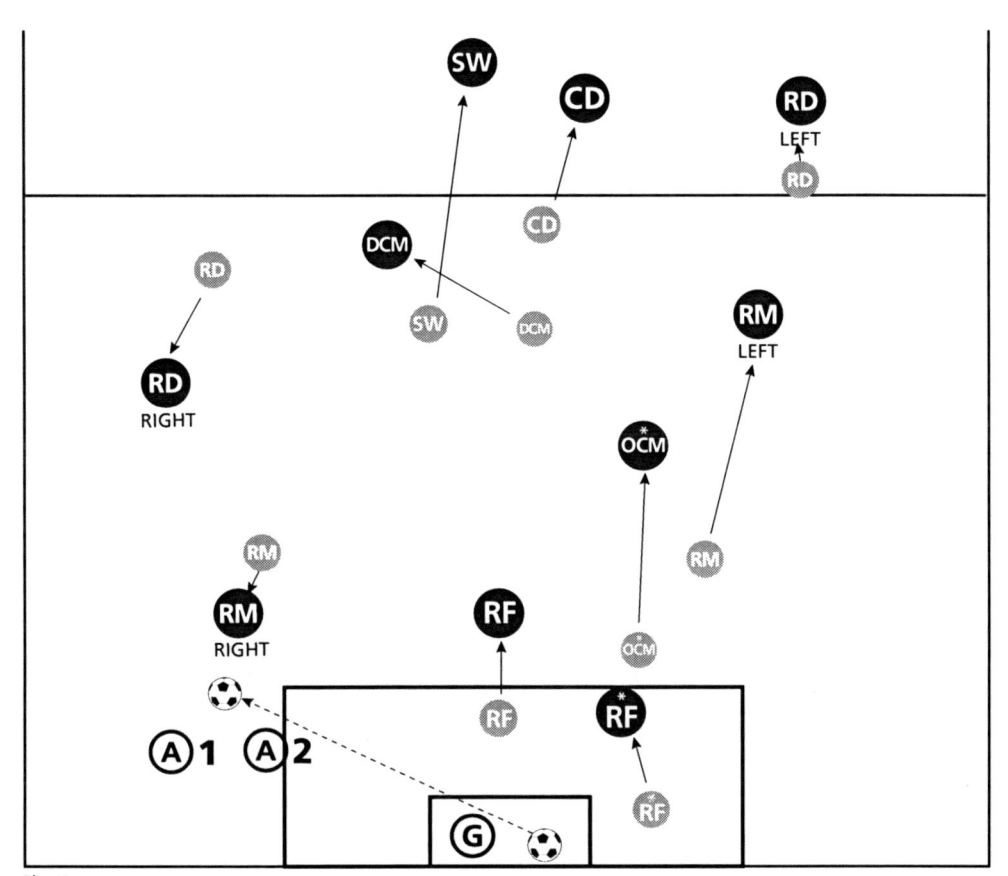

Fig. 4

- The attacking team will begin a counter attack on the right defensive side.
- The goalie plays the ball to the attackers who have taken a position on the outside.
- The attackers are there to teach the recovery defense how to recover the full length of the field.
- The attackers will advance by passing the ball back and forth.
- The right outside recovery midfielder will retreat and contain the two attackers.
- The outside right recovery defender will retreat to move into position to be in support of the right recovery midfielder.
- The center defensive midfielder recovers to a position near midfield and to defensive right outside.
- The center defender adjusts back over the midfield line and outside of the circle.
- The sweeper adjusts back, across the midfield line, behind the center defender, and takes position towards the right defensive side of the field.
- The left outside recovery midfielder recovers to a position near midfield.
- The left outside recovery defender recovers back over the midfield line.
- In 11v11 play, the center offensive midfielder moves back to take a position midway between the center line and the top of the opponent's box.
- The recovery forward recovers up the middle.
- In 11v11 play, a second recovery forward takes up a position at the top of the box.
- The defense does not take the ball from the attackers but works only on learning how to retreat and recover into their defensive third of the field.

FIGURE 5:

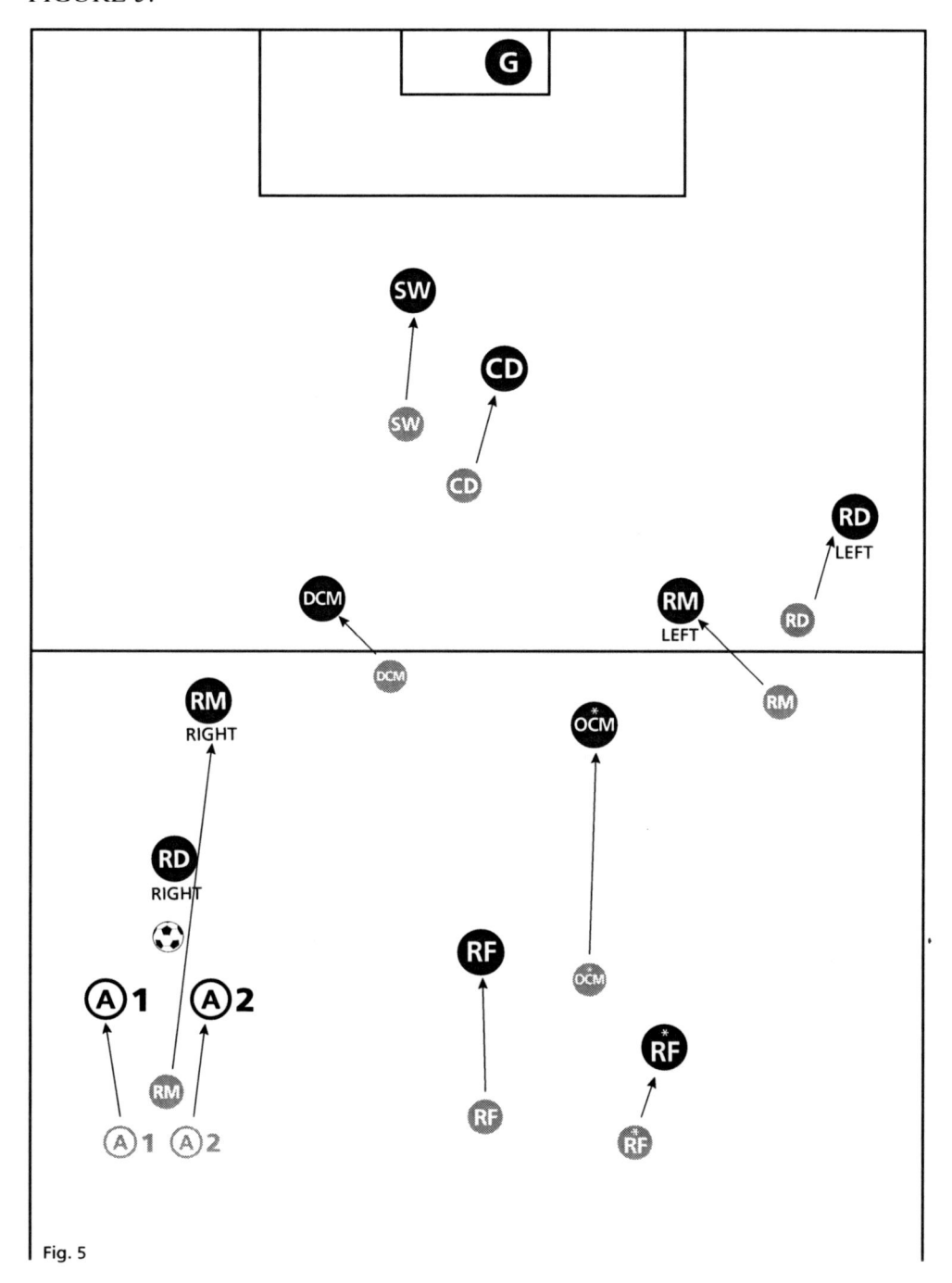

Fig. 5

- As the attackers 1 & 2 advance forward, the right outside recovery midfielder pretends to have been beaten by the two attackers and allows them to advance past.
- The right outside recovery midfielder then recovers to midfield.
- The right outside recovery defender now contains the attackers.
- The center defensive midfielder, the center defender, the sweeper, the left outside recovery midfielder, and the left outside recovery defender recover past midfield.
- In 11v11 play the center offensive midfielder and the second recovery forward begin to recover towards the defensive half of the field.

FIGURE 6:

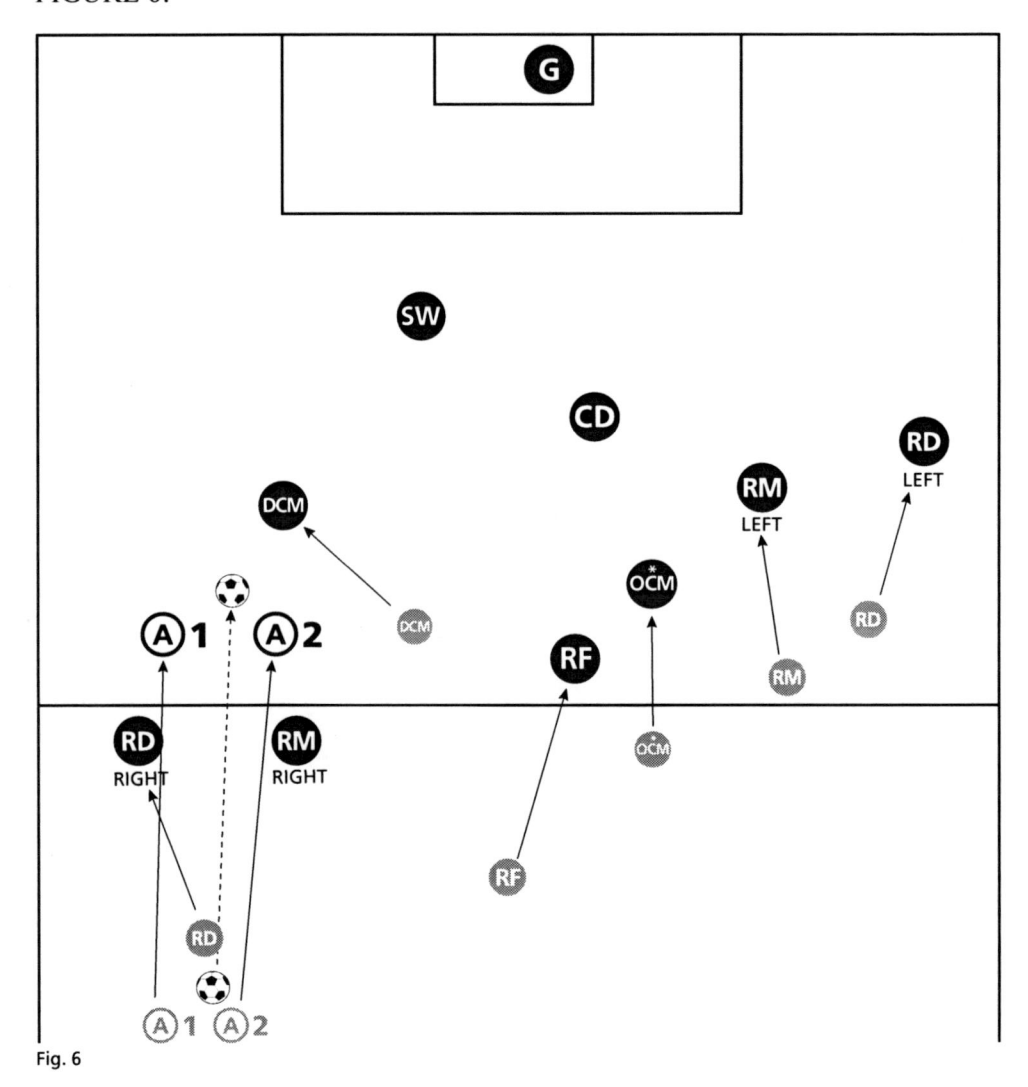

Fig. 6

- As the attackers 1 & 2 advance forward, the right outside recovery defender pretends to have been beaten by the two attackers and allows them to advance past.
- The right outside recovery defender then recovers to midfield.
- The center defensive midfielder will recover and take up the position as the contain defender in front of the attackers.
- The left outside recovery midfielder recovers back.
- The left outside recovery defender recovers back.
- The recovery forward recovers to the center and near the edge of the center circle.
- In 11v11 play, the center offensive midfielder recovers past midfield.
- The remaining recovery will be as previously described in YEAR TWO section VI. A. Figures 6 - 9.
- Once the sequence has reached back to the right defensive side of the penalty area, instead of beginning the left side transition with the center recovery run, the attackers pretend that they have lost possession of the ball and pass the ball back to the center defender.
- The center defender begins the transition sequence to the left defensive side of the field by passing the ball to the left outside recovery defender as described in YEAR TWO in the previous segment IV. Section A. Figures 1 through 8 and continues the play forward to midfield on the left defensive side.

FIGURE 7:

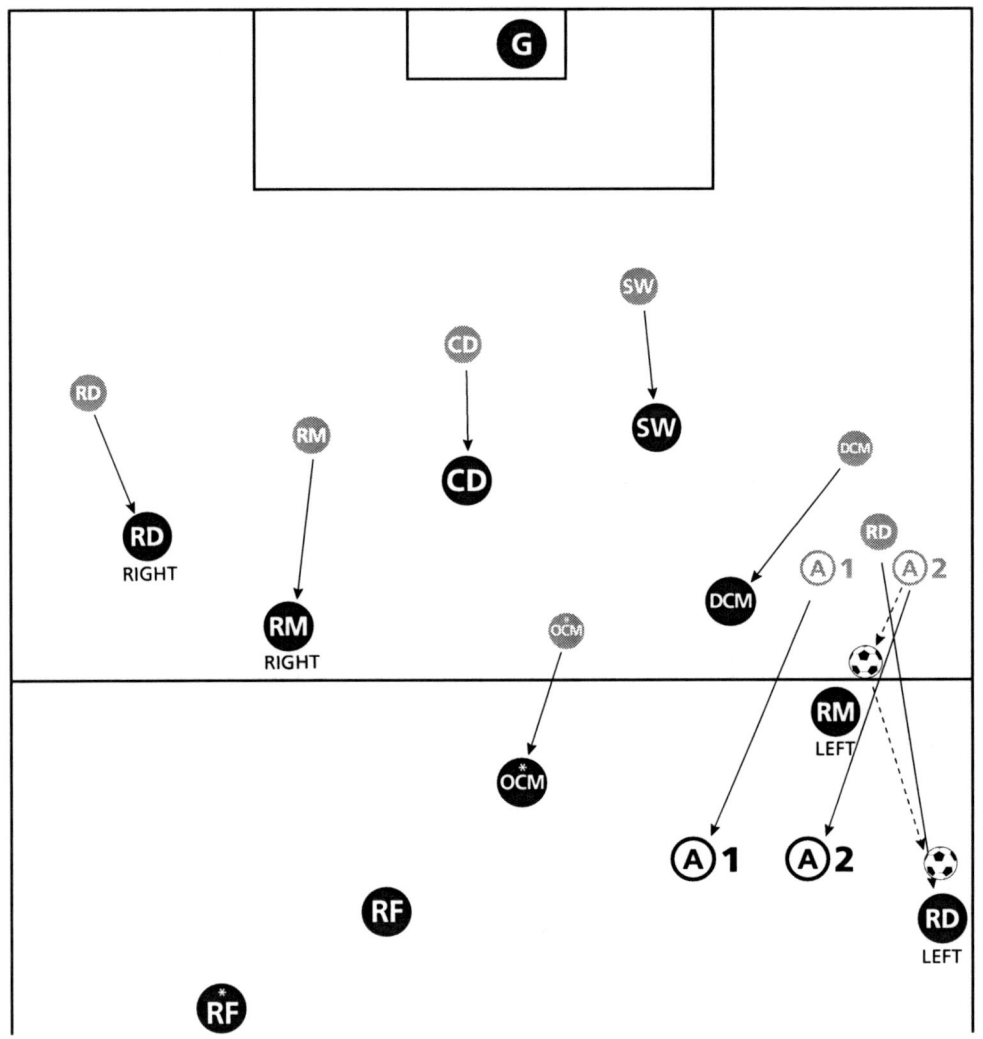

Fig. 7

- As soon as the ball is played by the left outside recovery defender to the left outside recovery midfielder, the left outside recovery defender makes a sprint up field, to the outside, and across midfield.
- The center defensive midfielder moves toward midfield and adjust towards the center but still somewhat on the left defensive side.
- The center defender adjusts forward and continues to defend the center.
- The sweeper adjusts forward but somewhat to the left defensive side.
- The right outside recovery midfielder adjusts to midfield.

- The right outside recovery defender adjusts forward.
- In 11v11 play, the center offensive midfielder crosses midfield.
- The recovery forward has now advanced to the top of the middle third of the field.
- In 11v11 play, a second recovery forward is introduced.
- The attack by the recovery defense has now crossed midfield and is moving forward towards the opponent's goal.
- The opposing attackers keep moving forward, to the right defensive side, and all the way to the opponent's box area.

FIGURE 8:

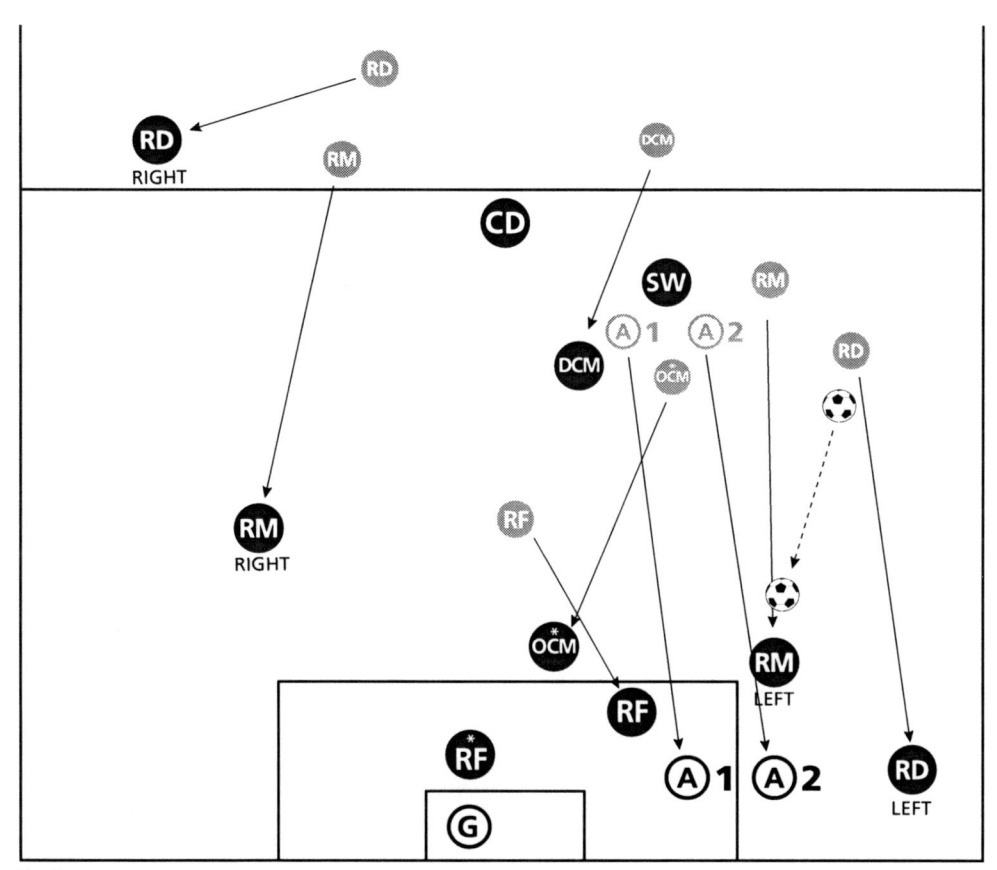

Fig. 8

- As soon as the ball is played by the left outside recovery defender to the left outside recovery midfielder, the left outside recovery defender makes a sprint forward to receive the ball from the left outside recovery midfielder.
- The left outside recovery defender and the left outside recovery midfielder continue this give-and-go passing play until the left outside recovery defender has reached the position outside the penalty area and almost to the goal line.
- Once the left outside recovery defender has reached this desired position, the left outside recovery midfielder passes the ball to the left outside recovery defender and then moves inside to take a position on top of the box and near the corner of the box.
- The center defensive midfielder moves across midfield and takes up a position towards the center of the field between the top of the opponent's box and the midfield line.
- The center defender adjusts forward to the midfield spot.
- The sweeper adjusts forward, across the midfield line, ahead of the center defender, and takes position towards the left defensive side of the field.
- The right outside midfielder moves forward to take up a position near the top of the opponent's box and right from the center of the field.
- The right outside recovery defender takes up a position at the midfield line but to the right of the center of the field.
- In 11v11 play, the center offensive midfielder moves forward to take a position on top of the opponents goalie box and in the center.
- The left outside recovery defender has been taught to go onto the attack and thereby the attacking recovery defensive team has now brought numbers into the attack.
- The midfielders are in position to attack the goal with the right recovery midfielder in position to pick up any ball played into the backside or be the first to contain any counter attack.
- The recovery forward has advanced into the goal area to threaten any ball played into the center of the goal.
- In 11v11 play, a second recovery forward takes up a position on the six yard box.
- The sweeper is brought forward enough to become a scoring threat yet is in position to defend a counter attack.
- The two attackers move forward and take up an outside position.

FIGURE 9:

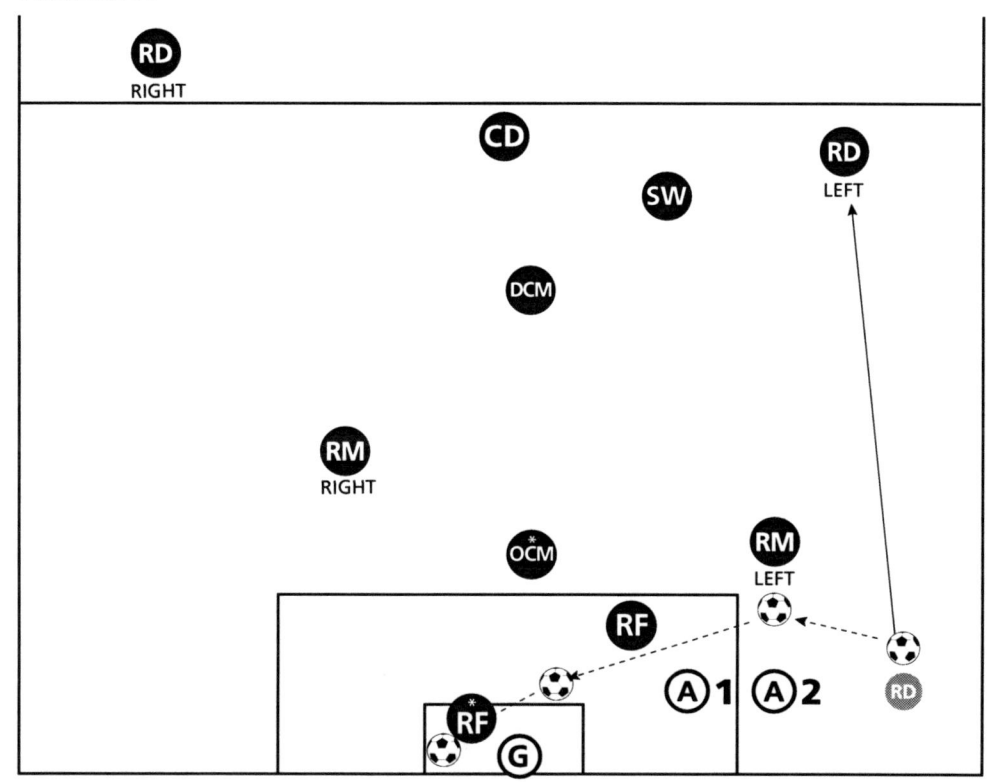

Fig. 9

- The left outside recovery defender plays the ball back to the left outside recovery midfielder who is positioned on top of the box near the corner of the box.
- Once the left outside recovery defender has made the pass back to the left outside recovery midfielder, the left outside recovery defender must make a recovery run and take position near midfield.
- The left outside recovery midfielder makes a pass to the recovery forward who takes a shot on goal.

EMPHASIZE:

- *The players have executed a set attacking play by transitioning on the defensive left side from the defensive third of the field, through the middle third of the field, and all the way to the attacking third of the field then finishing with a shot on the opponent's goal.*
- *The players have learned how to overload every third of the field with their own players on the defensive left side.*
- *The players have learned how to have a player in position in every part of the field on the defensive left side to either advance the attack or contain a counter attack.*

FIGURE 10:

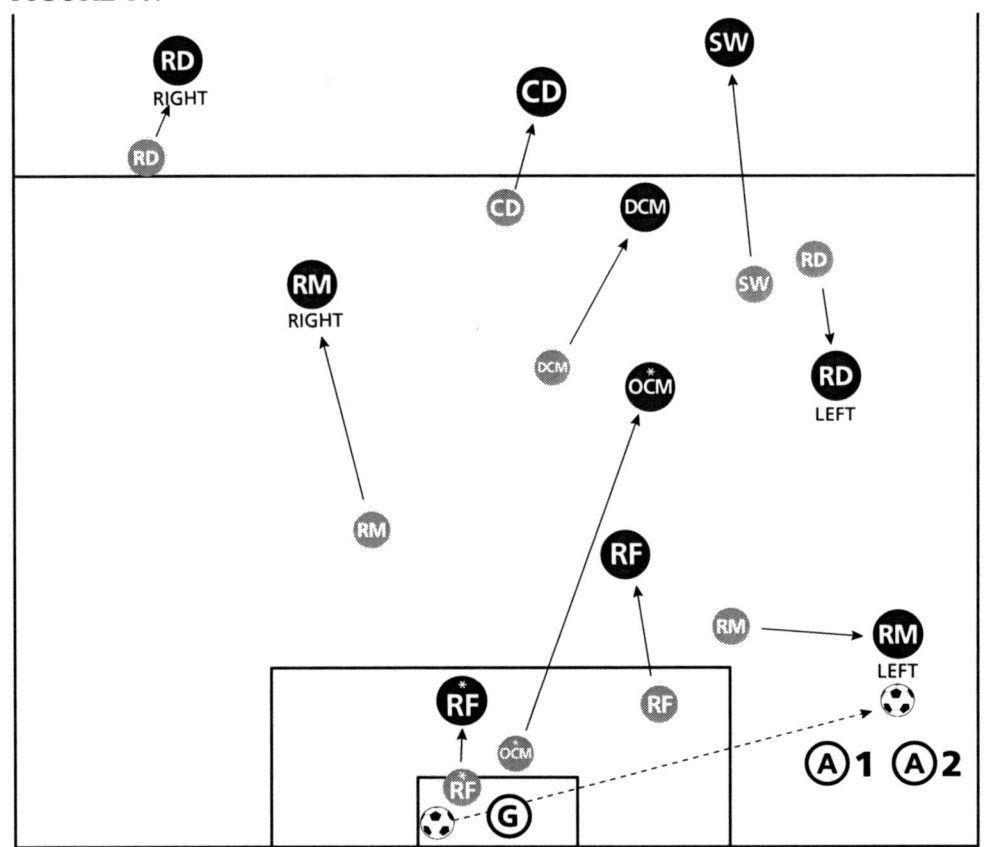

Fig. 10

- The attacking team will begin a counter attack on the left defensive side.
- The goalie plays the ball to attackers who had taken a position on the outside.
- The attackers are there to teach the recovery defense how to recover the full length of the field.
- The attackers will advance by passing the ball back and forth.
- The left outside recovery midfielder will retreat and contain the two attackers.
- The outside left recovery defender will advance to move into position to be in support of the left recovery midfielder.
- The center defensive midfielder recovers to a position near midfield and to defensive left outside.
- The center defender adjusts back over the midfield line and outside of the circle.
- The sweeper adjusts back, across the midfield line, behind the center defender, and takes position towards the left defensive side.

242

- The right outside recovery midfielder recovers to a position near midfield.
- The right outside recovery defender recovers back over the midfield line.
- In 11v11 play, the center offensive midfielder moves back to take a position midway between the center line and the top of the opponent's box.
- The recovery forward recovers up the middle.
- In 11v11 play, a second recovery forward takes up a position at the top of the box.
- The defensive team does not take the ball from the attackers but works only on learning how to retreat and recover into their defensive third of the field.

FIGURE 11:

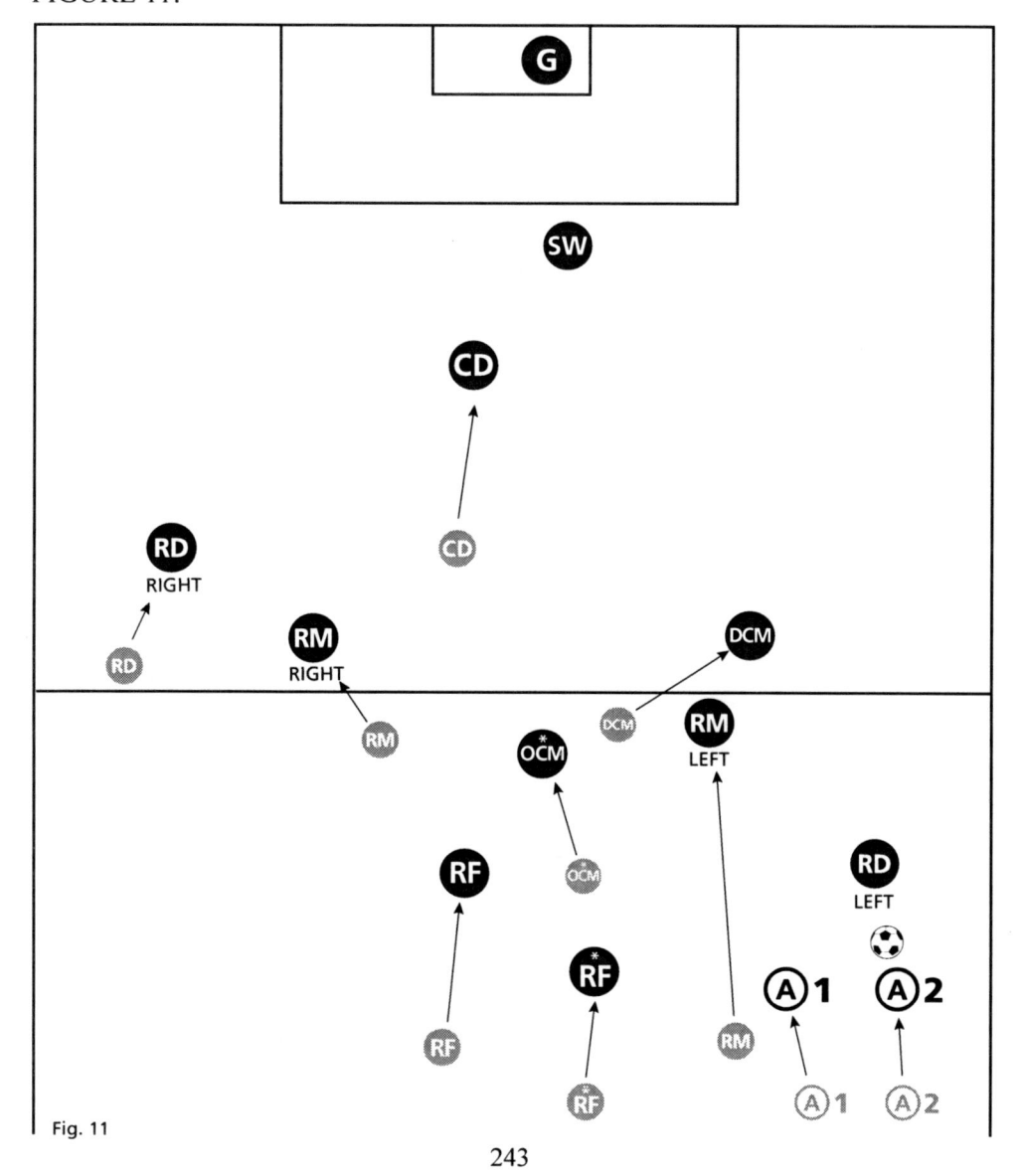

Fig. 11

243

- As the attackers 1 & 2 advance forward, the left outside recovery midfielder pretends to have been beaten by the two attackers and allows them to advance past.
- The left outside recovery midfielder then recovers to midfield.
- The left outside recovery defender now contains the attackers.
- The center defensive midfielder, the center defender, the sweeper, the right outside recovery midfielder, and the right outside recovery defender recover past midfield.
- In 11v11 play the center offensive midfielder and the second recovery forward begin to recover towards the defensive half of the field.

FIGURE 12:

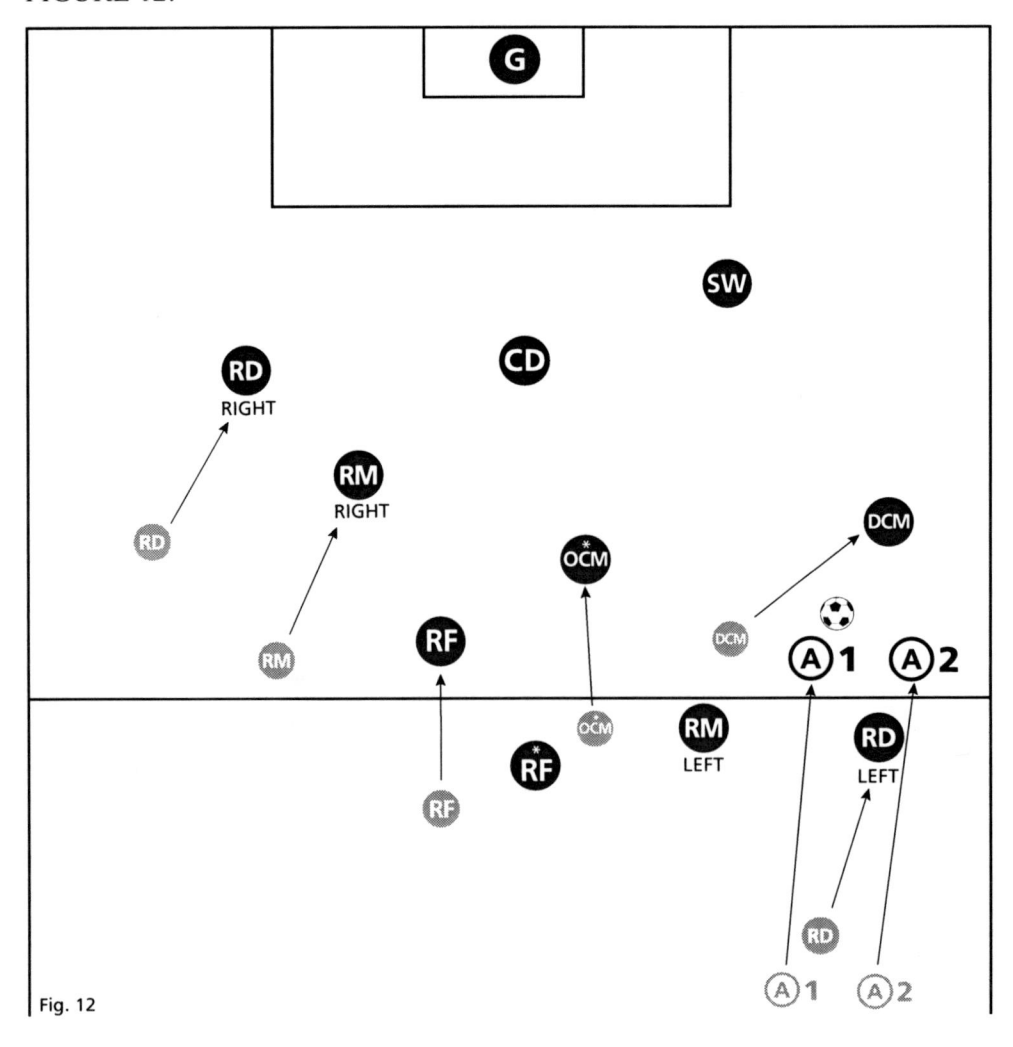

Fig. 12

244

- As the attackers 1 & 2 advance forward, the left outside recovery defender pretends to have been beaten by the two attackers and allows them to advance past.
- The left outside recovery defender then recovers to midfield.
- The center defensive midfielder will recover and take up the position as the contain defender in front of the attackers.
- The right outside recovery midfielder recovers back.
- The right outside recovery defender recovers back.
- The recovery forward recovers to the center and near the edge of the center circle.
- In 11v11 play, the center offensive midfielder recovers past midfield.
- The remaining recovery will be as previously described in YEAR TWO Section VI. A. Figures 6–9.
- Once the sequence has reached back to the left defensive side of the penalty area, instead of beginning the right side transition with the center recovery run, the attackers pretend that they have lost possession of the ball and pass the ball back to the center defender.
- The center defender begins the transition sequence to the right defensive side of the field by passing the ball to the right outside recovery defender as described in YEAR TWO in the previous Segment IV. Section A. Figures 1 through 5 and continues the play forward to midfield on the left defensive side.

NOTE:

1. The transition is now practiced uninterrupted between the right defensive side and the left defensive side of the field, from the defensive third of the field through the middle third of the field and into the attacking third of the field.
2. Once the players know the transition on the outside between the defender and the midfielder, other attacking sequences can be taught to the players such as:

a. Playing the ball from one outside of the field to the other outside of the field by passing it through the center midfielder.

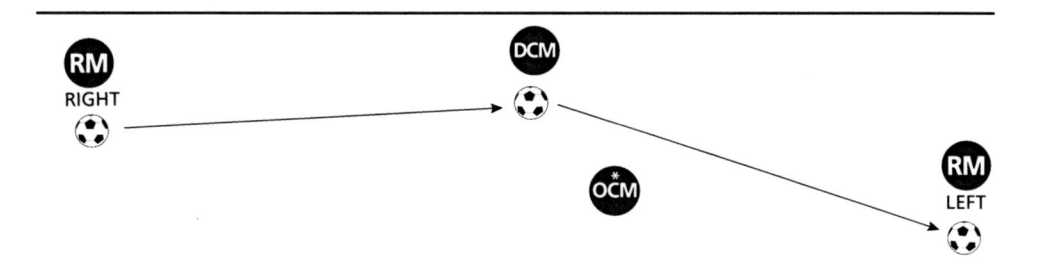

b. A give-and-go sequence can be developed between an outside player and the center offensive defender and the ball can be advanced that way.

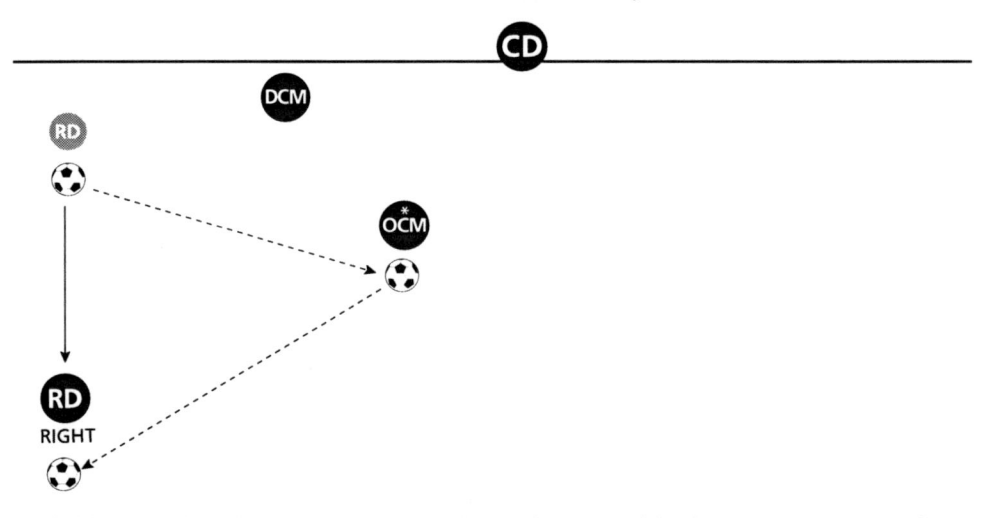

c. A ball can be played to any open center players by an outside player and the center player can play the ball forward and back outside to an overlapping defender who has move forward into the attack.

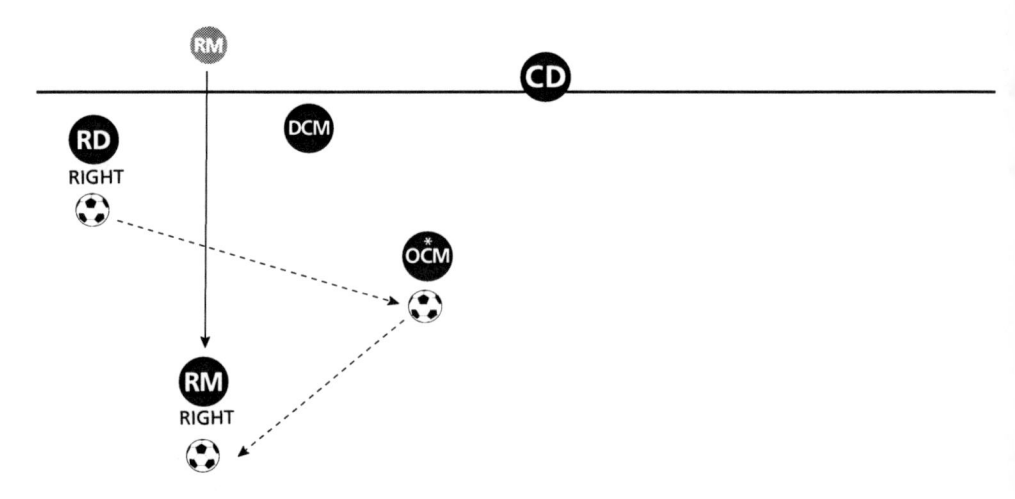

d. Any number of other combinations of playing the ball forward in the transition can be designed and practiced by the team.

e. Whenever a new combination of passing is taught to the team, it must be practiced by the full team who must learn how to advance together as a team.

VIII. FINISHING PLAY IN THE GOALIE BOX:

Play requirements:
- Four players who serve as feeders.
- Eight to twenty soccer balls.
- One player who will be the starting shooter.
- One goalkeeper.

A. SET UP THE PLAY:

1. This finishing play is designed for the forward players of a team.

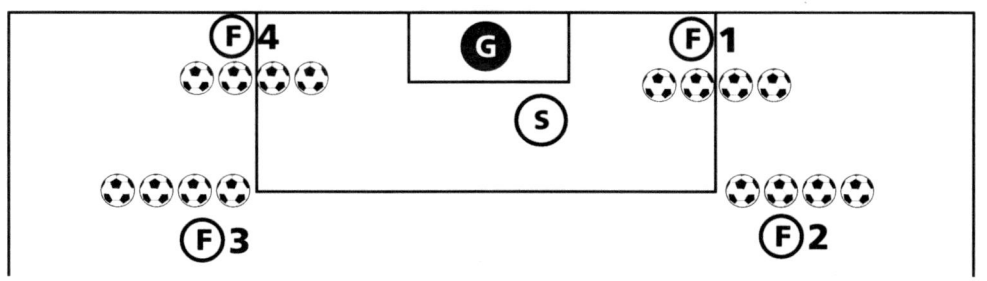

Fig. 1

a. One feeding player is stationed to the right of the goalpost at the spot where the six yard box line meets the end line.
b. One feeding player is stationed to the left of the goalpost at the spot where the six yard box line meets the end line.
c. Two players are stationed at the top of the goalie box and directly opposite the two feeders on the end line.
d. One player will start as the shooter who will shoot towards the goal and play within the area created by the four feeding players.
e. Each feeding player will have an equal number of soccer balls depending on how many total soccer balls are available for this play.
f. In a clockwise rotation starting with feeding player 1, the ball will be played to the shooting player.

2. Each ball must be fed to the shooting player in every conceivable manner such as on the ground pass, a bouncing ball, chest high balls, balls fed for heading, and so forth. The shooter must learn to handle and finish every type of ball.

3. The shooting player receives the ball from the feeding players and must then finish quickly with a shot on goal.
a. As soon as the ball is finished on the goal by the shooter, the shooting player must then turn quickly to receive the next ball from the feeding player in the clockwise rotation.
b. This continues until the shooting player has received all the balls from the four feeding players.
c. With each round of balls the shooting player will become increasingly tired. One of the objectives of this finishing play is for the shooting player to learn to finish under fatigue thereby simulating game conditions and accept that this limited space is sufficient room to finish a shot.
e. The shooting player must learn that there is very little time to finish a shot once penetration into the goalie area has occurred
f. The shooting player must learn to handle all types of balls played.
4. Once all the balls have been played by the feeders, the shooting player takes the place of feeding player #1 while feeding player #1 becomes the new shooter. This rotation continues until all players have had the opportunity to be shooting players.

B. AS THE SHOOTING PLAYERS BECOME INCREASINGLY CONFIDENT AND COMFORTABLE:
1. Instruct the shooting player to finish with a specific part of the shooting foot.
2. Instruct the shooting player to prepare the ball with a particular part of the body then finish the shot on goal with the second touch.
3. Instruct the shooting player to place the ball into a particular area of the goal thereby teaching the shooting player to aim the ball and shoot it with a particular touch on the ball.
4. Demand that the shooter finish each type of shot with the weak foot.

C. INCREASE THE FEEDING DISTANCE:
1. The four feeding players must spread out and feed longer balls from the outside and from the outside top of the box. See Figure 2.

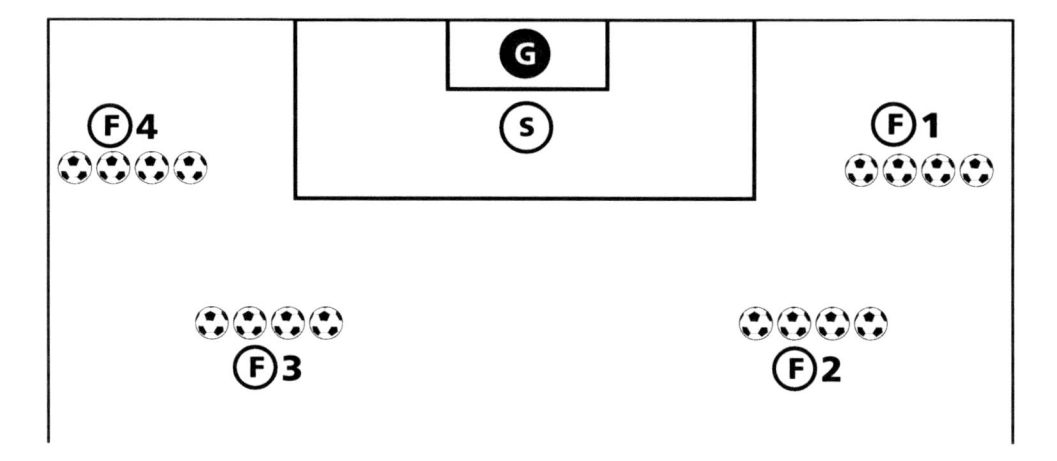

Fig. 2

2. Mix the finishing play with short balls and long balls by keeping the original four feeding players in position as described in Figure 1 and adding three feeding midfield players who are positioned near the top of the attacking third of the playing field. See Figure 3.

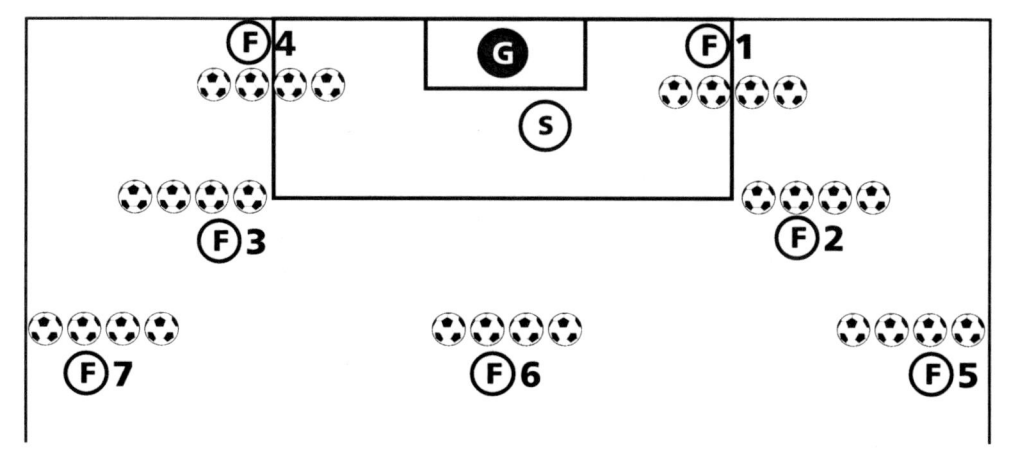

Fig. 3

3. As the shooting players increase their confidence and their comfort level at each of the shooting exercises previously described, a defender must be introduced into each exercise. This defender starts merely as a shadow defender and increases pressure on the shooting player as the confidence of the shooting player increases.

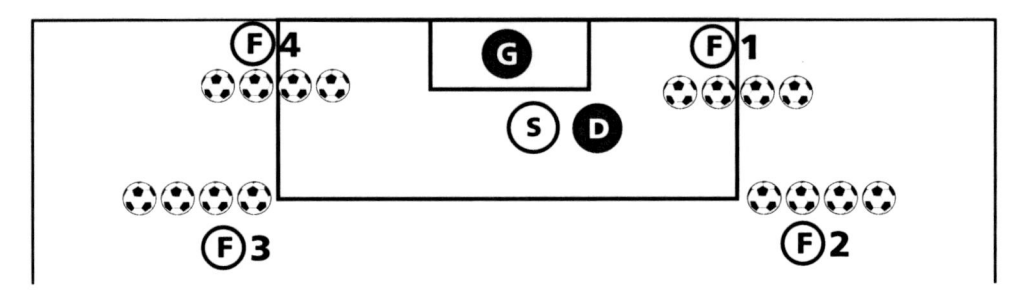

Fig. 1

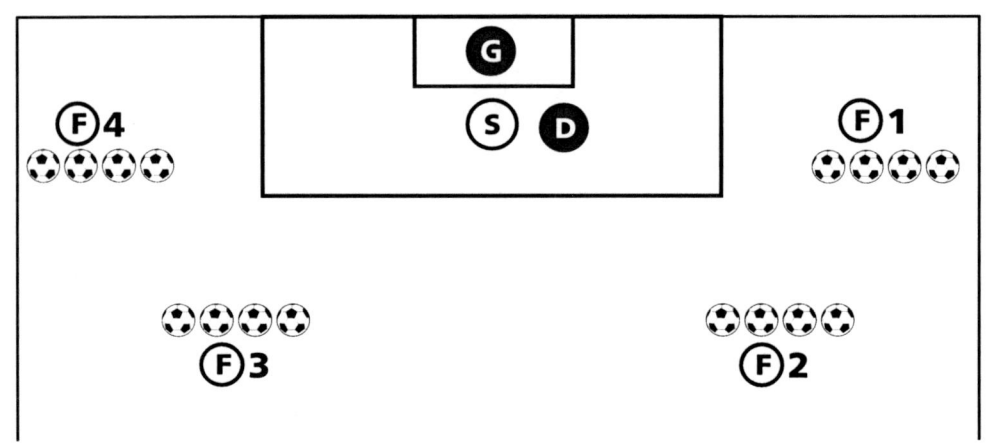

Fig. 2

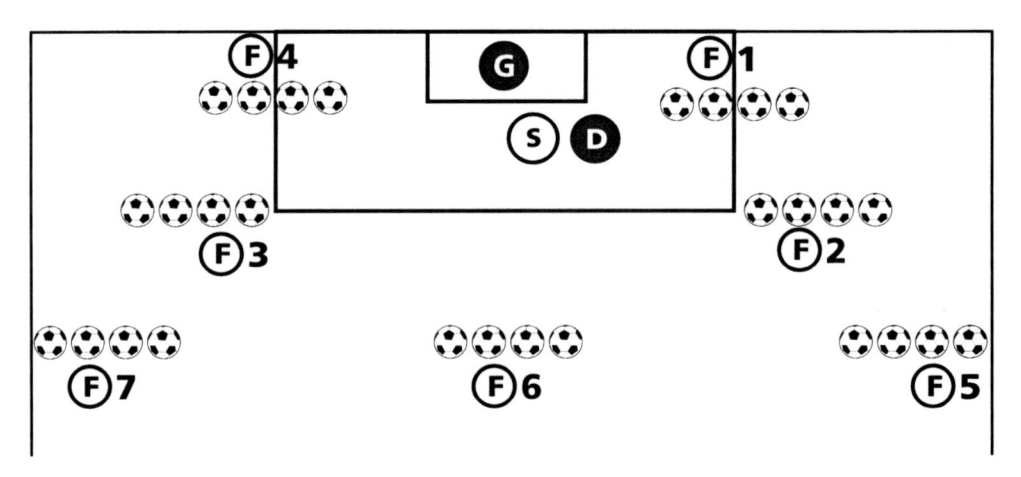

Fig. 3

4. As with all plays, players must switch roles from feeding player, to defender, and to shooting player.

IX. DEFENSIVE CLEARING PLAY:

A. THE FINISHING PLAY DESCRIBED IN THE PREVIOUS SECTION VIII. YEAR TWO CAN ALSO BE USED AS A CLEARING PLAY FOR THE DEFENDERS.

1. The play is set up exactly as described in section VIII with the feeding players positioned the exact same way.

2. The feeding players send every type of ball at the defender who is positioned in the middle and in the goalie box.

3. The defender must clear all the balls out of the goalie box by playing the ball UP field and OUTSIDE.

4. As the clearing defender becomes more confident and comfortable an attacker \ is introduced into this clearing play.

a. The attacker in the beginning serves as a shadow attacker and is merely an obstacle for the clearing defender.

b. The attacker increases the pressure as the clearing defender becomes confident in clearing the ball out of the goalie box.

B. TEACH AND DEMONSTRATE PLAY:

1. Players required:

a. Three feeding players.

b. One defender to clear the balls.

c. Six to fifteen soccer balls depending on the quantity of available soccer balls.

2. Set up the play:

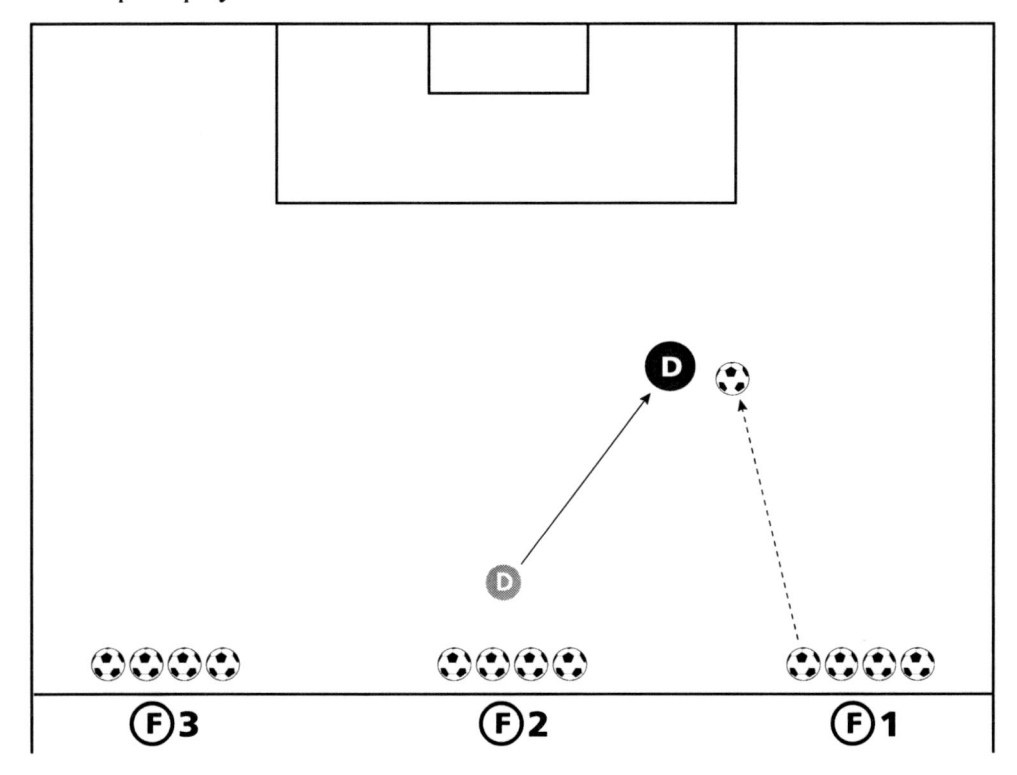

1. The three feeders are stationed at midfield with one feeding player stationed in the center and the other two feeding players are positioned on the outside and on either side of the center feeder.
2. Each feeding player has an equal number of soccer balls.
3. The clearing defender is stationed in the center and near the midfield line.
4. The feeding players will feed the ball clockwise beginning with feeding player #1.
5. One feeding player at a time will play the ball into the space ahead of the clearing defender.
6. The clearing defender must chase the ball down and clear the ball **up field** and towards the **outside.**
7. As soon as the ball is cleared, the clearing defender must turn and sprint back to where the feeding players are positioned.
8. As soon as the clearing defender has reached to where the feeding defenders are positioned then feeding player #2 plays the ball into the space ahead of the clearing defender.
9. This sequence **repeats** itself until all the balls have been played.

10. Players must change roles in order that each player learns to be a feeding player and a clearing defender.

11. As players become more confident and comfortable:
a. The feeding players must learn to feed balls in the air.
b. A forward is introduced who will put pressure on the clearing defender. In the beginning the forward is only a shadow forward but as the defender becomes comfortable, the forward increases the pressure.
c. Two or three defenders can be sent out to clear two or three balls that have been fed by each feeding player simultaneously.

EMPHASIZE:
- *The clearing defender must learn to get to the ball quickly and then recover back quickly to where the feeding players are stationed.*
- *The clearing defenders must learn to go to the ball directly and not to take a wide circle line to the ball.*
- *Clearing defenders must learn to get into proper position and behind the ball before striking the ball.*
- *Clearing defenders must learn to handle and clear different type of played balls.*
- *After the first or second round of balls has been fed, the clearing defender will become increasingly tired. One of the objectives of the clearing play is to learn to clear the ball under fatigue thereby simulating game conditions.*
- *The feeding player practices sending long balls by striking the ball from underneath and with the top part of the kicking foot and thereby lifting the ball into the air.*
- *Feeding players practice having the body weight over the ball and the plant foot enough distance from the ball so as to be able to strike the ball freely with the kicking foot.*
- *Feeding players should practice feeding the ball with their weak foot.*
- *Clearing defender must learn to clear the ball UP field and to the OUTSIDE.*
- *Clearing defenders must always be aware of the type of pressure from the opponent's attackers.*

YEAR THREE

Year Three in the development of youth soccer players will focus on playing as a team in the attacking third of the field of play. The play will center on organization. As always, the team that is better organized generally will win the game.

As has been demonstrated in Year One and Year Two, the playing of the game of soccer is not about one player or just a few players. The focus in the attacking third must never be on just the striker. The focus must be on sending an entire team on the attack. We have demonstrated this in Year Two with team transition from the defensive third through the middle third and all the way into the attacking third. At each stage a superior number of players must be in position.

Year Three will teach sets of attacking plays for the purpose of finishing the attack with a goal.

I. REVIEW YEAR ONE AND YEAR TWO:

As the coach of the team, one must never assume that because the players have been taught how to play in the defensive third or transition from the defensive third into the attacking third in Years One and Two that the youth players will remember how to implement these strategies. The younger the team the greater chance that they will have forgotten what had been taught. For this very reason the coach must take several weeks to review all the material taught in both of the previous years. Take the time to go over all of the material until you, as the coach, are satisfied that they understand completely what had been taught in the two previous years. **This material must be reviewed throughout the year. Success depends on REPETITION!**

II. WEAVE PLAY:

In Year Three the weave drill is expanded by placing three players in the center and five or more players are positioned on the outside. The principals of this play remain the same as taught in Years One and Two.

- Three balls are used in this Weave Play
- The ball is always first played from the outside player to the middle player. Any re-start always is played from the outside into the middle
- The balls are played by the outside players positioned directly opposite each other

Practice all the different plays described in the Weave Play sections in Years One and Two. They can now be practiced with three players in the center and with three balls. The speed of the play is now greatly increased.

III. LONG BALL—SHORT BALL—TAKE-OVER PLAY:

This play is an excellent play to demonstrate to players that they have the freedom to move all over the field of play. They are not rooted to only one area of the field. I do not know who first developed this play but it is an ideal play to demonstrate why soccer is called the "beautiful game." It deals with the "freedom" of the players.

1. Split the team into groups of five with each player receiving a number from 1 through 5.

a. Player sequence:
   - Player #2 will always play the ball from player #1.
   - Player #3 will always play the ball from player #2.
   - Player #4 will always play the ball from player #3.
   - Player #5 will always play the ball from player #4.
   - Player #1 will always play the ball from player #5.

b. Play sequence:
   - Player 2 will receive a short pass on the ground from player #1.
   - Player #3 must get into position to execute a take over of the ball from player #2
   - Player #3 will send a long ball in the air to player #4 who has moved into a position a good distance from player #3.
   - Player #5 needed to adjust the position towards player #4 to receive a short pass on the ground from player #4.
   - Player #1 must adjust to meet player #5 to execute a take over of the ball from player #5.
   - Player #1 will send a long ball in the air to player #2 who has moved into a position a good distance from player #1.

- Player #3 needed to adjust the position towards player #2 to receive a short pass on the ground from player #2.
- Player #4 must adjust to meet player #3 to execute a take over of the ball from player #3.
- Player #4 will send a long ball in the air to player #5 who has moved into a position a good distance from player #4.
- Player #1 needed to adjust the position towards player #5 to receive a short pass on the ground from player #5.

2. Continue this playing sequence which will always be:
   - A long ball between two players. The long ball is played in the air.
   - Followed by a short ball between two players. The short ball is played on the ground.
   - Followed by a take over.

3. By having an uneven number of players, the task between the same two players will always be a different sequence of the three tasks.

4. With this long ball-short ball-take over play, the five players have the freedom to play in an unlimited playing area. They should be constantly moving into another part of the playing field.

EMPHASIZE:

- *Player condition while using the ball.*
- *Players must play out this play under full game conditions.*
- *Players learn to be free and use any available space on the field.*
- *Players learn to develop field vision by having to locate their fellow players and adjusting their position accordingly.*
- *Players must constantly think in order to keep the sequence in order and continuous.*
- *Players must interact with each other while using different sequences.*

IV. FORWARD V FOUR DEFENDERS PLAY:

A. OBJECTIVE:

The purpose of this play is for the forwards to become comfortable in front of the opponent's goal when facing superior number of defenders. Forwards need to learn how to finish on goal quickly. Too often a youth forward will always take one more touch and one more step to be in a perfect position to shoot with no other players around them. It is necessary for a forward to view a very limited space as more than enough space to finish a shot on goal.

A forward's comfort level must develop to the point where being surrounded by defensive players produces no anxiety on the part of the forwards.

B. TEACH AND DEMONSTRATE:

1. Required Players: Goalie, Four Defenders, One Forward, Three Midfielders
2. Set Up Play:

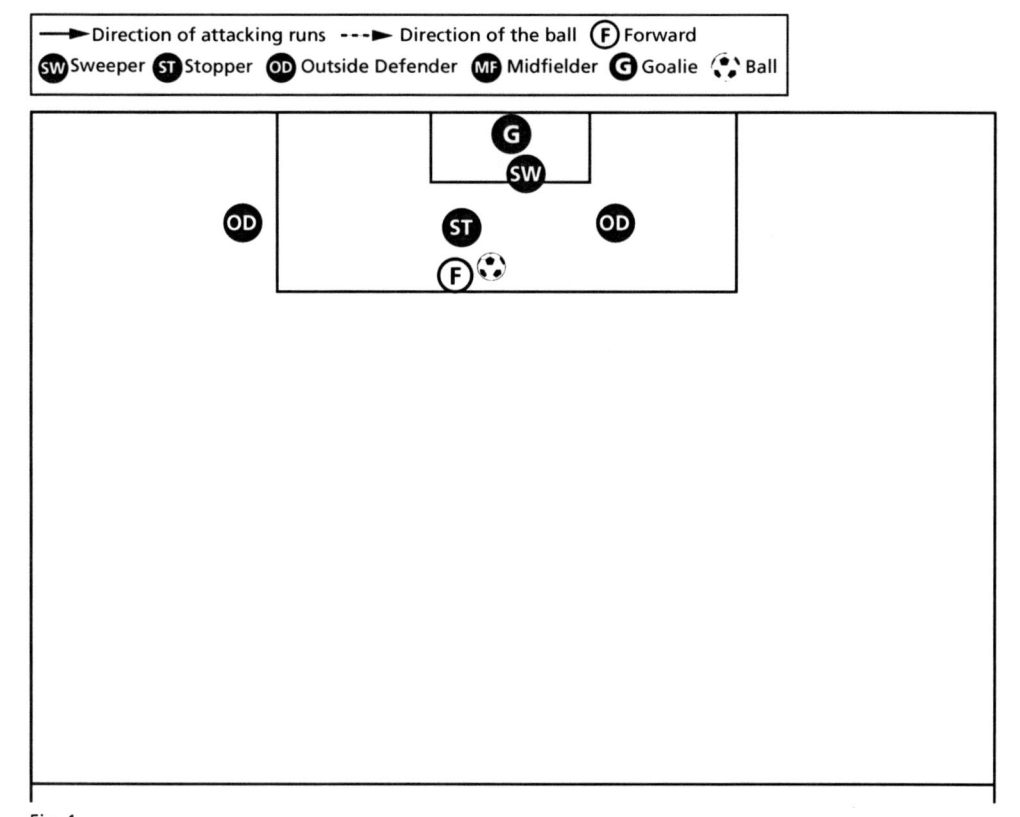

Fig. 1

FIGURE 1:

- Using individual ball handling skills, the forward must attempt to create enough space to finish with a shot on goal.
- The forward must learn to be quick and deceptive when attempting to maneuver between the defensive players.
- The forward can choose to attack into any available space.
- The forward must learn to **instantly** asses the available spaces and make an **instant** decision on how to attack those spaces.
- This play will teach the forward not to be intimidated when facing a superior number of defenders.
- The first task to be emphasized to the forward is for the forward to attack the defenders individually and finish with a shot on the opponent's goal.

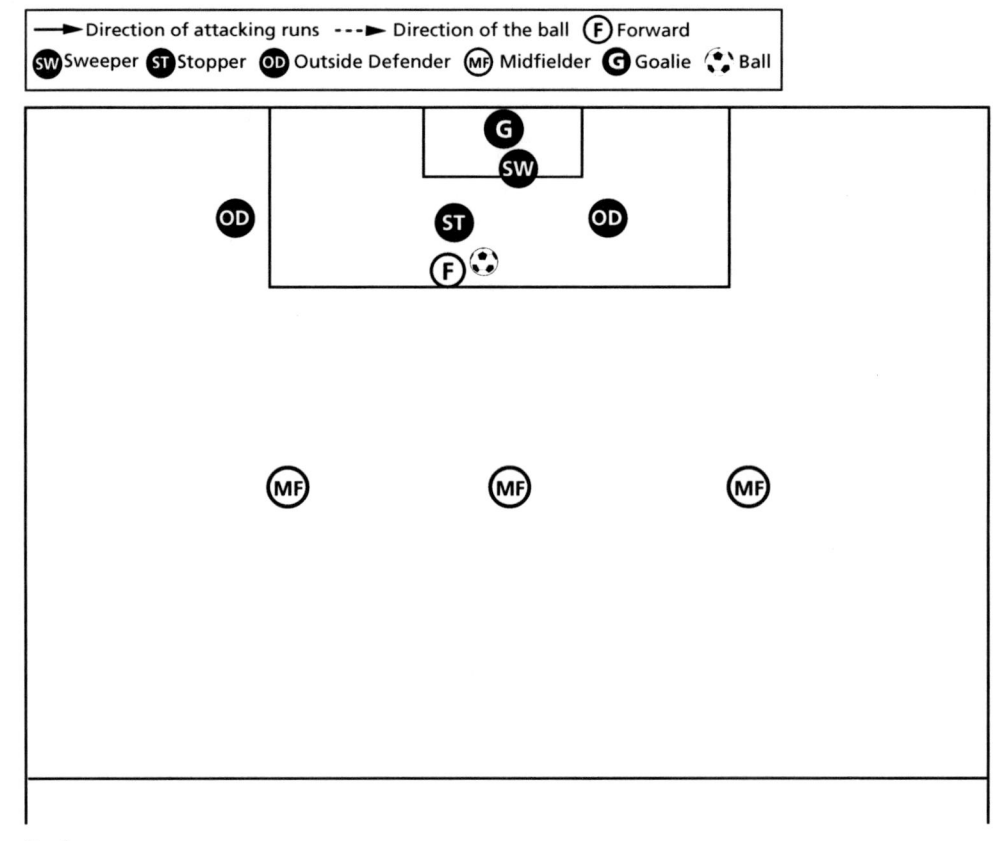

Fig. 2

FIGURE 2:

- Three midfielders will be positioned outside the goal area.
- The forward can use these three midfielders as support by passing the ball back to one of the midfielders.
- Once the ball is passed back to a midfielder, the forward must then make an instant decision to quickly attack into a space between the defenders.
- The midfielder must be aware of the forward's decision and pass the ball to the forward.
- The forward must finish with a shot on goal or pass the ball back to another midfielder before making another thrust on goal.
- Speed and quickness for the attack are the purpose of this play therefore the coach must not allow numerous passes between the forward and the midfielders.
- The midfielders should not be allowed to pass the ball back and forth between them.

3. Building onto this play:

a. A second forward can be added once the players become comfortable with attacking against superior numbers. Practice attacking only with the two forwards.

b. Introduce the three midfielders once again and allow the forwards to use them as support in their attack.

c. Allow the midfielders limited number of passes between the midfielders before they must make a pass to a forward.

EMPHASIZE:

- *This play is designed to make forwards comfortable in working against superior numbers of defenders.*
- *This play is designed to teach forwards to view a very limited space as sufficient space.*
- *This play is designed to develop the forward's foot skills.*
- *This play is designed to quicken player's decision process.*
- *This play is designed to develop timing and understanding between the forward and midfielder.*
- *This play is designed to develop speed of play.*

V. ATTACKING PLAYS:

A. OBJECTIVE OF ATTACKING PLAYS:

1. These attacking plays are for the benefit of the attack.

2. Defenders are not needed until the attackers can execute the attacking patterns flawlessly.

   a. Once the attackers can execute the attacking patters on instinct, defenders can be added to the attacking sequences.

   b. Once the defenders are added, at the beginning they will only be there to provide an obstacle for the attackers but no direct pressure.

   c. Defensive pressure must be gradual.

   d. Coaches make the mistake of adding defensive players almost immediately while the attackers are still in the learning stage. This takes away from the attacker's comfort zone to learn their assignments. If defenders are part of the attacking plays from the beginning, the attackers have now the additional burden to focus on the defenders as well as what their attacking assignment is. While learning the attacking patterns they should only have to focus on that one thing.

3. Attacking players are added until a full set of forwards and midfielders are running through the set of attacking plays.

4. Attackers must be made aware that each set of attacking plays are just one option and that during a game the player with the ball will have several options available in making a decision as to where to best play the ball.

5. With each set of attacking plays that are run, the attackers have to learn one particular option. Once the attackers are aware of several options their decisions will be that much easier.

6. Players are to execute only that particular attacking play that the coach has put onto the practice agenda. Attackers must understand that they must concentrate and learn each set of attacking plays individually.

7. Until the time when the attackers have learned the attacking patterns to the point of executing them on instinct, the coach will determine what specific attacking plays will be practiced. Once the attackers can execute the set patterns on instinct, the set play to be used will be executed by the attacker with the ball who will make the decision regarding the attacking pattern by where the ball is played.

8. When executing the attacking patterns, The attackers must always keep moving to create space and keep the defenders off balance. Make cuts quickly and sharp.

9. The coach must emphasize to the players that these attacking patterns begin with using three players just as the defensive sequences began with three players in Year One.

B. ATTACKING SET PLAYS:

1. Situation One:

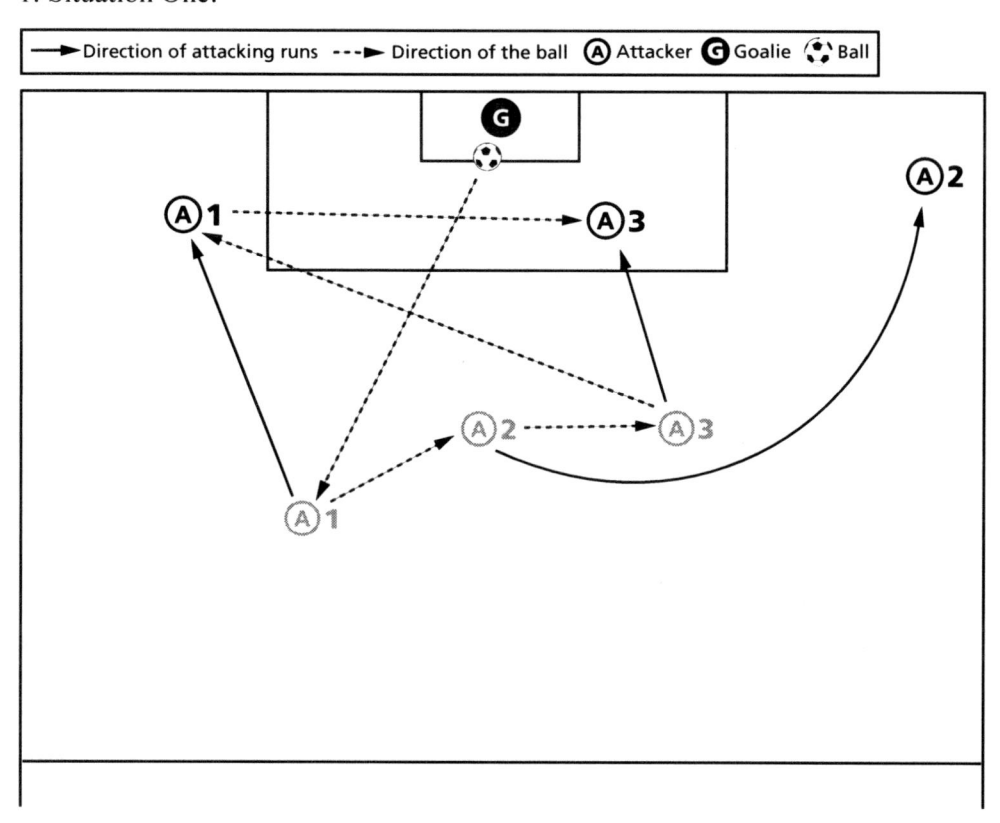

Fig. 1

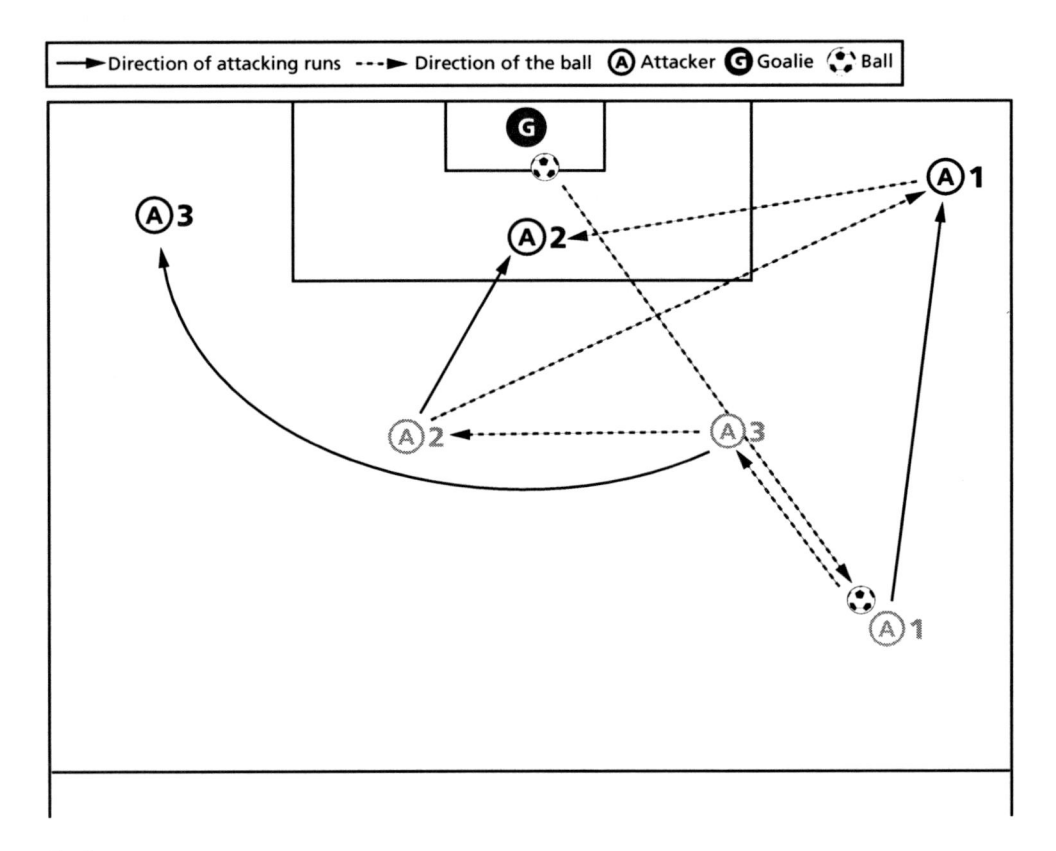

→ Direction of attacking runs   --▶ Direction of the ball   Ⓐ Attacker   Ⓖ Goalie   ⚽ Ball

Fig. 2

a. Players needed: Goalie and three Attackers. Attacker 1 is an outside midfielder, attackers 2 and 3 are forwards.

b. The goalie must punt the ball to Attacker 1.
   - It is imperative that the players learn to handle a ball out of the air and do not allow the ball to bounce in front of them before playing the ball.
   - Players must learn to play with speed.

EMPHASIZE:
With all the set attacking plays, the play begins with the goalie punting the ball to the attacker in order that players learn to handle the ball out of the air.

c. In Fig.1 the ball is played to the right defensive side. In Fig. 2 The ball is played to the left defensive side.

d. Outside midfielder A1 controls the ball out of the air and plays it to forward A2. After having made the pass to A2, the outside midfielder makes an arching run to the defensive right outside taking position outside the goalie area.

e. Forward A2 passes the ball across to the second forward A3 who is positioned in the middle area of the field. After the pass has been made to A3, forward A2 makes an arching run behind A3 taking position on the left defensive outside of the goalie area.

f. While outside midfielder A1 and forward A2 are making their runs to the outside, Forward A3 passes the ball to the outside midfielder A1. After the pass has been made, forward A3 penetrates into the goalie area taking up position in the middle of the goalie area directly in front of the goal.

g. Outside midfielder A1 crosses the ball to forward A3 who finishes on goal.

h. Repeat this same sequence only this time play the ball to the defensive left side as shown in Fig.2.

2. Situation Two:

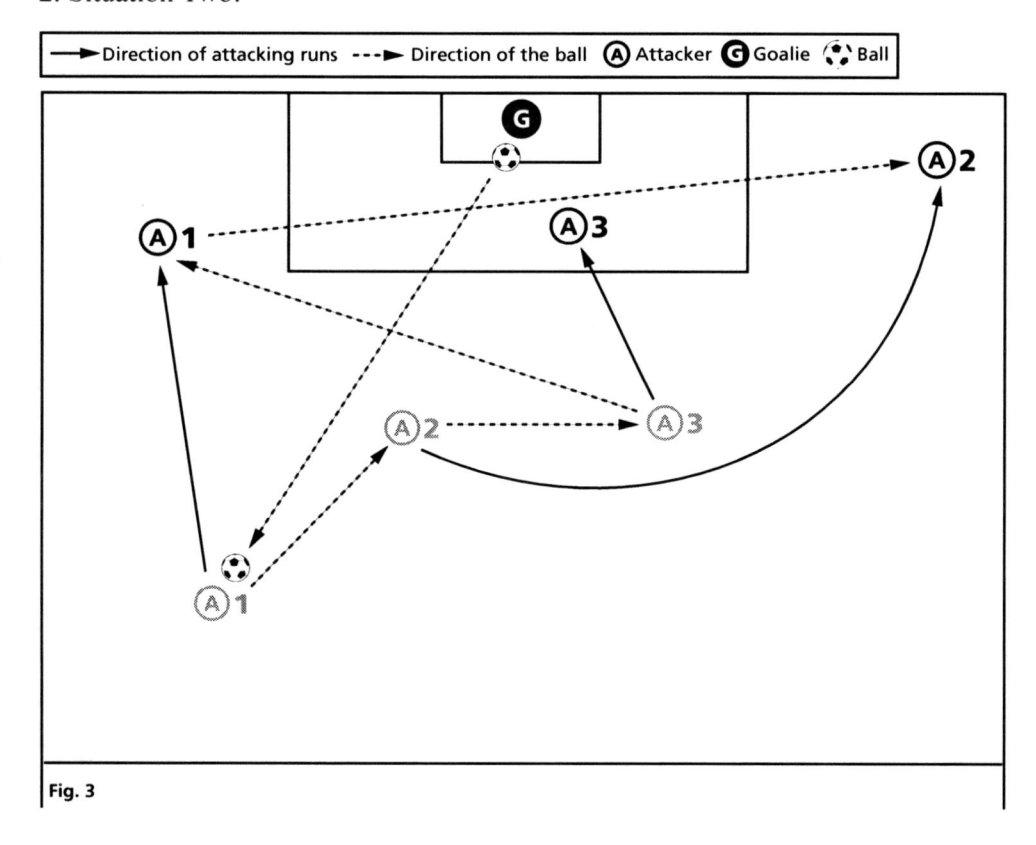

Fig. 3

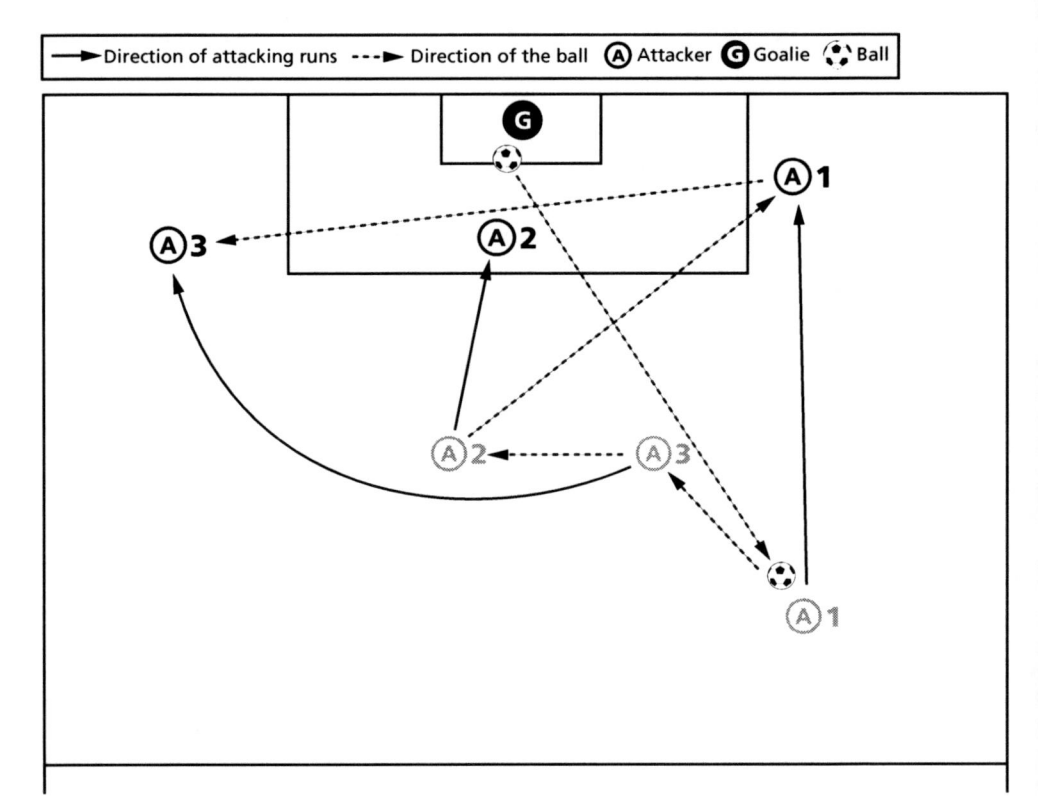

Fig. 4

a. Repeat the same sequence as described in Situation One.
b. The final cross from outside midfield attacker A1 will go to the weak side forward A2.
c. Forward A2 will finish on goal.
d. Repeat this sequence while playing the ball to the defensive right side as shown in Fig 4.

3. Situation Three: Add the attacking center midfielder A4.

In figure 5–8 the ball is played to the right defensive side

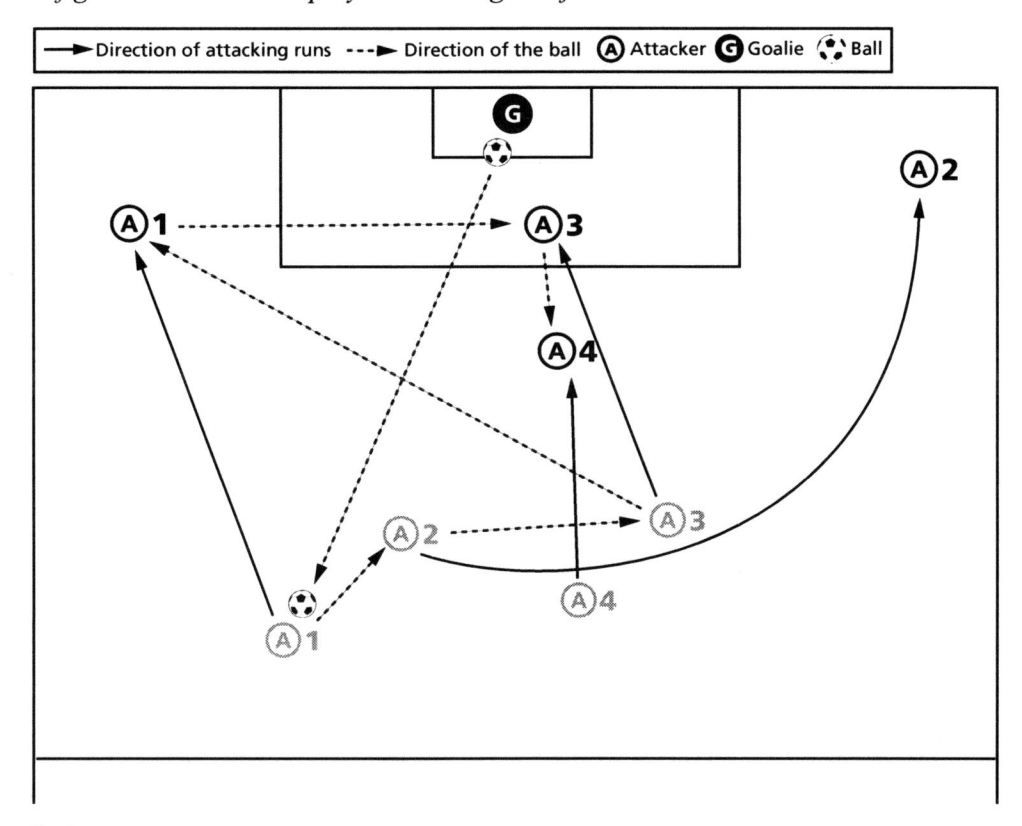

Fig. 5

Finishing the play, attacker 1 crosses the ball to attacker 3 who drops the ball back to attacker 4 who finishes on goal with a shot

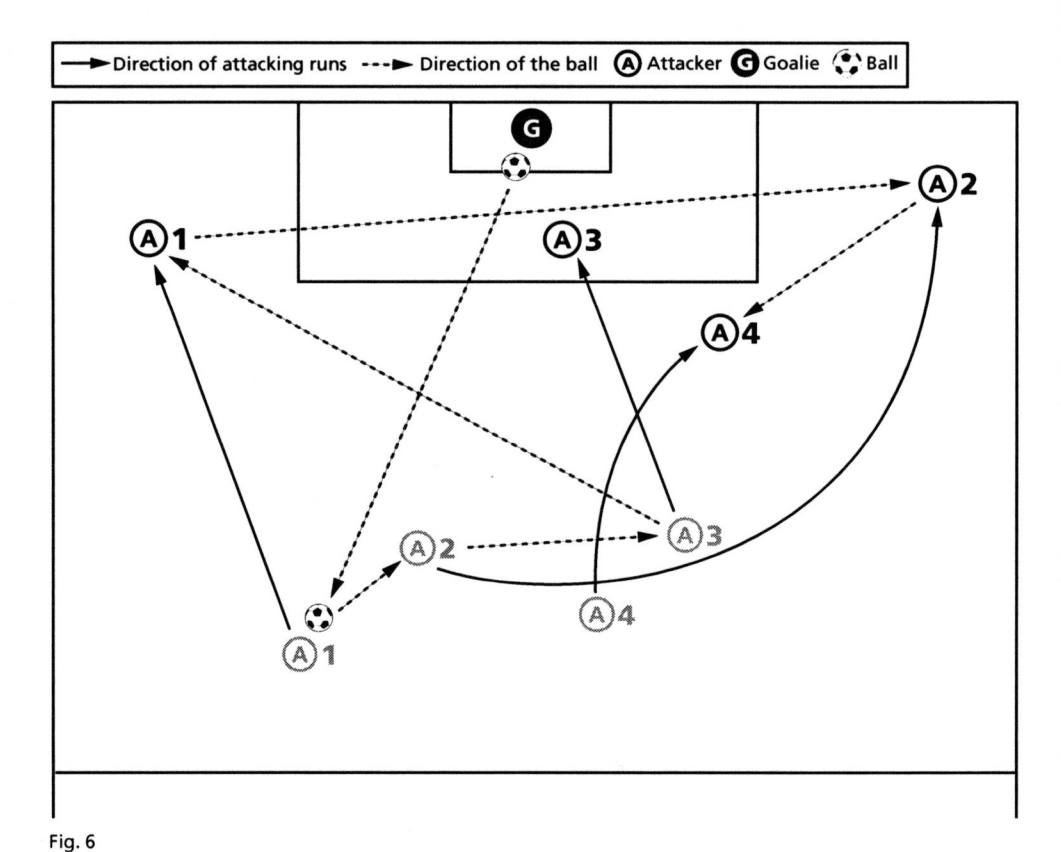

Fig. 6

Finishing the play, attacker 1 crosses the ball to attacker 2 who drops the ball back to attacker 4 who finishes on goal with a shot

Fig. 7

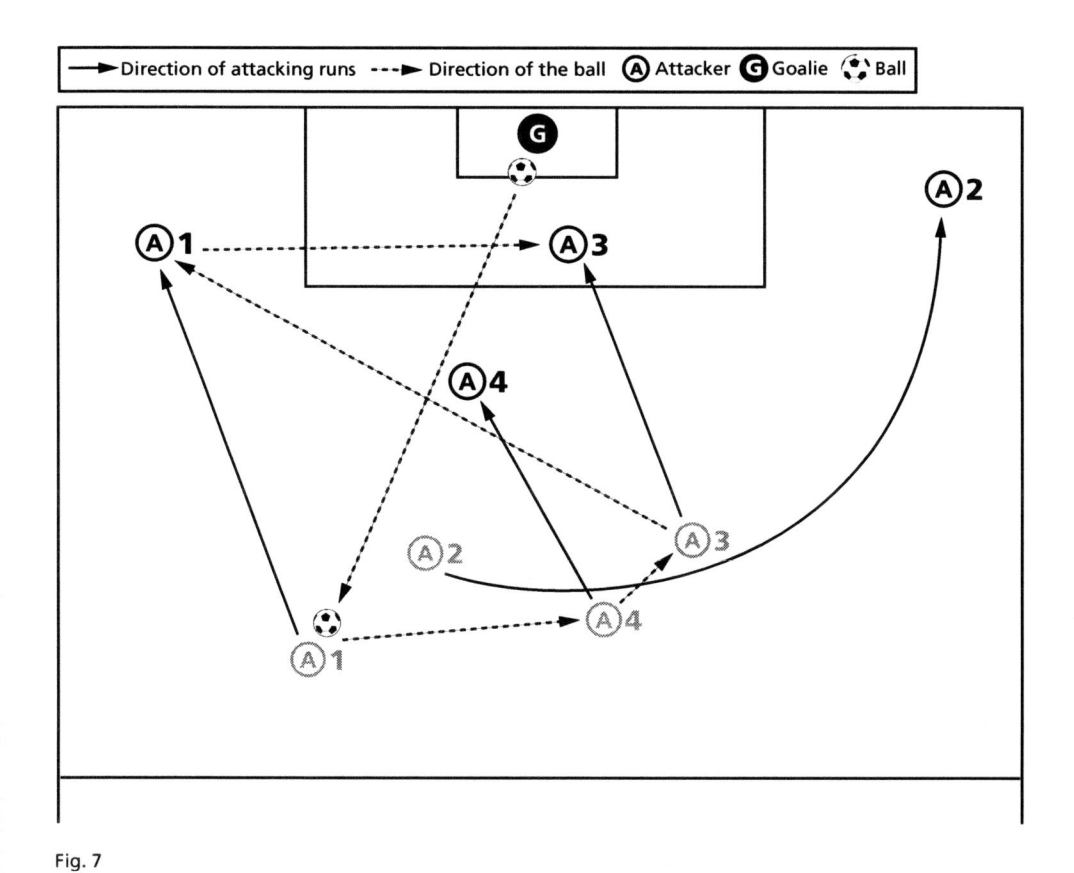

Finishing the play, attacker 1 crosses the ball to attacker 3 who makes the decision to either finish on goal or pass the ball back to attacker 4 who then finishes on goal.

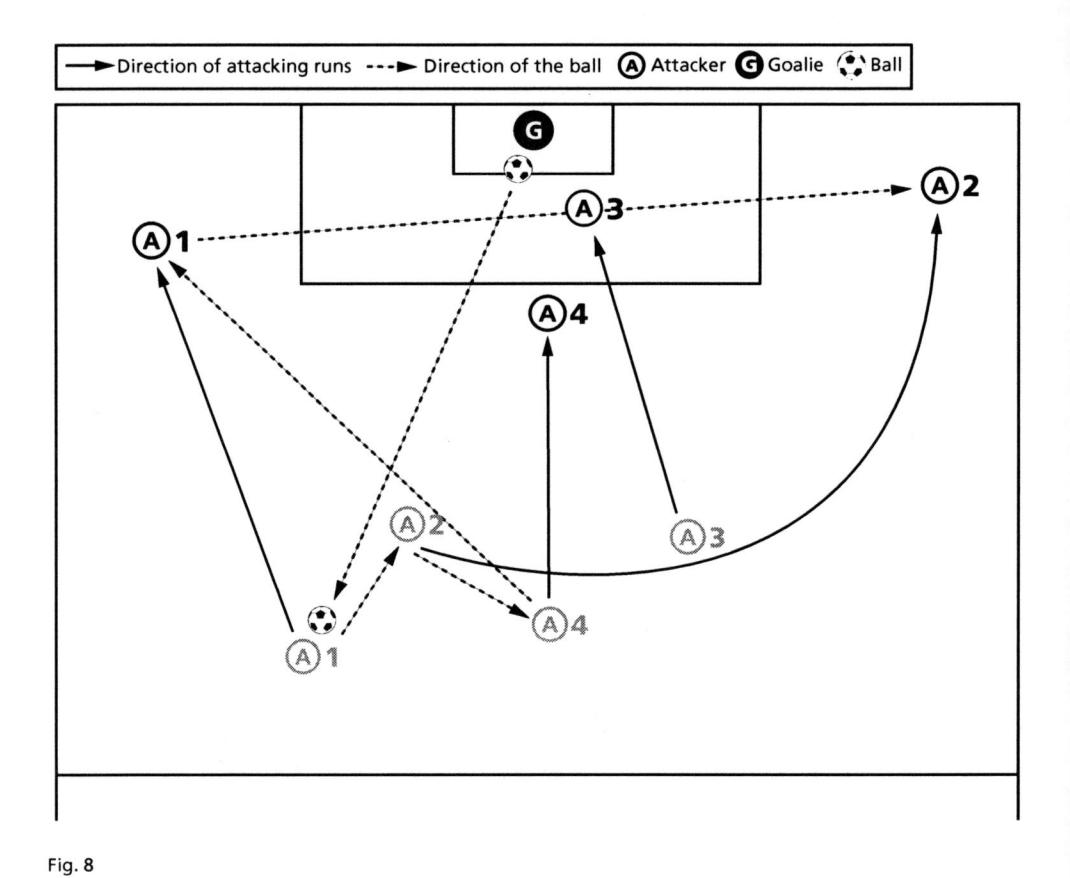

Fig. 8

Finishing the play, attacker 1 crosses the ball to attacker 2 who makes the decision to either finish on goal or pass the ball back to attacker 4 who then finishes on goal.

In figure 9–10 the ball is played to the left defensive side

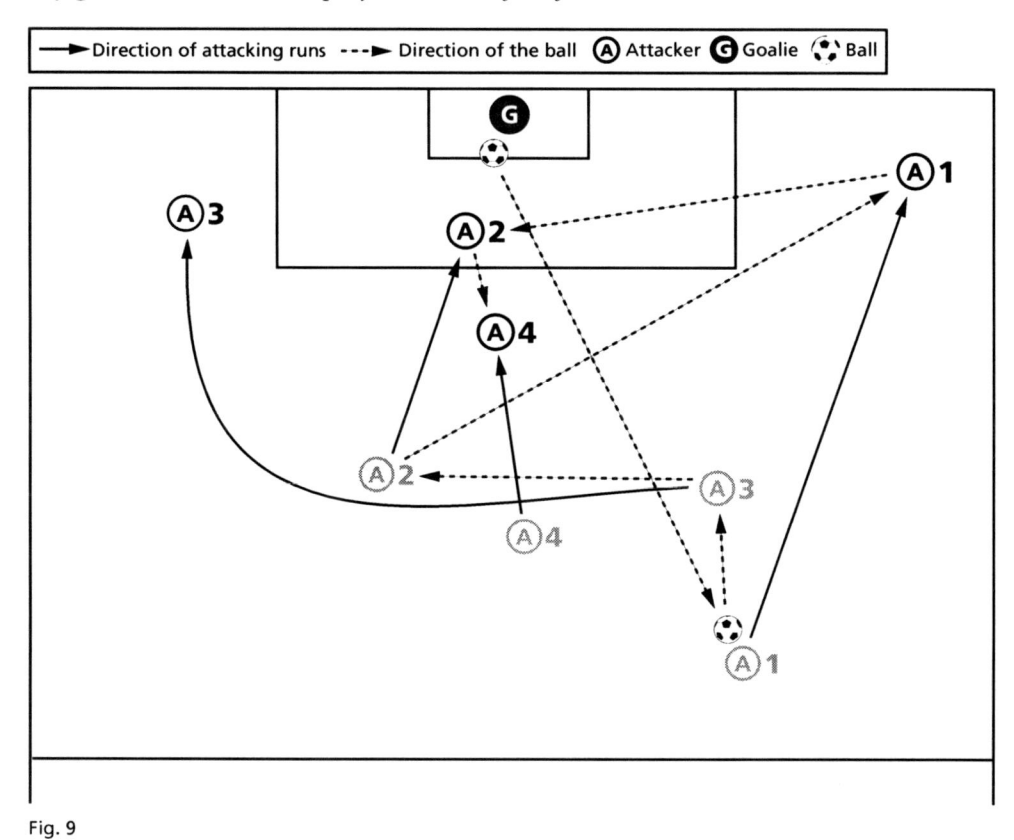

→ Direction of attacking runs ---► Direction of the ball (A) Attacker (G) Goalie ⚽ Ball

Fig. 9

Finishing the play, attacker 1 crosses the ball to attacker 2 who drops the ball back to attacker 4 who finishes on goal with a shot

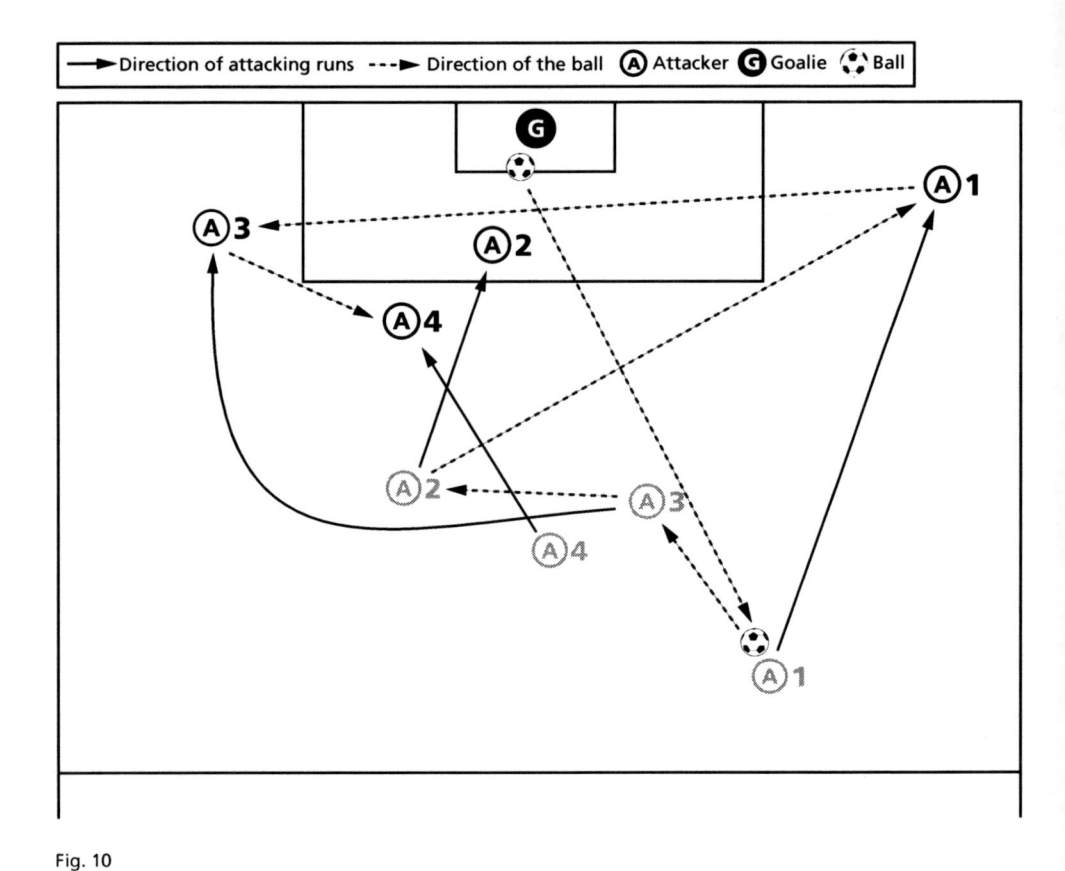

Fig. 10

Finishing the play, attacker 1 crosses the ball to attacker 3 who drops the ball back to attacker 4 who finishes on goal with a shot

Fig. 11

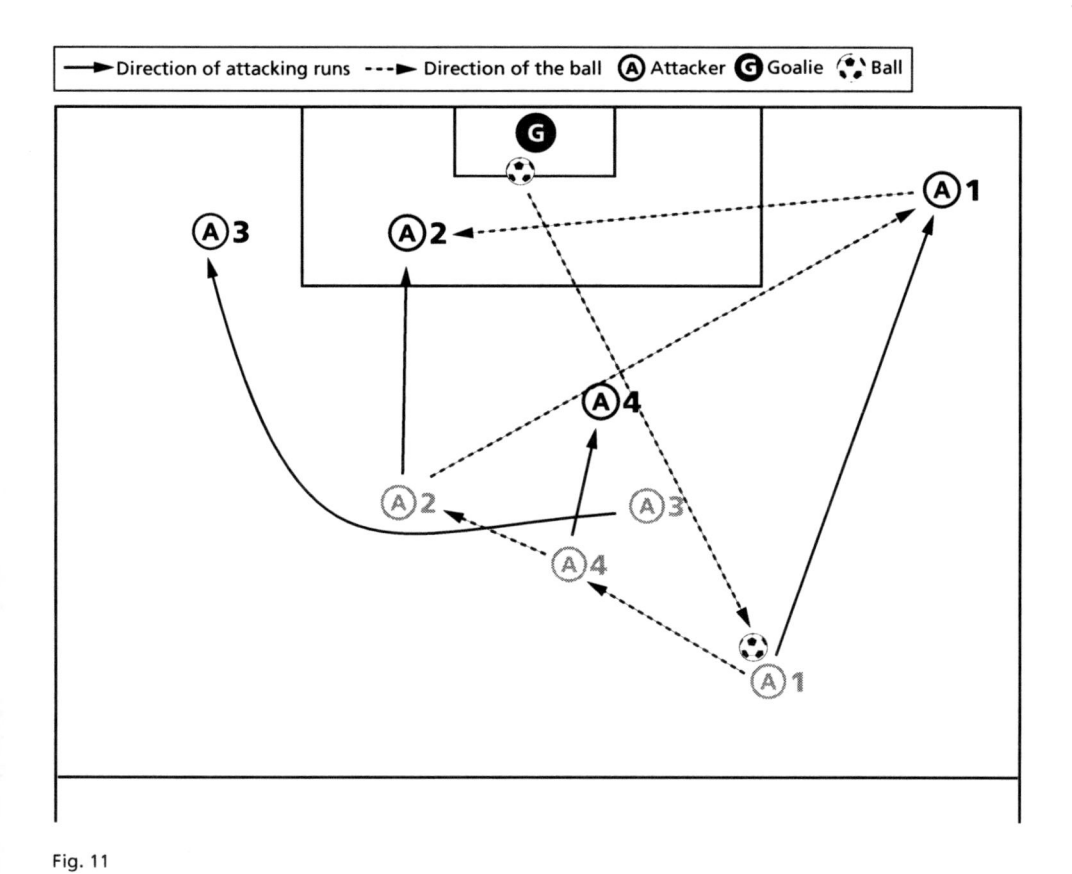

Finishing the play, attacker 1 crosses the ball to attacker 2 who makes the decision to either finish on goal or pass the ball back to attacker 4 who then finishes on goal.

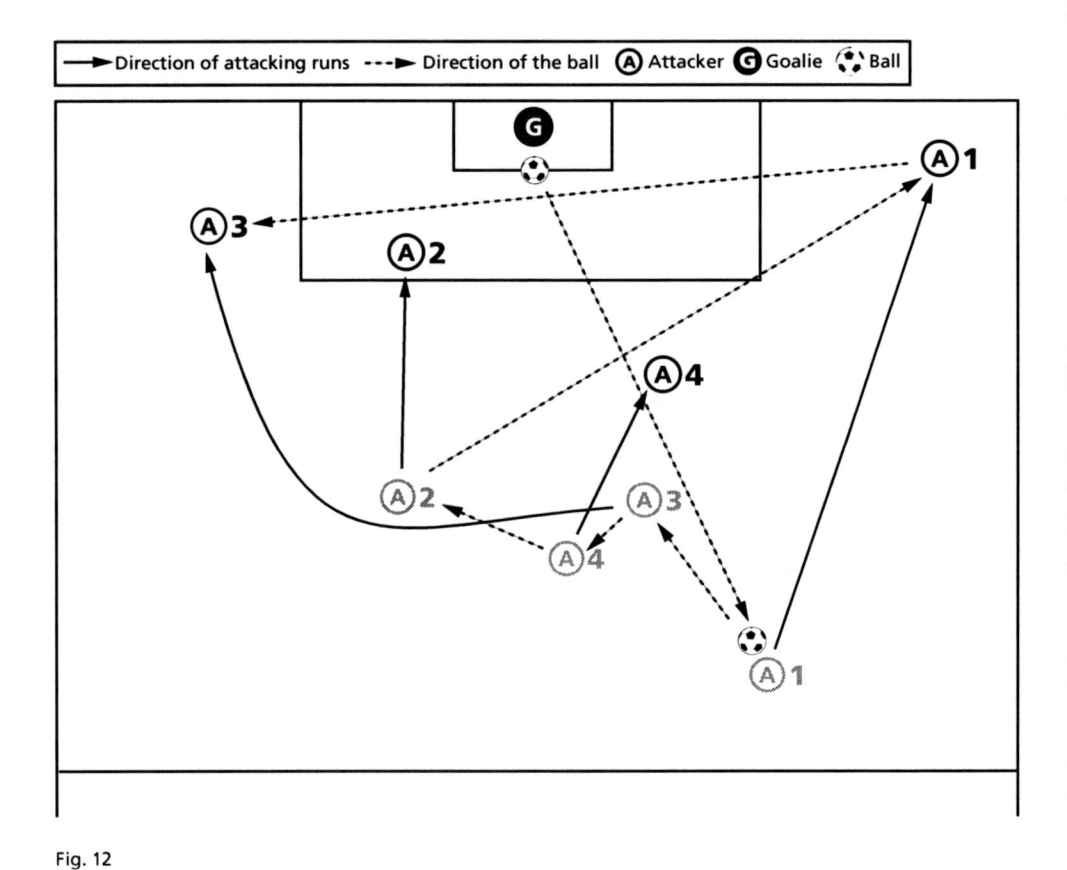

Fig. 12

Finishing the play, attacker 1 crosses the ball to attacker 3 who makes the decision to either finish on goal or pass the ball back to attacker 4 who then finishes on goal.

4. Situation Four. Add the attacking midfielder A5

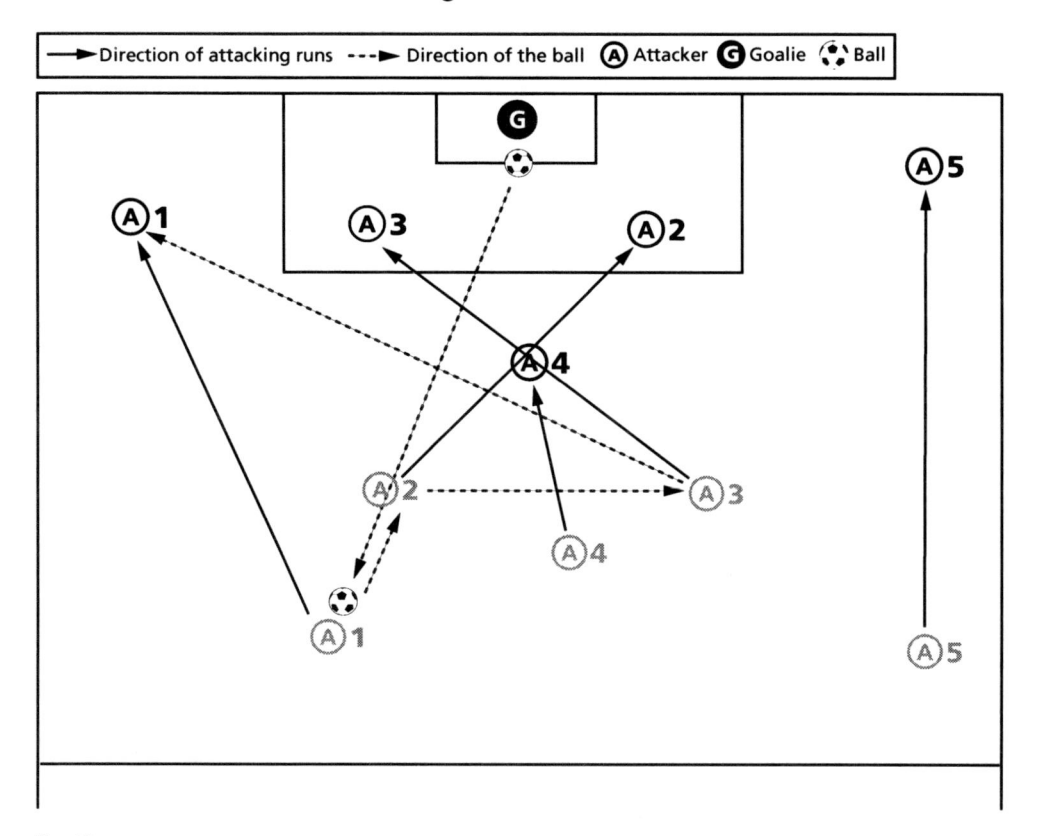

Fig. 13

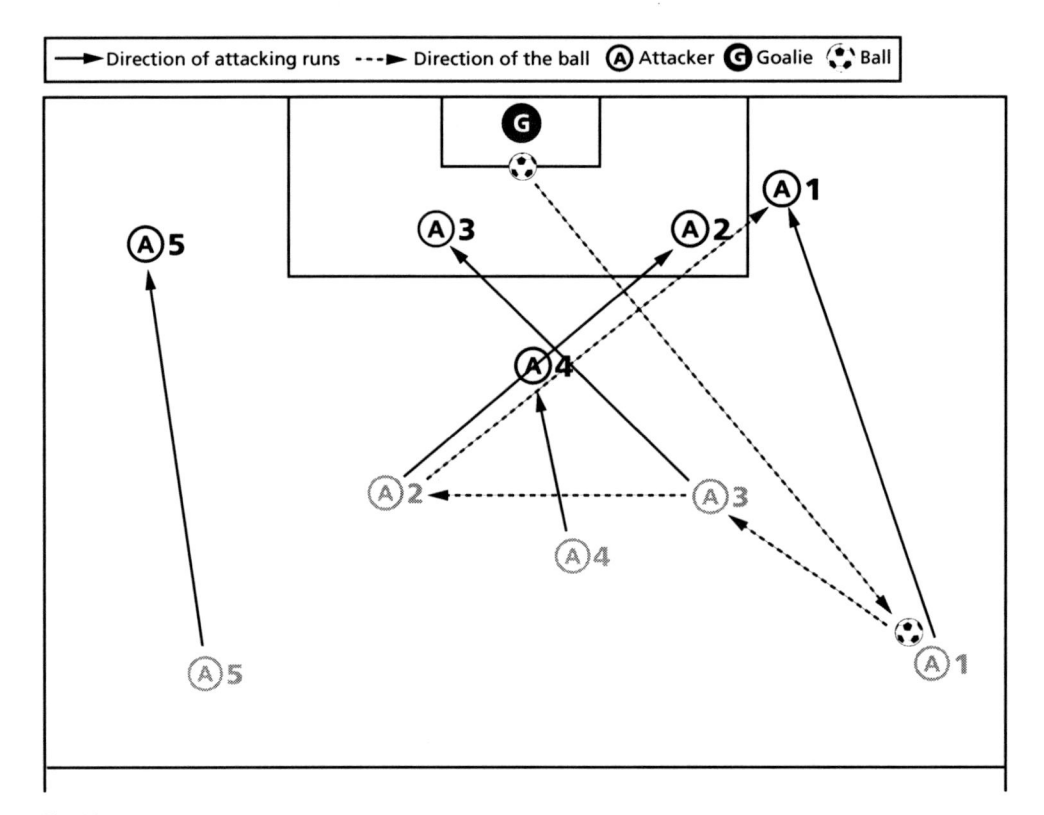

Fig. 14

a. Repeat the same attacking sequences as described in Situations One through Three.
b. Outside midfielder A5 will make the weak side attacking run into the attack and take up position on the outside of the goalie box area as shown in Figure 13.
c. Forward attackers A2 and A3 will make crossing runs and take up position inside the goalie box.
d. Attacker 1 will have four options:
   • Play the ball near post to attacker 3.
   • Play the ball far post to attacker 2.
   • Cross the ball to the weak side to attacker 5
   • Play the ball to attacker 4 who has taken up position at the top of the goalie box.
e. During practice the coach must first designate to which attacker the ball is played by attacker 1. Once players understand the options available for a crossed ball, the decision as to where to play the ball will be up to the attacker who has possession of the ball.

Repeat the same sequence only this time play the ball to the opposite side as shown in Figure 14.

5. Situation Five. Add Outside Defenders A6 & A7

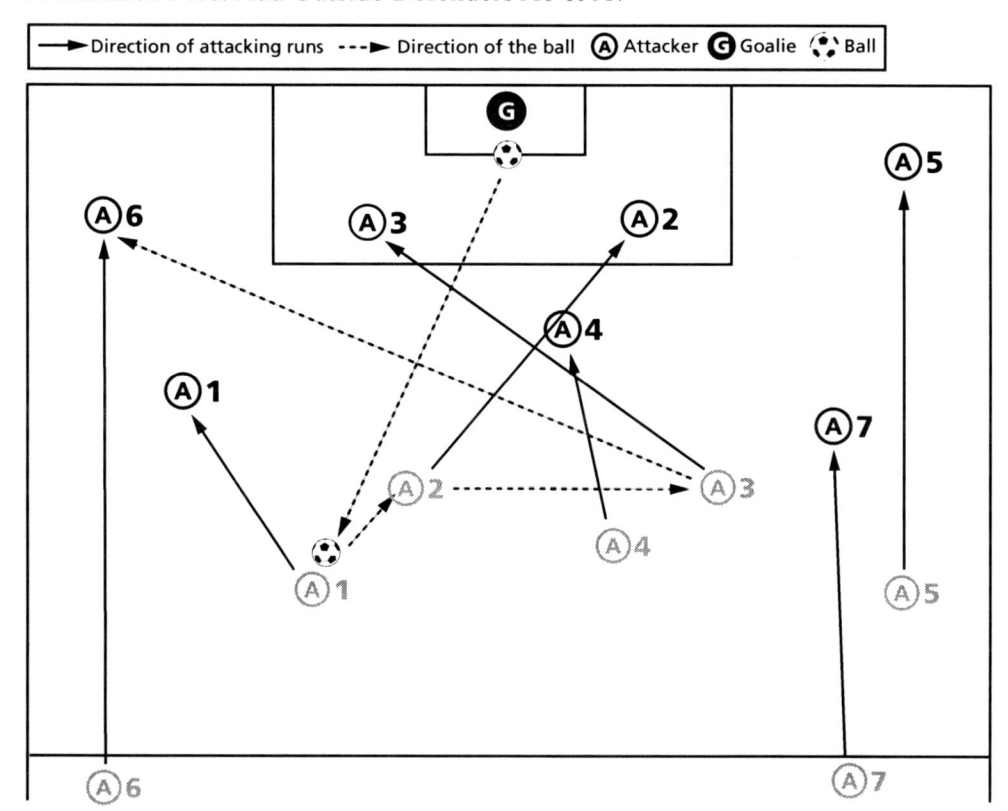

Fig. 15

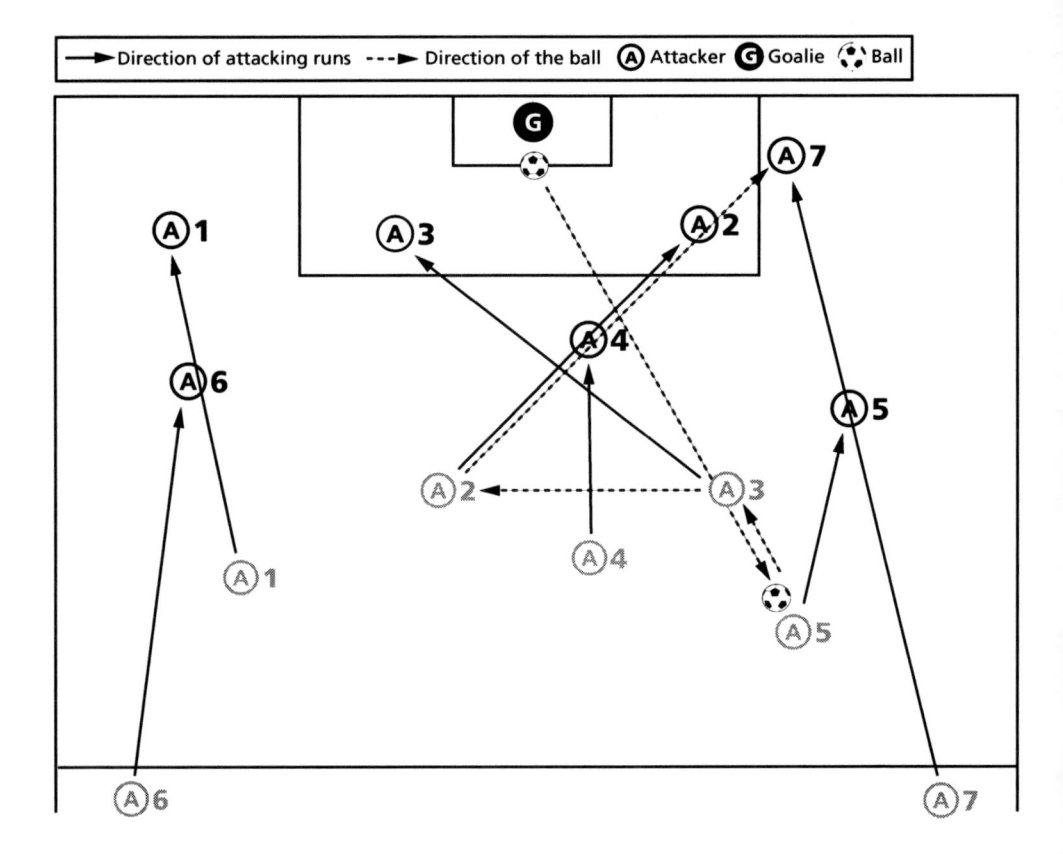

Fig. 16

a. Repeat the same attacking situations as described in Situations One through Four.
b. Additional attacking situations are now being created with the addition of defenders A6 and A7 moving into the attack as described in Figure 15.
   - Defenders A6 and A7 can push all the way to the goalie box and become attackers to either support the attack or actually finish on goal.
   - Run each attacking situation described previously working on the timing of the defenders run into the attacking positions.
   - Work a series of overlapping runs between the midfielders and defenders.
c. During practice the coach must first designate to which attacker the ball is played by attacker 1. Once players understand the options available, the decision as to where to play the ball will be up to the attacker who has possession of the ball. Players thereby learn to make decisions on their own.
d. Repeat the same sequence only this time play the ball to the opposite side as described in Figure 16.

EMPHASIZE:

The objective of this series of attacking sequences is to learn how to use the outside defenders to build and become part of the attack.

5. Situation Six. Add Defensive Center Midfielder A8, Stopper A9, and Sweeper A10.

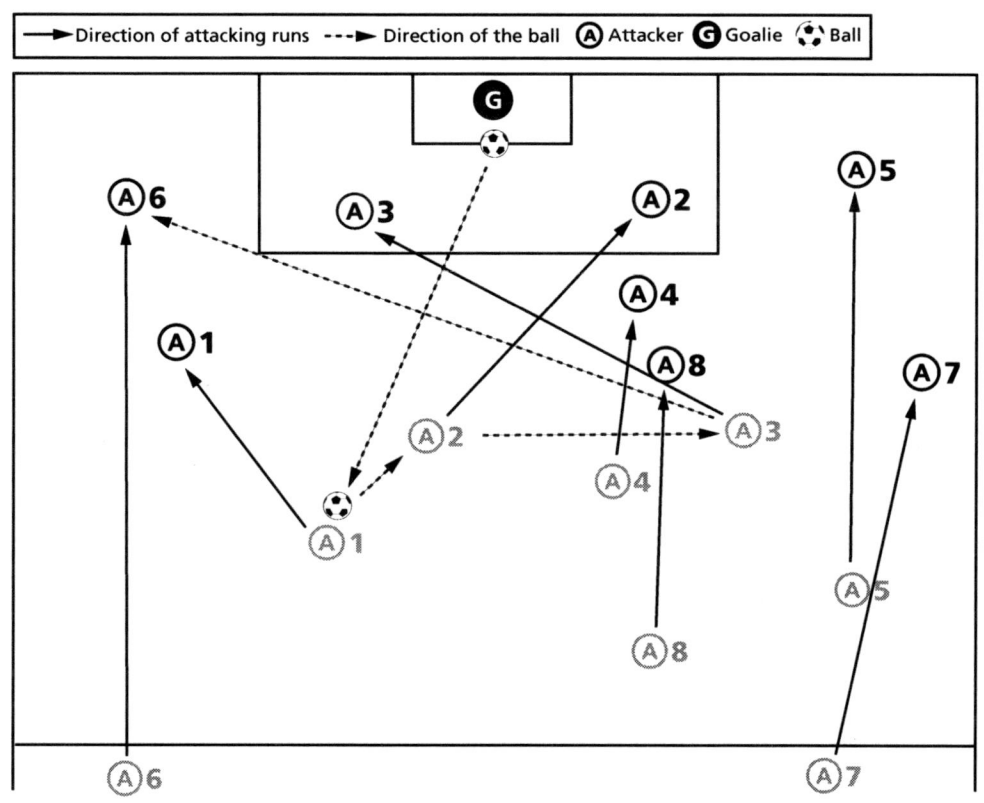

Fig. 17

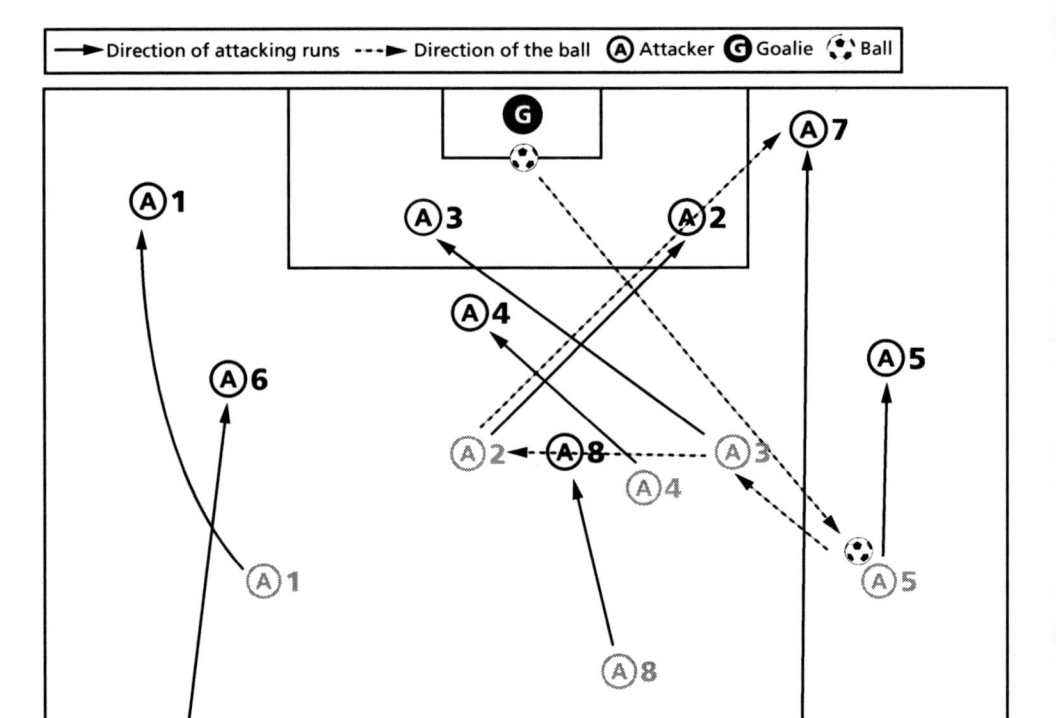

Fig. 18

a. Repeat the same sequences as described in Situations One through Five.

b. Additional attacking situations are now created.

- The sweeper, being the free man, is able to push out of the defense and into the attack to either be in a dangerous support position or actually finish on goal. The decision to go onto the attack is made when the attacking defense has pushed into the middle third of the field.
- Running the previously described attacking situations, the sweeper this time moves forward into an attacking position.
- The sweeper has the freedom to make runs to the outside as well as up the middle
- The sweeper's decision as to what attacking position to take will depend on the open spaces and which are most dangerous to the opposing defenders.
- Work on sequences of overlapping runs between the sweeper and the midfielders.

EMPHASIZE:

The objective of this series of attacking sequences is to learn how to use the sweeper to build and become part of the attack.

All set game play situations described in Year One through Year Three are only one specific option as to what players can develop in a game whether defensively, transitioning, or attacking. The coach must teach the players how to become creative players. The reason soccer is called the beautiful game is because any creative situation is possible. There are no limits to the freedom of play. Players will become creative if they are first taught ONE specific game play. Once they understand one specific game play they can then be shown how any number of combinations are possible.

Less is more!

OBSERVATIONS and COMMENTS

PASSION FOR THE GAME:

Recently my wife Lisa and I had the good fortune to travel to England with my friend Andrew Creathorn and his youth soccer team that he coaches. The team consisted of sixteen year old girls and for most of them it was their first trip overseas. The purpose of the trip was to play three girls teams from England, to train with some English coaches, and of course to take in the sights. It was a great educational experience for them especially since they won all three of their games and had only one goal scored against them.

Growing up in Europe, traveling is an important part in the education and development of a child. It is easier to achieve this end in Europe because each country is very reachable and has a completely different history and culture. If I were to drive for five hours from my home town in Austria I would be in Venice. In America if you drive for five hours from Rochester, New York, you will be in Pennsylvania with no cultural difference from Rochester. Having teams travel to a foreign country should be an objective of every soccer club.

While there, we were able to see one of the Semi-Finals of the FA Cup at Wembley Stadium. We were also able to see a Premiership regular league game at Old Trafford between Manchester United and Everton. The players from our team had never experienced such passion on the part of the fans from each team. The streets and pubs around the stadium were filled with people wearing the colors of their team. The chanting and singing of the theme songs for each team starts outside the stadium and continues inside the stadium growing louder as the game progresses. The stadiums are divided with the fans from each team all in one area of the stadium. Under no circumstance will a fan from one team ever dare to be seated in the same section as the fans from the opposing team. It would not be safe. We do not experience this at our sporting events in America where fans from each team are mixed together throughout the stadium. We lack the intense passion in this country because of the absence of...

HATE!

The passion is driven by hate. This hate towards one another goes back centuries. Recently I spoke with Andrew about this passion that the game of soccer produces in people. When I was growing up in Austria we hated the people in the village next to us even though the village was close enough to be able to walk to it. We did not consider them to be as good as us. They in turn hated us for the same reason. However, all of us in the State of Salzburg were united in our hatred for the people in the City of Salzburg because they thought that they were better than the rest of us in the State. All of us in the City and State of Salzburg were united in our hatred for the people in the State of Tyrol as well as the people in the State of Upper Austria, the State of Lower Austria, and the rest of the Austrian States. All the people in those states in turn also hated the people in the other states. But we were all united in our hatred of the people in Vienna because they thought that they were better than everyone else in Austria and in turn the people in Vienna hated everyone else in Austria. This same divisive hatred existed within the boarders of every other country.

Everyone in Austria was united in our hatred of the Italians, the Germans, the English, the Spanish, the Greeks, the people in the country of Portugal, and so on. Each country thinks that they are better than the others and thereby hated us Austrians and all the other countries. Hate is an abundant commodity.

However, every one in every country is united in our hatred for, but before I could say it, Andrew shouted out "The French!" Yes, we are all united in our hatred for the French and the French are united in their hatred for every other country. You see, Andrew was born and raised in Europe therefore he had grown up the same way as everyone else in those countries. He understood the dynamics of this hate.

This hate is crystallized through our soccer teams. The teams of each area represent the army of that area while the game of soccer represents the battle against those we hate from the other areas. Before the nineteenth century most big cities in Europe were city states and independent of each other. Over the centuries these city states waged wars against one another. Each person's dislike of people in other areas dates back many centuries. The soccer teams continue the battles once waged with weapons and armies. The only injuries now are the result of a fan from one team sitting in the section with the fans from the opposing team while wearing the wrong colors. But all in all, soccer is a bloodless battle that evokes the century old passions in each spectator.

In the United States this deep seated hatred for the opponent does not exist. We do not like the fans or the team from another city but we do not hate them to the point we do harm to those opposing fans. In our history the Civil War was the only time when two sections of the country hated one another to the point where we actually killed each other. But those wounds have now healed, at least for the most part. Fans from opposing teams find themselves sitting next to each other. There may be good natured chiding going on but there usually is no violence. This country has not had independent city states in our history. We all speak the same language and have had the same government. It is therefore hard for Americans to understand the passion that exists in other countries over the game of Soccer.

Today when I travel in Europe I am amazed to find no boarders and a common currency. When I was growing up, if someone had told me that one day I would be able to cross into Italy or Germany without having to spend some time at a boarder crossing I would have said that such a thing is impossible. Perhaps the hate has developed into a good natured hate.

For many years I have listened to Americans describe soccer as boring. They say that all they do is kick a ball around a field, there is no scoring, and the games end in ties. My answer to those people is that they shouldn't say any more because they will only show their ignorance. The sport of soccer has grown tremendously in the United States in the past decade. It is now the number one youth sport.

More Americans are beginning to see soccer for the beautiful game that it is. There is a freedom of play in soccer and yet it requires strategy, skill, fitness, and tremendous athleticism on the part of the players. Soccer is the number one sport in the whole world. This is so because soccer is the only team sport that comes closest to life itself. There are constant ups and downs, frustrations at near missed opportunities of scoring a goal or giving up a goal, successes as well as failures. Near misses such as a shot hitting the goal post add to the spectator's anticipation and frustration. Players and teams prepare and then it often is left to luck for the outcome.

These things that happen in a game of soccer are the things that happen in everyone's daily life. Yes, there are bad games in soccer as well as good games just as there are in every other team game.

All of these elements combine to create a tremendous passion in the people who follow soccer around the world because soccer is the game that most people can personally relate to. People from any walk of life regardless of their economic status or size can play soccer. How arrogant is it for Americans to basically say that our dislike of soccer is correct and the rest of the world is wrong?

ELITE TEAMS:

There is a growing trend in youth soccer with players leaving their area club teams to go and play on a team that they perceive to be a premier or elite team. The regular town soccer clubs are open to all players regardless of ability. These clubs usually have recreation teams for those players who lack skill, ability, and desire but who still wish to play the sport just for the entertainment of it. For those players who possess a greater athletic ability there are travel teams who play the same age teams from other towns in the area. In each case the club teaches their players the skills necessary for playing the game of soccer. The youth players are with their friends from their own area while participating in this team experience. The question that troubles me is why players from these general club teams feel it necessary to leave their friends whom they have known for a long time and go to join an elite team consisting of strangers?

Parents have the perception that their child will become a better player if he or she is playing with better players. A player unfortunately will only become better if that player possesses superior athletic ability and then works very hard at learning their sport. By simply winning games a false perception is often created that the player is getting better. In reality these teams may have already leveled off and are winning only because together with other gifted players they are strong enough to be winning games as a group. If this team is winning because at a particular stage in their growth this team has bigger, faster, and better skilled players then the necessity to further develop their ability as players is no longer emphasized.

Players who are selected by these elite programs are selected because they do have superior skill. They possess this superior skill because they have been developed in a town club program. By taking this skill to a premier team the local club does not benefit from their efforts. The premier team benefits from this player and yet the local club did all the work.

My friend Andrew had coached his team from the time they played travel soccer at the age of nine. When these players reached the age of seventeen, they wound up playing in a nineteen year old age bracket in Division One. For the previous seasons they finished first while playing in Division One in their proper age bracket and this coach felt that they should move up to this older division in order that they would be challenged to a greater degree. These players all started out just being average players with average skill but stayed together because they all were from the same town and all were friends. Within the town club program he had developed these players into a championship team and has given these players a love of soccer. This is a testament to Andrew's dedication and ability as a coach. Yet, Andrew is merely a so called travel team coach but the players were still able to flourish in this regular club travel team environment while learning life lessons and developing their soccer skills.

After all that has been accomplished, Andrew lost a player to a local so called premier team. It turned out that one of the local school coaches advised this player to switch to a premier program. Personally, I am very troubled by an own town school coach advising a player to leave the very local club team that had developed this player's ability for many years and had provided the coach, the program, and the atmosphere for this player to grow. This premier team gladly took this player who was a good player because of the work others had done.

It puzzles me why parents move their children from a local travel club team to an elite team especially when considering that the local team provided everything possible for this child to have achieved success. What reason could parents have for such a move?

Is such a move about winning?

The value of winning is achieved by going through a learning process whereby a player not only acquires the individual and the team skills but also develops the character traits such as focus, commitment, loyalty, and training habits. All these qualities the player found in the local travel club. Winning has been a regular habit for this team and their achievements have been many including beating an English team in London that had not lost in five years. Winning for these players had value because their achievements were due to many years of hard work together. What value is there in winning when a team consists of all players who are already good but who did not put in the labor together to become good players? If a player is able to develop the character skills while at the same time is on a winning team, then why switch to another winning team? Is this switch made because winning is not the only main objective but the group of players with whom a player wins is also important? Then, it is not only about winning but with whom you win. Sadly, if the focus of the player and the parents is on winning a meaningless soccer game then the real reasons of youth sports has been lost. Youth sports programs are for a child to learn life lessons and develop characteristics that will be beneficial throughout that child's life. Players must grow together to become a strong team.

Does a player and parents feel more special and proud because they are on a so called elite team?

These premier programs seem to breed elitism in people. It appears to give people some bragging rights. It may be harsh to say this because the people who have made such a switch are really good people. Unfortunately, a feeling of "I am" or "my child is" better than others rises to the surface when speaking to players or parents who are on such teams. I have found that when speaking with me they will always immediately let me know that they belong to one of these premier clubs. What is the need to tell me that? Does that information make any difference regarding the conversation? You may be proud that you are part of this elite organization but what you do not realize is that if this club should come upon a player who is better than you are, then this premier club will cut you from the team to make room for the new and better player. Developing the characteristic of loyalty has been lost by all concerned.

I have experienced player moves to an elite team and have seen first hand these players playing for a premier team the first year and getting cut from that team the following year because a better player had come along. The player is then placed into a different premier club but at the end of the season gets cut from that club also. The player moves from one elite team to another over a period of years. What has this player been taught by such constant changes? Certainly not loyalty and that player will never achieve a working bond or friendships with other players. These characteristics are great losses for a youth player that in many cases stifles the development of the player.

Is it coaching?

People are under the false assumption that since this is an elite team the coach must be of a higher level. Yes, many of these coaches have achieved a coaching license of a greater level. I am not convinced that just because a coach has a high level coaching license then that coach must be a good coach. These licensing programs are open to any person even a person who has never played the sport and has a very limited knowledge of the game. A person will learn the physical aspects of the sport through this licensing program but will not possess the "feel" of the sport which is the element that actually makes a good coach.

Andrew Creathorn is an excellent coach because he has this "feel" for the game. He is thereby able to give his players more than just teaching them how to kick the ball. When speaking with parents about what they wish for their child, everyone will say that they are looking for the type of approach and atmosphere that Andrew has provided. After having said that coaching is most important and having been exposed to a coach like Andrew, why then would a parent and player switch to a premier team where the coach is an unknown commodity?

Over the years I have observed countless practices by these elite teams and have not seen many that teach much of anything. They look good with a multitude of cones placed all over the practice area and moving from one drill to another. I suppose it is all relative as to what your actual understanding of the game is and what you are seeing. I do know this for certain, I have not seen many of these supposed premier coaches with whom I would have entrusted with my children's soccer education.

Did these premier teams recruit your child when this child had limited skills? Where are these elite programs then?

Is it about being seen by college coaches?

These elite clubs must give you something for the high price they charge parents to be part of their program. Having the players be seen by college coaches is the one area that creates the possibility that your child might win a scholarship for soccer to a college. This is merely a false perception. Parents must keep in mind that soccer is not a financial bonanza sport for colleges and therefore few actual soccer scholarships are given by the college. A player may be given financial aid which is based on family income. You can apply for this financial aid without playing soccer. The time would be better spent on studying hard and thereby achieving a scholastic scholarship.

What Division do these colleges play in whose coach is scouting your child? I doubt that many Division I college coaches who give those scholarships are there scouting the team your child plays on. Only one percent of players receive a scholarship. What do you think your child's chances are for you to invest your time and money into these premier club programs?

Most parents have no concept as to what athletic ability a child must possess to achieve the level that a scholarship is offered. Remember what is perceived to be an elite team in one area may only be a second level team in another area.

Is it about getting better by playing with "good" players?

A player can only become better if that individual player possesses a high degree of natural athletic ability, then is taught well, and finally trains very hard. Playing alongside other players who are "good" players does not in and of itself make you a better player.

One's athletic ability depends on the luck of BIRTH! If a youth player is an exceptional player then that youth player will stand out above the rest no matter what team that player plays on.

Presently there exist four premier clubs in the Rochester area alone. Does such an area really have enough players for four elite soccer clubs? I think not. If a parent really wants their child to receive better coaching, then instead of just assuming that because a club calls itself a premier club it will have great coaching and nothing but good players, that parent should do their homework by checking around as to what coach has a good reputation for teaching and developing youth players. The parent may just find out that it might not be a coach they first thought.

In the end what is it all for? Chances are very high that the child will never receive a scholarship, play on a college team, become a national team player, become a professional player, or for that matter even play on a high school varsity team. As the saying goes, "The cream will always rise to the top." If a player is outstanding then that player will be found.

SMALL SIDED GAMES (7V7, 9V9, 11V11):

The popular view in youth soccer has been that players should play 7v7 or 9V9 small sided games until and including to age twelve. At the heart of this view point is that through small sided games the youth player can develop the soccer skills better. The individual player will have the opportunity to touch the ball much more frequently than when playing 11v11 and it is only logical that if a player touches the ball constantly then the player's ability will increase.

The argument in favor of this small sided game concept continues by saying that more youth players can play since by having smaller teams a club can create numerous teams at an age group and players are not lost due to cuts. This will keep more players involved in the sport. At the same time the player is not burdened with learning numerous options. The kick and run option is taken away by utilizing a smaller group of players. By putting this smaller group of players onto a smaller field, those players do not get tired and worn out by the second half. We continue in support of this view by pointing to other countries that use this small sided game concept in their youth development of players. After all, if they do it in Europe and South America than that is proof that this is the way to go when developing our youth players in the USA.

We have not looked deeply enough at other sides of this popular small sided game concept which sounds great on the surface.

We must begin with the fact that the game of soccer is a sport that when played outside on a field it is a game that pits 11 players from one team against 11 players from another team. I cannot be more emphatic when saying that the actual game of soccer is 11v11 and never a lesser amount of players such 7v7 or 9v9. Therefore when we use these smaller sided games during the most formative learning years we lose most valuable time in teaching our players the correct game of 11v11. As with anything else, the younger we teach something to our children the better they will learn it.

I do not see why in soccer we seem to feel that it is necessary to delay until an older age, such as thirteen, the playing of 11v11. To the best of my knowledge, other sports play with the proper amount of players. Youth baseball plays with the same amount of nine players as the professional teams do. Youth hockey plays with the same amount of six players on the ice as the professional teams do. They develop their players and teach their game without changing their game. Why then does soccer find it necessary to change the game and play with lesser players in order to develop the players?

In the development stage for players, small sided games with the use of limited players is useful for teaching a concept during a practice. A practice is best suited for the smaller sided games because a practice is for teaching and learning. It is most important to point out to players how each soccer tactic being taught using fewer players actually relates to the real 11v11 game. Everything is easier to teach when you are able to break it down and practice. A game is not the forum to accomplish this.

By saying that all age players up to age 13 should play small sided games because of their learning capacity does players a disservice. Instead of once again playing down to their limited attention spans we should work to always expand their attention spans. They are capable of learning anything if it is being taught to them correctly. They learn best at a younger age. We as adults limit them when we say that they are only capable of learning reduced knowledge because of how old they are. Teach only one option at a time and remain with this one situation until the players understand it and can execute it. Then you should teach the next game situation. If the game is taught in a proper progression it does not become so complex that they do not understand how the game is played. If we adjust the game to fit the players lack of desire or discipline then the less skilled and knowledgeable the players will become. By teaching in a proper progression the challenges will be reachable goals.

Some players have greater ability than others. Should we limit their growth by teaching everyone the same? It is for that reason that we have different leagues in order to accommodate players of all ability levels. It is for that reason that players and parents must understand the difference between recreation, travel and premier teams. The games in recreations leagues would lend themselves to small sided games. It is a non competitive environment in which players of lesser ability or interest can play. All travel soccer is competitive and in that type of game, players should be taught to play the game properly with 11 players against 11 players. Why should recreation and travel soccer be the same by playing with reduced players at a younger age? We should expand the recreation soccer programs instead of lowering the level of travel soccer. Good and committed players must also receive our attention and they require a higher level of play regardless of age. If we are really interested in the well being of every player then we must have distinct programs for each of them in which they can succeed instead making all the programs the same. This will keep the children involved.

I agree that a limited group of players will enable each player to touch the ball more often. However, soccer is about the quality of touches and not the quantity of touches. Training and attending skills classes will enable a player to develop the quality touches. Quantity of touches does not guarantee a player will develop into a good soccer player. Does anyone really believe that by removing two to four players from a game the remaining players will now become excellent players because they have more touches on the ball?

The game of soccer is actually about learning to play without the ball and this is what should be focused on in practices. In travel soccer, a player should already arrive at team practice having a quality touch on the ball which is learned at skills development class and not at a team practice. With these small sided games the players are not taught the important part of a soccer game which is the playing without the ball. Even though a player might have more opportunity of movements off the ball in the small sided games these movements will be deceptive because the space that a player will have available will be limited. A false sense of space is created if the fields are also reduced for the small sided games. When playing on a larger field with 11v11, the spaces available are expanded and not recognizable to a player who is conditioned to playing with reduced players on a smaller field. The size of a field should be reduced according the age of the players but should always be able to accommodate 11v11 play. By reducing the field size and the length of the game according the age of the players, the fatigue that younger players would suffer would be eliminated as an argument for small sided games. If players become tired in the second half then those players have not been conditioned properly and conditioning is a major element to be learned.

These small sided games do not eliminate a kick and run style of soccer as some would argue. Kick and run can and will be played regardless if a team plays 7v7, 9v9, or 11v11. It does not so much matter the number of players but what you teach your players and how you teach the material so we might as well play 11v11 and have them learn the actual game of soccer right from the start.

THE GAME IS ALWAYS 11V11:

My wife Lisa gave me a DVD set as a Christmas present that covered every World Cup from the first one in 1930 to the present. As I watched these different World Cups it occurred to me that the scores in the outcome of these games have remained the same. The games were mostly 1-0, 2-0, 2-1 scores whether they were played in 1930 or in 2010. Yet early on, the formations with which teams played were with two defenders, three midfielders, and five forwards. Growing up I learned to play with this formation. It wasn't until the late 1950s and 1960s that the formations changed to four defenders, four midfielders, and two forwards. If we now play with only two forwards when the game used to be played with five forwards why did the games not produce higher scores then and much lower scores now? It would stand to reason that if you have five forwards attacking two defenders the scores should be high scores. Yet they were not. The scores were similar then as they are now because in the 2-3-5 formation two or three forwards were withdrawn into the midfield or defense while in the 4-4-2 formation some defenders and midfielders moved forward into the attack. The game of soccer is always played with eleven players on each team. It depends on whether players are moved back or are moved forward but in the end it is still an 11v11 game and therefore the outcome of these games produce the similar scores.

PLAYGROUND MENTALITY:

When driving around the city I have noticed that the basketball courts in these neighborhoods always have young people playing on them. Yet when I drive in the suburban areas I have noticed that soccer fields sit empty unless there is an official practice taking place with a coach being present. Unlike the city neighborhoods where the young are playing on their own, the suburban soccer fields do not have youth players simply playing on their own.

This is an unfortunate and disturbing trend for the sport of soccer that must change if we are ever going to produce creative soccer players in the United States. We are the country with the best basketball players because this playground mentality where our youth plays on their own has produced creative players that play a free flowing game. It is necessary to have formal instructional practices. However, our young soccer players will become creative and free flowing players when they can develop what they have learned in a playground setting with no coaches. They learn to organize themselves and play without restrictions.

I realize that today it is impossible to leave our youth unattended on these soccer fields. But we who attempt to develop our youth players must develop a playground setting for our players to become creative players. A team I once had coached had a picnic following a league game which we had lost. Sitting there drinking a diet cola I became aware that the players had gone back out onto the field, split into two teams and were playing a game by themselves. They were running and playing hard while during the game they were lethargic. They were having a great time. I wondered why they were playing so well now and not during the actual game? The thought came to me that now they were playing for themselves which provided them with the freedom of play.

There are several ways this playground mentality concept can be established. The soccer club can set time aside on their soccer fields such as an evening or a weekend day. A parent from the club would volunteer to be station near the fields to watch over the player's safety. If an injury should occur that required attention or a suspicious person is noticed lurking about then the parent would be there to make any necessary telephone calls. The local recreation department could also set time aside for the usage of the fields. A person from the rec. department would be assigned to watch over the players. Aside from this adult attendant no other adults would be allowed to be there and certainly no coaches. No equipment is provided. The players must bring their own soccer balls; pick their own teams; figure out how to recognize who is on what team; and decide what they wish to accomplish such as either skill work or play a game. All the choices must be left to be made by them. Team coaches must encourage their players to take part in the free play playground concept. They will gain a particular confidence from this play that they will not gain if they only play when being supervised.

In the rest of the world children are left to go and play on their own. Being on the soccer fields by themselves they develop this creativity necessary to play the game of soccer as it is intended to be played. Unless we develop this playground concept in the United States we will always continue to play a plotting style of soccer.

THE ELFREDO FACTOR:

Over the course of my coaching career I have witnessed many instances that have left me in a state of bewilderment. Time and again I have watched one of my players be five feet from an open goal only to see the ball go straight up in the air and over the cross bar. How is that possible when all the player had to do was breath on the ball and it would have been a goal? I have been part of games in which my team dominated the game. Shot after shot would go wide of the opponent's goal. My players couldn't score even the opponent's goalie was out of the goal. The other team would cross midfield once, score a goal and we would lose 1-0. An opposing player would take a shot from midfield and the ball would be perfectly placed into the upper corner of my team's goal for a score. The trajectory of the ball never changed. That player could not hit that shot again in a million years but it did happen in my game. One of my players would be on a breakaway towards the opponent's goal but suddenly stumble and fall over for no apparent reason. These incidents would leave me sitting in my chair long after the game had ended wondering how it was possibly that we lost this game?

It is human nature to find a reason for how these unexplainable events could happen. Having too much time on my hands to ponder this mystery, it finally occurred to me that the other team was always playing with an extra player. Not a player whom you could see but an invisible player. That player has played on the opposing team my entire life. Like the invisible rabbit in the story "Harvey", this invisible player is there if you look real hard. I have named this player "Elfredo." It is Elfredo who blocks all the shots on a wide open goal and makes the ball go straight up and over the crossbar; it is Elfredo who makes shot after shot go wide of the goal and who would allow the opponent's goalie to sit down; it is Elfredo who allows a goal for the opponent when they cross midfield only once during the game thereby making my team lose 1-0; it is Elfredo who is riding on the ball and steering it into the upper corner of the goal in a one in a million shots from midfield; and if look very closely you will see Elfredo's hand come out of the ground and trip up your player who is on a breakaway. It is Elfredo who has brought about the saying "I would rather be lucky than good."

The "Elfredo Factor" is that intangible element in soccer games that negates a coach's efforts in preparing the team to play and takes away your control. Every mean adjective that one can think of applies to Elfredo and believe me when I say I have used everyone that is imaginable and then some.

EPILOGUE

When I first took over as the Director of Coaching for the Penfield Strikers, I made it my goal to place a club team in the first division at every age level. This was going to be my measure of success. My friend Dito Garcia, the President of the Strikers, has researched the success of my program. Statistically he found that the goals against for the U11–U19 teams ranked the Striker teams' number 11 out of all 32 clubs in the league and number 4 out of the 15 big clubs. The goals against for the U11–U13 teams ranked the Striker teams' number 6 out of all 32 clubs in the league and number 2 out of the 12 big clubs. Dito goes on to state: "Our U8–U13 system delivers very low goals against per game. This results in higher levels of success. The effect persists in the older age groups. This is even more remarkable given our Town's small population."

Several years ago I reached my supposed goal of success. For the first time the Strikers placed a team into the first division of every age group. Yet, for me these great statistics do not symbolize success. Meaningful success in youth sports has to be much deeper and for which there are no surface statistics that one can easily touch. Three incidents over the past few years stand out to me and have become my symbols of success.

The first incident deals with my issue of making the players independent thinkers. In "The Coach" section under "Life Lessons", I speak of my method of confronting players when they make a good play. After players repeatedly back down when I sternly ask them as to what they were thinking when making this play, I finally tell them that they actually made a great play. The lesson is for the players to become independent thinkers and to stand up for their actions no matter who challenges them.

My U11 team had started the season on a high note. They were winning the league games, ranked on top of their division, and won their first tournament. After the tournament they promptly lost the next two games. They had hit the wall and had become satisfied although there was still halve the season to go. At the next practice, after the second loss, I called a team meeting. I told my players that they now "stink" (my exact word), that they won't win another game, and in fact that they won't even score another goal. As I was ranting on how terrible they were, one of my eleven year old players raised her hand. "What!" I yelled at her. She said, "We might still win." I wanted to jump with joy, but holding my excitement inside, I yelled back "Do you think you know more about soccer than me?" But she softly answered back a second time by saying "Well, you never know!"

It was a highlight moment for me that will stay with me forever. This eleven year old girl stood up to me. She had become an independent thinker who was willing to defend her position. THAT is success. They went on to win more games and in the end they were tied for first place.

The second incident deals with wanting to teach youth players to understand the game of soccer as being more than just a kick and run sport but that it is a game that requires strategy, endurance, intelligence, and athleticism. Even though most youth players will not go on to play at another level such as high school varsity, I wish for them to understand why soccer is called the "beautiful game."

One day I went to see my friend Bob Wells after his team practice had concluded. I had often mentioned to him how I wished for players to understand soccer at a deeper level. The first thing he told me that day was that he had asked the players on his U10 team if they watched any of the World Cup games which were on television daily that summer and many raised their hands. He then asked them if they had noticed anything. One ten year old said that she noticed how the players play the ball to the outside and attack from the outside just as they were learning to do in practice. THAT is what validates this method that I teach. Since then numerous coaches in the Strikers have told me how they now watch soccer differently from the way they had watched it before.

The third incident happened when I was still coaching high school. One fall day I had back spasms on the very day my high school team was to play a game. My back was so bad that I had to go to the emergency and I was bed ridden. The game had to be rescheduled. Three days latter I had the next game. I was able to walk very slowly with a shuffle and I was bent over. When I arrived at the opponent's high school there was a parent from the opposing team waiting for me with a van to drive me out to the soccer field, which was a great distance from where the bus was parked. When I arrived at the sideline Harry Duckworth, the opposing coach, had a comfortable lawn chair waiting for me to sit in during the game. The opposing players also presented me with a "Get Well" card that they had all signed. How often does something like this happen to an opposing coach? It was a complete surprise to me. Even today I am still overwhelmed with the kindness and generosity that Harry, his parents, and his players had shown me that day.

There are no statistics to measure these incidents yet they spell what for me is real success.

ACKNOWLEDGEMENTS

A special "Thank You" to George Hebert who as President of the Penfield Soccer Club, hired me. George had the foresight to be the first club in the area to hire a Director of Coaching to develop the youth players in the club.

Thank you to all on the Board of Directors of the Penfield Soccer Club who have stood behind me and allowed me to implement my program.

Thank you to the many coaches who volunteer so much of your time with the players of the Penfield Soccer Club and who had given me their trust enabling me to make my soccer theories reality.

Thank you to the terrific young ladies on my Striker teams whom I had the good fortune of coaching.

Thank you to Eric Pritchard who assisted me in implementing my soccer skills concept by teaching at my SKILLS Academy.

Thank you to my special friend Francisco "Pancho" Escos, a great professional player and coach from Argentina, whose friendship gave me soccer credibility.

Thank you to my friends Joe Borrosh and Jeff Farnsworth who during the years we coached high school would often sit on my bench because they had so many players that there was no room for them to sit on their bench. If we saw a parent walking by we would ask them to get us coffee. I will always treasure your kindness that you had shown me.

A VERY SPECIAL THANK YOU

*To my son **Erich Werner** whose outstanding soccer skill, knowledge, and teaching ability enabled me to implement my youth soccer development method.*